STUDIES IN CLASSICS

Edited by
Dirk Obbink & Andrew Dyck
Oxford University / The University of California, Los Angeles

A ROUTLEDGE SERIES

Studies in Classics

Dirk Obbink & Andrew Dyck, *General Editors*

Empedocles *Redivivus*:
Poetry and Analogy in Lucretius

Myrto Garani

Routledge
Taylor & Francis Group
New York   London

First published 2007
by Routledge
711 Third Avenue, New York, NY 10017

Simultaneously published in the UK
by Routledge
2 Park Square, Milton Park, Abingdon, Oxfordshire OX14 4RN

Routledge is an imprint of the Taylor & Francis Group, an informa business

First issued in paperback 2012

Typeset in Adobe Garamond by IBT Global

Library of Congress Cataloging-in-Publication Data

Garani, Myrto, 1975–
Poetry and analogy in Empedocles and Lucretius / by Myrto Garani.
    p. cm. — (Studies in classics)
Includes bibliographical references and index.
ISBN 0-415-98849-7
1. Empedocles.   2. Lucretius Carus, Titus.   3. Greek poetry—History and criticism.   I. Title.

PA3968.E6G37 2008
182'.5—dc22   2007031855

ISBN13: 978-0-415-98849-0 (hbk)
ISBN13: 978-0-415-54273-9 (pbk)

Contents

Abbreviations

Arr.²	G. Arrighetti, *Epicuro Opere*, 2nd ed., (Turin 1973).
CIAG	H. Diels (ed.), *Commentaria in Aristotelem Greaca* (Berlin, 1882–1909).
DK	H. Diels and W. Kranz, *Die Fragmente der Vorsokratiker*⁶ (3 vols.; Berlin, 1951–52).
Dox. Graec.	*Doxographi Graeci*, ed. H. Diels (Berlin, 1879; cited from 1965 reprint).
Ep. Hdt.	Epicurus, *Letter to Herodotus.*
Ep. Men.	Epicurus, *Letter to Menoeceus.*
Ep. Pyth.	Epicurus, *Letter to Pythocles.*
FHS&G	W. W. Fortenbaugh, P. M. Huby, R. W. Sharples, and D. Gutas (eds.), *Theophrastus of Eresus* (Leiden, 1992).
LSJ	H. G. Liddell and R. Scott, A Greek-English Lexicon⁹ rev. H. S. Jones, with supplement (Oxford, 1968) [rev. supplement by P. G. W. Glare (1996)]
M&P	A. Martin and O. Primavesi (eds.), *L'Empédocle de Strasbourg (P. Strasb. gr. Inv. 1665–1666)* (Berlin and Strasbourg, 1998)

OCD   *Oxford Classical Dictionary,* 3rd ed., eds. S. Hornblower and A. Spawforth (Oxford, 1996).

OLD   Oxford Latin Dictionary, ed. P. G. W. Clare (Oxford, 1982)

PHerc.   Papyri Herculanenses

SVF   H. von Arnim, *Stoicorum veterum fragmenta* (4 vols., Leipzig, 1903–24).

TLL   *Thesaurus Linguae Latinae* (Leipzig, 1887–)

Us.   H. Usener, Epicurea (Leipzig, 1887)

KΔ   Epicurus, *Principal Sayings.*

Fragments of the Presocratic philosophers are numbered according to DK. When Empedocles is identified by context, I am referring to his *testimonia* (labelled A) or extant fragments (labelled B) without naming him. There is a full list of the translations used in the end of the book.

Abbreviations for journal titles generally follow the system used in *L'Année Philologique;* lists of standard abbreviations for classical authors and works can be found in LSJ and the OLD.

Permissions

The translations of Empedocles' testimonia are reprinted by permission of University of Toronto Press from B. Inwood, *The poem of Empedocles: a text and translation with an introduction,* revised edition (Phoenix. Supplementary volume; 39), Copyright © 2001 by University of Toronto Press Incorporated.

Text and translation of Empedocles' extant fragments are reprinted by permission of Gerald Duckworth & Co. Ltd from Wright, M. R. (© 1981, 1995): *Empedocles, the extant fragments.*

The translation of Lucretius' *De rerum natura* is reprinted by permission of the publishers and the Trustees of the Loeb Classical Library from LUCRETIUS, Loeb Classical Library ® Volume 181, translated by W. H. Rouse, 1924, revised by Martin F. Smith, Cambridge, Mass.: Harvard University Press, Copyright © 1975, 1982, 1992 by the President and Fellows of Harvard College]

The translation of Diogenes Laertius is reprinted by permission of the publishers and the Trustees of the Loeb Classical Library from DIOGENES LAERTIUS: LIVES OF EMINENT PHILOSOPHERS–VOLUME II, Loeb Classical Library® Volume 185, translated by R. D. Hicks, Cambridge, Mass.: Harvard University Press, Copyright © 1925 by the President and Fellows of Harvard College. All rights reserved.

Acknowledgments

This book is a revised version of my Ph.D. thesis "Poetry and Analogy in Empedocles and Lucretius" (London 2004). The contribution of my supervisor, Professor Alessandro Schiesaro, in every step of this work is inestimable. I wish to express my sincere gratitude to him for initiating me to the studies of Lucretius and Empedocles. His clear view, deep insights and constructive criticism, his human understanding and constant encouragement "to stick my neck out" carried me on through difficult times and made this research possible.

I am also grateful to Professor Michael Trapp, who acted as my second supervisor, for being always very enthusiastic and generous with his time, comments and objections and for helping me to clarify my thoughts. Dr Han Baltussen meticulously read the whole first draft and offered stimulating suggestions, proving that genuine scholarly love can easily bridge geographical gaps. I would like to thank the examiners of my dissertation, Professors Philip Hardie and Bob Sharples for their invaluable comments.

I owe a great debt to Professor Dirk Obbink who accepted this book as co-editor to be published in the Routledge series. I am also profoundly indebted to Gordon Campbell who acted as my advisor for Routledge: he provided insightful and detailed criticism, patiently assisted me in various practical matters and saved me from many mistakes in the demanding process of turning my dissertation into a book; the errors that remain are, of course, my own.

Professor David Sider read parts of this work and offered useful comments. Throughout the years Professors Stratis and Eleni Kyriakidis and Evanthia Tsitsibakou-Vasalos, my undergraduate teachers in the Aristotle University of Thessaloniki consistently reminded me through their example what it genuinely means to be a scholar in Humanities; I am grateful to them for their academic and personal advice. Special thanks are also due to my colleague in Patras University, Dr Michael Lipka, for his encouragement and support.

Thanks are due to Professors André Laks, Damien Nelis, and David Sedley, and Drs Gordon Campbell and Efrossini Spentzou for kindly providing their work before publication. Many thanks go to all the staff of the Classics Department of the King's College London for creating such a friendly environment to which I was pleased to belong during my postgraduate studies. I would also like to thank the Institute of Classical Studies in London and the American School of Classical Studies at Athens, for providing an excellent environment in which I was happy to work. My friends, especially Dr Chris Christodoulou in London and Dr Chloe Balla in Athens made my return to Greece long before submission of my dissertation far easier than I first thought.

Funding for the thesis upon which this work is based was partially provided by A. G. Leventis Foundation, to which I express my thanks. I would also like to express my gratitude to University of Toronto Press, Gerald Duckworth & Co. Ltd, and the publishers and the Trustees of the Loeb Classical Library for permission to use material from their sources.

Lastly but most importantly, I am indebted to my parents Elias and Katerina Garanis for encouraging me to pursue postgraduate studies and supporting me every step along the way. Especially my father, even when in the intensive care, kept reminding me that "life without problems would be boring." Panagiotis and Charikleia Kavallaris were excellent parents-in-law, standing by me especially in times of difficult decisions. My brother-in-law, Dr Athanassios Efstathiou and my sister Dr Georgia Garani-Efstathiou offered valuable academic advice and moral support throughout my studies. There are not enough words to thank my husband, Paraskevas Kavallaris for his endless patience and love throughout this trying process, his assistance in several technical matters and for being always ready to juxtapose modern scientific theories with those of ancient cosmologists. This book is dedicated to both him and my father.

Myrto Garani
Athens
2007

Introduction

1.1 EMPEDOCLES' *CARMINA* AND *PRAECLARA REPERTA*

In his criticism of rival philosophical theories in Book 1 of his *De Rerum Natura*, it is Empedocles among the pluralists that Lucretius singles out (1.740–829).[1] What is particularly striking in the passage in question is the fact that Lucretius prefaces his harsh polemic with warm praise of the Presocratic philosopher (1.714–741):[2]

> et qui quattuor ex rebus posse omnia rentur
> ex igni terra atque anima procrescere et imbri. 715
> quorum Agragantinus cum primis Empedocles est,
> insula quem triquetris terrarum gessit in oris,
> quam fluitans circum magnis anfractibus aequor
> Ionium glaucis aspargit virus ab undis,
> angustoque fretu rapidum mare dividit undis 720
> Aeoliae terrarum oras a finibus eius.
> hic est vasta Charybdis et hic Aetnaea minantur
> murmura flammarum rursum se collligere iras,
> faucibus eruptos iterum vis ut vomat ignis
> ad caelumque ferat flammai fulgura rursum. 725
> quae cum magna modis multis miranda videtur
> gentibus humanis regio visendaque fertur,
> rebus opima bonis, multa munita virum vi,
> nil tamen hoc habuisse viro praeclarius in se
> nec sanctum magis et mirum carumque videtur. 730
> carmina quin etiam divini pectoris eius
> vociferantur et exponunt praeclara reperta,
> ut vix humana videatur stirpe creatus.

> *Hic tamen et supra quos diximus inferiores*
> *partibus egregie multis multoque minores,*   735
> *quamquam multa bene ac divinitus invenientes*
> *ex adyto tamquam cordis responsa dedere*
> *sanctius et multo certa ratione magis quam*
> *Pythia quae tripodi a Phoebi lauroque profatur,*
> *principiis tamen in rerum fecere ruinas*   740
> *et graviter magni magno cecidere ibi casu;*

"and those who think that all can grow forth out of four things, from fire, earth, air, and water. Foremost among whom is Empedocles of Acragas: who was born within the triangular coasts of that island, around which the Ionian deep, flowing with its vast windings, sprinkles the salt brine from its green waves, and the swift-moving sea in its narrow strait divides with its waves the shores of the Aeolian land from the boundaries of that isle. Here is wasteful Charybdis, and here Etna's rumblings threaten that the angry flames are gathering again, that once more its violence may belch fires bursting forth from its throat, and once more shoot to the sky the lightnings of its flame: which mighty region, while it seems wonderful in many ways to the nations of mankind and is famed as a place to see, fat with good things, fortified with mighty store of men, yet it seems to have contained in it nothing more illustrious than this man, nor more sacred and wonderful and dear. Moreover, the poems of his divine mind utter a loud voice and declare illustrious discoveries, so that he seems hardly to be born of mortal stock.

Nevertheless he and those whom I mentioned before, men very much below him by many degrees and far less than he, although in making many excellent and inspired discoveries they have given responses as it were from the holy place of the heart, with more sanctity and far more certainty than the Pythia who speaks forth from Apollo's tripod and laurel, nevertheless I say these have come to a crash about the beginnings of things; great they were, and herein great was their fall:"

First, Lucretius offers an elaborate description of Empedocles' birthplace, the three-cornered island of Sicily, which is surrounded by the Ionian Sea and separated by a narrow strait from Italy (1.717–725). While he praises Sicily for its numerous natural wonders, such as Charybdis and Aetna, as well as its wealth of things and the races of people that fortify it, he concludes that first and foremost this place owes the greatest part of its value to Empedocles (1.729–730). The pun that Lucretius makes on his own *cognomen* by attributing it to Empedocles (*carumque* 1.730) significantly adds to the warm and personal undertones of the passage.[3] Lucretius goes on to eulogize Empedocles' poems (*carmina*, 1.731) that expound illustrious discoveries (*praeclara reperta*, 1.732), emphasizing once more that Empedocles hardly seems to have been born of human stock (1.733). Finally, he compares Empedocles to a prophet (*vociferantur*, 1.732) and his discoveries with the responses of the Delphic Pythia (1.737–739).

These verses raise a considerable number of perplexing questions. Why does Lucretius present us with such a laudatory portrait of Empedocles, a philosopher so vehemently attacked by Epicurus? Why does he put forward such a lengthy description of Sicily? Why does he deify Empedocles, a status which is otherwise reserved for Epicurus alone in the course of the poem? What does Lucretius mean by referring to Empedocles' *carmina* and *praeclara reperta?*

Scholars mostly agree that Lucretius' reference to Empedocles' *carmina* suggests his acknowledgement of a profound debt to a predecessor whom he considers as the father of the genre of philosophical didactic epos and whom he follows in his rendering of Epicurus' philosophical writings into Latin, so as to make his principles easily absorbed by a Roman audience.[4] A letter of Cicero (*Q. fr.* II 9.4), which also reveals a revived interest in Empedocles' poem at the beginning of the first century B.C., strongly suggests that Lucretius' imitation would be obvious to the contemporary well-educated reader.[5] In fact, Sedley has gone so far as to reconstruct Empedocles' now lost proem to his poem from Lucretius' and to argue that the proem to *DRN* Book 1 is meant to be recognized as an imitation of Empedocles'.[6] Moreover, it has been argued that Lucretius purposely flanks his discussion of Empedocles with his attacks on Heraclitus and Anaxagoras; in this way he underlines the fact that Empedocles' poem constitutes an ideal model of philosophical language which, unlike Heraclitus' obscure style or Anaxagoras' technical jargon, can convey difficult philosophical ideas with clarity.[7]

Along these lines, one can proceed to explore how Lucretius embraces especially from Empedocles specific formulaic and stylistic elements, the ones conventionally required as essential ingredients of the epic and didactic genres. It has long been observed that Lucretius appeals to Empedocles' Muse, Calliope.[8] Moreover, just as Empedocles' didactic poem is addressed to a pupil called Pausanias, so Lucretius also aims at converting a specific intra-textual reader, Memmius.[9] We can also point to the similar function of standard ways of address and of formulaic expressions drawn from the didactic background that are used as a structural device in the articulation of the poem.[10] Likewise the repetitions of phrases, verses or complete passages equally serve, among other purposes, to facilitate and encourage memorization.[11] Other elements of Empedocles to be found in Lucretius are the compound adjectives[12] and especially the personifications, extended similes and metaphors, all of which will be discussed at length.

From a different point of view, it is quite remarkable that in verses 1.714–739 Lucretius condenses references to three of the roles with which Empedocles had credited himself, those of god, poet and prophet (B112).[13] Scholars have already discussed the fact that, when Lucretius introduces oracular imagery and compares Empedocles' heart to a shrine, he touches upon major issues pertaining to the nature of poetic creation and of philosophical truth and redefines the image of Roman *vates*. In the course of the poem, Lucretius fragments Empedocles' roles and associates Empedocles' portrait with that of Epicurus and of himself, thus creating a particularly complicated web of associations.[14] Lucretius associates Epicurus with Empedocles' divinity (5.6–12) and in a similar vein, Epicurus is said—like Empedocles—to be the great son of his *patria* (6.1–6).[15] In addition, while Lucretius embeds gigantomachic and triumphal imagery in Empedocles' praise by depicting a hurling lightning attacking the sky (1.722ff.), he conjures up Epicurus' similar assault on the sky (1.62–79).[16] In the opposite way, Lucretius praises Epicurus in Empedocles' words (cf. 1.72–74 with B129.4–6), pointing to Epicurus' primacy and downgrading the achievements of his predecessors, Empedocles included.[17] As for Lucretius, he himself appropriates Empedocles' fillets and garlands, regarding symbols of overpowering inspiration and mental strength, as well as the transforming effect of poetry (1.922–935).[18] Moreover, he represents himself as a prophet in a passage that bears strong Empedoclean connotations (5.104, 5.110–112).[19]

Nevertheless, since an exhaustive analysis of Empedocles' and Lucretius' intertextual interaction on the poetic and didactic level—still to be made—would require a larger-scale study,[20] the present study relies on the general scholarly consensus. Instead the focus will be on the more controversial issue of Empedocles' *praeclara reperta* (1.732).[21] Scholarly opinion on this issue is divided. On the one hand, there are those scholars who claim that Lucretius' intertextual engagement with Empedocles should be limited strictly to the poetical level and the formal similarities of the literary genre. This thesis could be summarized in Sedley's words: "following Epicurus, he [Lucretius] applauds the Presocratic tendency to seek physical, as opposed to theological, explanations for such cosmic phenomena as celestial motions, eclipses and earthquakes. [. . .] It is, I am convinced, only at this level of detail that the Epicureans, Lucretius included, are prepared to applaud the 'discoveries' of Empedocles."[22] As Sedley concludes: "His [Lucretius'] object?

To announce himself as the Roman Empedocles -the great Roman poet of nature." In short, he is laying claim to *a literary, not a philosophical heritage* [my emphasis]."[23] On the opposite side stand those who endorse the view that Lucretius' act of piety in the present context reveals also his appreciation of Empedocles' role as forerunner of the Atomists; hence, although their opinions vary as to what exactly this means, they argue that Lucretius' debt to Empedocles is both literary and philosophical.[24]

Although there are some respects in which Empedocles could be considered the precursor of Atomism, those who advocate the impossibility of any sort of intertextual engagement with Empedocles' philosophy by Lucretius' claim that Epicurus and his successors would never have acknowledged such a claim of philosophical debt, true as it may well have been.[25] They draw attention to the harsh polemics directed against the Presocratic philosopher within the Epicurean school.[26] Epicurus himself, as well as his pupils Metrodorus and Hermarchus wrote against Empedocles (Cic. *ND* 1.93). Demetrius of Laconia also opposed him in his writings (fr. 35, fr. 43 and fr. 46 de Falco). More precisely, from the extant fragments we can establish that Epicurus discusses Plato's reception of Empedocles' four elements in *Timaeus* (*ΠΦ* Book 14, fr. 60 col. xxxiv-xxxviii Leone = fr. 29.22–26 Arr.²). Elsewhere he raises his objections against a theory of vision which is based on effluences, probably targeting Empedocles (*ΠΦ* fr. 36.23 Arr.²). Colotes attacks Empedocles' mixture theory (Plut. *Adv. Col.* 10.1111F, 11.1112D, 12.1113A-D). Plutarch also speaks of the Epicureans mocking the monsters "with twisted feet and a hundred hands" and "man-faced ox-creatures" which feature in Empedocles' zoogony (*Adv. Col.* 28.1123B).[27] Hermarchus wrote 22 books against Empedocles, entitled Ἐπιστολικὰ περὶ Ἐμπεδοκλέους, in which he deals with matters of human cultural history, pertaining to the formation of the concepts of the divine, homicide, justice, and law among primitive men and attacks Empedocles' views on prehistory, religion and metempsychosis (Diog. Laert. 10.24–25).[28] Cicero's Velleius disapproves of Empedocles' ascription of divinity to his four elements (Cic. *ND* 1.29). Last but not least, Diogenes of Oinoanda criticizes Empedocles' four element theory (fr. 6 Smith), as well as his transmigration theory, along with that of Pythagoras (fr. 41, fr. 42 Smith).[29]

As a consequence, some scholars assert that Lucretius ought not to acknowledge Epicurus' philosophical similarities with Empedocles, in order to conform to the practice of his school. In Sedley's words "the unwritten rules of philosophical allegiance in the ancient world do not normally permit the imputation of authority to anyone other than the founder of your own school, or at most, to his own acknowledged forerunners."[30] Yet, without necessarily doubting Lucretius' loyalty to his master, one must bear in mind—as Sedley indeed does—the fact that he certainly was not a typical Epicurean.

The scholars who argue against Lucretius' debt to Empedocles' philosophy also stress the fact that directly after the eulogy of Empedocles, Lucretius places his refutation of Empedocles' theory of matter (1.734–829). Lucretius' discussion vividly echoes similar doxographical treatment of the Presocratic theories of elements, such as those that we find in Diogenes of Oinoanda (fr. 6 Smith) and Cicero (*ND* 1.29). His criticism may ultimately go back either to Epicurus' *On Nature* Books 14 and 15, or to Peripatetic doxography, or very plausibly to a later Epicurean critical text.[31] Whatever the case may be, it should be taken for granted that Lucretius knew Empedocles not only through his master's works or a doxographical—perhaps Epicurean—handbook, but also directly.

The key points of Lucretius' disagreement with Empedocles' theory of matter, articulated in these lines, are as follows.[32] To begin with, given Empedocles' denial of the existence of void (οὐδέ τι τοῦ παντὸς κενεὸν πέλει οὐδὲ περισσόν / "There is no part of the whole that is empty or overfull," B13), Lucretius denounces the Empedoclean combination of this precept with the acceptance of motion and the existence of soft and rarefied things (1.742–745).[33] Then, Lucretius criticizes Empedocles for not limiting division in his roots and not assuming a *minimum* (1.746–752). This concept runs counter to the fundamental Epicurean notion of indivisibility of minimal entities, which is explicitly denoted by the name ἄτομον, meaning something that cannot be cut any further, and the idea of the *minimae partes* (cf. 1.599–634). In order to illustrate the Epicurean principle, Lucretius puts forward the analogy of the extreme point of a visible thing (1.749 *extremum . . . cacumen*).[34] Moreover, as long as Empedocles' roots are soft this must entail that they are mortal and that the world must revert to nothing and be born anew from nothing, concepts both of which are erroneous (1.753–758). In a similar vein, Lucretius sketches the roots as mutually hostile; this would mean either that they disperse or—in case they aggregate—instead of generating a new creation, perish, as happens in a storm (1.759–762). In this way Lucretius—plausibly following his source—corrects Empedocles' teaching on the basis of sensory evidence; however, this distorts Empedocles' actual belief, since the Presocratic expressly states that the elements, though perishable in things, were in themselves imperishable (αἶψα δὲ θνήτ' ἐφύοντο, τὰ πρὶν μάθον ἀθάνατ' εἶναι, / "Immediately what were formerly accustomed to be immortal became mortal," B35.14). What is more, this interpretation completely disregards the impact of Love and Strife in the process of Empedocles' cosmogony that makes unlike elements unite.

Next, Lucretius objects to the idea of the continuous alternating process from elements to things and from things to elements (1.763–768); if this were true, we could not tell with certainty whether the four elements precede created things, or in the opposite way, things were simply the origin—the elements—of the elements.[35] On the other hand, if the four roots retain their character while they intermingle, i.e. what Lucretius considers as the secondary qualities of roots—as Empedocles actually thought—then they cannot produce anything (1.770–781). Moreover, if they are transformed and change their nature this means that they are not imperishable. As he concludes, only atoms have a secret and imperceptible nature. Then, Lucretius discusses a disagreement which pertains less to Empedocles and more to Heraclitus, the Peripatetics or the Stoics (1.782–802), the so-called "transformationist theory"; he states that if the four elements change one into the other (i.e. fire changes to air, air to water, water to earth and vice-versa), then again they cannot be eternal. In this way he puts forward one crucial Epicurean principle, that when something changes and passes out of its own boundaries it brings about the death of what it was before. Finally, Lucretius expresses his disapproval of Empedocles' and others' belief that fire, water, earth and air are the primary elements simply because they are necessary for the growth of things (1.803–829); on the contrary, as he claims by means of the famous analogy with the letters of the alphabet, the only true first beginnings are the atoms, which make our world through their varied forms, motions and arrangements.

On the basis of these hostile arguments it is understandable that some scholars should have concluded that Lucretius acknowledges no substantial conceptual debt to Empedocles. But this is not the only position that has been maintained.

Let us now turn to those scholars who interpret Lucretius' act of piety to Empedocles as having, in addition to literary implications, philosophical ones as well. In fact this is the position to which the present study adheres and aims to reinforce. This preliminary discussion of Lucretius' intertextual allusions to Empedocles' philosophical principles is not intended to be exhaustive, since we will come back to many of them in the course of the analysis that follows.

To begin with, when Lucretius differentiates the title of his poem from that of Epicurus by calling it "On the Nature of Things" (cf. 1.25 *de rerum natura*) instead of just "On Nature" it is very plausible to suppose that in doing so he is following the example of Empedocles who according to our sources entitled his poem *On nature of the things there are* (A2 = Suda, s.v. "Empedocles" Περὶ φύσεως τῶν ὄντων).[36] In this way he clearly places himself in the line of a specific physiological tradition inaugurated by his Presocratic predecessor.[37] As Sedley rightly remarks, Empedocles' title was above all "a pluralist manifesto" against the tradition of Eleatic monism.[38]

In line with this Furley stresses the fact that Lucretius' veneration of Empedocles can be seen as justified by the fact that the latter was the first to claim that everything is created out of unchanging minimal entities, his roots.[39] Empedocles redefines what mortals call "birth" and "death" as being in reality only a form of combination and dissolution (B8):

> ἄλλο δέ τοι ἐρέω· φύσις οὐδενὸς ἐστὶν ἁπάντων
> θνητῶν, οὐδέ τις οὐλομένου θανάτοιο τελευτή,
> ἀλλὰ μόνον μίξις τε διάλλαξίς τε μιγέντων
> ἐστί φύσις δ᾽ ἐπὶ τοῖς ὀνομάζεται ἀνθρώποισιν.

> "Here is another point: of all mortal things no one has birth, or any end in pernicious death, but there is only mixing, and separating of what has been mixed, and to these men give the name "birth.""

He also claims that nothing can arise from "what is not" or be completely destroyed:

> νήπιοι· οὐ γάρ σφιν δολιχόφρονές εἰσι μέριμναι,
> οἳ δὴ γίγνεσθαι πάρος οὐκ ἐὸν ἐλπίζουσιν,
> ἤ τι καταθνῇσκειν τε καὶ ἐξόλλυσθαι ἁπάντῃ. (B11)

> "Fools, for their meditations are not far-reaching thoughts, men who suppose that what formerly did not exist comes into existence, or that something dies and is completely destroyed."

> ἐκ γὰρ τοῦ μὴ ἐόντος ἀμήχανόν ἐστι γενέσθαι,
> καί τ᾽ ἐὸν ἐξαπόλεσθαι ἀνήνυστον καὶ ἄπυστον·
> αἰεὶ γὰρ †θήσεσθαι† ὅπῃ κέ τις αἰὲν ἐρείδῃ. (B12)

> "It is impossible for there to be a coming into existence from that which is not, and for what exists to be completely destroyed cannot be fulfilled, nor is to be heard of; for when and where it is thrust, then and there it will be."

Lucretius also believes that things are created out of unchangeable constituents and then are dissolved into them (*et rerum primordia pandam, / unde omnis natura creet res auctet alatque* / *quoque eadem rursum natura perempta resolvat* / "and I shall disclose the first-beginnings of things, from which nature makes all things and increases and nourishes them, and into which the same nature again reduces them when dissolved," 1.55–57).[40] Moreover, he himself stresses the impossibility of something being created out of nothing and of something being reduced to nothing (1.146–328: e.g. *nullam rem e nilo gigni divinitus umquam.* / "no thing is ever by divine power produced from nothing," 1.150; *Nunc age, res quoniam docui non posse creari* / *de nilo neque item genitas ad nil revocari* / "Now then, since I have taught that things cannot be created from nothing and, when brought forth, cannot be brought back to nothing," 1.265–266). Although in these fundamental propositions Lucretius unquestionably follows Epicurus (e.g. καὶ μὴν καὶ τὸ πᾶν ἀεὶ τοιοῦτον ἦν οἷον νῦν ἐστι, καὶ ἀεὶ τοιοῦτον ἔσται. οὐθὲν γάρ ἐστιν εἰς ὃ μεταβαλεῖ. παρὰ γὰρ τὸ πᾶν οὐθέν ἐστιν, ὃ ἂν εἰσελθὸν εἰς αὐτὸ τὴν μεταβολὴν ποιήσαιτο. / "Moreover, the sum total of things was always such as it is now, and such it will ever remain. For there is nothing into which it can change. For outside the sum of things there is nothing which could enter into it and bring about the change," *Ep. Hdt.* 39), scholars rightly call attention to Empedoclean echoes embedded in Lucretius' language. As a striking example one could point to the word *gigni* (1.150) which seems to echo Empedocles' γίγνεσθαι (B11.2).[41] It seems highly conceivable that Lucretius here recognizes points of philosophical agreement between Empedocles and Epicurus that can be justified by their common anti-Parmenidean heritage.[42] That is why he feels entitled to employ Empedocles' phrasing in order to expound the corresponding Epicurean precepts, underscoring their similarities as well as their differences. He thus hastens to add the unusual adverb *divinitus* (1.150) which brings in the Epicurean belief in the complete absence of divine intervention in human affairs.[43]

In a similar vein, it has also been pointed out that, when Lucretius asserts that the mass of matter (*summa rerum*) and the motion of atoms are constant and invariable and that the universe always was as it is now and will always be, he vividly recalls two Empedoclean fragments.[44] Thus, scholars often compare Lucretius' verses 2.296–302 with Empedocles' B16:

> *nam neque adaugescit quicquam neque deperit inde.*
> *quapropter quo nunc in motu principiorum*
> *corpora sunt, in eodem anteacta aetate fuere*
> *et post haec semper simili ratione ferentur,*
> *et quae consuerint gigni gignentur eadem*

300

condicione et erunt et crescent vique valebunt,
quantum cuique datum est per foedera naturai.   (2.296–302)

"For nothing increases it nor does anything perish from it. Therefore in whatsoever motion the bodies of first-beginnings are now, in that same motion they were in ages gone by, and hereafter they will always be carried along in the same way, and the things which have been accustomed to be born will be born under the same conditions; they will be and will grow and will be strong with their strength as much as is granted to each by the laws of nature."

ἔ<στ>ι γὰρ ὡς πάρος ἦν τε καὶ ἔσσεται, οὐδέ ποτ᾽ οἴω
τούτων ἀμφοτέρων κενεώσεται ἄσπετος αἰών. (B16)

"They are as they were before and shall be, and never, I think, will endless time be emptied of these two."

And then again they juxtapose Lucretius' verses 2.303–307 with Empedocles' B17.30–35:

nec rerum summam commutare ulla potest vis;
nam neque, quo possit genus ullum materiai
effugere ex omni, quicquam est extra, neque in omne   305
unde coorta queat nova vis inrumpere et omnem
naturam rerum mutare et vertere motus.   (2.303–307)

"Nor can any power change the sum total of things; for there is no place without into which any kind of matter could flee away from the all; and there is no place whence a new power could arise to burst into the all, and to change the whole nature of things and turn their motions."

καὶ πρὸς τοῖς οὐδ᾽ †ἄρ τι† ἐπιγίγνεται οὐδ᾽ ἀπολήγει·
εἴτε γὰρ ἐφθείροντο διαμπερές, οὐκέτ᾽ ἂν ἦσαν.
τοῦτο δ᾽ ἐπαυξήσειε τὸ πᾶν τί κε, καὶ πόθεν ἐλθόν;
πῇ δέ κε κἠξαπόλοιτο, ἐπεὶ τῶνδ᾽ οὐδὲν ἐρῆμον;
ἀλλ᾽ αὔτ᾽ ἔστιν ταῦτα, δι᾽ ἀλλήλων δὲ θέοντα
γίγνεται ἄλλοτε ἄλλα καὶ ἠνεκὲς αἰὲν ὁμοῖα.   (B17.30–35)

"Moreover, nothing comes to birth later in addition to these, and there is no passing away, for if they were continuously perishing they would no longer exist. And what would increase this whole, and from where would it come? How would it be completely destroyed, since nothing is without them? No, these are the only real things, but as they run through each other they become different objects at different times, yet they are throughout forever the same."

As Gale remarks, while the unusual verb *adaugescit,* meaning "coming into being in addition" (2.296), corresponds to Empedocles' ἐπιγίγνεται (B17.30), yet Lucretius also refers to *intervallis* (2.295), criticizing Empedocles' denial of the existence of void.[45]

It has also been argued that by his reference to Empedocles' *reperta,* Lucretius may refer to Empedocles' endlessly recurring cosmic cycle of unification and separation, the alternation in power between the cosmic principles of Love and Strife.[46] Trépanier aptly summarizes the version of Empedocles' reconstructed cosmic cycle that I embrace:[47]

> "Between two opposed, a-cosmic phases, characterized by the complete domination over the elements of Love and Strife, there come into being two separate worlds, containing mortal creatures, wherein the two forces vie for control over the elements. Under the full sway of Love, all the elements are harmoniously fused together into 'One,' also described by Empedocles as the Sphairos (fragments 27–9). Strife meanwhile, having retreated outside the elements(?), then reasserts itself by destroying this unity (fragments 30–1), thereby creating 'Many' and continues to assert itself until it has separated the four elements into pure or homogeneous bodies. This is the reign of Strife. Then once more it is Love's turn to take the initiative (fragment 35), reintroducing mixture into the cosmos, and blending the elements in ever increasing amounts until it has reconstituted the Sphairos. Having come full circle, the process begins anew, and so on ad infinitum."

Although a thorough discussion of the much vexed question of Empedocles' cycle is out of the scope of this study,[48] attention should be drawn here to Graham's important observation regarding Empedocles' style. According to Graham, when Empedocles discusses the recurrence of the cycle, he systematically repeats a specific AB motif, which corresponds to the dipoles of unification and separation, the one and the many, Love and Strife, while he makes variations in his phrasing and sentence structure; in this way, Empedocles employs a "mimetic structure" in order to reflect the image of the world he describes.[49]

As far as Lucretius is concerned, his poem is beyond any doubt permeated by images of the eternal cycle of growth and decay. In the first instance, Lucretius' evocation of Aphrodite, who reigns over creation in the proem, is full of terms pointing to nature's generating force (*genetrix,* 1.1; *exortum,* 1.5; *genitabilis aura favoni,* 1.11; *generatim,* 1.20; *exoritur,* 1.22). Clay correctly suggests that in his use of the word *natura* (*Quae quoniam rerum naturam sola gubernas,* / "Since therefore you alone govern the nature of things," 1.21), Lucretius is the first extant Latin author who reads the Greek word φύσις not only as nature, but also with its etymological implications as birth (γένεσις).[50] What is more, the most striking instance of φύσις explicitly used with the meaning of birth occurs in Empedocles' (φύσις οὐδενὸς ἐστιν ἁπάντων / θνητῶν, / "of all mortal things no one has birth," B8.1–2).[51]

In the course of the poem Venus, eventually equated with Nature, reveals her double face, both creative and destructive.[52] In this connection one can pinpoint several shorter or larger-scale cycles within the broader framework of the poem (e.g. 1.248–264, 2.77–79, 2.569–580, 2.1116, 3.964–971).[53] It suffices to recall here the contrast between the opening of the poem with the hymn to Aphrodite and its end with the gloomy picture of the Athenian plague. Although this idea of unremitting interchange between creation and destruction stems from Epicurus' writings and is conditioned by the Epicurean law of ἰσονομία (*Ep. Hdt.* 39), Empedocles rightly can put forward his claim for being its initiator. This is indeed how some scholars account for the un-Epicurean opening of the poem and the presence of Venus and Mars.[54]

What is more, Lucretius employs repetition in order to replicate the world's order in a way very similar to Empedocles. To use Schiesaro's words: "From the microtextual level of repeated sounds, to formulae, to passages and themes, Lucretius' poem presents its reader with a strong sense of repetition and continuity, as a series of material bodies whose components constantly rearrange themselves in cyclical fashion without ever being reduced *in nihilum.*"[55] It would seem rather implausible to consider this parallel use of a stylistic technique with identical semantic bearing as a mere coincidence. Still, Lucretius' mimetic representation of the natural workings is worked out in a more sophisticated way than his predecessor. What Graham identified regarding Empedocles' cosmic cycle as an AB pattern, figures in Lucretius inverted, since destruction does not always follow, but also precedes creation (e.g. 2.569–580: B = 2.569 *motus . . . exitiales* / "death dealing motions" → A = 2.571–572 *genitales auctificique* / *motus* / "motions that generate and give increase to things"; 5.826–836: B = 5.832 *namque aliud putrescit et aevo debile languet,* / "For one thing crumbles and grows faint and weak with age," → A = 5.833 *porro aliud concrescit et e contemptibus exit.* / "another grows up and comes forth from contempt"). Lucretius thus points to the fact that the two processes are inextricably linked and operate simultaneously. As Gale puts it "the two great cosmic forces exist, but it is in fact impossible to separate them. Empedocles' dualism is a mistake: creation and destruction are two sides of the same coin, two aspects of the 'goddess' Nature."[56] Besides,—unless more papyri fragments from his now lost poem prove the opposite—in Empedocles the technique does not function as an organizing principle for larger units of the poem as it does in Lucretius.[57]

Lastly, we should reconsider Empedocles' theory of four elements, against which Lucretius argues so emphatically (cf. especially 1.740–741). After establishing that the atoms and not the roots are the ultimate constituents of things, it seems that Lucretius regards Empedocles' roots as the world's basic atomic aggregations.[58] It has already been mentioned above that in opposing Empedocles' theory of matter Lucretius employs the simile with the letters of the alphabet (1.820–829):

> *namque eadem caelum mare terras flumina solem*   820
> *constituunt, eadem fruges arbusta animantis,*
> *verum aliis alioque modo commixta moventur.*
> *quin etiam passim nostris in versibus ipsis*
> *multa elementa vides multis communia verbis,*
> *cum tamen inter se versus ac verba necessest*   825
> *confiteare et re et sonitu distare sonanti.*
> *tantum elementa queunt permutato ordine solo;*
> *at rerum quae sunt primordia, plura adhibere*
> *possunt unde queant variae res quaeque creari.*

"for the same beginnings constitute sky, sea, earth, rivers, sun, the same make crops, trees, animals, but they move differently mixed with different elements and in different ways. Moreover, all through these very lines of mine you see many elements common to many words, although you must confess that lines and words differ one from another both in meaning and in the sound of their soundings. So much can elements do, when nothing is changed but order; but the elements that are the beginnings of things can bring with them more kinds of variety, from which all the various things can be produced."

Lucretius corroborates his main point by stating that just as there is an infinite supply of a limited number of letters in the alphabet which can produce an enormous number of various words by changing only their order, there must be an infinite quantity of each type of atoms greatly varying in size and shape that combine to create various objects by changing their order as well as their motions. By this analogy he may implicitly allude to Empedocles' simile of painters in order to refute the theory expressed in it and lay out the fundamental principles of the Epicurean philosophical system (B23.6–8):[59]

> δένδρεά τε κτίζοντε καὶ ἀνέρας ἠδὲ γυναῖκας,
> θῆράς τ' οἰωνούς τε καὶ ὑδατοθρέμμονας ἰχθῦς,
> καί τε θεοὺς δολιχαίωνας τιμῇσι φερίστους·

> "creating trees and men and women, animals and birds and water-nourished
> fish, and long-lived gods too, highest in honor;"

In this simile Empedocles spells out his doctrine of the four elements out of which everything that surrounds us is created when they are mixed in different proportions; he compares the process of creation with a picture of trees, men, women, birds, animals, water-nourished fishes and immortal gods painted out of just four colours.[60] Lucretius employs similar imagery to that of Empedocles, referring also to crops, trees and animals (*fruges, arbusta, animantis,* 1.821), only substituting letters for colours and therefore textualizing the visual image. What is particularly remarkable for our discussion is the fact that Lucretius completes his list by placing the four Empedoclean roots first (*caelum mare terras flumina solem,* 1.820). In this way he seems to suggest that while Empedocles' roots are not different in substance from any other mortal atomic combination, still they could be thought of as constituting the first stage in the creation of the world, from the microcosm upwards.[61]

In this spirit, Lucretius' poem is imbued with the Empedoclean four-fold division of the world in several of his descriptions. What is even more noteworthy, in a very Empedoclean way, instead of the four roots Lucretius uses their worldly manifestations, i.e. sea, rain, wind and sun.[62] To conjure up just two striking occurrences we should first refer to this phenomenon in the proem to Book 1, in which Lucretius interweaves twice within the very first ten verses the four Empedoclean roots, upon which Aphrodite exerts her catalytic power ([1] air: 1.2 *caeli,* water: 1.3 *mare navigerum,* earth: 1.3 *terras frugiferentis,* fire: 1.5 *lumina solis;* [2] air: 1.6 *venti,* . . . *nubila caeli,* earth: 1.7 *daedala tellus,* sea: 1.8 *aequora ponti,* fire: 1.9 *diffuso lumine*).[63] Likewise, Snyder remarks that the allusion to the four elements in the description of Empedocles' homeland, Sicily, should be considered entirely complimentary; while Lucretius refers to Empedocles' roots in an order reminiscent of B115.10–11, he offers us an explanation of how his predecessor came to develop his theory of the four elements (earth: 1.717 *insula . . . triquetris terrarum . . . in oris,* 1.721 *Aeoliae terrarum oras* → B115.10 ἐς χθονὸς οὖδας, B115.10 γαῖα; water 1.718–720 *aequor / Ionium . . . ab undis, / . . . rapidum mare . . . undis* → B115.10 πόντος; fire: 1.722–725 *Aetnaea . . . / murmura flammarum . . . iras, / . . . flammai fulgura* → B115.10–11 δ' ἐς αὐγὰς / ἠελίου φαέθοντος; air: 1.725 *caelum* → B115.11 ὁ δ' αἰθέρος).[64] In the pages to follow we will come across many other instances illustrating Lucretius' integration of Empedocles' four-element theory and consider how he applies unified figurative language in his description of atoms and roots.[65]

Last but not least, Furley explains Lucretius' lengthy praise of Empedocles in terms of the latter's physical theory about the random development of living forms. We know from Aëtius (Aët. 5.19.5 = A72) that Empedocles distinguished four stages in the emergence of animal life. Although Empedocles' zoogonical account will be discussed below in more detail,[66] it would be useful to make here a few preliminary remarks. According to this theory creatures were first created by the accidental combination of disparate limbs and organs that at an even earlier stage had sprung up and wandered about on their own, without the intervention of any divine power; if the correct "limbs" combine, then the creature will survive and go on to found a species, but if the wrong combination occurs then the creature will instantly perish.[67]

Lucretius actually puts forward a theory very similar to Empedocles', namely that originally a set of randomly composed monsters sprang up, of which only the fittest survived (5.837–877). It is true that there are clear differences between the two zoogonical accounts. Whereas in the very beginning Empedocles describes isolated limbs (B57), Lucretius describes whole organisms with congenital defects. Besides, as Campbell remarks, Lucretius' system is different in that his maladapted creatures are formed at the atomic level rather than at the macroscopic level of whole limbs.[68] More importantly, in Lucretius there is no inter-species mingling of limbs, as happens in Empedocles (B61). That is why, as we know from Plutarch (*Adv. Col.* 28.1123B), the Epicureans mocked Empedocles' monsters some of which were described "roll-walking creatures with hands not properly articulated or distinguishable" and as "ox-headed man-creatures" (εἰλίποδ' ἀκριτόχειρα καὶ βουγενῆ ἀνδρόπρωρα, B60; cf. B61.2).

At this point, one could claim that Lucretius' primary source for this theory might have been Epicurus' *On Nature* (Books 11 and 12),[69] which in turn interacts with and argues against Plato's *Timaeus,* since the latter text appropriates and subverts the Empedoclean and Democritean zoogonical doctrines.[70] However, we should not deny the fact that the whole Lucretian passage indisputably echoes Empedocles in terms of both theory and language.[71] That is why, after making such an intensive use of Empedocles' poem and attacking the compound creatures of myth, Lucretius also argues that the compound creatures of Empedocles never existed at any given time; he thus makes sure that he keeps his distance from his predecessor

(5.878–924).[72] In any case, as Campbell again acutely notes, "it is not clear to what degree Epicurus himself was influenced by Empedocles, or to what extent, Lucretius has on his own initiative returned to Empedocles the better to present Epicurus' zoogony."[73]

In general, I would thus endorse Campbell's concluding suggestion: "we should also not rule out the possibility that Lucretius sees a stronger Empedoclean influence on Epicurus than we can and in a circular progression injects further Empedoclean material into his poem on that authority."[74]

The present study argues that by applauding Empedocles' discoveries, Lucretius points especially to his predecessor's *epistemological methods of inquiry* into the unseen, methods which he extensively draws upon and creatively modifies. Faced with men's bewilderment in the face of seemingly inexplicable natural phenomena that bring about fear and religious superstition, Lucretius undertakes to communicate Epicurus' therapeutic message to his Roman audience and thus shake off the yoke of religion. In order to carry out this mission he composes a physiological poem in which he makes extensive use of analogical reasoning couched in various literary tropes (personifications, similes, metaphors) that are used with cognitive and probative force. In this way he successfully intrudes into the unseen natural world, decodes the laws that condition its terrifying aspects and offers valid scientific explanations. In line with this I will claim that Lucretius directly turns back to Empedocles' literary devices as one of his main sources of analogical methods and integrates his predecessors' methods of creating analogies within his philosophical discourse.

Lucretius' embracing of Empedocles' poetic devices is exactly what lays the foundation for his intensive intertextual play with the latter's thought both on the poetical and the philosophical level. In other words, while appropriating these devices, Lucretius inevitably has to take into consideration how inextricably they are linked and conditioned by his predecessor's doctrinal precepts. Specific philosophical principles that Epicurus has in common with Empedocles make the latter's poetical means especially convenient for Lucretius to employ as the conduit of similar concepts. Conversely, when it comes to analogies associated with philosophical disagreements, Lucretius has to clarify his stance towards Empedocles' philosophy before integrating them into his Epicurean poem. Similar theoretical claims about the use of tropes within a philosophical context that Empedocles and Lucretius share make the link between them even stronger. In this way Lucretius eventually departs from mythological interpretations which considered the gods as agents, demystifies anew the workings of the material cosmos and makes his pupil capable of confronting otherwise startling situations.

At this point committed proponents of the "exclusively poetic debt" view would counter that if we were to concede to this two-fold Lucretian engagement with Empedocles' philosophical poem, this would seriously threaten the stability of his devotion to the orthodox Epicurean tenets. At the same time, they would contend that Lucretius' intertextual relationship with Empedocles should be thought of as functioning in a totally straightforward way; in this way they exclude the interaction of Lucretius' text with other possible intertexts that had also assimilated Empedocles' imagery in parallel and perhaps in contrast to Epicurus. No matter how convenient such a rigid reading of Lucretius' poem may be regarding the nature of his relationship with his master, as Campbell very tellingly points out "certain themes will be so familiar and so resonant, that even Lucretius' aptitude for 'getting inside his opponents positions and then evacuating them of their prior content to refill them with Epicurean doctrine' will not remove all of their former associations. It is now a well known aspect of intertextuality that recontextualization of a topos does not cleanse it of all the accretions of meaning it gained from its former context."[75] We should, therefore, be ready to acknowledge that the presence of Empedocles' imagery simultaneously introduces disturbing philosophical hints both at Empedocles' thought as well as at other possible intertexts. From this point of view, for the prospective reader the border line between target texts remains quite vague and his expectations are often deceived. Within this framework possible tensions that Lucretius' intertextual hints at Empedocles bring about will be explored. I am aware that, due to the scantiness of our evidence about both Empedocles' poem and Epicurus' writings, my overall case about the extent of Lucretius' debt, along with the consequences this may entail, is meant to be a cumulative one, involving also a certain degree of speculation. Whatever the case may be, to quote Lyne's words "intertexts may offer opportunities for comparison or contrast: they may function like similes or contrast similes. They may also offer hints of ideology that agree with the new text -or disturb it. [. . .] There are these options of interpretation, the intertext is there and readable; and the reader must confront it."[76]

More generally, a detailed comparison between Empedocles and Lucretius should encourage the reading anew of Latin texts which condense simultaneous allusions to Empedocles and Lucretius, as well as echoes from other texts which are much indebted to Empedocles, such as Aratus, Apollonius Rhodius, the allegorists and Ennius. In this way more light will be shed upon Empedocles' reception by the Roman epicists, especially Vergil and Ovid, and it will become clearer why Lucretius was read as Empedocles Romanus *par excellence* in the Roman tradition of scientific didactic epos, what Hardie sees as "Empedoclean epos."[77]

1.2 EMPEDOCLES' AND LUCRETIUS' SCIENTIFIC METHOD: THINKING BY ANALOGY

The intrinsic similarities between Empedocles and Epicurus as regards their epistemology and perception theory will be here briefly reviewed, as a prelude to the detailed discussion that follows in the main part of this study. Although one could not claim that all of these principles are distinctive features only of these two philosophical systems, yet this essential approximation will turn out to be an indispensable prerequisite that made Empedocles' analogical strategy particularly convenient for Lucretius to adopt and adapt in his revealing and formulating of the arcane secrets of Nature. Pivotal tenets of Lucretius' own analogical method will be also brought up, along with specific terminology which will repeatedly recur in the subsequent chapters. Most significantly, it will be demonstrated that by explicit allusions to Empedocles Lucretius intentionally underlines his inner affinity with his predecessor's analogical methods, to which he is greatly indebted in various respects.

Following Epicurus' epistemological principles, Lucretius proposes that there are two aspects to the exploration of nature: the truth of things must be reached by means of sensory evidence as well as by mental projection and elaboration (2.61 *naturae species ratioque*).[78] Clay rightly points out that when Lucretius turns into Latin the Greek word φυσιολογία with a twofold phrase he underscores the necessity of combining both these actions within the investigatory process.[79]

More precisely, Epicurus claims that sensation is the primary standard of truth and cannot be refuted by any other criterion.[80] In accordance with this fundamental principle Lucretius sets great value on sensory evidence (*cui nisi prima fides fundata valebit, / haud erit occultis de rebus quo referentes / confirmare animi quicquam ratione queamus. /* "and unless our belief [in sensation] is first firmly established, there will be no principle of appeal in hidden matters, according to which we may establish anything by the reason," 1.423–425; *quo referemus enim? quid nobis certius ipsis / sensibus esse potest, qui vera ac falsa notemus? /* "For to what shall we appeal? What can we find more certain than the senses themselves, to mark for us truth and falsehood?," 1.699–700) and exhorts his pupil to use all his senses as a first step towards grasping the natural laws, without giving more credence to the one than the other (4.478–521).[81] Being an empiricist himself Empedocles too puts great confidence in sensory evidence. Among his extant fragments we come across a statement similar to that made by Lucretius, that every sense should be used according to the situation (B3.9–13):[82]

ἀλλ' ἄγ' ἄθρει πάσῃ παλάμῃ πῇ δῆλον ἕκαστον,
μήτε τιν' ὄψιν ἔχων †πίστει† πλέον ἢ κατ' ἀκουήν
ἢ ἀκοὴν ἐρίδουπον ὑπὲρ τρανώματα γλώσσης,
μήτε τι τῶν ἄλλων, ὁπόσῃ πόρος ἐστὶ νοῆσαι,
γυίων πίστιν ἔρυκε, νόει δ' ᾗ δῆλον ἕκαστον.

"But come, observe with every power in what way each thing is clear, without holding any seeing as more reliable compared with hearing, nor echoing ear above piercings the tongue; and do not keep back trust at all from the other parts of the body by which there is a channel for understanding, but understand each thing in the way in which it is clear."

Since the vocabulary that both poets use when they address their interlocutor pertains to our senses, it is also revealing of their doctrines about perception (e.g. in Empedocles: *κλῦθι*, B1; *ἄθρει*, B3.9; *ἄκουε*, B17.26; *δέρκευ*, B21.1; in *DRN possit cernere*, 2.250; *nonne vides*, 5.556).[83] What is particularly significant à propos Empedocles' and Lucretius' inner relationship is the fact that Lucretius—via Epicurus—follows Empedocles' belief that perception is based on the mechanism of pores and effluences (B84). Although specific aspects of this theory will be discussed in due course,[84] it suffices to point out here that, when Empedocles invites Pausanias to observe "by every device" (*πάσῃ παλάμῃ*, B3.1) he suggests the actual nature of our perceptual faculties; more precisely, the literal interpretation of this subtle metaphorical expression—i.e. "with all his palms"—ultimately equates every sense with that of touch. Similarly Lucretius stresses the pre-eminence of touch among our other senses (e.g. *tactus enim, tactus, pro divina numina sancta, / corporis est sensus, /* "For touch, so help me the holy power of the gods, it is touch that is the bodily sense," 2.434–435).[85] In addition, for both of them the acquisition of knowledge is a clearly material mechanism that entails the transformation of man's elementary structure by integrating new words and thoughts into one's heart (*γνῶθι, διατμηθέντος ἐνὶ σπλάγχνοισι λόγοιο. /* "do you learn, after the argument has been divided within your breast," B4.3; *πρὸς παρεὸν γὰρ μῆτις ἀέξεται ἀνθρώποισιν. /* "For man's wisdom grows according to what is present," B106). In a similar vein, Lucretius describes the absorption of knowledge in physiological terms as a process of "eating" or "spewing out" (e.g. *depascimur*, 3.12; *respuis ex animo*, 6.68).[86] At the same time knowledge is a gradual and cumulative process; the more one learns, the more one's receptiveness to new things is increased. Thus, Lucretius claims that (1.1114–1117):[87]

> *Haec sic pernosces parva perductus opella;*
> *namque alid ex alio clarescet, nec tibi caeca*   1115

nox iter eripiet quin ultima naturai
pervideas: ita res accendent lumina rebus.

"So you will gain a thorough understanding of these matters, led on with very little effort; for one thing will become clear by another, and blind night will not steal your path and prevent you from seeing all the uttermost recesses of nature: so clearly will truths kindle light for truths."

Nevertheless, when it comes to processes assumed to operate below the level of perception Lucretius acknowledges the limitation posed by the data of sense-perception in our ability to grasp the full spectrum of truth (*sed quae corpora decedant in tempore quoque, / invida praeclusit specimen natura videndi. /* "but what particles are separated on each occasion, our niggardly faculty of sight has debarred us from proving," 1.320–321).[88] The things called ἄδηλα can never be brought literally before our eyes,[89] either because they are located below our senses due to their size (e.g. atoms and the atomic structure of things) or too far off for us to obtain a near view of them and investigate (celestial things, τὰ μετέωρα), or even because they took place in the past (e.g. cosmogony).[90] In this precept he once more agrees with Empedocles (B2.1–8):

στεινωποὶ μὲν γὰρ παλάμαι κατὰ γυῖα κέχυνται,
πολλὰ δὲ δείλ᾽ ἔμπαια, τά τ᾽ ἀμβλύνουσι μέριμνας.
παῦρον †δὲ ζωῇσι βίου† μέρος ἀθρήσαντες
ὠκύμοροι καπνοῖο δίκην ἀρθέντες ἀπέπταν,
αὐτὸ μόνον πεισθέντες, ὅτῳ προσέκυρσεν ἕκαστος   5
πάντοσ᾽ ἐλαυνόμενοι, τὸ δ᾽ ὅλον <πᾶς> εὔχεται εὑρεῖν·
οὕτως οὔτ᾽ ἐπιδερκτὰ τάδ᾽ ἀνδράσιν οὔτ᾽ ἐπακουστά.
οὔτε νόῳ περιληπτά.

"The powers spread over the body are constricted, and many afflictions burst in and dull their meditations. After observing a small part of life in their lifetime, subject to a swift death they are borne up and waft away like smoke; they are convinced only of that which each has experienced as they are driven in all directions, yet all boast of finding the whole. These things are not so to be seen or heard by men or grasped with mind. But you now, since you have come aside to this place, will learn within the reach of human understanding."

In close connection with this general principle that both philosophers share in common, we should now turn to a passage in Lucretius' Book 5 (5.100–103):

> *ut fit ubi insolitam rem adportes auribus ante,* 100
> *nec tamen hanc possis oculorum subdere visu*
> *nec iacere indu manus, via qua munita fidei*
> *proxima fert humanum in pectus templaque mentis.*

"as happens when you invite a hearing for something hitherto unfamiliar, which you cannot bring within the scope of vision nor put into the hands, whereby the highway of belief leads straight to the heart of man and the precincts of his intelligence."

In this passage scholars have noticed a clear echo of Empedocles' B133.[91]

> οὐκ ἔστιν πελάσασθαι ἐν ὀφθαλμοῖσιν ἐφικτὸν
> ἡμετέροις ἢ χερσὶ λαβεῖν, ἧπέρ τε μεγίστη
> πειθοῦς ἀνθρώποισιν ἀμαξιτὸς εἰς φρένα πίπτει.

"It is not possible to bring (the divine) close within each of our eyes or to grasp him with the hands, by which the broadest path of persuasion for men leads to the mind."

In a way similar to Lucretius' statement, the Presocratic philosopher claims that the nature of the divine is also inaccessible to our senses (5.101 *nec tamen hanc possis oculorum subdere visu* → B133.1–2 οὐκ ἔστιν πελάσασθαι ἐν ὀφθαλμοῖσιν ἐφικτόν / ἡμετέροις; 5.102 *nec iacere indu manus* → B133.2 ἢ χερσὶ λαβεῖν); moreover, sense perception is described as a highway falling into the mind (5.102 *via qua munita* → B133.2–3 ἧπέρ τε μεγίστη / . . . ἀμαξιτὸς; 5.102 *fidei* → B133.3 πειθοῦς; 5.103 *proxima fert humanum in pectus templaque mentis.* → B133.3 ἀνθρώποισιν . . . εἰς φρένα πίπτει). Just before setting out to explain the perishability of our world, Lucretius strikingly recontextualizes the Empedoclean language. In this way, whereas he replaces the traditional religion with his divine doctrine, he stresses the difficulty of persuading his pupil about the invisible, since this cannot be seen or touched. What is even more, he reveals his awareness of Empedocles' concerns about the limits of our senses, concerns that he himself shares.

Lucretius warns his neophyte that in confronting such intriguing physical phenomena or philosophical issues our sight may contradict our mind, our eyes can blur the truth; hence, we may be led to wonder (*mirabile*, 2.1028; *mirantur*, 6.59; *mirari*, 6.654). In the same spirit Empedocles explains that the limited scope of our senses may let us fall prey to amazement (e.g. τὴν σὺ νόῳ δέρκευ, μηδ' ὄμμασιν ἧσο τεθηπώς· / "Contemplate her with the mind, and do not sit staring dazed," B17.21). So, how can we surmount the limitations posed by our sense organs, overcome the astonishment and thus achieve ultimate peace of mind?[92] In other words how can we inquire about the obscure and form preconceptions (προλήψεις, Epicur. *Ep. Hdt.* 37–38) about its various aspects?

It has long been observed that, as regards phenomena of which there is no hope of confirmation by actual examination, the Presocratic philosophers developed a process of inferring conclusions by appealing to analogies from familiar or easily accessible domains (τὰ φαινόμενα, τὰ ἐναργή, τὰ ἔνδηλα). This practice, which is encapsulated in Anaxagoras' famous dictum ὄψις τῶν ἀδήλων τὰ φαινόμενα (DK59 B21a) and was approved by Democritus (DK68 A111), was widely used not only in physics, but also in medicine, divination, law and rhetoric.[93]

Along the same lines, Epicurus embraced the method of reasoning about the unseen by resorting to signs (σημεῖα) from what could be directly observed (ὅθεν καὶ περὶ τῶν ἀδήλων ἀπὸ τῶν φαινομένων χρὴ σημειοῦσθαι. / "Hence it is from plain facts tht we must start when we draw inferences about the unknown," Diog. Laert. 10.32).[94] In essence, Epicurus claims that when direct sense evidence is not available any hypothesis must be submitted to the test of sensation and only accepted if it is not then contradicted (principle of οὐκ ἀντιμαρτύρησις). Moreover, Epicurus accepts multiple explanations for physical phenomena (τὸ μέντοι φάντασμα ἑκάστου τηρητέον καὶ ἔτι τὰ συναπτόμενα τούτῳ διαιρετέον, ἃ οὐκ ἀντιμαρτυρεῖται τοῖς παρ' ἡμῖν γινομένοις πλεοναχῶς συντελεῖσθαι. / "However, we must observe each fact as presented, and further separate from it all the facts presented along with it, the occurrence of which from various causes is not contradicted by facts within our experience," *Ep. Pyth.* 88). Yet, when it comes to basic tenets of atomism, he does not allow for alternative possibilities, but insists on just one valid mental model corresponding to one dogmatic scientific explanation. What is more, by Lucretius' day every major philosophical school had schematized formal theories of signs.[95]

In accordance with the Epicurean precepts of empirical investigation, Lucretius himself develops scientific methods of inference by analogy.[96] His ultimate aim is to penetrate into the invisible natural world and express its secrets in a code of communication decipherable by his uninitiated pupil. At the same time he endeavours to teach his student the way of further creating well-founded analogies in order to be capable of answering possible future queries himself and deepening his knowledge.

Lucretius' investigation is based on the fundamental principle that, since nature is gradually built out of the very same primary elements, i.e. the atoms, she is pervaded by the same laws, the so-called *foedera naturai,* which are active at every level of the universe: "The general laws he asserts and explains are to be proved valid in all and every circumstance. The act of interpretation will therefore consist in understanding the relationship between individual phenomena and the general law which can explain them."[97] The existence of this underlying *ratio* being taken for granted, Lucretius often appeals to the "manifest" in order to detect processes indicative and probative of what happens beneath our senses and thus bring the imperceptible before our eyes (e.g. *manifesta docet res* / "plain matter of fact teaches," 1.893).[98] That is why he systematically invites Memmius to set in motion the "eyes" of his mind and become a "penetrating reader," in order to see through the surface of things and mentally perceive their true nature (e.g. *perspicere,* 1.478).[99] Moreover, since the process of cognition of the universal atomic constitution is compared with vision (*res quibus occultas penitus convisere possis.* / "whereby you may see into the heart of things hidden," 1.145), it bears connotations of initiation into mysteries.[100]

From a more technical perspective, Gentner defines scientific analogies as follows: "[scientific] analogies can be characterized as structure-mappings between complex systems. Typically the target system to be understood is new or abstract and the base system in terms of which the target is described is familiar and perhaps visualisable."[101] By calculating the similarities and differences between source and target domains we are able to extract valid conclusions about the latter. More precisely, Lucretius envisages the structure of the universe as "a hierarchy of subordinated and coordinated levels," to use Hardie's words. Along these lines, on the one hand, "large scale events have strict analogues in small-scale events and vice versa."[102] So, through a process of magnifying or shrinking a visible phenomenon, we can mentally shift between subordinated levels and analogically project our knowledge from the visible world onto another level of microcosmic or macrocosmic reality. In order to descend into the microcosm, we should opt for an object from the visible world that is as neutral in qualities as possible and of limited dimensions; in other words a very basic atomic combination situated a level above the atomic in the scale of creation. Then, before visualizing the obscure atomic structure in question, a certain rational elaboration of the visible object should be made in order to deconstruct it further into its basic components.[103] On the other hand, when it comes to coordinated levels, "the gap to be bridged is not one of size, but of quality, although there may be a discrepancy of scale."[104] Last but not least, we should note that the more obscure the phenomenon under investigation is, the heavier the demand on analogical thinking; that is why such passages condense clusters of supplementary images.

When Lucretius integrates abundant personifications, similes and metaphors into his scientific discourse he therefore does not use them just as stylistic ornaments in order to facilitate the initiation of his pupil in the philosophical tenets they express. In so far as tropes assist him in articulating his scientific analogies, they become an indispensable element of the pedagogical process. Given the universal material homogeneity, as Hardie again notes, "the knowledge that the two things compared are analogous in an extra-literary sense encourages a more thorough exploration of the points of resemblance between the two; the detail of the object is tied in closely to the detail of the object to which it is compared."[105] As we will see in detail, Lucretius exploits the inherent potential of literary comparisons and disguises a wide range of source domains under the mask of literary "vehicles," and of target domains under that of literary "tenors."[106] In this way he effectively creates insight into reality, cogently demonstrates his theoretical assertions, as if drawing a diagram, and eventually substantiates them.

At this point I will focus on one simile, which in my view is highly revealing of Lucretius' stance towards Empedocles. While putting forward the Epicurean principle of the existence of void, Lucretius refuses to offer his pupil more proofs and encourages him to work them out for himself. In order to illustrate this process he compares the keen-scented reader's endeavour to perceive unseen reality with that of hunting dogs finding traces of mountain-ranging prey in the undergrowth that will eventually lead them to its unseen hiding places (1.402–409):[107]

> *verum animo satis haec vestigia parva sagaci*
> *sunt, per quae possis cognoscere cetera tute.*
> *namque canes ut montivagae persaepe ferai*
> *naribus inveniunt intectas fronde quietes,*　　　　　　　　405
> *cum semel institerunt vestigia certa viai,*
> *sic alid ex alio per te tute ipse videre*
> *talibus in rebus poteris caecasque latebras*
> *insinuare omnis et verum protrahere inde.*

"But for a keen-scented mind, these little tracks are enough to enable you to recognize the others for yourself. For as hounds very often find by their scent the leaf-hidden resting-place of the mountain-ranging quarry, when once they have hit upon certain traces of its path, so will you be able for yourself to see one thing after another in such matters as these, and to penetrate all unseen hiding-places and draw forth the truth from them."

As Clay astutely observes, here Lucretius develops into an elaborate simile the metaphor which was latent in Epicurus' expression ἴχνευσις τοῦ ἀδήλου (cf. *Ep. Pyth.* 96).[108] In addition, Lucretius does not describe just a vague process of conquering knowledge. He rather grants his comparison a specific programmatic function since he brings up essential points of his scientific method, such as its rational character and the value of empirical evidence (1.402–403), with the aid of which we gradually derive information about the invisible world through the process of σημείωσις.[109] This pattern of "hunting," or the "venatic" paradigm for investigation, to use Fowler's term, centred on the image of *vestigia,* is applied throughout the poem.[110]

It has long been observed that this simile is hinted at in Empedocles' B101 which refers to dogs "tracking with nostrils fragments of animal bodies (which they) left from their paws on the soft grass" (κέρματα θηρείων μελέων μυκτῆρσιν ἐρευνῶν, / . . . ἀπέλειπε ποδῶν ἁπαλῇ περὶ ποίῃ . . .).[111] Even more notably, Lucretius is the first extant Latin author to employ the compound adjective *montivagus.* It is thus highly probable that he invents it in order to translate the corresponding Greek compound adjective ὀρίπλαγκτος which was also an Empedoclean coinage (θηρῶν ὀριπλάγκτων, fr. a (ii) 26 M&P) and may have been used in the broader context of B101.[112]

It seems very plausible to suggest that, by means of such a clear allusion to Empedocles within the framework of this key simile regarding his scientific methodology, Lucretius makes tangible the focal intertextual source, to which he is about to resort systematically. In other words, Lucretius proclaims here that, in expounding the Epicurean philosophical system and analyzing fundamental concepts of the imperceptible world, he will use Empedocles not only as a poetic model, but also as a scientific one. And in fact, thanks to the partial overlapping of their philosophical precepts, Lucretius can draw from his predecessor a whole series of techniques which he then creatively appropriates as an organic component of his poem. Elsewhere, he inevitably deviates from Empedocles' literary means of thought and subordinates them to his didactic purposes and to Epicurean tenets.

1.3 EMPEDOCLES, ENNIUS AND LUCRETIUS

In his article "Philosophy and Literature in Lucretian Intertextuality," Don Fowler stresses the fact that "in considering literary intertextuality, we should certainly return to the original texts for our comparison and contrast, because this will often suggest traces present in our target-text under erasure, but we should also consider the way in which these literary texts may have already been used within the context of philosophical discourse, and how they may thus have acquired further associations in the history of their reception."[113] A brief digression on how Empedocles' poem was first received and appropriated by a poet who preceded Lucretius and considerably influenced his poem is therefore needed.

More specifically, by looking at Ennius' works, via which Empedocles presumably found first his way into Latin literature and thought,[114] an attempt will be made further to counterbalance those scholars who like to regard Lucretius strictly as an orthodox Epicurean devotee, who was using as his sole source of philosophical material his master's writings alone, and as a consequence uncritically closed his eyes to any other external philosophical influence. Along these lines, evidence of Empedocles' poetry and philosophy being tightly interwoven in the literary tradition upon which Lucretius so extensively draws will be offered; in this way it will become clear how implausible it would be for Lucretius to have distinguished the content of Empedocles' poem from its form when he himself directly turns to the latter's poem and initiates an intensive intertextual dialogue at various textual levels. Then I will look at Lucretius' own discussion of Ennius' poetry, which will also reinforce my main claim about Lucretius' conscious reading of Empedocles as a natural philosopher as well as a poet.

To begin with, the Empedoclean four elements appear to be the model for *Annales* 7 (*Cui par imber et ignis, spiritus et grauis terra* / "for whom water and fire and breath and heavy earth are equal," fr. 221 Skutsch). Bignone also argued that Ennius' dream of Homer in his *Annales* 1, in which the latter remembers that he became a peacock before his soul passed into Ennius (*memini me fiere pavom* / "I remember becoming a peacock," fr. 11 Skutsch), shows close affinity with Empedocles' account of the transmigration of souls.[115] In addition, Norden has persuasively demonstrated that the demonic *Discordia taetra* who opens the *Ianus Geminus* at the outbreak of the Second Punic War in *Annales* 7 (*postquam Discordia taetra* / *Belli ferratos postes portasque refregit* / "After foul Discord broke open the ironclad doors and doorposts of war,," frs. 225–226 Skutsch) or the *Paluda virago* (*Corpore tartarino prognata Paluda virago* / "<Discord,> of hellish body daughter bred, woman of war in warrior's cloak," fr. 220 Skutsch) is the Latin version of Empedocles' principle of Strife.[116] It is noteworthy that in this context a philosophical idea serves to explain a historical event. Bignone takes Norden's remark further and assumes that this transition from peace to war in Roman history may have been connected by Ennius with the cyclic alternation between cosmic Love and Strife.[117] Concerning the philosophical colour of Homer's speech in *Annales* 1, Hardie rightly notes that "the general sequence of natural philosophy followed by history may have been designed to provide a generalized cosmic overture for the detailed Roman themes that followed."[118] From this point of view, Ennius should be considered the decisive intermediary for the introduction into later Roman literature of Empedocles' integration of cosmological-philosophical order with historical.[119]

Likewise, in Ennius' *Epicharmus,* which was the Latin version of a work assigned to the fifth century Sicilian comic writer of that name, Ennius dreams that he is dead and learns, probably from Epicharmus himself, the truth about nature and the four elements, with a section on the nature of living beings, whose body is earth and whose soul is fire from the sun.[120]

Scholars have long ago discerned a significant number of Ennian echoes in Lucretius' poem.[121] For the purposes of the present discussion the focus will be placed on just one passage of Lucretius' proem to Book 1 (1.102–126), which will prove particularly enlightening about his reading of Ennius as an Empedoclean poet. In fact, as will be shown, Lucretius' treatment of his Latin predecessor parallels that of the Presocratic philosopher. In these verses Lucretius apostrophizes his pupil and warns him not to be terrified by the superstitious tales of priests (*vatum,* 1.102, 1.109) about the survival and transmigration of soul after death; Memmius should always bear in mind the true nature of the human soul, which, according to a fundamental Epicurean principle, is mortal. As a striking example of such erroneous beliefs about after-life Lucretius evokes "our own Ennius" (*Ennius ut noster,* 1.117).

There are two major issues that Lucretius touches upon here. First, he acknowledges a poetic debt to Ennius, as his poetic predecessor in Latin hexameter verse, who "first brought down from pleasant Helicon a chaplet of evergreen leafage to win a glorious name through the nations of Italian men" (*qui primus amoeno / detulit ex Helicone perenni fronde coronam / per gentis Italas hominum quae clara clueret;* 1.117–119). Then he brings up Ennius' belief in the existence of Acheron and recalls Ennius' dream of Homer, with which Ennius probably opened his *Annales* (*Ann.* frs. 2–10 Skutsch). According to Lucretius, Ennius claimed that the phantom of everlasting Homer expounded to him the "nature of things" (*rerum naturam,* 1.126).[122]

It has already been pointed out that here "Lucretius' homage is mingled with an element of rivalry and even with criticism."[123] On the poetic level, while Lucretius points to Ennius' everlasting garland (*coronam,* 1.118), thus recognizing his predecessor's indisputable value as the first to introduce poetry into Italy, he claims for himself an illustrious chaplet (*insignemque . . . coronam,* 1.929), usurping in this way the other's pioneering role.[124] At the same time, since he presents Ennius' Homer as a poet writing "on the nature of things," he draws a very specific line of poetic succession within the genre of natural-philosophic didactic epic, with Homer being the first inventor and he himself the last link in this long chain. In any event, relying on firm Epicurean grounds Lucretius denounces Ennius' ideas of transmigration.[125]

This is the moment when Empedocles enters again to take up his position in the line of literary heritage that Lucretius prominently grants him. One can easily detect Empedoclean echoes on the level of philosophical ideas; in fact this is what leads Sedley to assume that this passage should be taken as a direct attack on Empedocles' explanation of his doctrine of transmigration (B115), which should then form part of the proem of Empedocles' *On Nature*.[126] Gale has pointed out that the etymological pun on Ennius' name (*perenni fronde,* 1.118)[127] may recall Empedocles' own play on his name in B77–78.1 (<δένδρεα δ'> ἐμπεδόφυλλα καὶ ἐμπεδόκαρπα τέθηλεν / "evergreen and 'constantly bearing' trees flourish"),[128] with the epithet ἐμπεδόφυλλα translated by *perenni fronde* and ἐμπεδόκαρπα by the expression *semper florentis* (1.124), which is attributed to Homer. Moreover, since Empedocles' name can be analysed into ἔμπεδος and κλέος and the suffix *-κλης* is etymologically associated both with the word κλέος and the Latin *clueo,* the expression "destined to bring him bright fame" in the next line (*clara clueret,* 1.119) turns out to be another etymological play that makes the link—both poetic and philosophical—of both Ennius and Homer with the Presocratic philosopher noticeably stronger.[129]

Sedley concludes that "Lucretius is here distancing himself from Ennius' beliefs, while revering his poetry, in a way that pointedly parallels his treatment of Empedocles."[130] While Sedley's remark that Lucretius makes a distinction between his poetic and philosophical debt to Ennius, a distinction which is similar to that à propos Empedocles, holds true, one could raise an objection against the general validity of this claim. Although Lucretius specifically rejects Ennius' eschatological ideas of metempsychosis for which the latter is presumably indebted to Empedocles, Ennius still remains a crucial intertextual channel for his reception of other Empedoclean philosophical ideas, such as the notion of unity between cosmic and historical order that we have just discussed above. Once again, in Hardie's words, "Lucretius is an efficient predator, who digests those parts of his victim which are beneficial to his system and ostentatiously rejects the indigestible."[131] In this sense, Lucretius' attitude towards Ennius constitutes proof that his intertextual engagement with Empedocles is both poetic and philosophical.

Chapter One
Personification

2.1 INTRODUCTION

Since the very beginning of mythology and literature, in an effort to comprehend the perplexing world around him, man has found in himself a convenient model, with which to concretize the abstract and unveil the unseen. So, he ascribed to inanimate things an anthropomorphic appearance, human capabilities or emotions.[1] In the first part of this chapter (2.2), I will explore how Lucretius uses personification in order to sketch abstract natural forces and to enlarge the invisible first beginnings of things. In the second (2.3) and third part (2.4) respectively it will be seen how Lucretius envisages the world and the earth as human beings, in order to reduce their size so that his audience might visualize and conceive their unseen workings.

Lucretius, while resorting to personification, widely employed in poetry and prose, found in Empedocles' poem a specific model for turning this literary device into an effective philosophical tool, and thus exploited it widely for heuristic and demonstrative purposes. Although several points related to this particular aspect of Empedocles' and Lucretius' intertextual relationship have been repeatedly noted, an overall study is still needed. In what follows I will examine anew the extent of Lucretius' intertextual debt to Empedocles, which in the case in question should not be restricted only to the latter's poetical method. It is in this spirit that Lucretius' overall stance towards this specific Empedoclean device will be sketched and the general impact upon *DRN* that this choice entails will be considered. Given the common principles in their philosophical doctrines, in his effort to communicate similar ideas, Lucretius could resort to Empedocles' device in a more concrete way and adopt specific instances of personification, which anyhow were inextricably linked with the latter's precepts. There are in fact several instances in which Lucretius could validate his device by turning to Epicurus' writings, where similar anthropomorphic wording occurred, albeit in an embryonic state.

Even so, Epicurus' serious disagreement with specific aspects of Empedocles' philosophy could render this specific intertextual borrowing inappropriate for Lucretius' philosophical and didactic construction and even imperil his stable rapport with his master. A detailed analysis of how Lucretius constantly tries to clarify Epicurus' doctrinal discrepancies with regard to Empedocles and seems to effectively surmount any such obstacle that he encounters will be postponed for the sections to follow. At this point, however, it is imperative to explore in more general terms whether it was acceptable for an Epicurean philosopher to resort to the literary mechanism of personification. The focus will principally be on one issue which directly pertains to all four concepts that Lucretius describes in anthropomorphic language (motive forces, atoms, the world and the earth), following Empedocles' example. One should not forget that they were already heavily charged with specific mythographical and religious connotations. In fact, Empedocles himself as well as Epicurus' rival philosophical schools of thought considered them not simply animate entities, but divine.[2]

Epicurus had very specific ideas about the nature of divinity. Although he himself believed in the existence of gods, according to our sources he plausibly located them in the *intermundia* (= μετακόσμια)[3] and denied them any interest or intervention in human affairs.[4] His natural world was governed by strictly mechanistic principles. Therefore, not only did these four concepts that Lucretius treats in human terms not share anything with divinity, but actually—apart from the abstract natural forces—they were all simply considered aggregations of inanimate matter (cf. 5.110–145).

In Epicurus' view, despite the fact that at the outset of history men had the right notion of the divine, in the course of time religious beliefs had been distorted by religious rites and poetic performances and then even further by theologians and philosophers, who wickedly used them to misguide people.[5] That was actually the reason for Epicurus' disapproval of poetry and myths, even when they were used alongside their allegorical interpretations, since he considered them all contagious vehicles of false religious ideas.[6] It would perhaps be superfluous to note here that, given his attitude towards the use of mythological language, it is highly improbable that he himself would have appropriated Empedocles' phrasing in his writings. In the same spirit, Philodemus in his *On Piety* argues that the poetic or philosophical reduction of gods to some entity or principle or the assimilation of a god with one or more divinities amounts to atheism.[7]

Therefore, by no means could Lucretius accept any kind of "religious personification,"[8] as this could certainly cause a conflict with his master, contradicting his theological precepts. In other words, by imitating Empedocles' personifications he runs the risk of introducing into his text theological and teleological connotations that could prove rather unsettling within an Epicurean context. In what follows, it will be seen how Lucretius, instead of completely rejecting the use of personification alongside myth and allegorism, creatively assimilates it as an indispensable part of his didactic project, and also why Empedocles could be a particularly convenient model in this instance.[9] Whatever the case may be, it seems that Lucretius plays on dangerous ground.

In order to dispel any doubts about his method and his actual goals, Lucretius provides us with self-referential comments and invites us to use them as our reading guidelines throughout *DRN*. Just after the account of the *Magna Mater* cult, in which myth has been provocatively used to illustrate his arguments (2.598–643),[10] Lucretius explains in detail the workings of his device (2.644–660):

Quae bene et eximie quamvis disposta ferantur,	
longe sunt tamen a vera ratione repulsa.	645
omnis enim per se divom natura necessest	
inmortali aevo summa cum pace fruatur	
semota ab nostris rebus seiunctaque longe;	
nam privata dolore omni, privata periclis,	
ipsa suis pollens opibus, nil indiga nostri,	650
nec bene promeritis capitur neque tangitur ira.	
terra quidem vero caret omni tempore sensu,	
et quia multarum potitur primordia rerum,	
multa modis multis effert in lumina solis.	
hic siquis mare Neptunum Cereremque vocare	655
constituet fruges et Bacchi nomine abuti	
mavolt quam laticis proprium proferre vocamen,	
concedamus ut hic terrarum dictitet orbem	
esse deum Matrem, dum vera re tamen ipse	
religione animum turpi contingere parcat.	660

"But well and excellently as all this is set forth and told, yet it is far removed from true reasoning. For the very nature of divinity must necessarily enjoy immortal life in the deepest peace, far removed and separated from our affairs; for without any pain, without danger, itself mighty by its own resources, needing us not at all, it is neither propitiated with services nor touched by wrath. The earth indeed lacks sensation at all times, and only because it receives into itself the first-beginnings of many things does it bring forth many in many ways into the sun's light. Here if anyone decides to call the sea Neptune, and corn Ceres, and to misapply the name of Bacchus rather than to use the title that is proper to that liquor, let us grant him to dub the round world Mother of the Gods, provided that he forbears in reality himself to infect his mind with base superstition."

Metonymy or "deification" of physical objects is acceptable, provided that we have a clear conception of divinity. Abusing the name of Neptune when referring to the sea, of Bacchus instead of wine, or of Ceres instead of corn, should not imply anything erroneous about the inanimate structure of the object. Lucretius takes pains to establish the essence of the divinity, which in fact is far removed from human affairs, enjoys eternal peace and cannot be touched by any sacrifice or propitiating ceremony (2.646–651).[11] Likewise Mother-Earth is not a god. Moreover, one should always bear in mind that for each thing there is a literal meaning (*proprium . . . vocamen*, 2.657), which should be juxtaposed whenever the metonymy alone would obfuscate the truth. Only if a personification fulfils these preconditions can it be employed as a useful explanatory device. Similar instructions are given in 5.795–796:

> *Linquitur ut merito maternum nomen adepta*
> *terra sit, e terra quoniam sunt cuncta creata.*

> "It remains, therefore, that the earth deserves the name of mother which
> she possesses, since from the earth all things have been produced."

Lucretius comments on his account of the first creation of life that precedes (5.772–877) and emphatically repeats that the Earth is not divine; she has just rightly gained this name, thanks to specific functions she shares with female living organisms.[12] This kind of comment serves him as a safety valve in many places in the poem.

Here, we should recall that, while unlike Lucretius Empedocles believed that his motive forces and the roots are truly divine, he himself made it clear that, for example, Hephaestus is another name for fire (τέσσαρα δ᾽ Ἡφαίστοιο· τὰ δ᾽ ὀστέα λευκὰ γένοντο, / "[of the eight parts] and four of Hephaistos; and these came to be white bones," B96.3) and Aphrodite symbolizes the creative forces (Γηθοσύνην καλέοντες ἐπώνυμον ἠδ᾽ Ἀφροδίτην· / "giving her the name Joy, as well as Aphrodite," B17.24). Although Empedocles' theory of metaphorical language in general will be revisited,[13] it should be stressed here that his technique of using instances of personification and then explaining them may have influenced Lucretius in presenting Epicurus' philosophy.[14]

In sum, in what follows it will be shown that Lucretius interplays with Empedocles' method and ideas in such a cunning way that he eventually turns personification into an essential tool of communicating to his pupil the Epicurean truth of freedom and salvation. While so doing, he strives to clarify his beliefs and ensure his fidelity to Epicurus' orthodox doctrine.

2.2 PERSONIFICATION OF NATURAL FORCES AND MINIMAL ENTITIES

Empedocles generally resorts to personification in order to present his pupil with a comprehensible image of both the *motive forces* of creation and destruction and the unchangeable *first beginnings* of things, i.e. his roots. Lucretius, too, makes use of similar images in order to sketch the Epicurean physical system, regulated by self-prompted actions and obscure mechanistic processes. In this section, it will be argued that Empedocles' and Lucretius' systems of personifications overlap in important respects and specific affinities in their use will be expounded. Moreover, it will be shown that, following Empedocles' example, Lucretius applies this literary device in a more systematic way. Like his predecessor, he does not limit himself to treating unseen primary elements and natural forces as isolated animate units; rather, by means of a more articulated imagery that reflects different manifestations and facets of human relationships, he succeeds in conveying a variety of philosophical notions as well. As this cannot be a mere coincidence, I will attempt to answer the question why Empedocles was particularly suitable for Lucretius as a model in this respect, what obstacles their philosophical discrepancies pose for Lucretius in this context, and how the Epicurean poet disentangles himself from the trap of deviating from his master's doctrine.

Our starting point will be rather basic occurrences of personification (deification 2.2.1, simple animation 2.2.2). Then, a more complex web of relationships from which both philosophers draw their imagery will be gradually sketched, a web that reflects the pyramid of human relations. In other words, while man himself is always at the centre, as we ascend the stages of human relations, interrelations may vary ranging from more primitive and unconscious processes of attraction and repulsion (sexual imagery or images of friendship and hostility 2.2.3.1) to more complicated and structured associations; those, depending on the identity and number of persons involved, necessitate formal legal agreements in order to acquire a certain temporary coherence (socio-political imagery 2.2.3.2). Conversely, as the equilibrium in human relationships can be easily disturbed, images of disorder complete the overall picture (images of war 2.2.3.3). Moreover, while some stages are independent and can coexist (e.g. friendship and sexual relationships or marriage and alliances between states), in other cases the existence of one stage presupposes that of the next one (e.g. the existence of several couples as a prerequisite for the creation of societies). A certain overlapping and ambivalence in the vocabulary used with reference to different types of human relationships should be therefore expected, as this reflects their actual structure and interdependence.[15] Nevertheless, as will emerge once the overall picture is completed, both Empedocles and Lucretius make use of the whole range of relationships in order to highlight various aspects of their philosophy.

2.2.1 Personification and Deification of Cosmic Forces

Empedocles' motive forces are believed to possess divine nature.[16] The creative power is concretized as Aphrodite or Kypris. When Empedocles refers to her reign during the Golden Age (B128), he seems to express some kind of preference for her, as he implies that she is the only Goddess truly worthy of worship.[17] Ares also figures in the extant fragments, most probably identified with Strife (οὐδέ τις ἦν κείνοισιν Ἄρης θεὸς οὐδὲ Κυδοιμός / "They did not have Ares as god or Kydoimos," B128.1).

In general terms, deification of motive forces for Empedocles, is not just a poetic device; it rather denotes his critical stance towards traditional religion and the inherited mythical world. In fact, elsewhere Empedocles directly attacks Homer's anthropomorphism and proposes instead a new kind of divinity (B134):[18]

> οὐδὲ γὰρ ἀνδρομέῃ κεφαλῇ κατὰ γυῖα κέκασται,
> [οὐ μὲν ἀπὸ νώτοιο δύο κλάδοι ἀΐσσουσι,]
> οὐ πόδες, οὐ θοὰ γοῦν', οὐ μήδεα λαχνήεντα,
> ἀλλὰ φρὴν ἱερὴ καὶ ἀθέσφατος ἔπλετο μοῦνον,
> φροντίσι κόσμον ἅπαντα καταΐσσουσα θοῇσιν.   5

> "For he is not equipped with a human head on a body, [two braches do not spring from his back,] he has no feet, no swift knees, no shaggy genitals, but he is mind alone, holy and inexpressible, darting through the whole cosmos with swift thoughts."

In the later tradition, he is said to have replaced traditional hymns for the anthropomorphic gods with scientific hymns (ὕμνοι φυσιολογικοί).[19] Empedocles himself entreats the immortal Muse, Calliope, to stand by him in his endeavor to reveal a good account about the blessed gods (εὐχομένῳ *νῦν αὖτε παρίστασο, Καλλιόπεια, / ἀμφὶ θεῶν μακάρων ἀγαθὸν λόγον ἐμφαίνοντι.* / "now once more, Kalliopeia, answer a prayer, and stand by as a worthy account of the blessed gods is being unfolded," B131.3–4).[20] Besides, the Homeric tradition, in which Empedocles was writing, already had an established image of personified gods to offer; hence, a similar representation of motive forces and the roots, as we will see in the following section, was for him a natural choice. In order to create the link with the traditional divinities, Empedocles incorporates into his physical poem direct references to the traditional Olympic Pantheon, in this case Aphrodite and Ares; he strips it of its familiar traits and dislodges it from its throne, while he replaces it with what he considers truly eternal, granting his new gods the pivotal role of the Homeric ones.

Empedocles' deification of motive forces, as can be seen from his account of zoogony, entails further specific consequences. According to Aëtius' testimony Empedocles distinguished four zoogonical stages, two taking place under the influence of Love—on which the focus will be here placed—and two under that of Strife (A72a = Aët. 5.19.5 = *Dox. Gr.* 430).[21] In the first stage disjoined limbs and other body parts sprung out of the earth and roamed around (B57):[22]

> *ᾖ πολλαὶ μὲν κόρσαι ἀναύχενες ἐβλάστησαν.*
> *γυμνοὶ δ' ἐπλάζοντο βραχίονες εὔνιδες ὤμων,*
> *ὄμματά τ' οἶ' ἐπλανᾶτο πενητεύοντα μετώπων,*

> "Here many heads sprang up without necks, bare arms were wandering without shoulders, and eyes needing foreheads strayed singly."

Sedley believes that these first creations should be thought of not so much as "detached body parts as very simple organisms, each with just one specialization."[23] Although Aëtius' account is not very informative in this respect, as Sedley persuasively continues, it seems that in this preliminary phase of the transition from roots to the first structures Aphrodite's intervention is decisive. Simplicius (*In Cael.* CIAG 7, 528.3–530.26) informs us that the introduction of Love's increasing power (B35) was followed by three passages all describing her work (*ἐξ ὧν ὄμματ' ἔπηξεν ἀτειρέα δι' Ἀφροδίτη.* / "Out of these the goddess Aphrodite fashioned untiring eyes," B86; *γόμφοις ἀσκήσασα καταστόργοις Ἀφροδίτη* / "Aphrodite, having fitted [them] with rivets of affection," B87; *Κύπριδος (φησίν) ἐν παλάμῃσιν ὅτε ξύμ πρῶτ' ἐφύοντο.* / "When they first grew together in the hands of Kypris," B95). Sedley adds to these B84, which plausibly describes Aphrodite's creation of the eye during the same period. What is important for the present discussion is the fact that the

Goddess' fashioning of human organs and tissues out of the primary elements seems to be a purposeful activity. Inevitably, such an illustration of the creative force introduces teleological connotations into Empedocles' philosophical system, especially if viewed in the light of later teleological accounts.[24]

In the second stage these separate limbs (B58 μουνομελῆ) were combined into composite beings, described by Aëtius—who plausibly quotes Empedocles' phrasing—as "apparition-like" (εἰδωλοφανεῖς). Aristotle (*Phys.* 198b29–32) and Simplicius (*In Cael.* CIAG 7.586.5–587.26, *In Phys.* CIAG 9, 371.33–372.9) explain that there was a random combination of single-limbed organs. The product were monstrous joined-up hybrids:

> αὐτὰρ ἐπεὶ κατὰ μεῖζον ἐμίσγετο δαίμονι δαίμων,
> ταῦτά τε συμπίπτεσκον, ὅπῃ συνέκυρσεν ἕκαστα,
> ἄλλα τε πρὸς τοῖς πολλὰ διηνεκῆ ἐξεγένοντο. (B59)

"But as god mingled further with god they fell together as they chanced to meet each other, and many others in addition to these were continually arising."

> πολλὰ μὲν ἀμφιπρόσωπα καὶ ἀμφίστερν' ἐφύοντο,
> βουγενῆ ἀνδρόπρῳρα, τὰ δ' ἔμπαλιν ἐξανέτελλον
> ἀνδροφυῆ βούκρανα, μεμιγμένα τῇ μὲν ἀπ' ἀνδρῶν
> τῇ δὲ γυναικοφυῆ, †σκιεροῖς† ἠσκημένα γυίοις. (B61)

"Many creatures with a face and breasts on both sides were produced, man-faced bulls arose and again bull-headed men, [others] with male and female nature combined, and the bodies they had were dark."

During this process Aphrodite's role is superseded by chance. The formation of living forms is now sketched as a random natural process in which most of them proved non-viable and perished, but a few successful forms were able to survive. In other words, only if the "correct" limbs combine, then the creature would survive and go on to reproduce its own species. From this point of view, Empedocles' nature seems to be governed mainly by mechanistic Darwinian-like principles, without any design or pattern. Actually, as this was exactly contrary to Aristotle's view of nature, according to which processes take place for the sake of the resultant forms, it was this that impelled Aristotle to complain about Empedocles' failing to introduce a consistent pattern of teleology into his account.[25] Aristotle's judgment has been very influential, and as Furley notes "Empedocles was sometimes regarded as the paradigm case of an anti-teleological philosopher of nature."[26] All in all, this mutation in Aphrodite's role in favor of contingency that takes place during the two first stages of Empedocles' cosmogony has been viewed as an instance of internal conflict in his doctrine and has accordingly become the cause of much debate among scholars on the question as to whether we should totally eliminate teleology from his philosophy or not.[27]

Bearing the above discussion in mind, we should now turn to Lucretius' proem and his famous invocation to Aphrodite (1.1–49):

> *Aeneadum genetrix, hominum divomque voluptas,*
> *alma Venus, caeli subter labentia signa*
> *quae mare navigerum, quae terras frugiferentis*
> *concelebras, per te quoniam genus omne animantum*
> *concipitur visitque exortum lumina solis:* 5
> *te, dea, te fugiunt venti, te nubila caeli*
> *adventumque tuum, tibi suavis daedala tellus*
> *summittit flores, tibi rident aequora ponti*
> *placatumque nitet diffuso lumine caelum.*
> *nam simul ac species patefactast verna diei* 10
> *et reserata viget genitabilis aura favoni,*
> *aeriae primum volucris te, diva, tuumque*
> *significant initum perculsae corda tua vi.*
> *inde ferae, pecudes persultant pabula laeta*
> *et rapidos tranant amnis: ita capta lepore* 15
> *te sequitur cupide quo quamque inducere pergis.*
> *denique, per maria ac montis fluviosque rapacis*
> *frondiferasque domos avium camposque virentis,*
> *omnibus incutiens blandum per pectora amorem,*
> *efficis ut cupide generatim saecla propagent.* 20
>   *Quae quoniam rerum naturam sola gubernas,*
> *nec sine te quicquam dias in luminis oras*
> *exoritur neque fit laetum neque amabile quicquam,*
> *te sociam studeo scribendis versibus esse,*
> *quos ego de rerum natura pangere conor* 25
> *Memmiadae nostro, quem tu, dea, tempore in omni*
> *omnibus ornatum voluisti excellere rebus.*
> *quo magis aeternum da dictis, diva, leporem.*
>   *Effice ut interea fera moenera militiai*
> *per maria ac terras omnis sopita quiescant;* 30
> *nam tu sola potes tranquilla pace iuvare*

mortalis, quoniam belli fera moenera Mavors
armipotens regit, in gremium qui saepe tuum se
reiicit aeterno devictus vulnere amoris,
atque ita suspiciens tereti cervice reposta   35
pascit amore avidos inhians in te, dea, visus,
eque tuo pendet resupini spiritus ore.
hunc tu, diva, tuo recubantem corpore sancto
circumfusa super, suavis ex ore loquellas
funde petens placidam Romanis, incluta, pacem;   40
nam neque nos agere hoc patriai tempore iniquo
possumus aequo animo nec Memmi clara propago
talibus in rebus communi desse saluti.
omnis enim per se divom natura necessest
inmortali aevo summa cum pace fruatur   45
semota ab nostris rebus seiunctaque longe;
nam privata dolore omni, privata periclis,
ipsa suis pollens opibus, nihil indiga nostri,
nec bene promeritis capitur nec tangitur ira.

"Mother of Aeneas and his race, darling of men and gods, nurturing Venus, who beneath the smooth-moving heavenly signs fill with yourself the sea full-laden with ships, the earth that bears the crops, since through you every kind of living thing is conceived and rising up looks on the light of the sun: from you, O goddess, from you the winds flee away, the clouds of heaven from you and your coming; for you the wonder-working earth puts forth sweet flowers, for you the wide stretches of ocean laugh, and heaven grown peaceful glows with outpoured light. For as soon as the vernal face of day is made manifest, and the breeze of the teeming west wind blows fresh and free, first the fowls of the air proclaim you, divine one, and your advent, pierced to the heart by your might. Next wild creatures and farm animals dance over the rich pastures and swim across rapid rivers: so greedily does each one follow you, held captive by your charm, whither you go on to lead them. Then throughout seas and mountains and sweeping torrents and the leafy dwellings of birds and verdant plains, striking alluring love into the breasts of all creatures, you cause them greedily to beget their generations after their kind.

Since therefore, you alone govern the nature of things, since without you nothing comes forth into the shining borders of light, nothing joyous and lovely is made, you I crave as partner in writing the verses, which I essay to fashion on the Nature of Things, for my friend Memmius, whom you, goddess, have willed at all times to excel, endowed with all gifts. Therefore all the more grant to my speech goddess, an ever-living charm.

Cause meanwhile the savage works of war to sleep and be still over every sea and land. For you alone can delight mortals with quiet peace, since Mars mighty in battle rules the savage works of war, who often casts himself upon your lap wholly vanquished by the ever-living wound of love, and thus looking upward, with shapely neck thrown back, feeds his eager eyes with love, gaping upon you, goddess, and, as he lies back, his breath hangs upon your lips. There as he reclines, goddess, upon you sacred body, do you, bending around him from above, pour from your lips sweet coaxings, and for your Romans, illustrious one, crave quiet peace. For in this time of our country's troubles neither can I do my part with untroubled mind, nor can the noble scion of the Memmii at such a season be wanting to the common weal. [I pray to you for peace,] for the very nature of divinity must necessarily enjoy immortal life in the deepest peace, far removed and separated from our affairs; for without any pain, without danger, itself mighty by its own resources, needing us not at all, it is neither propitiated with services nor touched by wrath."

Epicurus' attitude towards the true nature of the Gods and his objections to the use of allegory has already been discussed above.[28] As the epic poem in question specifically claims that its didactic and philosophical objective is to convert the reader to Epicureanism, such an invocation may seem to be a deviation from tradition which would entail significant implications. Hence, in an Epicurean context just the presence of Venus, who is burdened so strongly with intertextual connotations of purposeful divine intervention, turns out to be highly problematic or even impossible. Not only are the expectations of any educated reader subverted, but more importantly, for the philosophically illiterate pupil to whom the poem is primarily addressed, such a proem could easily obfuscate orthodox doctrine or even seriously undermine it.

So, what does Lucretius' Venus symbolize? Moreover, why does Lucretius resort to the highly unsettling process of deification and why does he choose this specific goddess? Since the texture of the proem has been dissected in various ways, the main aim here will not be its overall evaluation anew.[29] Without underestimating the complexity of Aphrodite's identity, it will be rather attempted to re-examine her intertextual association with Empedocles and the extent to which this determines the overall relationship between himself and Lucretius.

From a certain point of view, there should be nothing surprising about such an opening to an epic poem. Venus could easily be considered as standing in for the traditional epic Muse, who is called upon to bestow inspiration on the poet and assist him in his labor.[30] Yet, the specific figure to which Lucretius grants the leading role of the Muse is a goddess, and consequently the whole proem takes on the form of a prayer. Again, this is in accordance with the openings of literary hymns. One could parallel here Philodemus' hymnic invocation of Ino's son Melicertes, Leucoteha (=Ino), a chorus of Nereids, Poseidon, Waves and the Thracian wind Zephyr (*Anth. Pal.* 6.349 = Epigram 34 Sider), an invocation which is consonant with his Hellenistic associations.[31] Lucretius' choice of Venus could be justified also by the fact that she is the national goddess of the Romans (1.1) and even the protector of Memmius' family. Venus is also the figure who governs generation and natural order in general (1.21). Scholars have thus pointed out her character as a "cosmic" deity, and inferred that Lucretius is alluding here to divinities invoked in other philosophical poems with more or less clear teleological implications, namely Parmenides' Goddess, Cleanthes' Stoic Zeus and especially Empedocles' Aphrodite.[32]

In fact, the association with Empedocles becomes more tangible by means of direct linguistic and poetic allusions: the adjective *alma* (1.2) may reflect Empedocles' adjective "life-giving" (ζείδωρος, B151), which is attested by Plutarch (*Amat.* 756E) or even better another one meaning "nurturing" (φυτάλμια, fr. d 13 M&P), recently read in the Strasbourg papyrus.[33] More importanly, as Sedley has persuasively argued, the pairing of two compound epithets in line 1.3 (*quae mare navigerum, quae terras frugiferentis*), which is a characteristic technique of Empedocles' poetry, suggests that Lucretius is here translating into Latin a verse directly drawn from Empedocles' poem. Sedley calls this phenomenon the "Empedoclean fingerprint" and argues that in the present context the—now lost—Greek verse could plausibly have the form: πόντον ναυσίπορον καὶ γαίας καρποφορούσας.[34] So, as Gale aptly summarizes it, "Venus is represented as the force which, like Empedocles' *Philia*, brings things together. [. . .] She has dominion over the four Empedoclean elements; and, finally she is the force that inspires peace, just as Philia is the source of 'friendly thoughts' among men."[35]

As the proem unfolds, Lucretius draws a tableau of Venus propitiating belligerent Mars in her embrace (1.31–40). The intertextual hint at Empedocles, already discernible from the very first verses of the poem, becomes here even stronger; both *Venus* and *Mars* directly allude to Empedocles' Love and Strife, his creative and destructive powers. In turn, Lucretius may be echoing an allegorical reading of Homer's song of Demodocus about the scene of the divine lovers Aphrodite and Ares, who were caught in bed and bound by Hephaestus.[36] He could even be inspired by a contemporary work of art.[37]

Sedley goes so far as to argue that Empedocles would have used the image of Aprhodite and Ares' reconciliation "not so much as an attempt to interfere with the inevitable progression of the cosmic cycle, as a plea to human beings to let their peaceful tendencies calm and suppress the bloodthirsty side of their nature."[38] It is, however, significant that this idea of the harmonious coexistence of Aphrodite and Ares runs counter to the dualistic alternation between the power of Love and Strife to which Empedocles adheres. As Gale puts it, this tableau "is a tribute to Empedocles, but once again it is perhaps not uncritical. This may be a way of suggesting that Empedocles' creative and destructive forces are in fact eternally and indissolubly linked and that his theory of alternation on a cosmic scale is superfluous."[39] Whatever the case may be, as Gale again rightly remarks, Lucretius seems to embrace Empedocles' allegorical use of the same myth in order to represent abstract, albeit dissimilar ideas.[40] As has already been discussed above, this constitutes a serious deviation from Epicurus' practice. Sedley goes on to infer more correspondences between Empedocles' and Lucretius' proems. In fact, the overall affinity seems to be here so patent that Sedley, relying closely on Lucretius' proem, can present us with a remarkable reconstruction of Empedocles' now lost proem to his own poem.[41] According to this, Empedocles' poem would similarly open with a hymn to Aphrodite and might even include a scene of reconciliation, similar to that occurring in Lucretius.[42]

We should now focus on the impact that the presence of the figure of Empedocles' Aphrodite has on Lucretius' didactic poem, as well as the tension possibly caused within the Epicurean philosophical system. Given Epicurus' hostility towards Empedocles, the important question here is: why should Lucretius open his poem in such a strongly Empedoclean and thus seemingly un-Epicurean way? In exploring this question, we should bear in mind both Aphrodite and Ares' divine identity within Empedocles' poem and their role in representing the motive forces of the cosmic cycle.[43]

This is the point to go back to Sedley's arguments against Furley's thesis according to which Lucretius' homage to Empedocles in Book 1 can be considered as the acknowledgement of the former's philosophical debt to the latter's physical theory about the random development of living forms.[44] Against Furley's assertion, Sedley objects that Lucretius could not view Empedocles as an anti-teleologist; quite the opposite, there were many elements in the latter's doctrine which would place him among the teleologists instead. As Sedley characteristically writes: "since Lucretius certainly knew Empedocles' physical poem at first hand and did not have to rely exclusively on Aristotelian-influenced doxography, it certainly should not be assumed that he read Empedocles as a pioneering opponent of teleology"; and again: "the architectonic role of Love in Empedocles' cosmic cycle makes it a very hard task indeed to portray him as a pure mechanist."[45]

Sedley rightly puts forward the inherent ambivalence of Empedocles' mechanics. In fact, Empedocles' passages at which Lucretius hints in his proem to Book 1 are those in which the Presocratic philosopher seems to figure as a teleologist. Nevertheless, instead of tipping the balance towards Empedocles the teleologist and thus annihilate Furley's thesis, it could rather be argued that Empedocles should not be called either a pure mechanist or a teleologist. What is more significant, such a claim does not acquit Lucretius from his choice to present Empedocles' Aphrodite as holding the leading role in the proem and to introduce thus teleological connotations. Anyhow, in an effort to tone down the unsettling reference to Empedocles' divinities, Sedley adds that Lucretius himself actually comments on the gods' true nature, which is "tranquil and detached, instead of angry and warlike" (1.44–49) and thus does not leave any doubt about his intentions in his use of allegory.[46] In my view, whereas Sedley is right in seeing an element of teleology in Empedocles, I would find it hard to follow his claim that intertextuality in the proem works exclusively on a literary level and not on a philosophical one. In other words, instead of arguing in this context merely for a literary debt which Lucretius incurs with Empedocles as founder of the genre, one should rather consider the possibility that Lucretius' borrowing of Empedocles' imagery carries over the latter's teleological implications.

In the course of the poem the reader may piece together several clues that partly solve the enigma of Lucretius' proem and thus are intended to soothe the tension caused by the allusion to Empedocles' Love and Strife. At the same time, even with a considerable delay, given the didactic purposes of *DRN,* by means of the *Magna Mater* digression (2.655–660) Lucretius attempts to disperse any possible doubts about his metonymic use of the deities and retrospectively provides us with reading guidelines.[47]

The figure of Aphrodite undergoes a gradual metamorphosis. Whenever she reappears after the proem she is assigned her more conventional role, that of ensuring the continuity of the human species through sexual reproduction (e.g. 2.173, 5.962). Eventually, the Goddess is totally degraded, and when Lucretius embarks on his famous attack on the passion of love, he identifies her with the purely physiological passion of sexual intercourse (4.1037–1287: *Haec Venus est nobis; hinc autemst nomen amoris;* / "This is our Venus; from this also comes love's name," 4.1058). At the same time, her multifaceted functions are shifted to other *personae,* mainly female ones, such as Cybele (2.598–643), Mother Earth (2.589–599, 5.795–836) and the muse Calliope (6.92–95) or even Epicurus himself, as Lucretius' genuine source of knowledge and inspiration (5.1–12).

What is more important, Aphrodite's generating and governing role is soon transferred to nature, which embodies both creative and destructive forces (e.g. 1.55–57 quoted above).[48] Quite surprisingly, nature herself is also personified, being granted several roles.[49] At first glance, it seems that Lucretius finds it difficult to eliminate from his poem the disturbing teleological connotations that he first introduced by alluding to Empedocles' Aphrodite. However, even Epicurus himself, who by no means would leave any space for teleological interpretation in his mechanics, in his ethical writings inevitably yielded to the personification of nature (χάρις τῇ μακαρίᾳ Φύσει, ὅτι τὰ ἀναγκαῖα ἐποίησεν εὐπόριστα, τὰ δὲ δυσπόριστα οὐκ ἀναγκαῖα. / "Thanks be to blessed Nature because she has made what is necessary easy to supply, and what is not easy unnecessary," fr. 469 Us. = Stob. *Flor.* XVII 23). In his turn, Lucretius completely demystifies nature when he assigns to her a monologue against those who are reluctant to die (3.931–977).[50] Hence, he makes explicit that the personification of nature forms part of the poem's rhetorical discourse in his effort to decipher and then communicate the secret workings of nature.

To conclude, it is under Empedocles' influence that Lucretius brings both anthropomorphic divinities and suggestions of teleology into his proem. It is also true that as the poem advances, both the anthropomorphism and the teleology are somehow defused. Nevertheless, whereas by his intertextual engagement with Empedocles Lucretius enjoys the advantage of a striking opening to his work, despite his precautions—which actually follow the proem—he runs the risk of damaging in the long run the clarity of his Epicurean message or even his Epicurean credentials.

2.2.2 Simple Animation of the Primary Elements

Both Empedocles and Lucretius animate the unseen primary elements in their effort to enlarge them; in this way, they both turn again personification into an effective philosophical weapon. Although it would be difficult to claim that in this respect Lucretius follows Empedocles' example, this section should be considered as the prelude to the following one (2.2.3), in which Lucretius' direct debt to Empedocles' probative and illustrative method will be more deeply and firmly established.

In Empedocles there are several passages in which the roots are depicted as tiny living creatures.[51] They are envisaged as having their own bodies, which can be enlarged by the addition of similar matter (e.g. αὔξει δὲ χθὼν μὲν σφέτερον δέμας, αἰθέρα δ' αἰθήρ. / "Earth increases its own bulk, and air increases air," B37). In performing human activities, they are portrayed as particularly agile and active, reflecting at the same time both their inherent tendency to move and the temporary existence of the elementary structures they form, under the power of Love and Strife. In his description Empedocles takes a wide range of verbs and adjectives from Homer and transplants them into his philosophical poem. During their incessant mixing, his roots can change the direction of their motions (ζωρά τε πρὶν κέκρητο, διαλλάξαντα κελεύθους. / "and formely unmixed things were in a mixed state, owing to the exchanging of their ways," B35.15); they "enter" (ὄμβρος ἐσέρχεται, B100.12) or "rush down" (αἰθὴρ παφλάζων καταΐσσεται, B100.7), they "spring up" (εὖτε δ᾽ ἀναθρώσκῃ, B100.8), or "spit out" (πόντος δ᾽ ἐς χθονὸς οὖδας ἀπέπτυσε, B115.10), they "run into each other" (δι᾽ ἀλλήλων δὲ θέοντα, B26.3).[52] Empedocles also refers to the roots with adjectives proper to the portrayal of human beings, which are often original coinages after Homer (e.g. ἡ δὲ φλὸξ ἱλάειρα / "the gentle flame," B85; ἡ δὲ χθὼν ἐπίηρος / "the kindly earth," B96.1; εὐρυμέδοντος / αἰθέρος / "wide ruling air," B135).[53] The main representations of the roots within the world are similarly personified: Empedocles talks about the swift limbs of the sun and the shaggy might of earth (ἔνθ᾽ οὔτ᾽ ἠελίοιο διείδεται ὠκέα γυῖα, / οὐδὲ μὲν οὐδ᾽ αἴης λάσιον μένος, οὐδὲ θάλασσα. / "There the swift limbs of the sun are not distinguished, nor the shaggy might of earth, nor sea," B27),[54] the sharp arrowed sun (ἥλιος ὀξυβελής / "sharp-arrowed sun," B40) which moves around the sky (ἀλλ᾽ ὁ μὲν ἁλισθεὶς μέγαν οὐρανὸν ἀμφιπολεύει. / "but [the sun], after being collected together, moves round the great sky," B41) is viewed as a lord (ἄθρει μὲν γὰρ ἄνακτος ἐναντίον ἀγέα κύκλον. / "she [the moon] contemplates the bright circle of her lord facing her," B47).[55]

More significantly, Empedocles truly believes the roots to possess divine natures. Apart from explicit references in his extant fragments (e.g. αὐτὰρ ἐπεὶ κατὰ μεῖζον ἐμίσγετο δαίμονι δαίμων, / "But as god mingled further with god," B59.1; αἰθέρι δ᾽ αἰθέρα δῖον, / "with air divine air," B109.2),[56] deification in Empedocles is achieved by a twofold process. On the one hand, the roots are named after Homeric Gods. Various divinities drawn from the Olympic Pantheon which are identified with the roots turn up in several fragments (e.g. τέσσαρα γὰρ πάντων ῥιζώματα πρῶτον ἄκουε· / Ζεὺς ἀργὴς Ἥρη τε φερέσβιος ἠδ᾽ Ἀϊδωνεύς, / Νῆστίς θ᾽ ἣ δακρύοις τέγγει κρούνωμα βρότειον. / "Hear first the four roots of all things: bright Zeus and life-bringing Hera and Aidoneus and Nestis, whose tears are the source of mortal streams," B6).[57] Conversely, epithets previously assigned to the traditional Gods are now transferred to the roots. It is significant that the epithet "cloud-gatherer" (νεφεληγερέτην, B149), which in Homer designated Zeus, now qualifies air, perhaps in a meteorological context; and the moon acquires Athena's distinctive epithet "grey-eyed" (γλαυκώπιδος . . . μήνης, B42.3).[58]

As far as Lucretius' use of personification with regard to primary elements is concerned, more factors should be taken into consideration. As we have already seen, the Epicureans openly attacked Empedocles for his theory of divine roots, because, according to them, by no means can atoms bear a divine nature.[59] At the same time, Lucretius inherited from Epicurus the word σῶμα as an established alternative term when referring to atoms (e.g. *Ep. Hdt.* 39, 40). He thus had to deal with the fact that, although atoms were actually inanimate, the Greek term already carried uneasy connotations of life and could cause unwelcome doctrinal confusion.

Like Empedocles, Lucretius uses a range of terms to describe microcosmic atomic reality.[60] Among these, we find the word *corpus,* which is the exact Latin translation of the Greek σῶμα.[61] In order to dispel any doubt about the actual nature of the atoms, he contrasts them directly with mortal animals; he makes it explicit that unlike Empedocles' roots, atoms lack any human trait or feeling (2.865–990; cf. 1.915–920). Within this context, it is significant that he twice uses the key verb *adsimilare* (2.914, 2.980), thus revealing the conclusion of his reasoning: for the sake of philosophical clarity alone can immortal atoms be visualized as *resembling* living things; in fact, they should never be thought of as capable of speaking, thinking or arguing, weeping or laughing and in general of performing any activity characteristic of human beings.

Bearing the above clarification in mind, we can see how Lucretius develops further the metaphorical potential of Epicurus' terminology. He uses the word *corpus* with reference to things of various sizes at all cosmic levels (e.g. world: 5.65, clouds: 5.466, ether: 5.468, stars: 5.476), thereby disclosing the hidden homogeneous structure of everything. At the same time, by means of qualifying adjectives, some of which are used in pairs of opposites, he initiates the interplay among the different "atomic *personae*" and draws various vertical distinctions among them. As will be seen in the following chapters, this thorough strategy of "embodiment" is used as the basis for many of his similes and metaphors.

At the ultimate level of existence, "atomic bodies" are called either *genitalia corpora* or *corpora prima*. Both terms are used with reference to simple as well as compound bodies.[62] Like Empedocles' roots, these bodies are envisaged as infinitesimal human beings. In order to emphasize the compactness of the compound, the atoms are even depicted with limbs and are "tripped up by their own feet" (e.g. *indupedita*, 2.102).[63] Invisible bodies are also granted their own power and thanks to their solidity, they spit out blows (*respuere,*

3.807). Moreover, in a passage which appears to echo directly Empedocles' theory of elementary mixture (e.g. δι' ἀλλήλων δὲ θέοντα, B26.3), "atoms interpenetrate one another in their motions," in order to form one single body, in this case the soul (3.258–272: *Inter enim cursant primordia principiorum,* 3.262). In this context, Lucretius inserts comparative conjunctions and carefully warns us about the use of personification (*sed quasi multae vis unius corporis extant.* / "but they are, as it were, the many forces of a single body," 3.265). The pun is further developed, in the juxtaposition of soul (already described as body) and of the archetypal body, the human one (*quod genus in quovis animantum viscere volgo* / *est odor et quidam calor et sapor, et tamen ex his* / *omnibus est unum perfectum corporis augmen,* / "Just as in the flesh of any living creature there is a scent and a certain heat and flavour, and yet from all these is made one body grown complete," 3.266–268).

Lucretius also identifies three major features that differentiate the primary elements from compound structures and emphasizes their distinct characteristics. In contrast with composite bodies which are visible to the naked eye (*aperto corpore,* 1.297), atoms are invisible (*corpora caeca,* 1.277). Lucretius apparently exploits the ambivalence of the word *caecus,* which either brings to mind a blind person or refers to imperceptible things. This distinction is made sharper by bringing into play another set of adjectives that define the intrinsic nature of atoms; whereas the archetypal body, i.e. the human one, and any other atomic construction are proved to be doomed to dissolution due to their mortal nature (e.g. *mortali corpore,* 1.232; *nativo corpore,* 2.542), atoms are treated as belonging to a different category; only their body is eternal and indestructible (e.g. *inmortali . . . natura,* 1.236; *aeterno corpore,* 1.242; *incolumi . . . corpore,* 1.246). Finally, Lucretius uses adjectives literally denoting some sort of deficiency regarding human beings in order to convey the concept that atoms lack primary qualities; they are described as bereft and despoiled, because stripped of colour (*orba colore,* 2.838; *spoliata colore,* 2.842) and then again as "sterile" of sound and "barren" of taste (*et sonitu sterila et suco ieiuna feruntur,* 2.845), when moving through the void.

Lucretius also depicts the Empedoclean roots as possessing their own bodies. Yet, although in terms of structure roots should be placed first in the hierarchy of mortal things on the scale from the microcosm upwards, one level above that of the atoms, unlike the atoms, roots are not immortal. This image is truly essential, as it will turn out to be distinctive of Lucretius' overall attitude towards his predecessor's doctrine and will constitute a basis for explaining the nature of the roots. The same idea will be conveyed in several ways in the course of the poem. Already in Book 1, Lucretius had directly juxtaposed atoms and roots on the basis of their solidity or softness (*solidissima,*

1.565; *mollia,* 1.567).[64] In another passage which echoes Empedocles' catalogues even more closely, as we have recently learned from the new Empedocles' Strasbourg papyrus, Lucretius enumerates various mortal bodies in order to prove that nothing is unique (2.1077–1089);[65] among these we find Empedocles' roots (*quapropter caelum simili ratione fatendumst / terramque et solem lunam mare, cetera quae sunt, / non esse unica, sed numero magis innumerali, /* "Therefore you must in like manner confess for sky and earth, for sun, moon, sea and all else that exists, that they are not unique but rather of number innumerable," 2.1084–1086).[66] The same statement is revisited later in the poem, in Book 5, where Lucretius embarks upon a more elaborate denial of the divinity of the Empedoclean elements and discusses the mortality of the earth, water, air and fire (5.235–323: *terrai corpus,* 5.235; *omnia nativo ac mortali corpore constant,* 5.238; *corpore toto,* 5.273; *nativo ac mortali corpore,* 5.321).[67]

2.2.3 The Web of Human Relationships

A system of metaphorical images "drawn from social and political life in order to describe the physical processes of the Epicurean universe" has long been detected in Lucretius.[68] It was Don Fowler in his article "Lucretius and Politics," and even more explicitly in his remarkable posthumous commentary who pointed out that this is a device that goes back to the origins of Greek philosophy.[69] Yet, despite this general assertion, there has never been a more systematic attempt to identify Lucretius' specific model.

It will now be attempted to demonstrate that, by using specific terms (e.g. *cupido, concilium, foedera, condicio, nexus, pactum, concursus*), Lucretius creates a concrete web of sexual, socio-political and warlike images. It will be shown that their use as cognitive tools in his didactic poem is a conscious choice and, above all, that it is a choice inspired by the example of Empedocles. For, in using this imagery, Lucretius both places himself firmly in the cosmological tradition in general, and specifically evokes Empedocles, on the grounds of common principles in their doctrines. In doing so, however, Lucretius takes account of discrepancies between Epicurus' and Empedocles' philosophy. After refuting the points with which he does not agree and making the necessary deviations and adaptations, he incorporates the Empedoclean images into his doctrine.

Such images seem to have been absent from Lucretius' atomic predecessors (Leucippus, Democritus) and in particular from Epicurus' writings, being actually drawn in all probability from the same Presocratic sources. Yet, it will be demonstrated to what extent Lucretius was the first to systematize Empedocles' imagery and make it an integral part of his poem, taking at the same time into consideration his Roman audience. Finally, in the last part of this section, I will show how certain political images, common both in Empedocles and Lucretius, do not describe the cosmic order, but rather are imposed by it.

Although the sexual and the socio-political imagery are closely interdependent, as has already been explained above, they will be treated here separately, due to their different function in revealing nature's obscure workings. On the one hand, the otherwise inexplicable attraction between the primary elements along with their intrinsic properties can be better perceived if viewed as basic human instincts. On the other, the patterns of regularity which recur in nature are better illustrated by similar images which are dominant within a lawful society.

2.2.3.1 Sexual Imagery–Imagery of Friendship

Empedocles uses images of sexual intercourse and friendship, in order to schematize specific characteristics of the two factors that control the mixture of the primary elements, i.e. the *external* creative forces that stimulate matter and cause attraction and the *inherent* and *automatic* propensity of like roots to unite. The source of those images can be easily traced back within the earlier tradition; they had already been used by Homer, Hesiod and especially Parmenides, who introduced Eros into his philosophical poem.[70]

Apart from the traditional representations of Love (*Φιλότης*) in the figure of Aphrodite, Empedocles personifies this abstract notion directly. The poet designates her with alternative names (*Στοργή, Ἁρμονία, Γηθοσύνη*).[71] At the same time, Love is portrayed as immortal, gentle, without reproach (*ἠπιόφρων φιλότητος ἀμεμφέος ἄμβροτος ὁρμή*, B35.13), and serene (*θεμερῶπις*, B122.2).[72]

Only under Love's impact are dissimilar roots made more alike and mutual desire is born within them (*σὺν δ' ἔβη ἐν φιλότητι καὶ ἀλλήλοισι ποθεῖται.* / "they come together in love and are desired by one another," B21.8; *ὡς δ' αὕτως ὅσα κρῆσιν ἐπαρκέα μᾶλλον ἔασιν / ἀλλήλοις ἔστερκται ὁμοιωθέντ' Ἀφροδίτῃ·* / "In the same way, those that are more ready to combine are made similar by Aphrodite and feel mutual affection," B22.4–5); and so, they gather together to form compounds. It should not escape us that in the fragments in which Empedocles describes processes of "mixture" the word *μιγνύναι* unmistakably carries over from Homer connotations of sexual union (e.g. *τῶν δέ τε μισγομένων χεῖτ' ἔθνεα μυρία θνητῶν,* / "And, as they were being mixed, countless types of mortal things poured forth," B35.7).[73] All in all, Love figures as an external agent that imposes her power onto the roots and incites the passion of coming together. Yet, there is an inverse process; disruptive Strife dissolves these harmonious formations and struggles to keep them apart (e.g. B22.6–9).

In addition to Love's impact that diametrically opposes the divisive one of Strife, another crucial factor operates in nature, namely the inner tendency of the roots for like to join with like; apparently this is at odds with Love's role. In fact, it seems that Strife assists the roots in externalizing their innate predisposition and brings about creation in a way different from Love.[74] Nevertheless, figurative language, used elsewhere to describe the outcome of Aphrodite's force, is also applied to portray the sexual-like interaction between alike roots or similar elementary structures. A worldly manifestation of this mechanism is the creation of the four elementary masses (e.g. *ἄρθμια μὲν γὰρ ταῦτα ἑαυτῶν πάντα μέρεσσιν,* / "For all these [sun and earth and sky and sea] are one with the parts of themselves," B22.1; *βύσσῳ δὲ †γλαυκῆς κρόκου† καταμίσγεται ἀκτίς,* / "And the gleam of bright saffron mixes in with the linen," B93).[75]

As has been seen above, Lucretius' Venus stands for the creative power, just as in Empedocles, and in the proem to Book 1 that power is fully and richly personified.[76] In the course of the poem, however, Empedocles' imagery of Love and Strife is gradually given less importance. So thorough is this process that contrary to Empedocles' account in which the roles of Love and Strife are dominant during cosmogonical and zoogonical processes, this imagery of creative and destructive forces is absent in Lucretius' corresponding accounts of the creation of the world (5.416–508) and the generation of animals (5.783–820). In the latter passage, Venus, already degraded to mere sexual love in the end of Book 4, is replaced by Mother-Earth; sexual metaphors are at this juncture notably absent, as Furley rightly remarks, probably in order to lay extra emphasis on the spontaneity of the procedure.[77] This differentiation from Empedocles should not surprise us. It should be bore in mind that Lucretius aims at bringing out the concealed picture of a natural world within which atoms move accidentally of their own accord; for him, motive forces are only the weight, collisions and swerve of atoms. Accordingly, the tension caused by the Empedoclean bipolarity between innate tendency and imposed movements would be quite alien to an Epicurean description of the universe. In fact, Lucretius seems to perceive that the use of sexual imagery in the same way as Empedocles would enfeeble the power of his argument.

Yet, Lucretius' stance towards Empedocles' sexual imagery changes when it comes to the portrayal of the atoms. For this Lucretius could find support in Epicurus' writings, from where he could even retrieve a model. The latter, in his account of hearing and vision, talks about the affinity that atoms must display in order to maintain a certain coherence in terms of affinity (συμπάθεια).[78] Moreover, the vocabulary of Plutarch, who talks about "unyielding and unresponsive atoms" (τὰς ἀτρέπτους καὶ ἀσυμπαθεῖς ἀτόμους, *Adv. Col.* 10.1112B), could strengthen further our inference that similar illustrations of atomic behaviour in terms of friendship were familiar in the Epicurean tradition.

Nevertheless, even assuming that Epicurus used more such images in his now lost writings, it seems conceivable that Lucretius turned also to Empedocles' sexual imagery and thus depicted the atoms as craving one another, as this would better convey the vigor of the movement. In *DRN*, we spot two such instances in which the intrinsic properties of atoms are conveyed in terms of desire. In Book 1, the image is used in the negative form: as there is no middle, atoms do not actually display a yearning for the middle (*haud igitur possunt tali ratione teneri / res in concilium medii cuppedine victae. / "*Therefore, things cannot be held in combination together in any such way, overcome by a yearning for the middle," 1.1081–1082). Similarly, in Book 2 the mechanical force eagerly pushes things upwards (*tam cupide sursum revomit magis atque remittit, / "*the more eagerly does [the water] vomit them back and shoot them back up," 2.199).

In conclusion, it appears that Lucretius retained Empedocles' sexual imagery at the level of the behaviour of individual atoms, even if he could not do so at the level of cosmological forces.

2.2.3.2 Relationships Based on Agreements: Socio-Political Imagery

By the systematic deployment of specific verbs and nouns with socio-political connotations, Lucretius fleshes out the dormant metaphorical meanings of corresponding words already used by the Atomists and then by Epicurus, and he thus goes back to similar socio-political imagery deployed by the Presocratic cosmologists and once again plausibly alludes to Empedocles. At the same time he establishes up to a point a unified terminology and consequently a coherent imagery for both monists (Heraclitus) and pluralists (Empedocles, Anaxagoras); in using similar vocabulary to develop and criticize the doctrines of his predecessors he draws a continuous line from the beginnings of philosophical thought up to Epicurus. In a way he empties these Presocratic images to invest them with the new Epicurean ideas, in order to make the differences more explicit. Then he uses these images again in contexts where Empedocles could have used them, in order to describe the coming together of his roots.

It should briefly be noted that in general terms socio-political and legal imagery were one of the principal means by which the Presocratics described the universal order and the rational principles that both these and the primary substance obey. Vlastos, for instance, pointed out that the Presocratics envisaged harmony in terms of equality.[79] Thus, political concepts are projected onto the universe in order to describe something new expressed in comprehensible notions. Starting from this general background to cosmological poetry, it is time to focus on Empedocles' extant fragments.

Although we are unfortunately dealing with scant evidence, a close look at Empedocles' fragments is revealing. For him there is no birth or death, but just a mingling and separating of unchanged, eternal primary roots (e.g. B8); hence the roots are illustrated as regularly coming together in order to unite into the Sphairos under the power of Love and then as gradually separating under the power of Strife. In describing the behaviour of elements Empedocles uses vocabulary with connotations of socio-political gathering, i.e. words such as *σύνοδος* and *συνέρχομαι*.[80] Especially during the reign of Love, roots are explicitly depicted as coming together as if to form an assembly (*τὴν μὲν γὰρ πάντων σύνοδος τίκτει τ᾽ ὀλέκει τε,* / "for the uniting of all things brings one generation into being and destroys it," B17.4; *ἄλλοτε μὲν φιλότητι συνερχόμεν᾽ εἰς ἓν ἅπαντα,* / "at one time all coming together into one through love," B17.7). The same phrasing is found in the new Strasbourg papyrus fragment and in many other fragments where Empedocles describes the uniting of the roots under Love (e.g. *[π]ρῶτον μὲν ξύνοδόν τε διάπτυξίν τ[ε γενέθλης]* / "first the coming together and the unfolding of the stock," fr. a (ii) 24 M&P; *<τῶν δὲ συνερχομένων ἐξ> ἔσχατον ἵστατο νεῖκος.* / "Strife was retreating from them to the extremity as they were coming together," B36).[81] Thus, before total unity, the roots come together into smaller congregations, which become manifest on a larger scale by the creation of men, animals, birds, fishes and plants.[32] Such elementary "societies" can also be created under the increasing power of Strife, as Love still exercises her power, though gradually roots are more and more prevented from participating in them (e.g. B22).

The term *σύνοδος* now used with reference to the gathering of atoms is also found in Leucippus' and Democritus' testimonia.[83] More significantly, there are at least two occurrences in Epicurus. For example he employs the word when he describes the formation of the dew by the gathering of particles productive of moisture from the atmosphere, from moist regions or from those regions containing water (*Ep. Pyth.* 108): [84]

Δρόσος συντελεῖται καὶ κατὰ σύνοδον πρὸς ἄλληλα ἐκ τοῦ ἀέρος τῶν τοιούτων, ἃ τῆς τοιαύτης ὑγρασίας ἀποτελεστικὰ γίνεται· καὶ κατ᾽ ἀναφορὰν δὲ ἢ ἀπὸ νοτερῶν τόπων ἢ ὕδατα κεκτημένων, ἐν οἷοις τόποις μάλιστα δρόσος συντελεῖται, εἶτα σύνοδον τούτων εἰς τὸ αὐτὸ λαβόντων καὶ ἀποτέλεσιν ὑγρασίας καὶ πάλιν φορὰν ἐπὶ τοὺς κάτω τόπους, καθά περ ὁμοίως καὶ παρ' ἡμῖν ἐπὶ πλειόνων τοιαῦτά τινα <συντελούμενα θεωρεῖται>.

"Dew is formed when such particles as are capable of producing this sort of moisture meet each other from the air: again by the rising from moist and damp places, the sort of place where dew is chiefly formed, and their subsequent coalescence, so as to create moisture and fall downwards, just as in several cases something similar is observed to take place under our eyes."

Turning now to Lucretius, it will first be established that, while he describes the coming together of the atoms and the aggregations they form by means of words that in other contexts were mainly employed to describe the coming together of living things to form an assembly (see verbs such as *coeo, consocio, convenio, congredior* and especially the nouns *concilium, coetus / coitus, conventus, congressus*), he personifies the atoms and presents us with systematic images of miniature atomic societies. By doing so Lucretius consciously alludes to Empedocles' socio-political imagery. This claim could possibly encounter the objection that Epicurus' metaphorical language, which at any rate bears a close intertextual relationship with Empedocles, would suffice Lucretius and thus a direct link with Empedocles would be superfluous. That is why in the second part of this section a more detailed comparison of Empedocles' and Lucretius' images will be offered in order to give further evidence of the fact that Lucretius is aware of Epicurus' debt to Empedocles' language and he himself adapts it into his Latin translation as well; more notably, he draws more heavily and independently from his Presocratic original and enriches the poem with Roman colour.

While scholars comment on the use of the word *concilium,* they generally confine themselves to pointing out that by means of this term Lucretius seeks to fill the terminological gap in the Latin philosophical language by translating two distinct Epicurean terms and merging them into one, i.e. the word σύγκρισις which denotes the intermingling of the atoms and the word ἄθροισμα which points to the compound thus formed.[85] Nonetheless, this interpretation disregards the socio-political implications of the word which would rather correspond to the Greek word σύνοδος, a word which was employed also by Epicurus, but as it seems not in a systematic and technical way. In any case, Lucretius follows Epicurus in endowing atoms with bodies capable of performing human actions; this atomic "embodiment" is particularly vivid in contexts where the atoms are envisaged as coming together. As Cabisius has noted, Lucretius gives a picture of the atoms as if "they demonstrate social characteristics and a natural tendency to engage in political relationships."[86]

In order to avoid any misunderstanding caused by his imagery, Lucretius strives to take precautions by using this personification in a simile about the atomic lack of sensation, which, however, comes quite late in the course of the poem (2.920–923):

> *quod tamen ut possint, at coetu concilioque*   920
> *nil facient praeter volgum turbamque animantum,*
> *scilicet ut nequeant homines armenta feraeque*
> *inter sese ullam rem gignere conveniundo.*

> "And even supposing they could be so, yet by conjunction and combination they will produce nothing but a throng and crowd of living things, exactly as men, cattle and wild beasts could not produce a new thing amongst themselves by coming together."

The words *coetus, concilium* and *convenio* are used emphatically in the two parts of the simile to state the actual difference in the constituents between atomic aggregations and those of animate beings (atoms: *coetu concilioque*, 2.920 → animate beings: *conveniundo*, 2.923). In this way Lucretius, conscious of the confusion such a metaphoric image of personified atoms could produce, makes a self-referential comment to clarify that it is only for the sake of his argument that such a representation is chosen, as it is also the case with his use of the names of the gods (2.644–660).

In addition, Lucretius states that this imagery cannot be applied to describe the parts of the atoms due to the principle of indivisibility (*non ex illorum conventu conciliata,* / "[the first beginnings] not compounded by the gathering of these parts," 1.611).[87] On the contrary, while referring to the "coming together" of the atoms he uses the term *concilium* for the first time in lines 1.182–183 (*genitali concilio*) and henceforth repeatedly, in alternation with other words which bear analogous connotations (e.g. *coetus, coeo, congredior*). To cite only one example, he refers to the rejection of the atoms from the aggregations as a kind of ostracism from the atomic communities (*multaque praeterea magnum per inane vagantur,* / *conciliis rerum quae sunt reiecta nec usquam* / *consociare etiam motus potuere recepta.* / "And many besides wander through the great void which have been rejected from combination with things, and have nowhere been able to obtain admittance and also harmonize their motions," 2.109–111).[88]

It is worth noting that Lucretius applies the very same vocabulary when in Book 1 he refers to his other predecessors alongside Empedocles and attacks their views. Heraclitus, Lucretius tells Memmius, thought of his miniature societies as formed only by fire in union (*ignis in coetu,* 1.666). Yet, if fire contracts and thus gets quenched—Lucretius objects among other things—this entails that it changes into something else and is destroyed. What follows is the refutation of Empedocles' theory, the pluralism of which bears closer affinity to Lucretius' atomic theory. However, Lucretius emphasizes that in Empedocles' doctrine the coming together of elementary "roots" would only result in a discordant heap and not in a harmonized society (*coire,* 1.770; *in concilio,* 1.772; *in coetu variantis acervi,* 1.775). Last but not least, Lucretius places the refutation of Anaxagoras' heterogeneous particles, which are also described as coming together (*coeuntibu',* 1.838).[89] By means of a vocabulary which bears socio-political connotations and is almost established within his poem as technical terminology, Lucretius seems to make use of a coherent system of imagery and straightforwardly juxtaposes his atomic societies with those of his predecessors, which were thought of as formed by the coming together of fire, roots or seeds. Thus, he succeeds in placing himself more firmly in the cosmological tradition and at the same time in differentiating himself from it.

Along the same lines, Lucretius also uses the imagery of elemental societies when he describes how at the very beginning of this world the earth, sea, sky and ether were formed randomly by the aggregation of the right kind of atoms (5.422–429):[90]

> *sed quia multa modis multis primordia rerum*
> *ex infinito iam tempore percita plagis*
> *ponderibusque suis consuerunt concita ferri*
> *omnimodisque coire atque omnia pertemptare,*   425
> *quaecumque inter se possent congressa creare,*
> *propterea fit uti magnum volgata per aevom,*
> *omne genus coetus et motus experiundo,*
> *tandem conveniant ea quae convecta repente*
> *magnarum rerum fiunt exordia saepe,*   430
> *terrai maris et caeli generisque animantum.*

"but because many first-beginnings of things in many ways, struck with blows and carried along by their own weight from infinite time up to the present, have been accustomed to move and to meet in all manner of ways, and to try all combinations, whatsoever they could produce by coming together, for this reason it comes to pass that being spread abroad through a vast time, by attempting every sort of combination and motion, at length those come together which, being suddenly

> brought together, often become the beginnings of great things, of earth
> and sea and sky and the generation of living creatures."

Having made clear again the distinction between the atomic level, which is the ultimate level of existence, and the one just above it, which is formed out of Empedocles' roots, Lucretius goes on to describe the coming together of what Empedocles thought of as primary elements by using the same wording and therefore drawing similar images. Lucretius appears to be integrating Empedocles' philosophy into that of Epicurus, placing it properly in the cosmic scale from the microcosm upwards. In the same direction Lucretius draws other comparable pictures of the Empedoclean elements coming together to "form an assembly" in several contexts (e.g. *aut quia conveniunt ignes* / "or because there is a gathering together of fires," 5.660).[91]

Therefore, it seems that when Lucretius describes the formation of Epicurus' atomic aggregations his choice to give preference to a secondary Epicurean term is not simply initiated by his own creative imagination and the *patrii sermonis egestas* (1.832); rather, he directly hints at Empedocles' elemental "societies," with which they share a certain degree of similarity.

In order to establish further that Lucretius takes consciously and directly from Empedocles rather than *just* from Epicurus the vocabulary he uses to create a coherent imagery of elementary congregations organized as human societies, it will be helpful to compare the two philosophers further on the grounds of their overall socio-political systems of imagery. Firstly, the images that Empedocles uses in order to describe cosmic order will be reviewed. There are two levels on which he makes use of them; his images for the relationship between the cosmic principles, Love and Strife, and that of the relationship within the "societies" formed by roots. Afterwards, it will be examined the imagery by means of which Lucretius conveys the *notion of law* that pervades his universe and how he illustrates the atomic *concilia*.

In B30 Empedocles refers to *a broad oath* between Love and Strife (πλατέος . . . ὅρκου, B30.3). However, what does this *oath* stand in for and what are the consequences involved in Empedocles' specific choice of metaphor? On the one hand, Love and Strife seem to undertake voluntarily an agreement as equals rather than one imposed upon them by a higher authority. As Vlastos has persuasively argued, Empedocles sees harmony in the universe in terms of equality; this harmony is based on the "equalitarian justice of rotation of office." The dominance of Strife, then, is an established right (τιμάς, B30.2), a lawful portion for a certain period (τελειομένοιο χρόνοιο, B30.2), an office that both Strife and Love undertake successively for an allotted number of years (ἀμοιβαῖος, B30.3).[92] On the other hand, as Lloyd remarks, this image of the successive rule of Love and Strife is, rather, consistent with an oligarchic or aristocratic ideology.[93]

Aristotle rightly identifies the oath with necessity (*Metaph.* 1000b9–17).[94] However, when Empedocles describes the obscure relationship that conditions the successive alternation of motive forces by means of an oath (B30), he intentionally sketches the abstract situation without specifying it as necessity. Hence, it seems that this metaphorical image enables Empedocles to maintain within his system the dualism between Love and Strife and the equal status that he tries to accord to them; otherwise these forces would appear subject to a higher authority, to the existence of which Empedocles does not seem ready to explicitly concede. In the opposite way, since the oath between Love and Strife about their successive alternation illustrates the fixed regularity and harmony of nature, unlike human oaths that in practice can be transgressed, this oath deceptively appears to be eternal and thus by no means can it be broken. In this respect his choice reveals his approval of this specific political institution.[95]

What is important for the comparison with Lucretius that follows is that Empedocles borrows the mundane notion of the *oath* in order to conceptualize the immutability of natural laws and the obscure notion of necessity by which his cosmic cycle is ultimately conditioned.[96] In other words, he employs an institution of the society he lives in as a cognitive tool to explain the unseen workings of the universe.

Equality is the principle among the roots within the congregations as well (ταῦτα γὰρ ἰσά τε πάντα, B17.27). The roots are of equal age (B17.27 ἤλικα γένναν ἔασι); each has its peculiar honour (τιμῆς δ' ἄλλης ἄλλο μέδει, B17.28), its own inalienable characteristics (πάρα δ' ἦθος ἑκάστῳ, B17.28), which parallel Lucretius' primary qualities of the elements, and they rule in turn as the time comes round (ἐν δὲ μέρει κρατέουσι περιπλομένοιο χρόνοιο, B17.29. Cf. also B26.1). As Wright points out, Empedocles' description of the individual τιμαί of the roots and their equality directly recalls Homer's language in the equality of privilege and allotment of power enjoyed by Zeus, Poseidon and Hades, and distances the Presocratic philosopher from the traditional religion.[97] Again Vlastos rightly discerns here the same principle of successive supremacy that we have just seen between Love and Strife. He goes on to point out that elementary societies cannot be monarchies, as no power within them possesses the qualifying primogeniture.[98] Once again the image is that of an oligarchy or of a primitive democracy. Nevertheless, the more the elements mix under the power of Love, the more they are subdued into their congregations until they are totally subordinated into the unity of the Sphere (e.g. B26.7).

Jobst was the first to suggest that when Lucretius presents us with the image of a universe organized according to certain agreements, the so-called *foedera naturai,* he directly hints at Empedocles' oath. Here it will be discussed in more detail how Lucretius embraces from Empedocles this innovative metaphor, which quite plausibly did not occur as such within Epicurus' writings, and how he articulates his imagery while at the same time integrating the Presocratic metaphors into the Roman context.[99]

In the proem to Book 1, Lucretius asks Venus to persuade her lover Mars to grant peace (1.29–40). As the poem progresses, Venus, gradually equated to *Natura,* is presented as shouldering both the roles of creator and destroyer (e.g. *et rerum primordia pandam, / unde omnis natura creet res auctet alatque / quove eadem rursum natura perempta resolvat, /* "and I shall disclose the first-beginnings of things, from which nature makes all things and increases and nourishes them, and into which the same nature again reduces them when dissolved," 1.55–57).[100] Keeping this picture in mind, it should not come to us as a surprise that, when Lucretius describes the Epicurean universe and the order that pervades it in political terms, there is no place for any solemn oath between *Venus* and *Mars* like the one exchanged in Empedocles' B30. Since in *DRN* the two processes i.e. creation and destruction, are simultaneous rather than linear, there could not be an equal rotation of power as in Empedocles.

Despite this fundamental difference at a philosophical level, Lucretius' universe too is organized according to certain eternal *foedera naturai.* Unlike Empedocles, who avoids identifying his oath with necessity in B30, Lucretius attaches to *foedera* the word *natura* to signal the coalescence of the two forces, Love and Strife: their combination constitutes in his system the natural law. While it is beyond the scope of this study to define the exact similarities and discrepancies between Empedocles' necessity and Lucretius' Nature,[101] it should be remarked that, thanks to a certain degree of affinity that these notions share, Lucretius can borrow Empedocles' metaphor of the oath and deploy it, with partial modifications, as a philosophical tool.[102]

As not all the atomic combinations are possible, the *foedera naturai* determine which *motus convenientes* the atoms are able to perform, according to their intrinsic characteristics (2.712–713). In Schiesaro's definition "the laws of nature are the projection in the infinity of time of the prevailing forms of association among compatible atoms which obtained at the very beginning of the world and that natural reproduction has inherited."[103] Moreover, the Lucretian natural pacts are sanctioned formally (*sancitum,* 1.587), and so they bear a solemnity similar to the Empedoclean oaths. At the same time, exactly like the eternal primary qualities of the atoms (namely size, shape, weight), natural decrees are eternal. Hence, in his choice of metaphorical imagery, Lucretius disregards the fact that the actual mundane agreements can be cancelled; by so doing, he further validates and honors the Roman institutions. Moreover, the use of metaphors with Roman colour forms an integral part of the contemporary Roman communication code and a necessary means of transmission of such a strange and rather indigestible philosophical doctrine.[104]

A close reading of the passages in which the phrase *foedera naturai* is found reveals that it is mainly used in contexts where Lucretius discusses the regularity of species and the limits of change, growth and length of life within the world.[105] For example, while refuting Empedocles' zoogony, Lucretius discusses what the barriers set by the fixed natural laws are, namely the impossibility of the existence of creatures such as Centaurs, monsters made of different species (5.916–924):[106]

> *nam quod multa fuere in terris semina rerum*
> *tempore quo primum tellus animalia fudit,*
> *nil tamen est signi mixtas potuisse creari*
> *inter se pecudes compactaque membra animantum,*
> *propterea quia quae de terris nunc quoque abundant—*
> *herbarum genera ac fruges arbustaque laeta—*   921
> *non tamen inter se possunt complexa creari,*
> *sed res quaeque suo ritu procedit, et omnes*
> *foedere naturae certo discrimina servant.*

"For although there were many seeds of things in the soil at the time when first the earth poured forth the animals, that is nevertheless no proof that creatures of mixed growth could be made, and limbs of various creatures joined into one; because the various kinds of plants and the corn and the luxuriant trees, which even now spring in abundance from the earth, nevertheless cannot be produced interwoven together, but each thing proceeds after its own fashion, and all by fixed law of nature preserve their distinctions."

The same metaphor is employed in a context referring to what nature allows. Lucretius writes about the permanence of matter and motion (2.300–302):

> *et quae consuerint gigni gignentur eadem*   300
> *condicione et erunt et crescent vique valebunt,*
> *quantum cuique datum est per foedera naturai.*

> "and the things which have been accustomed to be born will be born
> under the same conditions; they will be and will grow and will be strong
> with their strength as much as is granted to each by the laws of nature."

In this passage, another legal metaphor supplements of Lucretius' imagery system, which pertains to fixed natural laws. The word *condicio,* which is found only here in the *DRN,* is usually translated in a very abstract way as "condition." However, as in other contexts it is used to denote a contract, an agreement, a pact or even a marriage relationship,[107] in the present case as well it could be invested with this rather common meaning and would form, thus, part of Lucretius' political imagery.[108]

There are further terms, drawn again from the contemporary legal system that Lucretius adopts in his effort to convey the obscure notion of natural laws (5.55–58):

> *Cuius ego ingressus vestigia dum rationes*   55
> *persequor ac doceo dictis, quo quaeque creata*
> *foedere sint, in eo quam sit durare necessum*
> *nec validas valeant aevi rescindere leges*

> "His steps I trace, his doctrines I follow, teaching in my poem how all
> things are bound to abide in that law by which they were made, and
> how they are impotent to annul the strong statutes of time;"

In this context, *foedera naturai* are equated to *aevi leges,* laws that exist from the outset and cannot be broken and that are above and beyond the potential atomic *concilia* (5.58). Here we should note the double substitution, i.e. the use of *aevum* for *natura* and *leges* for *foedera.* Whereas the notion of time here bears a close affinity to that of nature,[109] the use of *leges* clearly alludes to the similar Stoic metaphor used also with reference to the natural law (φυσικὸς νόμος).[110] Still, as the Stoic notion of law presupposes a lawgiver, by and large Lucretius gives preference to the more democratic metaphor of the treaty (*foedera*) in order to tone down any teleological implications and stress the mechanistic nature of the Epicurean system.

Lastly, the word *pactum* is also abundantly employed with similar metaphorical connotations (e.g. *quo pacto fiant et qua vi quaeque gerantur,* / "how [all those things which are soft] are formed, and by what force each is directed," 1.568).[111]

On the other hand, the atomic *concilia* are not created because of these natural laws. The atoms did not form *concilia* of their own accord; they did not come together because they agreed to do so, but by chance, due to the *clinamen* (swerve) and the collisions thus caused (*Nam certe neque consilio primordia rerum / ordine se quo quaeque sagaci mente locarunt / nec quos quaeque darent motus pepigere profecto,* / "For certainly neither did the first-beginnings place themselves by design each in its own order with keen intelligence, nor assuredly did they make agreement what motions each should produce;," 1.1021–1023). So, by their combinations atoms do not break the *foedera naturai,* but the *foedera fati* (2.254). Lucretius applies the metaphor of treaty to the Stoic notion of fate instead of the more common one of law in order to reject fate's everlasting validity and Stoic determinism; therefore, he directly juxtaposes it with the fixed Epicurean natural law.[112] Here we should also point out the contrast with the Empedoclean roots, which are said to come together willingly, probably due to their alleged divine nature (οὐκ ἄφαρ, ἀλλὰ θελημὰ συνιστάμεν' ἄλλοθεν ἄλλα. / "not immediately, but coming together from different directions at will," B35.6).

The atomic clusters are depicted as miniature states. At this point a parallel could be drawn between the *concilia* and Empedocles' κόσμος, i.e. the root cluster, which was sketched as a well-ordered microcosm (cf. B26.5).[113] Nevertheless, the web of political relationships within the *concilia* is broader than in Empedocles, depicted in more concrete terms with metaphors which are drawn from the contemporary context and thus are tinted in Roman colour. The atoms themselves are personified like Roman magistrates; they are presented as miniature soldiers who can get despoiled (*spoliata colore,* 2.842) and administer public affairs in peace or in war under the supervision of nature (cf. the formulaic expression *res in quo quaeque geruntur / gerantur* in 1.472, 1.482, 1.505 and 1.955).[114] Their properties of resisting and obstructing or of depressing everything downwards are called *officium* (e.g. *corporis officiumst quoniam premere omnia deorsum,* / "since it is the property of body to depress everything downwards," 1.362).[115] Furthermore, while the atoms that participate in the congregations retain their primary qualities unaltered, still within the newly formed "society" they comply with certain rules in order to achieve common goals. What results from such a union of atoms with different shapes, combined differently and performing different movements, are the secondary qualities of things, the so-called *coniuncta* (i.e. the accidents of the *concilia:* e.g. colour, sound, taste, smell, heat or cold, sensation). These are changeable and cannot be removed without the destruction of the thing to which they belong.[116]

From a different point of view, each atomic cluster is restricted in its variety, change and growth by boundaries that it cannot transcend (*fines:* e.g. *nam quodcumque suis mutatum finibus exit, / continuo hoc mors est illius quod fuit ante.* / "for whatever by being changed passes outside its own boundaries, at once this is the death of that which was before," 1.670–671).[117] Cabisius points out that the word *fines* is used in other contexts to mean the boundaries of a country and sometimes its territory.[118] The same meaning is conveyed by a metaphor drawn also from the Roman context, the image of the deep-set stone pillar marking the boundary between properties (*alte terminus haerens*: e.g. *finita potestas denique cuique / quanam sit ratione atque alte terminus haerens. /* "in a word, how each thing has its powers limited and its deep set boundary mark," 1.76–77).[119] The cluster is similarly said here to hold a *finita potestas* (1.76), a phrase which, as Cabisius again remarks, recalls the notion of Roman magisterial *potestas*, primarily belonging to the office and only at a second level to the magistrate himself. In other words, this collocation suggests that each atomic aggregation possess a certain potential for growth which is analogous to certain political power. It thus has a fixed *imperium* that it cannot overstep.[120]

Still, the coherence of the *concilia* is based on temporary agreements, namely the *nexus*. Commenting on this term, Davies remarks that the word in other contexts is always used in its legal meaning, denoting the relationship between debtor and creditor, slave and master.[121] What is most essential it that this kind of pact is not eternal (*discidium parere et nexus exsolvere posset. /* "to cause disruption [of its parts] and dissolve their connexions," 1.220). Fowler stresses that here Lucretius hints at the cohesive force of social institutions; just as the *concilia* are dissolved, once the *nexus* are destroyed, in the same way the foundation of a society begins to totter once these bonds disintegrate.[122] Finally, it is noteworthy that the disbanding of the atomic cluster is also described in legal terms as *discidium*, which to most Romans would mean a violent end of an agreement or, more specifically, divorce.[123]

In sum, while Lucretius uses as his starting point Empedocles' social and political imagery in order to define the abstract notion of natural law, he resorts to a broad range of metaphorical images (*foedera naturai, condiciones, pacta, leges, fines, alte terminus haerens*). At the same time, while he sketches the atomic *concilia* as small states again inspired by Empedocles' example, he uses words such as *nexus* or *discidium*, which denote a less permanent agreement, in order to point to the precarious nature of atomic compounds.[124]

2.2.3.3 Warfare Imagery

As the Empedoclean cycle is one of regular change between creation and destruction, images of warfare are also indispensable so as to complete his description of reality. Very tellingly, several of the alternative names that designate Νεῖκος,[125] the cosmic destructive power, such as *Δῆρις αἱματόεσσα* (B122.2), *Κυδοιμός* (B128.1), *Ἔρις* (B20.4, B124.2), *Κότος:* (B21.7), are literally used for human battles. In contrast to Love's figure, characterizations of Strife are persistently negative; it is called destructive (B17.19 νεῖκός τ' οὐλόμενον), baneful (νείκεϊ λυγρῷ, B109.3), mad (νείκεϊ μαινομένῳ, B115.14). A bipolar distinction is thus established between them.

War seems to constantly threaten the "societies" of the roots (ἐν δὲ κότῳ διάμορφα καὶ ἄνδιχα πάντα πέλονται, / "Under strife they have different forms and are all separate," B21.7); as soon as one root comes into power, the destruction of the roots' congregation is brought about; they all become separate, reminiscent of a society in the aftermath of civil war. As a result, the image of equality within a society organized according to democratic principles is undermined. After the destruction of the Sphairos in particular, when Strife advances more and more the roots become totally incompatible due to a lack of proportion in their composition and their shape (B22.6–9):

> ἐχθρὰ μάλιστ' <ὅσα> πλεῖστον ἀπ' ἀλλήλων διέχουσι
> γέννῃ τε κρήσει τε καὶ εἴδεσιν ἐκμακτοῖσι,
> πάντῃ συγγίγνεσθαι ἀήθεα καὶ μάλα λυγρά
> †νεικεογεννέστησιν† ὅτι σφίσι †γένναν ὀργᾶ†.

> "But such as are most different from each other in birth and mixture and in the molding of their forms are most hostile, quite inexperienced in union, and grieving deeply at their generation in strife, in that they were born in wrath."

In this way they cannot come together to form societies; rather, they start joining their likes in order to form the four separate masses, which are similar to the sun, earth, sea and sky we perceive. The image is one of conflicting opposites, even if their conflict is involuntary.[126] On the other hand, if one may rely on the cumulative evidence of testimonia, one could conjecture that Empedocles described a storm or battle of the elements just before cosmogony:[127]

> κατὰ γὰρ Ἐμπεδοκλέα τὸν φυσικὸν καὶ μετὰ τὸ γῆν φανῆναι καὶ θάλασσαν ἀτάκτως καὶ ἔτι τὰ στοιχεῖα κεκίνητο ποτὲ μὲν τοῦ πυρὸς ὑπερνικῶντος καὶ καταφλέγοντος, ὀτὲ δὲ τῆς ὑδατώδους ὑπερβλυζούσης καὶ κατακλυζούσης ἐπιρροῆς. (Tzetz. *Exeg. Iliad* p. 42.17ff. Hermann = A66b = Bollack 390).

> "For according to Empedocles the natural philosopher, even after the earth and sea appeared, the elements even still moved in a disorderly fashion, with fire sometimes winning out and burning things up and the watery flow sometimes overflowing and flooding things."

Ἐπεὶ δ,' ὥσπερ ἐν τοῖς Ἐμπεδοκλέους στοιχείοις διὰ τὸ νεῖκος καὶ τὴν φιλίαν ἔνεστι διαφορὰ πρὸς ἄλληλα καὶ πόλεμος, μᾶλλον δὲ τοῖς ἀλλήλων ἁπτομένοις καὶ πελάζουσιν, οὕτω τὸν πᾶσι τοῖς Ἀλεξάνδρου διαδόχοις πρὸς ἀλλήλους ὄντα συνεχῆ πόλεμον αἱ τῶν πραγμάτων καὶ τῶν τόπων συνάφειαι πρὸς ἐνίους ἐποίουν ἐπιφανέστερον καὶ μᾶλλον ἐξέκαον, ὥσπερ Ἀντιγόνῳ τότε πρὸς Πτολεμαῖον (Plut. *Vit. Demetr.* 5.890E-F = Bollack 233)

"But just as among the elements of the universe according to Empedocles, love and hate produce mutual dissension and war, particularly among those elements which touch or lie near one another, so the continuous wars which the successors of Alexander waged against one another were aggravated and more inflamed in some cases by the close proximity of interests and territories, as at this time in the case of Antigonus and Ptolemy."

Thus, close to Heraclitus' War, which was "the father of all things" (DK22 B53), Empedocles' Strife is credited with a binary role, being the agent not only of dissolution, but of creation as well.

As far as Lucretius is concerned, a bipolar situation is being delineated: our world is the product of the incessant atomic war, but at the same time its life is meant to be terminated by war. Hence, along with images of social gathering, he also employs images of war in order to convey the creative processes. Moreover, Lucretius presents us with military images as typical of the atomic behaviour in order to sketch the destructive natural forces as well.[128]

Such words, bearing connotations of hostile confrontation or civil strife (e.g. *σύγκρουσις, στασιάζειν, συμπλέκειν, συμπλοκή*), are already used metaphorically in the Atomists' *testimonia* and also in Diogenes of Oinoanda's fragments.[129] However, it may be plausibly suggested that it is again greatly in line with Empedocles' system of imagery that Lucretius translates and incorporates them into his poem.[130] Yet, unlike Empedocles' linear alternation between the total dominance of Love and Strife, Lucretius stresses that these opposite processes are simultaneously in progress in different places.

In order to elucidate further the process of atomic combination Lucretius establishes next to *coetus* and *conexus* another alternative term, the word *concursus,* which literally can mean hostile collision (*varios conexus pondera plagas / concursus motus, per quae res quaeque geruntur. /* "the variety of connexions, weights, blows, concurrences, motions, by which all things are brought to pass," 1.633–634).[131] In the same way, Lucretius employs also the words *congredior* and *congressus,* which can mean either "to meet" and "social intercourse" or "to join battle" and "encounter with an enemy." This inherent semantic ambiguity, however, serves Lucretius in order to sketch atomic combination simultaneously in both socio-political and martial terms (e.g. *omnimodisque coire atque omnia pertemptare, / quaecumque inter se possent congressa creare,* / "[the first beginnings of things have been accustomed] to meet together in all manner of ways, and to try all combinations, whatsoever they could produce by coming together," 5.190–191).[132] On the other hand, Lucretius following his Epicurean source corrects Empedocles' theory of mixture when he argues that in their coming together the four roots cannot but be mutually destructive (*deinde inimica modis multis sunt atque veneno / ipsa sibi inter se; quare aut congressa peribunt / aut ita diffugient ut tempestate coacta / fulmina diffugere atque imbris ventosque videmus.* / "Then again, these elements are at war together in many ways, and poison to one another; therefore when they meet they will either perish, or will fly apart, as when a tempest has gathered we see lightnings and rain and winds fly apart," 1.759–762); hence Lucretius overlooks the power of Strife and the principle of like joining like.[133] He may plausibly base his reading of Empedocles' theory also in the twofold sense of the words συνέρχομαι and σύνοδος (e.g. B17.4), a sense which corresponds with that of *congredior* and *congressus;* in this way he wrongly prioritizes the connotations of aggressive meeting over the socio-political ones that the words seems to bear in the Empedoclean context, so as to serve his version of his predecessor's doctrine: according to this, unlike the atomic war, the battle of roots may only end up with their destruction. At the same time, as has been discussed above, he himself appropriates the very same vocabulary, so as to sketch the constructive forces of the atoms.

Moreover, on the macroscale Lucretius conflates Empedocles' image of the storm of elements with that of a cosmogonic battle of atoms at the beginning of the world (5.436–442):[134]

> *sed nova tempestas quaedam molesque coorta*
> *omnigenis e principiis, discordia quorum*
> *intervalla vias conexus pondera plagas*
> *concursus motus turbabat proelia miscens,*
> *propter dissimilis formas variasque figuras*   440
> *quod non omnia sic poterant coniuncta manere*
> *nec motus inter sese dare convenientis.*

"but a sort of strange storm, all kinds of beginnings gathered together into a mass, while their discord, exciting war amongst them, made a confusion of intervals, courses, connexions, weights, blows, meetings, motions, because, on account of their different shapes and varying

> figures, not all when joined together could remain so or make the
> appropriate motions together."

This war takes place at a level beneath Empedocles' roots; actually, the latter, designated as members of the world, are the product of this atomic war (5.445–448).

Conversely, when it comes to *images of disorder and disintegration*, it is Nature who is identified very significantly with the instigator of civil war, a war which will ultimately lead to universal disaster (*quid moliretur rerum natura novarum.* / "whether nature was in travail to work some universal disaster," 6.646).

On the level of the Lucretian *concilia* the equilibrium within seems to be rather fragile (e.g. 4.939–948): [135]

> *quare utrimque secus cum corpus vapulet, et cum*
> *perveniant plagae per parva foramina nobis*   940
> *corporis ad primas partis elementaque prima,*
> *fit quasi paulatim nobis per membra ruina;*
> *conturbantur enim positurae principiorum*
> *corporis atque animi. fit uti pars inde animai*
> *eiiciatur, et introrsum pars abdita cedat,*   945
> *pars etiam distracta per artus non queat esse*
> *coniuncta inter se neque motu mutua fungi;*
> *inter enim saepit coetus natura viasque;*

"Therefore, since the body is beaten on both parts, and also blows coming in through the tiny passages penetrate to the primary particles and elements of our bodies, by degrees there comes about as it were a collapse all through the limbs. For the positions of the first-beginnings of both body and mind are disordered. Next, part of the spirit comes to be cast forth, and a part recedes within and is hidden; a part again, being drawn abroad through the frame, cannot remain in conjunction or perform a combine motion; for nature shuts off the communications and paths;"

The atoms of a compound that has been stable and harmonious may suddenly become a *turba,* a crowd (*conturbantur,* 4.943). Within the atomic societies Lucretius even identifies the existence of *partes* (4.944–946), which, just as the political factions in the political life of the Republic, often lead to disruption and open violence.

Lucretius conveys more vividly the concept of the atomic civil war by means of two extended similes. In the first one he unfolds the principles of Epicurus' kinetics and puts forward the famous simile with the motes in the sunbeam; these, by their diverse movements, resemble the movement of troops in a battle (2.112–141). Lucretius hastens to make explicit that what he illustrates as eternal atomic conflict is just figurative (2.118–120):

> *et velut aeterno certamine proelia pugnas*
> *edere turmatim certantia nec dare pausam,*
> *conciliis et discidiis exercita crebris;*

> "and as it were in everlasting conflict struggling, fighting, battling in troops
> without any pause, driven about with frequent meetings and partings;"

He thus reveals that he himself is responsible for the atoms being dressed up with human characteristics. Cabisius rightly singles out words that bear connotations of a political disturbance; the invisible particles of dust or atoms are indeed imagined as plotting an undercover conspiracy (2.125–128):[136]

> *Hoc etiam magis haec animum te advertere par est*
> *corpora quae in solis radiis turbare videntur,*   126
> *quod tales turbae motus quoque materiai*
> *significant clandestinos caecosque subesse.*

> "Even more for another reason it is proper that you give attention
> to these bodies which are seen to be in turmoil within the sun's rays,
> because such turmoil indicates that there are secret and unseen motions
> also hidden in matter."

Anyhow, despite its vivid Homeric echoes,[137] the image has been filtered through the cosmological tradition and acquired broader implications.[138]

Moreover, when Lucretius discusses how animate things arise from non-sensible atoms he calls to mind the example of worms that are produced from rotten wood. Here again he sketches the changed relationship among the atoms through a rather elaborate image of political disturbance and of the established new order (2.898–901):[139]

> *et tamen haec, cum sunt quasi putrefacta per imbres,*
> *vermiculos pariunt, quia corpora materiai*
> *antiquis ex ordinibus permota nova re*   900
> *conciliantur ita ut debent animalia gigni.*

> "yet these, when they have become rotten as it were by rain, bring forth
> little worms, because the bodies of matter, being moved from their

ancient arrangements by a new condition, are combined together in
they way by which living things must be produced."

The atomic clusters are subverted as if they were the Roman classes (*ordini-
bus*, 2.900); the established order, denoted by *antiquis* (2.900), has been
left behind. The phrase *permota nova re* (2.900) points to the way that this
change has taken place, namely by civil strife and revolution. Then, the word
conciliare is used to connote the new atomic society and to lend an opti-
mistic tone to the simile. A miniature Empedoclean cycle indeed, although
depicted in Roman terms. Nevertheless, that is how, according to the Epicu-
rean principles, harmony and *isonomia* are achieved.[140]

Images of civil strife are also applied to a range of microcosmic and
cosmic levels in order to describe the incompatibility of certain atomic forms
and the resulting failure to form harmonious combinations (e.g. *aere inter-
posito discordia tanta creatur* / "When the bronze comes between, all this
quarrel is caused," 6.1048).[141]

After unfolding at length his doctrine about the war within the atomic
cluster, Lucretius comes to the discussion of the perishability of our world; he
describes another sort of civil war (*pio nequaquam . . . bello*, 5.381), one which
takes place within our world between earth, fire, water and air (5.380–395):

> *Denique tantopere inter se cum maxima mundi*   380
> *pugnent membra pio nequaquam concita bello,*
> *nonne vides aliquam longi certaminis ollis*
> *posse dari finem? vel cum sol et vapor omnis*
> *omnibus epotis umoribus exsuperarint;*   384
> *quod facere intendunt, neque adhuc conata patrantur:*
> *tantum suppeditant amnes ultraque minantur*
> *omnia diluviare ex alto gurgite ponti—*
> *nequiquam, quoniam verrentes aequori venti*
> *deminuunt radiisque retexens aetherius sol,*
> *et siccare prius confidunt omnia posse*   390
> *quam liquor incepti possit contingere finem.*
> *tantum spirantes aequo certamine bellum*
> *magnis inter se de rebus cernere certant,*
> *cum semel interea fuerit superantior ignis*
> *et semel, ut fama est, umor regnarit in arvis.*   395

"Again, since the greatest members of the world fight so hard together,
stirred by most unrighteous war, do you not see that some end may be
given to their long strife? Either when sun and all heat shall prevail,

having drunk up all the waters; which they are striving to do, but so far they are unable to accomplish the attempt: so plentiful a supply do the rivers bring up, and further threaten to deluge the whole from the deep gulf of the sea—all in vain, since the winds sweeping the surface of the waters diminish them, as does the ethereal sun unravelling them by his rays, and these are confident that they can dry up all before the water can attain the end of its endeavour. So fierce is their warlike spirit, as in well-matched contest they strive to win a decision upon a mighty cause; although in the meanwhile fire won the mastery once, and once, as the story goes, water was king over the fields."

The soldiers now are no longer the atoms, but Empedocles' primary elements, which Lucretius considers as forming the level above his atomic societies on the scale from the microcosm upwards. Very much in Empedocles' way (e.g. κρατέουσι, B17.29), the war of the roots may one day cease with the victory of one, a tyranny resulting in the destruction of the "social" coherence. Lucretius once again explains to what extent Empedocles' theory of roots could reflect reality; this war can take place among Empedocles' elements, but this is not the ultimate level of reality. One level below the atoms are indestructible; only their *concilia,* their combinations, can be dissolved. The personification is further emphasized by the use of the Homeric phrase "breathing courage" (*tantum spirantes . . . bellum,* 5.392; cf. μένεα πνείοντες, *Il.* 2.536). However, this phase will again be something temporary, as this battle is *aequum,* the warfare of creation and destruction is balanced. Perhaps a world will be destroyed by some atomic motions, but according to the principle of ἰσονομία, the total sum of motions is the same; somewhere else these destructive motions will be counterbalanced by other, creative ones (2.569–580):

> *Nec superare queunt motus itaque exitiales*
> *perpetuo neque in aeternum sepelire salutem,*   570
> *nec porro rerum genitales auctificique*
> *motus perpetuo possunt servare creata.*
> *sic aequo geritur certamine principiorum*
> *ex infinito contractum tempore bellum:*
> *nunc hic nunc illic superant vitalia rerum*   575
> *et superantur item. miscetur funere vagor*
> *quem pueri tollunt visentes luminis oras;*
> *nec nox ulla diem neque noctem aurora secutast*
> *quae non audierit mixtos vagitibus aegris*
> *ploratus mortis comites et funeris atri*   580

"And therefore, neither can death-dealing motions lord it for ever and for ever bury existence, nor further can motions that generate and give increase to things for ever preserve them when made. Thus the war of first-beginnings waged from infinity is carried on with doubtful issue: now here, now there the vital elements gain the mastery, and in like manner are mastered. With the funeral dirge is mingled the wail that children raise when they first see the borders of light; and no night ever followed day, or dawn followed night, that has not heard mingled with their sickly wailings the lamentations that attend upon death and the black funeral."

Empedocles' linear cycle, Lucretius tells us, is true only in what we see around us, counterbalanced, though, by its opposite elsewhere.[142]

Finally, by means of a siege metaphor Lucretius draws the image of a fortified city inhabited by atoms being stormed. Therefore, our world is continually subject to attacks from atoms outside the *moenia mundi* (*Sic igitur magni quoque circum moenia mundi / expugnata dabunt labem putrisque ruinas. /* "So therefore the walls of the mighty world in like manner shall be stormed all around, and shall collapse into crumbling ruin," 2.1144–1145).

Strangely enough, insight into this reality should not be a reason for Memmius to worry: although the atomic upheaval is unending, it results only in changes of the atomic order within the clusters; the atoms themselves are not destroyed. Has Lucretius a specific reason to use these particular images? His insistent reference to the civil war and its aftermath should put us on the alert.

2.2.3.4 Appendix: Parallel Life Experiences

So far, it has been seen how images of political order, social organization and disorder are used in order to describe the natural processes both on the macrocosmic and the microcosmic level (i.e. the universe and atomic clusters correspondingly). However, this relation works both ways; by unveiling its laws, nature, for the Presocratics, becomes the example according to which human societies should be organized and the stages they are destined to go through can be justified. Moreover, by applying the principle of analogy, not only can the cosmos be explained through political images, but also different political choices are justified by reference to the alleged cosmic order. This seems to be a common concept among the Presocratics. The images each philosopher uses in order to describe the universal order are accordingly drawn from his experience or even reflect in a way his political beliefs; at any rate, the Presocratics strive to show that this secular order is an integral part of the universal one; in fact this is how the former gains its validity.[143]

As far as Empedocles is concerned, his democratic beliefs are attested by Timaeus of Tauromenium and Neanthes of Cyzicus through Diogenes Laertius.[144] According to this testimony, Empedocles incited internal struggles in Acragas in order to subvert the oligarchic regime, dissolve the assembly of a Thousand and restore democracy. To those who blamed him for doing so the philosopher replied with a description of the macrocosmic order, where Love is established only after slowly eliminating the opposite principle, Strife. What he had done was suggested by natural laws, as "civil Strife is the inevitable intermezzo between phases of peace and well being."[145] This civil war was worthwhile if now order had been established again, albeit temporarily.

Whatever the degree of historical truth in Diogenes Laertius' account, this democratic profile of Empedocles' personality seems to be the image which was handed down in antiquity. Furthermore, it is significant that, while Ennius in his *Annales* 7 described a historical event, the second Punic War, he modelled *Discordia* (fr. 225 Skutsch) or *Paluda virago* (fr. 220 Skutsch), i.e. the demon who opens the *Ianus Geminus* and hurls Rome into the chaos of war with Carthage on Empedocles' Strife; in fact, this indicates that already before Lucretius Empedocles' cosmic powers had been transferred to the vision of the human society and applied in order to describe and explain by analogy the "natural" order of historical events.[146]

It is true that, when Lucretius deploys political and legal terms metaphorically and names the eternal universal laws after Roman ones, he pays homage to his homeland.[147] However, Lucretius seems to warn his fellow citizens that like certain Roman political institutions, natural processes are dynamic: *nexus*—for instance—can be dissolved (1.220). Hence, while Empedocles justifies his political choices and actions, Lucretius seems to refer to another civil war, one in which he is not directly involved. Already in the proem we read about his country's present troubles (1.41–43). What Lucretius seems to hint at is the political disturbance of his days, the imminent or recently started civil war.[148] The Epicurean seeks to ensure peace of mind by analogy and thus alludes to that linear succession between Love and Strife that Empedocles suggested. He then projects this cosmological image onto the society of his day in order to present his fellow citizens with a more optimistic message. He warns them not to be taken aback if they experience such a social subversion because, as the universe by analogy implies, this is part of natural law. In this phase of our world Strife starts becoming dominant; yet in due course the creative forces which are now active in another world will counterbalance the destruction we are experiencing (e.g. 2.899–901 discussed above).

Thus, while Empedocles figures as protagonist in the political life of Acragas, the Epicurean is just a spectator, reflecting from a distance on the actual situation (2.1–6). Despite the fact that their involvement in politics is totally different, they both appear to share similar experiences. Therefore, when Lucretius turned to Empedocles' philosophical principles he may have found more points of contact with his predecessor. Through analogy with earlier phases of history, which are also fragments of cosmic history, Lucretius was taught that civil strife is an inevitable period within each world. His pupil should rather embrace Epicurean philosophy in order to ensure his inner *ataraxia,* no matter which phase of the "cycle" the world around him is going through.[149]

2.3 *MUNDUS* AS *MAKRANTHROPOS*

The archetypal model of man has been widely used in several ways by philosophers in order to reflect upon the universe and describe a wide range of cosmological processes. Hence, the world is envisaged as a supernatural human being, a *Makranthropos.* As a result, various aspects of man, now bestowed upon the world, acquire value as interpretative tools of its past, present and future states. Accordingly, the philosopher is able to make conjectures or even to perceive processes which are remote in terms of time and distance and inconceivable because of the world's size.

There are three major types of the personification of the world, all of which have clear Presocratic origins. Embryological analogies are used in order to infer the process of cosmogony, by means of comparison with the birth of an infant.[150] Biological analogies are deployed in order to describe the possibility and the process of growth out of minimal entities; in this case, what serves as vehicle is the concept of sperm along with its implications.[151] Finally, the vitalist notion of the universe presupposes both previous analogical concepts and inevitably ensues from them. According to this notion the *cosmos* is envisaged as a living being, regarding not only its growth, decay and its final dissolution, but also its structure and functions: this is the so-called Organic or *Makranthropos* model.[152] Inevitably, these categories overlap to some extent. On the whole, both Empedocles and Lucretius make use of a wide range of such analogies in their cosmological poems. Yet, while Empedocles by and large believes in the actual validity of these images, Lucretius regards them just as a handy demonstrative device.

The section will be limited to the various usages of the *Makranthropos* analogy within *DRN*. First, it will be seen how Lucretius' depiction of the world as *Makranthropos* serves as a means of proving its mortal nature. In the main part, the focus will be on Lucretius' illustration of the formation of the four elemental masses (i.e. earth, air, water, fire) by means of language which denotes anthropomorphic articulation. Although such analogies are not absent from Epicurus, Lucretius deploys them in a more systematic way. In hunting down his source, scholars easily turned to Empedocles' poem. Here it will be claimed that in this particular case such an approach proves too narrow, and therefore this assertion is true only up to a certain extent. Empedocles' poetical imagery misguidingly serves as a safety-valve in an effort to cleanse Lucretius' poem from any possible connection with other intertexts, which would unsettle his firm relationship with his master. On the contrary, a more complete image of Lucretius' intertextual relationship is required as well as a reassessment of the complexity of this poetic and didactic choice.

Lucretius sketches the world as a *Makranthropos* in order to better establish its mortality. In three instances (1.551–564, 1.1038–1041, 2.1105–1174) he describes the duration of the world's life in terms of the life-span of a human being, which grows as long as it absorbs more matter than it gives off and thus gets nourished, but starts getting older and in due course passes away when the balance between incoming and outgoing quantities is reversed (e.g. 2.1118–1127):

> *ut fit ubi nilo iam plus est quod datur intra*
> *vitalis venas quam quod fluit atque recedit.*
> *omnibus hic aetas debet consistere rebus,*   1120
> *hic natura suis refrenat viribus auctum.*
> *nam quaecumque vides hilaro grandescere adauctu*
> *paulatimque gradus aetatis scandere adultae,*
> *plura sibi adsumunt quam de se corpora mittunt,*
> *dum facile in venas cibus omnis inditur, et dum*   1125
> *non ita sunt late dispessa ut multa remittant*
> *et plus dispendi faciant quam vescitur aetas.*

"as happens when no more is now given into the arteries of life than what flows out and passes away. At this point the life of all things must come to a stand, at this point nature by her power curbs back growth. For whatever you see growing with merry increase, and gradually climbing the steps of mature life, assimilates to itself more bodies than it discharges, so long as food is easily absorbed into all the veins, and so long

> as the things are not so widely spread open as to let go many elements
> and to spend away more than their age feeds on."

Along the same lines, as long as the cosmos absorbs atoms from outside, it grows; then, it reaches its acme (*summum aetatis . . . finem,* 1.555; *extremum crescendi . . . finem,* 2.1116; *alescendi summum . . . cacumen,* 2.1130) and from that point on matter taken in is less than that flowing out and hence the cosmos gradually falls into pieces.[153]

Epicurus himself compared the world to a living creature as well as a plant, in order to prove that it perishes (*Ἐπίκουρος πλείστοις τρόποις τὸν κόσμον φθείρεσθαι, καὶ γὰρ ὡς ζῷον καὶ ὡς φυτὸν καὶ πολλαχῶς.* / "Epicurus, [says] that the world perishes in many ways, as an animal and as a plant and in many ways," fr. 305 Us. = Aët. 2.4.10 = *Dox. Graec.* 331,24). Without deviating from his master's theory, Lucretius develops the analogy further. Solmsen has shown the correspondences of 2.1105–1174 with Plato's account of the nutrition process which is found in his *Timaeus* (*Ti.* 77c5–79e9; 80d1–81e5), correspondences which, however, may just suggest that this was the dominant medical theory; in any case, Plato does not draw the parallel between man and world, since this would contradict his belief in world's immortality.[154] More importantly, Solmsen persuasively suggests that ultimately this parallel between *anthropos* and *Makranthropos,* according to which in the course of nutrition and growth particles of earth unite with earth, those of water join the water and so on (*umor ad umorem, terreno corpore terra / crescit, et ignem ignes procudunt aetheraque aether,* / "liquid goes to liquid, earth grows by earthy elements, fires forge out fires and air air," *DRN* 2.1114–1115; *ὁ δὲ τρόπος τῆς πληρώσεως ἀποχωρήσεώς τε γίγνεται καθάπερ ἐν τῷ παντὶ παντὸς ἡ φορὰ γέγονεν, ἣν τὸ συγγενὲς πᾶν φέρεται πρὸς ἑαυτό.* / "And the process of filling and evacuating take place just as the motion of everything in the Universe take place, namely according to the law that every kindred substance moves towards its kind," Pl. *Ti.* 81a2–4), goes back to Empedocles' theory of growth and decay according to the principle of "like joining with like" (*αὔξει δὲ χθὼν μὲν σφέτερον δέμας, αἰθέρα δ' αἰθήρ.* / "Earth increases its own bulk, and air increases air," B37).[155] This theory, apart from its validity for the distribution of food, could be applied equally to different levels of reality, including the *cosmos* on the macroscale. Yet, whereas in Empedocles this process was performed under the operation of Love and Strife, in an Epicurean context it becomes completely mechanistic. In this case, therefore, Lucretius justifies his use of the *Makranthropos* model by turning to Empedocles' physical theory and integrating it within the atomic context.[156]

The same parallelism between the world and the human body can be found in a more condensed image (5.338–350). Lucretius states that just as the same diseases which have been fatal to others in the past threaten us now, likewise the present afflictions of our world should suffice to assume its mortality.

Furthermore, when Lucretius reconstructs the initial formation of the major parts of the world during cosmogony, he delineates a vague image of human limbs and parts (*membraque dividere et magnas disponere partes,* / "to put its members in place and to arrange its great parts," 5.445). The same expression occurs in two other instances in relation to the mortality of elemental cosmic masses (*quapropter maxima mundi / cum videam membra ac partis consumpta regigni,* / "Therefore, when I see the grand parts and members of the world being consumed and born again," 5.243–244) and their unremitting rivalry, which points to the imminent destruction of our world (*Denique tantopere inter se cum maxima mundi / pugnent membra, pio nequaquam concita bello,* / "Again since the greatest members of the world fight so hard together, stirred by most unrighteous war," 5.380–381).[157]

It is true that Epicurus himself had also depicted the articulation (διαρθρώσεις, *Ep. Pyth.* 89) of atoms at this stage of creation.[158] Yet Lucretius breathes new life into Epicurus' term. Unlike his master, he places the emphasis not only on the process of atomic combination, but more firmly on the very first outcome that this combination entails, i.e. the four elemental masses and, above all, their anthropomorphic shape. Scholars have tried to identify Lucretius' source of inspiration for his creative development of the potential metaphorical meaning of Epicurus' vocabulary. Empedocles' poem has been pinpointed once more as the most probable intertext and the image of anthropomorphic articulation of the world has been repeatedly and unquestioningly registered as Lucretius' direct allusion to Empedocles' poetical imagery.[159]

This certainty can be challenged. By questioning the scholarly conviction that Lucretius' elaboration of the *Makranthropos* analogy is limited to and entirely conditioned by his poetical debt to Empedocles, it should be reconsidered how easily and to what extent this allusion should be taken for granted. Moreover, one should weigh up further the consequences of Lucretius' choice. Unlike the Stoic animate universe, the Epicurean claimed that the world is an aggregation of *inanimate* matter (e.g. 5.110–145). On the other hand, the *Makranthropos* analogy is heavily loaded with specific philosophical implications, namely Platonic and especially Stoic. Hence, when Lucretius embraces it, his choice cannot simply be justified by claiming that the Epicurean poet reconstructed Empedocles' poetic illustration exclusively for his own purposes; on the contrary, Lucretius inevitably insinuates alongside it images which derive from rival philosophical systems.[160] It should be, therefore, explored how he endeavors to resolve the tension caused by these "contagious" images and ingeniously transform them into indispensable philosophical vehicles with heuristic and didactic value. As we will see, they are actually turned into the basis for a more elaborate deployment of the *Makranthropos* model in order to minimize the world's size and greatness.

It is now time to turn back to Empedocles' poem and re-evaluate the validity of the scholarly claim regarding the link with Empedocles. Where does Empedocles like Lucretius talk about "limbs" of the world and what kind of ideas does he try to transmit? I will focus on three key-words: μέρη, μέλη and γυῖα, all of which can be used to illustrate the parts of the human body. The evidence indicates that Empedocles attributes a spherical image to the Sphairos, which is by no means anthropomorphic (οὐ γὰρ ἀπὸ νώτοιο δύο κλάδοι ἀΐσσονται, / οὐ πόδες, οὐ θοὰ γοῦν', οὐ μήδεα γεννήεντα, / "For two branches do not spring from his back, he has no feet, no swift knees, no organs of reproduction," B29; ἀλλ' ὅ γε πάντοθεν ἶσος <ἐοῖ> καὶ πάμπαν ἀπείρων, / σφαῖρος κυκλοτερὴς μονίη περιηγέι γαίων. / "but he is equal to himself in every direction, without any beginning or end, a rounded sphere, rejoicing in encircling stillness," B28). Nor are the limbs of the sun distinguishable during Love's total reign (ἔνθ' οὔτ' ἠελίοιο διείδεται ὠκέα γυῖα, / "the swift limbs of the sun are not distinguished," B27.1). Yet, with reference to the Sphairos Empedocles twice introduces the idea of a frame with limbs, once negatively (οὐ στάσις οὐδέ τε δῆρις ἀναίσιμος ἐν μελέεσσιν. / "no discord or unseemly warring in the limbs," B27a) and once while Strife comes into this frame when he regains power (αὐτὰρ ἐπεὶ μέγα νεῖκος ἐνὶ μελέεσσιν ἐθρέφθη, / "But when great strife had grown in the frame," B30.1).[161] In line with this, we read about Strife's attack on the Sphairos; movement in the Sphairos initiates cosmic articulation (πάντα γὰρ ἐξείης πελεμίζετο γυῖα θεοῖο. / "For one by one all the parts of god began to tremble," B31). During the reverse process, Strife retreats from the members of the world and lets the elements ultimately reunite (ἀλλὰ τὰ μέν τ' ἐνέμιμνε μελέων τὰ δέ τ' ἐξεβεβήκει. / "but part remained within and part had gone out of the frame," B35.11). Moreover, Empedocles refers to the basic masses as "parts" (ἄρθμια μὲν γὰρ ταῦτα ἑαυτῶν πάντα μέρεσσιν, / "For all these [sun and earth and sky and sea] are one with the parts of themselves," B22.1).[162]

Upon closer scrutiny, only B35.11 (and perhaps B22.1) could support the idea that Empedocles even vaguely handed down to Lucretius and subsequently to other Latin writers the idea of cosmic articulation and the description of the four elemental masses as limbs. On the contrary, the majority of fragments in which Empedocles deploys the picture of limbs pertain to the deified Sphairos. Perhaps this choice can be explained by the fact that Empedocles implicitly conforms to the traditional anthropomorphic image of God, even if it is explicitly rejected elsewhere. It is arguably more likely that in this case his language anticipates the image of the world which is about to be created similar to a *Makranthropos*.[163] Either way, it seems that a certain degree of ambiguity and obscurity pervaded Empedocles' phrasing and the ideas lying beneath it.

Whatever the genuine significance of Empedocles' imagery, it was Plato in his *Timaeus* and afterwards the Stoics who explicitly believed that the universe was a living animal or organism.[164] In addition, very much in Empedocles' way (cf. B22.1), the Stoics systematically refer to the parts of the world as τὰ μέρη τοῦ κόσμου.[165] Therefore, despite our vague information about Empedocles' specific ideas, in all probability his imagery provided the Stoics with the appropriate conduit in order to communicate their own ideas. In fact, it was so vividly coloured with Stoic connotations that henceforth it ended up being mainly used to denote the vitalist concept of the universe, a concept to which an Epicurean philosopher should be radically opposed. For example, this is the phrasing of the Academic Cotta when in Cicero's *De Natura Deorum* he refutes the arguments of the Epicurean Velleius that gods do not play any role in the creation or the guidance of the universe as the Stoics believe (*ND* 1.100):

> *Et eos vituperabas qui ex operibus magnificis atque praeclaris, cum ipsum mundum, cum eius membra caelum terras maria, cumque horum insignia solem lunam stellasque vidissent, cumque temporum maturitates mutationes vicissitudinesque cognovissent, suspicati essent aliquam excellentem esse praestantemque naturam quae haec effecisset moveret regeret gubernaret.*

> "Then you censured those who argued from the spendour and the beauty of creation, and who, observing the world itself, and the parts of the world, the sky and earth and sea, and the sun, moon and the stars that adorn them, and discovering the laws of the seasons and their periodic successions, conjectured that there must exist some supreme and transcendent being who had created these things, and who imparted motion to them and guided and governed them."

It would be difficult to accept the unlikely assumption that the subsequent reception of the expression *membra mundi*, which was used in Latin to denote the four elemental masses firstly by Lucretius, and was in any case so tightly interwoven with his philosophical ideas, could be received completely independently from them. At this point, it is worth discussing in brief how the expression was crystallized in later Latin poetry. A characteristic instance can be found in the cosmogony at the beginning of Ovid's *Metamorphoses* (*Sic ubi dispositam quisquis fuit ille deorum / congeriem secuit sectamque in membra coegit,* / "When he, whoever of the gods it was, had thus arranged in order and resolved that chaotic mass, and reduced it, thus resolved, to cosmic parts," *Met.* 1.32–33).[166] Even more remarkably in Ovid's *Fasti* the poet portrays the literal articulation of the God Ianus out of the original Chaos; Ianus' *membra* directly recall the four Empedoclean roots (*Fast.* 1.105–112):[167]

> *lucidus hic aer et quae tria corpora restant,*   105
> *ignis, aquae, tellus, unus acervus erat.*
> *ut semel haec rerum secessit lite suarum*
> *inque novas abiit massa soluta domos,*
> *flamma petit altum, propior locus aëra cepit,*
> *sederunt medio terra fretumque solo.*   110
> *tunc ego, qui fueram globus et sine imagine moles*
> *in faciem redii dignaque membra deo.*

"Yon lucid air and the three other bodies, fire, water, earth, were huddled all in one. When once, through the discord of its elements, the mass parted, dissolved, and went in diverse ways to seek new homes, flame sought the height, air filled the nearer space, while earth and sea sank in the middle deep. 'Twas then that I, till that time a mere ball, a shapeless lump, assumed the face and the members of a god."

Given the similarities that these cosmogonies share with the one narrated by Lucretius in Book 5, which have been long noticed by scholars,[168] these passages should be considered examples of what Hardie calls Ovid's technique of "double allusion," i.e. simultaneous conflation of Empedoclean and Lucretian elements.[169] What is more, it is important that this fusion takes place within a context which basically echoes Stoic ideas.[170]

Let us now see how Lucretius, after having vaguely sketched the world as *Makranthropos* by means of the phrase *membra mundi,* manipulates this image and uses it systematically in order to substantiate his assumptions about the structure of the world and the suggested interconnection between its parts.

First, Lucretius explains why after cosmogony the sun and moon were situated in between the stationary earth and the sky and were still able to revolve in the air (5.471–479):

> *Hunc exordia sunt solis lunaeque secuta,*
> *interutrasque globi quorum vertuntur in auris;*
> *quae neque terra sibi abscivit nec maximus aether,*
> *quod neque tam fuerunt gravia ut depressa sederent,*
> *nec levia ut possent per summas labier oras;*   475
> *et tamen interutrasque ita sunt ut corpora viva*
> *versent et partes ut mundi totius extent;*
> *quod genus in nobis quaedam licet in statione*
> *membra manere, tamen cum sint ea quae moveantur.*

"This was followed by the beginnings of sun and moon, whose globes revolve in the air between the two; which neither earth nor the great ether adopted to itself, because they were neither so heavy as to sink down and settle, nor so light that they could glide through the uppermost regions, and yet they remain between both in such fashion that they revolve like living bodies and abide as parts of the whole world; in the same way as in us some members may remain at rest, while yet there are others moving."

Lucretius personifies the sun and moon as living bodies (*corpora viva*, 5.476) and immediately changes the picture by incorporating them as organic limbs into the larger picture of the world. He then puts forward an explicit analogy with the human body, in which some limbs can move without preventing others from remaining still, thus suggesting that the macrocosmic phenomenon could be grasped more easily if we were to visualize it through this lens (5.477–479). This analogy foreshadows the discussion about the actual causes of the motions of the celestial bodies which will be explained in detail in the following verses by means of extended similes.

Lucretius then turns to the Earth, which he considers to be the motionless member of *Makranthropos* (5.534–563). By way of three analogies Lucretius explains why it has rested in the middle since the beginning of the world, forming a single whole with the atmosphere.[171] He justifies first his assertion that the earth does not depress the air beneath it by its weight. So, he evokes the similar behaviour of human limbs, which apparently were also created as a whole (5.534–549):

> *Terraque ut in media mundi regione quiescat,*
> *evanescere paulatim et decrescere pondus*   535
> *convenit atque aliam naturam subter habere*
> *ex ineunte aevo coniunctam atque uniter aptam*
> *partibus aeriis mundi quibus insita vivit.*

propterea non est oneri neque deprimit auras,
ut sua cuique homini nullo sunt pondere membra,
nec caput est oneri collo, nec denique totum   541
corporis in pedibus pondus sentimus inesse;
at quaecumque foris veniunt inpostaque nobis
pondera sunt laedunt, permulto saepe minora.
usque adeo magni refert quid quaeque queat res.   545
sic igitur tellus non est aliena repente
allata atque auris aliunde obiecta alienis,
sed pariter prima concepta ab origine mundi
certaque pars eius, quasi nobis membra videntur.

"That the earth may rest in the middle region of the world, it is proper that the weight should vanish away by degrees and grow less, and that it should have another substance beneath, joined together with it from the beginning of its life and united into one with the airy parts of the world on which it is engrafted and lives. This is why it is no burden and does not depress the air; just as to a man his limbs are no burden, the head no burden to the neck, nor in a word do we feel the whole weight of the body to be pressing upon the feet; but all weights that come from without and are placed upon us annoy, although often very much smaller. So important is it what each thing can do. In this way then the earth is not something alien suddenly brought and thrown upon alien airs from some other quarter, but it was conceived along with them from the first beginning of the world and a fixed part of it, as in us the limbs are seen to be."

Apart from the close correlation between earth and air, the analogy conveys the latent power of each thing as well as the fixed place of earth within the world. Significantly, given the Stoic connotations of the *membra mundi*, both those analogies, which describe the structure of our world and the interrelation of its parts with reference to the human body, can easily recall similar Stoic images that were used to describe cosmic stability thanks to the relationship of the parts of the world, the so-called συμφυΐα.[172] Lucretius, however, focuses on the structure of the world itself rather than the transmission of every movement to all its parts because of this structure. That is why he reiterates thrice the phrase "joined together with it and united into one" in a formulaic way (*coniunctam atque uniter aptam*: 5.537, 5.555, 5.558).

Lucretius suppresses further the *Makranthropos* model (5.550–555).[173] Instead of applying the picture of Stoic συμπάθεια, according to which every part of the cosmos transmits its movements to all the others,[174] a picture which might seem convenient in this case, he rather derives his proof from a meteo-rological observation, the transmission of an earthquake's shock to the atmo-sphere (5.550–554), simultaneously employing the binding metaphor (*revincta*, 5.553) and a botanical analogy (*communibus . . . radicibus*, 5.554); air and earth are interrelated by common roots, as if they form parts of the same plant.[175]

In the third and last analogy, Lucretius again takes up the *Makranthro-pos* model (5.556–563):

> *Nonne vides etiam quam magno pondere nobis*
> *sustineat corpus tenuissima vis animai*
> *propterea quia tam coniuncta atque uniter apta est?*
> *denique iam saltu pernici tollere corpus*
> *quid potis est nisi vis animae, quae membra gubernat?*
> *iamne vides quantum tenuis natura valere*   561
> *possit, ubi est coniuncta gravi cum corpore, ut aer*
> *coniunctus terris et nobis est animi vis?*

> "Do you not see also how the most thin essence of the spirit sustains our body for all its great weight, just because it is so joined together and knit up with it into one? Again, what is able actually to lift the body in a vig-orous leap, except the power of the spirit which guides the limbs? Now do you see how great can be the power of a thin nature when it is joined together with a heavy body, as air is joined together with earth and the power of mind joined together with us?"

Thanks to air's inner power, not only is its thin nature not depressed by the earth's weight; quite the opposite, for it can exercise its power upon the lat-ter, in spite of the fact that the earth is a heavier body. Lucretius proposes the analogous supremacy of our soul over our body, taking their interconnection for granted, as established in 4.898–906. The picture of the soul govern-ing earth could easily echo the Stoic theory of πνεῦμα and its permeation through the whole universe (σύμπνοια).[176] However, the air that Lucretius is referring to has nothing to do with the divine substance of the Stoic airy soul; on the contrary, it is explicitly degraded to one of the four mortal ele-ments. Therefore, just before concluding his account, Lucretius creates an anticlimax by gradually fading out the Stoic colour.

In conclusion, although Lucretius may ultimately derive the image of the limbs of the world from Empedocles, as he adopts it, he treads on a dangerous ground, since he echoes similar, if divergent, Stoic ideas. In this interplay, Lucretius artfully creates crescendos and diminuendos, as far as the Stoic presence is concerned, while he refutes his opponents' ideas and replaces them with his atomic explanation.

2.4 TURNING THE EARTH INTO A WOMAN

The conceptualization of Earth as a human being[177] or even more specifically as a Mother[178] was very common in the Greek mythological and philosophical tradition. Given that the same natural forces are active at different levels within nature and that unchangeable laws condition both the earth and the human body, by means of observing a woman's external structure, her behaviour and her inward operations, we are in a position to compare the earth with her. The analogy is thus deployed so as to minimize the earth and to account for a specific category of obscure natural phenomena directly pertaining to her.[179] In particular with the personification of Earth as Mother, characteristics that belong to a specific category of creatures, i.e. mammals are automatically transferred to her. Consequently, conclusions can be drawn about the inner structure of Earth, her formation and her functions. This serves as a scientific tool with retrospective value. At the same time, present events can be explained and Earth's future behaviour may be inferred.

Lucretius uses the Mother-Earth analogy in four instances: a) twice in the description of the image of the *hieros gamos* between Mother-Earth and Father Aether (1.250–264, 2.991–998); b) in his illustration of Mother-Earth who contains the seeds of all things as Cybele-*Magna Mater* (2.598–660); c) in his explanation of how everything was first born out of Mother-Earth (5.772–836).

A full discussion of the Mother-Earth personification, which is already weighted down with rich intertextual ramifications, as well as the implications of its deployment in an Epicurean context, are beyond the scope of this section.[180] It is, however, worth mentioning the fact that Lucretius feels the need to justify the use of this device and explicitly states that by no means should the Earth be treated as a God, nor even as a living being (5.821–825):

> *Quare etiam atque etiam maternum nomen adepta*
> *terra tenet merito, quoniam genus ipsa creavit*
> *humanum atque animal prope certo tempore fudit*
> *omne quod in magnis bacchatur montibu' passim*
> *aeriasque simul volucres variantibu' formis.*   825

"Therefore again and again the earth deserves the name of mother which she has gained, since of herself she created the human race, and produced almost at a fixed time every animal that ranges wild everywhere over the

> great mountains, and the birds of the air at the same time in all their
> varied forms."

He himself defines the significance of his option, as a means of disentangling perplexing natural phenomena and thus assuaging men's fears. In fact, generation is caused only by spontaneous motion and the rearrangement of various types of atoms, without any divine intervention.[181]

To begin with, Lucretius directly alludes to Empedocles when he depicts the Earth as a Living Creature. When Lucretius defines the Earth as a body and describes it in anthropomorphic terms (e.g. *in gremium matris terrai* / "into the lap of mother Earth," 1.251; *sub tergo terrai* / "beneath the earth's back," 6.540), in all probability, this is in accord with Epicurus' descriptions, who also spoke of the Earth's limbs ([κ]ατὰ σχῆμα κώλω[ν] / "according to the shape of the members," *ΠΦ* fr. 26.32.19 Arr.²).[182] However, when he refers to the formation of the Earth during cosmogony (*tam magis expressus salsus de corpore sudor* / "so much the more did the salt sweat, squeezed out of its body," 5.487) he directly alludes to a specific analogy used by Empedocles, who first called the sea "the sweat of the Earth" (γῆς ἱδρῶτα θάλασσαν, B55).[183]

Let us now focus on Lucretius' account of *generatio spontanea* (5.772–836). As will be discussed below in more detail, both Empedocles and Epicurus believed in the autochthonous generation of plants, animals and human beings from the earth.[184] Despite certain changes in Lucretius' theory in comparison with that of his predecessors, intended to make it more credible, there is a scholarly consensus that the passage bears a close intertextual association with Empedocles' language. Yet, what will be questioned here is the suggestion that it also mirrors Empedocles' analogies between the vegetable and the animal kingdom.

More precisely, Empedocles' botanical analogies were ultimately based on the similarities between plants, animals and human beings in their elementary constitution and subsequently on their homogeneous structure. It is well-known that these analogies were widely embraced by the Hippocratic writers as heuristic and demonstrative devices.[185] Yet, Empedocles used also the theory of homology as a basis for his doctrine on pampsychism and metempsychosis (e.g. ἤδη γάρ ποτ' ἐγὼ γενόμην κοῦρός τε κόρη τε / θάμνος τ' οἰωνός τε καὶ ἔξαλος ἔλλοπος ἰχθύς. / "For before now I have been at some time boy and girl, bush, bird, and a mute fish in the sea," B117).[186] This theory had been the target of severe criticism within the Epicurean school. Hermarchus wrote 22 books against Empedocles, in which he attacked his theory of transmigration (Diog. Laert. 10.24–25).[187] Lucretius in turn explicitly refutes it in Book 3, in his account of the mortality of the soul.

It seems plausible that Lucretius' stance in the present passage is implicitly related to this particular aspect of his intertextual relationship with Empedocles. Within this framework, one may identify scholarly inaccuracies made as a result of the conjecture that botanical analogies after Empedocles' example would certainly be appropriate for Lucretius' demonstration. Yet Lucretius does no such thing. On the contrary, it will be argued that Lucretius' suppression of Empedocles' botanical model and minimization of its importance constitutes a characteristic case of conscious departure from Empedoclean tenets. Instead, Lucretius favors a different literary device, i.e. Earth's personification. All in all, the present reading of this passage assumes that within it all preceding echoes, intratextual and extratextual, and all mythological and philosophical elements ultimately coalesce.

Lucretius starts his account with the explanation of the spontaneous generation of plants (*Phytogenesis*), in line with Epicurean mechanics (5.783–791):

> *Principio genus herbarum viridemque nitorem*
> *terra dedit circum collis camposque per omnis,*
> *florida fulserunt viridanti prata colore,*   785
> *arboribusque datumst variis exinde per auras*
> *crescendi magnum inmissis certamen habenis.*
> *ut pluma atque pili primum saetaeque creantur*
> *quadripedum membris et corpore pennipotentum,*
> *sic nova tum tellus herbas virgultaque primum*   790
> *sustulit, inde loci mortalia saecla creavit*
> *multa modis multis varia ratione coorta.*
> *nam neque de caelo cecidisse animalia possunt*
> *nec terrestria de salsis exisse lacunis.*

"In the beginning the earth gave forth the different kinds of herbage and bright verdure about the hills and all over the plains, and the flowering meadows shone with the colour of green; then to the various kinds of trees came a mighty struggle, as they raced at full speed to grow up into the air. As feathers and hair and bristles first grow on the frame of four-footed creatures or the body of strong-winged birds, so then the new-born earth put forth herbage and saplings first, and in the next place created the generations of mortal creatures, arising in many kinds and in many ways by different processes. For animals cannot have fallen from the sky, nor can creatures of the land have come out of the salt pools."

Grass came first and then trees grew of their own accord. In the present context, Lucretius does not have to throw light *just* upon the generation of plants from the earth as such, since the process has remained almost unchanged till the present day. Rather, he has to formulate an analogy by means of which he will elucidate what caused their very *first* spontaneous growth.

Lucretius compares the first herbage and saplings with feathers, hair and bristles that grow for the very first time on the skin of young animals and birds (5.788). The analogy is very striking, given the fact that we find a similar one among Empedocles' extant fragments (ταὐτὰ τρίχες καὶ φύλλα καὶ οἰωνῶν πτερὰ πυκνά / καὶ λεπίδες γίγνονται ἐπὶ στιβαροῖσι μέλεσσιν. / "As the same things, hair, leaves, the close-packed feathers of birds, and scales on strong limbs grow," B82).[188] Empedocles breaks the boundaries between animal and plant kingdoms; his focus is placed upon the homology in the elementary constitution of hair, feathers, scales and leaves and their analogous function as integral parts of living beings. The pairing of two compound adjectives in the following verse (*quadripedum membris et corpore pennipotentum*, 5.789) makes the Empedoclean echo indisputable.[189]

Despite this close linguistic association, Sedley is hesitant to acknowledge some kind of connection between Lucretius' account and Empedocles' doctrine in this context; unlike Lucretius, nothing actually confirms that Empedocles transferred the analogy to the cosmic level, i.e. to the spontaneous sprouting of whole plants directly out of the Earth. On the contrary, as Sedley remarks, although Empedocles was a follower of the doctrine of spontaneous generation, he himself put forward a different analogy from the one to which Lucretius resorts by comparing the relationship of trees with the earth to that of an embryo which forms part of the womb in the stomach (αὔξεσθαι δὲ ὑπὸ τοῦ ἐν τῇ γῇ θερμοῦ διαιρόμενα, ὥστε γῆς εἶναι μέρη καθάπερ καὶ τὰ ἔμβρυα τὰ ἐν τῇ γαστρὶ τῆς μήτρας μέρη. / "They grow by being raised out by the heat in the earth, so that they are parts of the earth, just as embryos in the abdomen are parts of the womb," A 70a = Aët. 5.26.4 = *Dox. Gr.* 439).[190] Therefore, Sedley concludes that "it is simply the list of animal kinds that echoes an Empedoclean original."[191]

In spite of this claim, in the very same article Sedley eventually allows for Lucretius' hinting at Empedocles' philosophical ideas, with which the Epicurean seems to agree, namely the survival of the fittest in the zoogonical account (5.864–867):[192]

> *at levisomna canum fido cum pectore corda,*
> *et genus omne quod est veterino semine partum,*   865
> *lanigeraeque simul pecudes et bucera saecla,*
> *omnia sunt hominum tutelae tradita, Memmi;*

> "But the intelligent dog, so light of sleep and so true of heart, and all the various kinds which are sprung from the seed of beasts of burden, woolly sheep also, and horned breeds of oxen, all these have been entrusted to men's protection, Memmius."

In this passage, Lucretius employs two compound adjectives in a distinctively Empedoclean way (5.864: *levisomna*, 5.866: *lanigeraeque*).[193] Therefore, going back to the *Phytogenesis* passage in question, it is tempting to reassess Sedley's suggestion and to ask whether Lucretius' use of the same technique indicates a closer affinity with Empedocles' doctrine. The double allusion to Empedocles within one hundred lines makes a stronger case for Lucretius' conscious dialogue with the ideas of his predecessor. While adapting Empedocles' language from this or from another, now lost, Empedoclean passage as Sedley believes, Lucretius shifts the balance and makes a significant distinction: he keeps in the source domain of the analogy only animals and birds and thus eliminates the presence of plants. At the same time, he places in the target domain the Earth and the plants which grow out of her. The result is a biological analogy based on the personification of the Earth. It is worth pointing out that, within the framework of this analogy, the validity of Lucretius' conclusion is limited to describing the Earth as *just a Young Creature* and not yet as a *Mother*. Moreover, the emphasis is placed upon a process that takes place at a certain point in a creature's life, the very *first* appearance of hair according to fixed natural laws.

Such an adjustment should put us on the alert. Lucretius does not seem to accept the kind of homology between human beings, animals and plants that was suggested by Empedocles. On the contrary, it could be argued that this change seems to signal his negative stance towards Empedocles' pampsychism; in a way, Lucretius quotes and at the same time refutes his predecessor. This will become even more obvious later in this section.

Lucretius places next his version of *zoogony* (5.795–924). In order to make his strange theory about the spontaneous generation of life sound reasonable he transforms the figure of the *young person* that he sketched in the explanation of plants into that of a *mother* and uses this image as the backbone of his explanation. Moreover, as the phenomena that Lucretius endeavors to clarify require intense analogical thinking due to their mechanistic nature, he also combines various analogical images drawn from everyday experience. Hence, he fills in certain logical gaps in his explanations and provides his pupil with more persuasive evidence.

In establishing his assumption about the original spontaneous generation of life, Lucretius takes for granted the Earth's motherhood and appeals to a phenomenon from present-day experience while disregarding its mechanical nature: even today worms can arise from the earth spontaneously, depending on an adequate quantity of moisture and warmth (5.797–800):[194]

> *multaque nunc etiam existunt animalia terris,*
> *imbribus et calido solis concreta vapore;*
> *quo minus est mirum, si tum sunt plura coorta*
> *et maiora, nova tellure atque aethere adulta.*   800

"And even now many living creatures arise from the earth, formed by the rain and the warm heat of the sun, so that it is less wonderful if then more and larger ones arose, which grew up when earth and air were young."

Lucretius singles out two different aspects of past and present processes, which, however, form part of the general picture of animals' spontaneous generation that he is trying to piece together. In the second part of the analogy, which refers to the past, Lucretius does not describe the ubiquitous abundance of rain and heat then; he suspends it till later, as part of the overall setting of that distant era (5.806), and instead he introduces another characteristic aspect of this period, the earth's and air's infancy (5.800).[195] The coupling of earth and air alludes to the *hieros gamos* of *Pater Aether* and *Terra Mater*[196] and brings in Mother-Earth's embodiment, which constitutes the scaffolding of the story he is about to expound. Lucretius uses this reference, in order to clarify differences in the size and quantity of animals now and then (5.799–800). However, he suppresses this explanation and postpones direct juxtaposition between young and old Earth till the last part of this section.

In order to deal with the obscure theory of spontaneous generation of birds and animals and make his account more plausible, Lucretius systematizes it. He distinguishes two separate categories and accordingly presents us with two different, yet co-existing mechanisms. At this primary stage of the world's creation, he first endows the Earth with the power of bringing forth eggs, out of which birds then hatched. In this case, Lucretius resorts to an analogy with a contemporary phenomenon, the emergence of cicadas out of their husks (5.801–804).[197]

Lucretius continues his account with the generation of human beings. In the present context he strikingly modifies the traditional theory to which Empedocles clings; according to that, men were thought to have sprung *directly* out of the earth. More specifically, Empedocles believes in the immediate springing of "whole natured forms" out of the earth (οὐλοφυεῖς μὲν πρῶτα τύποι χθονὸς ἐξανέτελλον. / "First, whole-nature forms, [having a share of both water and heat] sprang up from the earth," B62.4).[198]

According to a testimonium, he gave a plausible explanation of the remote phenomenon, claiming that "men are born from the earth, like blite" (*Empedocles natos homines ex terra ait ut blitum*, A72c = Varro *Sat. Men.: Eumenides* fr. 150 vol. 4 Cèbe). Since for him the affinity between plants, animals and human beings bears deeper roots, it is not surprising that this botanical analogy alone would suffice as a valid explanation of human origins. Accordingly, when Empedocles describes birth and creation he deploys metaphorical vocabulary in order to demonstrate this very homology; human birth is twice equated with sprouting (ᾗ πολλαὶ μὲν κόρσαι ἀναύχενες ἐβλάστησαν. / "Here many heads sprang up without necks," B57.1; πολλὰ μὲν ἀμφιπρόσωπα καὶ ἀμφίστερν᾽ ἐφύοντο, / "Many creatures with a face and breasts on both sides were produced," B61.1). Elsewhere, he draws a parallel between human limbs and branches (οὐ γὰρ ἀπὸ νώτοιο δύο κλάδοι ἀΐσσονται, / "For two branches do not spring from his back," B29.1; νῦν δ᾽ ἄγ᾽, ὅπως ἀνδρῶν τε πολυκλαύτων τε γυναικῶν / ἐννυχίους ὅρπηκας ἀνήγαγε κρινόμενον πῦρ, / τῶνδε κλῦ᾽· / "And now hear this—how fire, as it was being separated, brought up by night the shoots of men and pitiable women," B62.1–3).

However, while Lucretius following Epicurus agrees with Empedocles zoogonical doctrine about spontaneous generation, very significantly he does not resort to Empedocles' botanical analogies to support his account. Instead, Lucretius introduces the image of "wombs rooted in the earth" and explains the creation of men by means of the Earth's Pregnancy (5.805–820):[199]

tum tibi terra dedit primum mortalia saecla;	805
multus enim calor atque umor superabat in arvis.	
hoc ubi quaeque loci regio opportuna dabatur,	
crescebant uteri terram radicibus apti;	
quos ubi tempore maturo patefecerat aetas	
infantum, fugiens umorem aurasque petessens,	810
convertebat ibi natura foramina terrae	
et sucum venis cogebat fundere apertis	
consimilem lactis, sicut nunc femina quaeque,	
cum peperit, dulci repletur lacte, quod omnis	
impetus in mammas convertitur ille alimenti.	815
terra cibum pueris, vestem vapor, herba cubile	
praebebat multa et molli lanugine abundans.	
at novitas mundi nec frigora dura ciebat	
nec nimios aestus nec magnis viribus auras.	
omnia enim pariter crescunt et robora sumunt.	820

"The earth, you see, first gave forth the generations of mortal creatures at that time, for there was great abundance of heat and moisture in the fields. Therefore, wherever a suitable place was found, wombs would grow, holding to the earth by roots; and when in due time the age of the infants broke these, fleeing from the moisture and seeking the air, nature would direct thither pores of the earth and make it discharge from these open veins a liquid like a milk, just as now when a woman has brought forth she is filled with sweet milk, because all that rush of nourishment is directed towards the breasts. Earth gave food for the children, warmth gave the raiment, the herbage a bed with abundance of down rich and soft. But the infancy of the world produced neither hard cold nor excessive heat nor winds of great force; for all things grow and gain strength together."

Evidence on Epicurus' views about this stage of spontaneous generation is very scanty. A controversial passage from Censorinus, reports a situation very close to what we read in *DRN*, attributes the idea to Epicurus, and points out the similarities with Democritus' anthropogony, but seems to describe Epicurean ideas dressed in Lucretius' vocabulary (Censorinus *DN* 4.9 = Epicur. fr. 333 Us.):[200]

> *Democrito Abderitae ex aqua limoque primum visum esse homines procreatos. nec longe secus Epicurus. is enim credidit limo calfacto uteros nescio quos radicibus terrae cohaerentes primum increvisse et infantibus ex se editis ingenitum lactis umorem natura ministrante praebuisse, quos ita educatos et adultos genus humanum propagasse.*

"Democritus of Abdera thought that humans were first produced from water and mud. Epicurus' opinion is not very different, for he believed that when mud was heated some sort of wombs grew and clung to the earth by roots, and when the infants had been produced, ministering nature provided a naturally occurring milky liquid for them. Thus they were reared and grew up and propagated the human race."

Lucretius' divergence from Empedocles' tradition signals his distancing from it. By introducing the image of wombs, Lucretius manages to give a more realistic account than Empedocles, as his predecessor's idea would be quite implausible or even repulsive. In addition, wombs would provide an intermediate stage between sexual production and spontaneous generation.[201] Yet while this is true as far as the credibility of his theory is concerned, his choice has further implications and thus the passage deserves a closer analysis.

The following scheme will be useful in order to unlock Lucretius' passage.

Table 1.

1ˢᵗ source domain (SD)	2ⁿᵈ source domain (SD)	3ʳᵈ source domain (SD)	Target domain (TD)	Lucretius' image (LI)
Earth	Mother	Womb	Earth	Mother-Earth
Roots	Vein/Nerves	Umbilical cord	Roots	Roots
Plants	Womb	Embryo	"Wombs" (like plants)	Wombs (+Embryo)

Lucretius draws a parallel between the Earth and a *mother*, who carries and nourishes her embryo long before it comes to light; more precisely, he endows the former with wombs, which is an organ that is a characteristic exclusively of mammals. The Earth's metamorphosis into a mother is actually so thorough that the reader may be deceived into taking for granted and trusting that in the remote past the Earth could have had real wombs. Yet by this transference Lucretius arbitrarily conflates source (2ⁿᵈ SD: mother) and target domains (Earth). So he cunningly disregards the fact that each analogy can be used as a cognitive tool only in a limited way. The mere fact that Earth behaves in *some* aspects like a mother does not necessarily entail the existence of wombs, which would account for the generation and growth of the first men. Therefore, the reader should always bear in mind that this image is legitimized only by the personification of the Earth and that it is used as a heuristic tool which aims at imposing conjectures about past events as valid. However, this observation alone does not suffice to solve the riddle of the actual nature of those "wombs."

At this point it is time to take into consideration a detail that has so far consciously been left aside: Lucretius' wombs are depicted as *rooted* in the earth. The word *radicibus* (5.808) is the key for deciphering the puzzle in question. This word thus far has been taken as a reference to Empedocles' botanical analogies between the life of plants and embryos (cf. A70a); according to this interpretation, the nourishment and growth of embryos by means of the umbilical cord (cf. 3ʳᵈ SD, which is used in this case as the target domain) could be grasped by comparing it to that of plants by means of roots (cf. 1ˢᵗ SD).[202] In line with this, it is often taken for granted that Lucretius implies a similar parallel between plants and mammals, according to which *radicibus* would be functionally equal to the umbilical cord and would account for the nourishment of the very first embryos. However, this mistakenly constitutes a logical jump: although in this passage the roots are probably responsible for some kind of nourishment, in fact they do not join up *a womb* with the infant (cf. 3rd SD), but *several wombs* with earth (cf. TD, LI). This suggests that their function cannot directly parallel that of an actual umbilical cord. Rather, the analogy pertains only to *the way in which* wombs are connected to the mother's body (2nd SD), which resembles the way plants are connected to the earth. At the same time, the parallel between plant kingdom and man is limited, as the object of Lucretius' inquiry is only *wombs,* not embryos. Still, despite the erroneous mapping of Lucretius' analogy, we cannot deny that in this case he appears to draw a botanical analogy similar to those we find in Empedocles in order to supplement the personification of Earth.[203]

However, allusion to Empedocles by means of the metaphor of roots is only part of the story. Lucretius had his own reasons for introducing this image. If we leave aside for a moment the personification of the Earth as Mother (cf. 2nd SD, LI), roots do not have to carry any metaphorical meaning (cf. TD); according to ordinary experience, they are actually the only way for something to be connected to the earth and draw its nourishment from it (cf. 1st SD). From this point of view, there is nothing disturbing in the image of wombs *rooted* in the Earth. Lucretius aims at disclosing Mother-Earth's true identity, which is simply the inanimate earth. That is why he makes a literal statement about the way "wombs" are connected to her. From this point of view there seems to be only one clear botanical analogy in the passage: wombs are depicted as some kind of *plant.* Additionally, this is how one could account for the plural (*uteri*), whose presence was also problematic in view of the figure of Mother-Earth. No real mother, unless a monstrous one, could have more than one womb. At this point one could object that according to Lucretius' zoogonical doctrine the existence of such creatures could have been possible at some point in the past; in this case in particular, the force of the botanical analogy would be further weakened, given that the reference to roots would just be subordinated to Lucretius' focal device, i.e. the Earth's personification.

Once "pregnant" Earth gives birth to the first infants, Lucretius needs to provide evidence about how the first human beings could have been brought up without parents. Hence, the Earth acquires the role of a *nourishing mother* and produces a milk-like liquid (5.809–815). Archelaus used a similar image, although in a more abstract form (DK60 A1 = Diog. Laert. 2.17):[204]

> γεννᾶσθαι δέ φησι τὰ ζῷα ἐκ θερμῆς τῆς γῆς καὶ ἰλὺν παραπλησίαν
> γάλακτι οἷον τροφὴν ἀνιείσης· οὕτω δὴ καὶ τοὺς ἀνθρώπους ποιῆσαι.

> "Living things, he holds, are generated from the earth when it is heated and throws off slime of the consistency of milk to serve as a sort of nourishment, and in this same way the earth produced man."

Table 2.

1st Source Domain (SD)	2nd Source Domain (SD)	Presocratics (Archelaus)	Lucretius' image (LI)
Nourishing Mother	Plants	Earth	Mother-Earth
Veins-Breasts	Roots	–	Veins-Breasts
Maternal Milk	Milky Liquid	Milky Liquid	Maternal-like milky juice
Infants	–	First Men	First Men

The table above will also assist us in reading the passage:

Lucretius integrates the Presocratic reference to the existence of some kind of milky liquid during this primitive stage of creation into his "Mother Earth" model, given that the mechanism of lactation forms part of it. According to Lucretius' account, thanks to Nature's providence the pores of the Earth are transformed in due course into open veins, from which flows a milky liquid (cf. LI) exactly like the milk that mothers produce for their newborn children to suckle (cf. 1st SD). In this context the personified *natura* (5.811) should be considered as equivalent to the *foedera naturai*. The personification of Earth will actually constitute the basis for the validity of the conclusion of the simile that Lucretius puts forward: if we take for granted the Earth's embodiment as a mother, there is no reason to wonder why, according to the immutable laws of nature, she produced a milky juice, just when first human beings were born out of her wombs.[205]

A further botanical analogy between plants and men has been read here. If correct, this would lend extra support to the suggestion about Lucretius' debt to this specific aspect of Empedocles' analogical thinking. More precisely, the *maternal-like milky liquid* within the Earth's veins (cf. LI) is connected with the *sap* in the roots of plants (2nd SD). This assumption is based on the fact that the word *sucum* (5.812)—although it can mean "liquid" in general—is often used to denote specifically the "plant juice."[206] In the other way round, Aristotle and others after him called this kind of sap "milk."[207] In addition, as this primary interpretation necessarily entails the identification of *venis* mentioned in 5.812 with *roots,* from which the milky liquid surges, it has been observed that Aristotle too drew such a comparison between the roots of plants and the veins of animals (e.g. *Gen. an.* 740a33–34).[208] However, nowhere does Aristotle combine these two analogies that scholars cite (i.e. sap like milk, roots like veins) to illustrate that the milky liquid which flows in the roots resembles the milk, especially the maternal one, flowing within veins. Let us now consider further the validity of this analogy.

If we were to accept this assertion, we would run the risk of committing a serious logical slip. Nowhere does Lucretius explicitly refer to the Earth's veins in terms of roots. In addition, maternal milk has nothing to do with plants' milk, since the former is produced at a fixed time for the sake of specific recipients, i.e. the new-born children, whereas in reality the latter constitutes by itself a scientific metaphor and describes just the texture of a certain vegetable juice. This interpretation disregards the fact that Lucretius has by now firmly established the image of the Earth as a Mother (cf. LI). So, he refers to the existence and function of veins—which afterwards change into breasts—only in connection with her. In fact, it is by means of this image that Lucretius justifies the production of this proto-liquid, that is through its similarity with maternal milk. Therefore, primarily relying on the meaning of *sucus* as juice, one could only allow for a subtle hint at this similarity between the growth of humans and plants; still, this constitutes a disconnected metaphorical image, not integrated into Lucretius' elaborated imagery. On the other hand, even if we were to accept the assertion that Lucretius implicitly compares Mother-Earth's veins with roots, then at a second—though extratextual—level Mother-Earth would be envisaged as a *gigantic Plant* (cf. 2nd SD). On the contrary, since in the second part of the simile Lucretius refers just to the Earth as a nourishing mother (5.813–815), he clearly restricts his probative mechanism exclusively to one source domain, i.e. that of a Mother (cf. 1st SD). Finally, Lucretius resorts to the description of the primeval climate (5.818) only additionally in order to make his argument more credible.

Before completing his account Lucretius has to secure the validity of his explanation against every possible objection: if once upon a time the Earth was capable of generating animals automatically, how could he explain the fact that today only worms and such like creatures can emerge from her? The question pertains to a contemporary phenomenon, which, due to its mechanical nature, can be clarified only analogically.

Lucretius completes the picture of the Earth's maternity and sketches the portrait of a menopausal woman (5.826–836):

Sed quia finem aliquam pariendi debet habere,
destitit, ut mulier spatio defessa vetusto.
mutat enim mundi naturam totius aetas,
ex alioque alius status excipere omnia debet,

> *nec manet ulla sui similis res: omnia migrant,* 830
> *omnia commutat natura et vertere cogit.*
> *namque aliud putrescit et aevo debile languet,*
> *porro aliud concrescit et e contemptibus exit.*
> *sic igitur mundi naturam totius aetas*
> *mutat, et ex alio terram status excipit alter,* 835
> *quod tulit ut nequeat, possit quod non tulit ante.*

"But because she must have some limit to her bearing, she ceased, like a woman worn out by old age. For time changes the nature of the whole world, and one state of things must pass into another, and nothing remains as it was: all things move, all are changed by nature and compelled to alter. For one thing crumbles and grows faint and weak with age, another grows up and comes forth from contempt. So therefore time changes the nature of the whole world, and one state of the earth gives place to another, so that what she bore she cannot, but can bear what she did not bear before."

This model will assist him in giving adequate reasons for the changes in the Earth's fertility:[209] it is no wonder why after a certain period the Earth cannot bear living beings any more; actually, this should be expected, as it happens in accordance with the natural life-cycle of every mother when she comes to the end of her child-bearing years (5.826–827). Once more, in his explanation Lucretius arbitrarily takes for granted the Earth's motherhood and articulates his argument accordingly. Finally, Lucretius subordinates the analogy between the different stages that are common in life-span of both a woman and Mother-Earth, to the natural law of limit and of continuous and cyclical change.[210] Thus, he integrates his account within his general philosophical doctrine. Moreover, after his long implicit refutation of certain principles in Empedocles' doctrine, Lucretius ends his account by approvingly alluding to Empedocles' cycle of growth and decay.

In conclusion, Lucretius consistently tries to keep only men and not plants in the source domain and so gives preference to the device of personification. As a result, he describes the whole life-cycle of a Mother throughout its different stages, from her first childhood to her adolescence, motherhood and old-age. In this way he handles personification as a dynamic process, which serves him equally well to clarify past and present events. His ultimate aim consists in clarifying the differences between plants and animals, without resorting to Empedocles' thorny biological analogies. This very choice implicitly may signal Lucretius' rebuke of Empedocles' theory of transmigration.

2.5 CONCLUSIONS

Empedocles should be considered one of Lucretius' main models in his use of the device of personification. In line with this statement, Lucretius' intertextual debt to Empedocles has been analyzed in three different instances of its occurrence within the poem. At the same time, given the fact that this device is burdened with specific mythological and religious connotations, and Lucretius' choice could thus be judged particularly hazardous as far as his rapport with his master is concerned, the possible consequences that this otherwise literary choice may entail for his philosophical poem have been discussed, along with the question of how Lucretius attempts to overcome them.

First, it has been explored how Lucretius employs personification in order to conceptualize the abstract motive forces of nature and the minimal entities of matter. Regarding the powers of creation and destruction, Lucretius follows Empedocles' example in sketching them in anthropomorphic terms; as a consequence, he inevitably introduces teleological implications which are incompatible with orthodox Epicurean teaching; that is why he takes pains to tone them down in the course of the poem. Within the same framework, a concrete web of sexual, socio-political and martial images has been traced down, images which are employed in connection with the formation and destruction of elementary congregations as well as abstract natural law. Although in this case Lucretius could have drawn his wording just from the Atomic and Epicurean tradition, he seems to be aware that this vocabulary and the corresponding imagery ultimately goes back to Empedocles' poem; hence, he himself turns directly to his Presocratic predecessor and enriches his Epicurean rhetoric with further images. Still, in this case as well, he alters them so as to adjust them to his Epicurean beliefs and the Roman context and thus successfully articulates a system of images with cognitive and illustrative function.

Regarding the visualization of world as *Makranthropos,* although Empedocles' poem is often thought of as the ultimate intertext at which Lucretius hints, it has been shown that the latter's choice simultaneously may introduce uneasy Stoic implications—often disregarded—which Lucretius attempts to defuse. Last but not least, by personifying the Earth not only does Lucretius not follow Empedocles' botanical analogies as is often thought, but on the contrary, he avoids them, probably revealing his negative stance towards the latter's theory of reincarnation which ensues from the homology between plants and men.

In this way, Lucretius turns personification into an indispensable philosophical vehicle with heuristic and didactic value.

Chapter Two
Similes

3.1 INTRODUCTION

From the earliest documented period, it was common practice for physical philosophers to rely on their senses and resort to models and comparisons with objects from common experience in order to speculate about invisible meteorological and astronomical phenomena, physiological issues or other obscure physical processes that could not be investigated directly.[1] At this preliminary stage of science, it seems that the philosophers did not look for any heuristic value in these comparisons, nor did they conduct any systematic experiments. Instead of revealing the actual nature of the unseen phenomenon in question, these explanatory models were rather deployed in order to corroborate a suggested hypothesis, often intentionally overlooking the differences between illustration and illustrandum.[2] In line with this tradition Empedocles' and Lucretius' poems abound with such comparisons.

Nevertheless, both Empedocles and Lucretius stand out from the other cosmologists, since they shape their explanations into long similes in dactylic hexameters after the Homeric model.[3] Several scholars have already pointed out Lucretius' debt to Empedocles' similes.[4] However, this debt is often assumed to extend only to the poetic form of the similes that Empedocles as a pioneer inherited from Homer and adapted to his didactic and scientific purposes. Therefore, Lucretius' incorporation of Empedocles' similes is considered as part and parcel of his choice of genre, a philosophical account in dactylic hexameters.

In this chapter it will be suggested that while Lucretius turns directly to Empedocles' extended similes, he does not appropriate them just because the Presocratic provided him with a convenient model of how to dress difficult philosophical truths in an attractive attire and thus make them digestible for his student. On the contrary, Lucretius artfully assimilates these similes as an organic part of his cosmological account for very specific reasons. After briefly reviewing the Homeric form of both Empedocles' and Lucretius' similes as well as the Homeric echoes within them (Section 3.2), it will be considered why Empedocles' differentiation from Homer in this regard was particularly significant for Lucretius' didactic and scientific goals. First (Section 3.3), the interrelation between poetic form and scientific content will be explored and the articulation and the structure of Empedocles' and Lucretius' scientific similes will be discussed in detail. In this connection, certain techniques that Lucretius takes from Empedocles' similes will be examined and it will be investigated how and to what extent he enhances them. In the last part (Section 3.4) it will be suggested that Lucretius discerns within Empedocles' similes specific probative methods, albeit in an embryonic state, which are closely related to his philosophical principles, and appreciates their force as effective philosophical and scientific tools. Within this framework, it will be analyzed how Lucretius shapes his arguments accordingly, so as to present us with plausible explanations of the physical world.

At the same time, Lucretius' intertextual engagement with authors, such as the writers of the Hippocratic corpus, Aristotle and above all Theophrastus will be taken into consideration, since in those writings occur analogies similar to those of Empedocles, which may have been influenced—directly or indirectly—by the latter's example.

Certain preliminary remarks should be taken for granted for the discussion to follow. Empedocles' interest in medical matters is well known. Moreover, his influence upon the Hippocratic corpus, even if varied, is well attested.[5] One group adopted his philosophy along with his scientific method and applied it to medicine; others opted only for the method, ignoring or rejecting the theory of the four elements.[6] What is more, there are several instances in *DRN* which make it highly probable that Lucretius knew at least some of the Hippocratic treatises.[7] By the same token, Aristotle's treatises abound in analogical explanations, which resemble those of Empedocles.[8] As I will show, Lucretius appropriates into his similes analogical material directly drawn from both the Hippocratic corpus and Aristotle, which he alters in accordance with the Empedoclean methods and subordinates to his own purposes.

Even more significantly, Theophrastus' *Metarsiologica* too is loaded with numerous analogies, which are reminiscent of the Empedoclean ones.[9] In fact, it is remarkable that Theophrastus was not just the compiler of Presocratic explanations of natural phenomena; on the contrary, in this work he adds on his own account several analogies, which are not found—or at least not so systematically articulated—in his predecessors. It seems that his ultimate intention was not just to summarize existing accounts of the phenomenon in question, but rather to further explain and visualize it for the potential pupil. It has been argued that Lucretius draws his material from Theophrastus—probably as it is assumed via Epicurus' now lost account—in the account of atmospheric and terrestrial phenomena in Book 6. There are several reasons to endorse this supposition. To begin with, the two accounts share many specific explanations in common. Moreover, Theophrastus himself, deviating from Aristotle's practice of seeking one cause for a phenomenon, anticipates Epicurus in the practice of giving multiple explanations of natural phenomena. Whereas for Theophrastus this principle reflects the variety of similar phenomena, according to Epicurus, it is due to the limitations of human perception that no single explanation is sufficient; all are equally right, as long as they do not contradict our experience. This is what Epicurus calls the principle of οὐκ ἀντιμαρτύρησις.[10] It is also noteworthy that Theophrastus' account includes a theological excursus which denies any divine intervention in the sublunary world, a passage that clearly corresponds to *DRN* 6.379–422.[11]

Sedley remarks that, given the different organization of explanations in Lucretius' Book 6, in all probability Epicurus does not follow Theophrastus' *Metarsiologica,* but rather the same author's now lost *Physical Opinions.*[12] Even if this is the case, one should still account for the remarkable lack of correspondence between Theophrastean and Lucretian analogies. Did Epicurus also find them in Theophrastus' *Physical Opinions?* Yet we should not overlook the fact that there is an instance in Lucretius' explanations of thunder in which he employs as his model the image of a bladder instead of a vase which, however, was the analogy used by both Theophrastus and Epicurus (6.121–131).[13] Although there are unfortunately two missing texts in our chain of reconstruction, i.e. Theophrastus' *Physical Opinions* and Epicurus' *On Nature,* it still seems plausible that it was Lucretius who first modified Theophrastus' meteorological account—be it the *Metarsiologica* or the *Physical Opinions*—in this respect and opted for different analogies. In fact, as I am going to argue, these changes reflect and are entailed by Lucretius' appropriation of Empedocles' analogical method.

3.2 EPIC FORM

While writing an epic after the Homeric model, Empedocles inevitably integrates the extended epic simile into his philosophical poem as an integral constituent of the epic genre. Although we have unfortunately only few such long similes (B23 the painters simile, B84 the lantern simile and B100 the clepsydra simile), it seems most probable that Empedocles made systematic use of them.[14] From the extant fragments, it is clear that he adopted Homer's bipartite structure;[15] moreover, he invested them with formulaic vocabulary and resonances drawn from various Homeric passages.[16]

As far as Lucretius is concerned, this aspect of his direct relationship with Homer has often been overemphasized.[17] It is true that in his comparisons Lucretius often adopts the extended form of Homeric similes.[18] Nonetheless, unlike what we find in Empedocles' extant fragments, Lucretius does not confine himself to the rigid form of the bipartite Homeric simile; on the contrary he often formulates his analogies in such a loose way that some scholars end up simply talking about an analogical imagery, which, however, bears the function of a Homeric simile; in other cases they go so far as to mistakenly eliminate any association with the latter.[19] Moreover, in several similes commentators have no difficulty in pinpointing echoes of specific Homeric similes, now creatively modified and appropriated in the new physical context.[20]

For example, in 2.308–316 Lucretius claims that atoms move incessantly in the void. Yet why does this relentless motion remain concealed and macrocosmic bodies seem at rest? Schiesaro formulates the answer as a mathematical-like function: "The perceptibility of the motion depends on the size of the body in motion, which is in turn diversely perceptible in relation to the distance of the point of the observer."[21] On the grounds that we may rely upon τὰ πρὸς καιρὸν ἄδηλα, so as to form a prolepsis of τὰ φύσει ἄδηλα (Sext. Emp. *Adv. Math.* 8.145), Lucretius resorts to an analogy with two artificial microcosms in order to demonstrate this illusory paradox (2.317–332):

> *nam saepe in colli tondentes pabula laeta*
> *lanigerae reptant pecudes quo quamque vocantes*
> *invitant herbae gemmantes rore recenti,*
> *et satiati agni ludunt blandeque coruscant;*   320
> *omnia quae nobis longe confusa videntur*
> *et velut in viridi candor consistere colli.*
> *praeterea magnae legiones cum loca cursu*
> *camporum complent belli simulacra cientes,*
> *fulgor ubi ad caelum se tollit totaque circum*   325
> *aere renidescit tellus subterque virum vi*
> *excitur pedibus sonitus clamoreque montes*
> *icti reiectant voces ad sidera mundi*
> *et circumvolitant equites mediosque repente*
> *tramittunt valido quatientes impete campos—*   330

et tamen est quidam locus altis montibus unde
stare videntur et in campis consistere fulgor.

"For often on a hill, cropping the rich pasture, woolly sheep go creeping whither the herbage all gemmed with fresh dew tempts and invites each, and full-fed the lambs play and butt heads in fun; all which things are seen by us blurred together in the distance, as a kind of whiteness at rest on a green hill. Besides, when great legions cover the outspread plains in their manoeuvres, evoking war in mimicry, and the sheen rises to the sky and all the country around flashes back the brilliancy of bronze, and beneath, the ground quakes, resounding with the mighty tramp of men's feet, and the mountains, stricken by the clamour, throw back the sounds to the stars of heaven, and horsemen gallop around and suddenly course through the midst of the plains, shaking them with their mighty rush, yet there is a place on the high mountains, from which they seem to stand still, and to be a brightness at rest upon a plain."

Lucretius describes the images of a flock of sheep on a hillside and then army manoeuvres in a mock battle on a plain, both of which seem to form one mass of light when seen from a distance. It is true that both those vehicles, which bear supplementary probative force, are drawn from the stock examples of a σῶμα ἐκ διεστώτων (Sext. Emp. *Adv. Math.* 9.78). However, given their epic subject-matter, Lucretius restores them back to their original poetic form; what is more important, they are both evocatively interwoven by tangible threads drawn from various Homeric passages.[22] It is in this form that they eventually get fully assimilated into Lucretius' philosophical argument.[23]

Although both Empedocles and Lucretius draw extensively on Homeric similes, they essentially deviate from them. While Empedocles rewrites the Homeric similes, he consciously filters them through his scientific and philosophical method in order to turn them into a valid scientific tool that is endowed with a distinct rhetorical, pedagogical and thus functional role. By means of it not only does Empedocles decipher the secrets of nature, but is also empowered to transmit them to his pupil in an enlightening way. On these grounds, as it will be claimed in what follows, Lucretius turns to Empedocles' similes with reference to structural features (Section 3.3) as well as to the content of his comparisons (Section 3.4).[24]

3.3 POETRY VERSUS SCIENCE

Empedocles' and Lucretius' choice of medium, i.e. versified similes, entails certain consequences for the validity of their scientific comparisons. A shift within a simile towards poetry or science could easily result in its balance being overthrown and this could obfuscate the clarity of the analogy. As a result, its usage within a poem with didactic aspirations may turn out to be problematic. On these grounds, their similes should be evaluated by exploring the interaction of the poetic form with the scientific content, the effectiveness of the ensuing combination and certain ways by which balance within them can be maintained. On the one hand, there are features within their similes that, although they are innate in their poetic form, could endanger the scientific principle of clarity and which each poet handles in a different way. On the other, there are specific techniques that Empedocles uses to enhance the structure and the systematicity of Homeric similes in order to turn his similes into effective cognitive tools for disclosing unseen reality and which Lucretius embraces in his similes.

Regarding Empedocles' similes, O'Brien has pointed out that there lurks "a fresh metaphorical stratum which is introduced within an already established simile."[25] In other words, besides the main vehicle that the poet employs in order to shed light upon the nature of the tenor, an additional one intrudes, often in the form of an ambiguity in the meaning of the tenor itself. The contamination within, from which stems what will be henceforth called *multi-dimensional similes* and which is otherwise imposed and legitimized by their poetic claims, may turn out to be so powerful that it could constitute a potential cause of confusion, while identifying the similarities between vehicle and tenor. As a result, this could violate the clarity of a simile and undermine its scientific value.

When Empedocles explains the structure of the human eye by comparing it to the structure of a lantern, he refers to the former as *κούρην* (B84.8). There should be nothing strange in it, as "eye" was the regular poetic meaning of the word in the fifth century B.C.[26] In the same way, from the point of view of the scientific comparison the phrase *ἐν μήνιγξιν ἐεργμένον ὠγύγιον πῦρ / λεπτῇσιν <τ'> ὀθόνῃσι . . . κύκλοπα κούρην* (B84.7–8) is primarily meant to be literally interpreted as "the elemental fire, wrapped in membranes and delicate tissues . . . in the round eye."[27] However, this wording by which Empedocles describes the linen screens and the delicate tissues of the lantern is rich in Homeric resonances and brings to mind the dresses worn by the dancing girls depicted by Hephaestus on the shield of Achilles (*τῶν δ' αἱ μὲν λεπτὰς ὀθόνας ἔχον, οἱ δὲ χιτῶνας / εἵατ' ἐϋννήτους, ἦκα στίλβοντας ἐλαίῳ.* / "These wore, the maidens long light robes, but the men wore tunics of finespun work and shining softly, touched with olive oil," *Il.* 18.595–596).[28] Therefore, since such metaphorical connotations seem to be embedded in the phrase, on a further level it could also be translated as "a round-eyed little girl wrapped in membranes and in delicate garments."[29] Consequently, the metaphorical dimension that intrudes into the simile and the concomitant ambiguity regarding its overall meaning shifts the balance towards poetry and thus detracts from its scientific transparency. In addition, another poetic element which could be considered as a possible cause of scientific confusion is the expression ὕδατος . . . βένθος . . . ἀμφινάοντος (B84.9), which literally denotes the deep or the ocean of the circumfluent water. As Sedley remarks, this is of course "an extravagant term for a thin film of water."[30] Despite the fact that such oscillations, when referring to different manifestations of the same primary element, are a common practice for Empedocles and otherwise should not surprise us, its strong poetic flavour here may result in exaggeration and thus in disturbing imprecision.[31]

Again, Empedocles illustrates in the form of a long simile an obscure mechanism of human physiology (respiration), by comparing it with the workings of a model, a clepsydra (B100). A clepsydra was a common household apparatus with a narrow opening at the top which could be plugged by hand, and a perforated base through which it was filled; it was used for transferring small amounts of liquid from one container to another.[32] As the interpretation of this simile has caused much discord among scholars, I will consider here some possible causes for this suspension of clarity. In the spirit of Homer, Empedocles unnecessarily gives elaborate details about the vehicle; thus, he periphrastically describes the clepsydra, along with the water in which it is immersed (κλεψύδρη . . . διειπετέος χαλκοῖο· / "a clepsydra of shining bronze," B100.9; εἰς ὕδατος . . . τέρεν δέμας ἀργυφέοιο, / "into the smooth body of shining water" B100.11), [33] This alone should not obscure the simile to such an extent as to destabilize the validity of the model itself. However, this may not be the case with the military metaphor that occurs further down in the description of the air that keeps the water within the clepsydra (πορθμοῦ χωσθέντος, B100.17; ἀμφὶ πύλας ἠθμοῖο δυσηχέος, ἄκρα κρατύνων, B100.19).[34] Literally, Empedocles says that, when the neck of the clepsydra is blocked then air presses against the perforations. But the expressions can also mean that "the gates are blocked" and that "a general controls the defences." Here as well, Empedocles seems to sacrifice a degree of clarity in favour of the overall poetic effect.

In Lucretius also we can detect instances of similes in which the straightforward comparison between the tenor and the vehicle is contaminated by the intrusion of a supplementary level of comparison. However, as it will turn out below, Lucretius employs what we called regarding Empedocles multiple-dimensional similes in a more systematic way. Instead of abolishing from his similes the implications of a supplementary vehicle, Lucretius cunningly manipulates it so as to establish the scientific precision of his comparisons. Whereas in Empedocles the metaphorical connotations were lurking within the meaning of the tenor itself, Lucretius explicitly transfers them to a new vehicle. In other words, within the limits of a single simile he simultaneously brings into play two or more vehicles and thus sheds light upon the tenor from different angles. In brief, Lucretius endows the multi-dimensional similes with a functional role rather than just a poetical one and turns them into another probative device of his didactic poem. Here, we will have a close look at two such instances.

Such an instance of a vehicle ramified in several directions occurs in Lucretius' first explanation of the possible causes of thunder (6.108–115):

> *Dant etiam sonitum patuli super aequora mundi,*
> *carbasus ut quondam magnis intenta theatris*
> *dat crepitum malos inter iactata trabesque,*　　　　　　　　　　110
> *interdum perscissa furit petulantibus auris*
> *et fragilis sonitus chartarum commeditatur*
> *(id quoque enim genus in tonitru cognoscere possis),*
> *aut ubi suspensam vestem chartasque volantis*
> *verberibus venti versant planguntque per auras.*　　　　　　　115

"They make a noise also over the stretches of wide-spreading firmament, as at times the canvas awning stretched over a great theatre cracks flapping between poles and beams, sometimes tears and flies wild under the boisterous winds, imitating the rendering sound of paper (for that kind of sound also you may recognize in the thunder); or as when a garment hung on the line or flying sheets of paper are beaten by the blows of the breeze and slapped through the air."

When clouds are buffeted by winds so that different parts are blown in different directions, the result is a flapping or rolling noise like that produced when wind beats the awnings of a theatre (6.109–111). After this first comparison of clouds with awnings, Lucretius introduces a new simile, which is embedded within the main one: in its turn the sound of the canvas awning imitates that of paper (6.112). In this way, the role of the first vehicle is inverted and turned for a moment into that of a tenor. Then, in a parenthetical comment, paper is linked directly to the primary tenor of the simile, i.e. the clouds (6.113), to be resumed in the following line, along with an additional vehicle, clothes hung up to dry (6.114). In this way, while paper dominantly serves as the main point of reference throughout, the various vehicles are clarified by each other and eventually become tightly interwoven (6.109–111, 6.114) and hence further light is retrospectively thrown upon the phenomenon of thunder. So the distinction between tenors and vehicles is further elided. In other words, Lucretius puts forward a straightforward rapid succession of multiple vehicles, which not only does not obscure his explanation or imperil the validity of the scientific model, but rather reinforces it.

Lucretius expounds his second explanation of lightning by means of a particularly dense passage in terms of analogical thinking (6.173–203). According to this passage for a stroke of lightning to occur two things are necessary: wind within the cloud must grow hot by its whirling motion, and a cloud must be thick in order for the wind to hollow out its centre and make its walls dense. Lucretius initially resorts to separate analogies in order to establish his point about the nature of winds and clouds, and only at the end do the two images become integrated. First he describes the formation of lightning from wind by evoking that a leaden bullet also ignites when rotated (6.173–179).[35] After a digression about its expulsion and the simultaneous production of thunder (6.180–184), Lucretius focuses on the *structure* of clouds (6.185–203):

scilicet hoc densis fit nubibus et simul alte   185
extructis aliis alias super impete miro;
ne tibi sit frudi quod nos inferne videmus
quam sint lata magis quam sursum extructa quid extent.
contemplator enim, cum montibus adsimulata
nubila portabunt venti transversa per auras,   190
aut ubi per magnos montis cumulata videbis
insuper esse aliis alia atque urgere superne
in statione locata sepultis undique ventis:
tum poteris magnas moles cognoscere eorum
speluncasque velut saxis pendentibu' structas   195
cernere, quas venti cum tempestate coorta
conplerunt, magno indignantur murmure clausi
nubibus in caveisque ferarum more minantur;
nunc hinc nunc illinc fremitus per nubila mittunt,
quaerentesque viam circum versantur, et ignis   200
semina convolvunt e nubibus atque ita cogunt
multa rotantque cavis flammam fornacibus intus,
donec divolsa fulserunt nube corusci.

"You may be sure that this is what happens, when clouds are thick and at the same time piled high one above another in a wonderful mass,

that you may not be deceived because from below we see more read-
ily how wide they are than how far they extend piled upwards. For do
but apply your scrutiny when the winds carry clouds like mountains
across through the air, or when you see them piled about the great
mountains one above another, pressing down from above, and lying
still with the winds deep buried on every side: then you will be able
to recognize the great masses of them, and to perceive the similitude
of caverns reared with vaulted roofs, which when a tempest arises the
winds fill, and with loud roaring resent their imprisonment in the
clouds, menacing like wild beasts in their cages: now this way now
that way they send their growlings through the clouds, roaming round
in quest of a way out, and rolling together the seeds of fire from the
clouds, and thus they collect many such and send the flame rushing
about the hollow furnaces within, until they have shattered the cloud
and flashed forth coruscating."

Regarding the height of the clouds, Lucretius asks his pupil to bring to
mind their obvious similarity to mountains (6.189); the juxtaposition of this
image with that of real mountains above which clouds are actually hanging
effectively lends to the illustrative force of the comparison (6.191). In the
following lines he puts a twist into the image by visualizing clouds as huge
vaulted halls (6.195). Then a new turn in the vehicle comes, that from cav-
erns into cages (6.198). At this moment Lucretius picks up winds again and
compares their behaviour with that of wild animals in a cage, in order to illu-
minate their movement and their roaring. The transference of the vocabulary
is revealing; the winds are angry and growl, they threaten, they move up and
down growling, looking to escape from their prison and going out in circles
(6.197–200). The description ends up with an implied comparison of clouds
with hollow furnaces, within which lightning is forged (6.202).[36]

Therefore, the pupil is called upon to map the clouds consecutively
onto mountains–caverns–cages–furnaces. More precisely, Lucretius shifts the
focus away from the external appearance (i.e. mountains), to the internal
structure (i.e. vaulted caves), then to the agent (winds like animals in cages)
and finally to the function of the container (furnace). At first glance, Lucre-
tius' multi-dimensional simile seems to violate the principle of clarity. How-
ever, while describing one single tenor by means of several different vehicles
in alternation, the poet turns each image from being just ornamental and
superfluous into an organic part of the simile. Such a dense image, besides its
poetical beauty, seeks to shed light on different aspects of his explanation of
the cause of lightning and critically adds to the value of Lucretius' scientific

explanation. Nevertheless, it is down to the alertness of the pupil to follow the thread of Lucretius' complicated imagery.

West discusses at length the simile through which Lucretius attempts to prove the corporeality of the wind, which is invisible, by comparing its destructive effects with those of water; at a second level, this comparison will ultimately prove the corporeality of the unseen atoms (1.271–297):[37]

> *Principio venti vis verberat incita pontum*
> *ingentisque ruit navis et nubila differt;*
> *interdum rapido percurrens turbine campos*
> *arboribus magnis sternit montisque supremos*
> *silvifragis vexat flabris: ita perfurit acri*   275
> *cum fremitu saevitque minaci murmure ventus.*
> *sunt igitur venti nimirum corpora caeca*
> *quae mare, quae terras, quae denique nubila caeli*
> *verrunt ac subito vexantia turbine raptant;*
> *nec ratione fluunt alia stragemque propagant*   280
> *et cum mollis aquae fertur natura repente*
> *flumine abundanti, quam largis imbribus auget*
> *montibus ex altis magnus decursus aquai,*
> *fragmina coniciens silvarum arbustaque tota,*
> *nec validi possunt pontes venientis aquai*   285
> *vim subitam tolerare: ita magno turbidus imbri*
> *molibus incurrit validis cum viribus amnis,*
> *dat sonitu magno stragem volvitque sub undis*
> *grandia saxa, ruit qua quidquid fluctibus obstat.*
> *sic igitur debent venti quoque flamina ferri,*   290
> *quae veluti validum cum flumen procubuere*
> *quamlibet in partem, trudunt res ante ruuntque*
> *impetibus crebris, interdum vertice torto*
> *corripiunt rapidoque rotantia turbine portant.*
> *quare etiam atque etiam sunt venti corpora caeca,*   295
> *quandoquidem factis et moribus aemula magnis*
> *amnibus inveniuntur, aperto corpore qui sunt.*

"First the mighty wind when stirred up beats upon the ocean and overwhelms huge ships and scatters the clouds, and at times sweeping over the plains with rapid hurricane strews them with great trees and flogs the topmost mountains with tree-crashing blasts: so furious and fierce its howling, so savage and threatening the wind's roar. Therefore undoubtedly there are unseen bodies of wind that sweep the sea, that sweep the earth, sweep the clouds of the sky also, beating them suddenly and catching them up in a hurricane; and they flow and deal devastation in the same way as water, which, soft as it is, suddenly rolls in overwelling stream when a great deluge of water from the high mountains swells the flood with torrents of rain, dashing together wreckage of forests and whole trees, nor can strong bridges withstand the sudden force of the coming water, with so mighty a force does the river, boiling with rain-torrents, rush against the piers; it works devastation with loud uproar and rolls huge rocks under its waves, and sweeps away whatever stand in its path. Thus therefore the blasts of the wind also must be borne along, which, like a strong river, when they have borne down in any direction, thrust all before them and sweep all away with frequent attacks, and at times catch things up in a swirling eddy and whirling them round carry them off in a swift tornado. Therefore I say again and again, there are unseen bodies of wind, since in deeds and ways they are found to rival great rivers, which possess a body which can be seen."

West points out several—conscious or coincidental, as he says—correspondences between the parallel descriptions of wind and water in the two parts of the simile (e.g. wind's action: *ruit,* 1.272; *ruunt,* 1.292 → flood's action: *ruit,* 1.289; wind: *percurrens,* 1.273 → flood: *decursus,* 1.283; *incurrit,* 1.287; wind's impact: *silvifragis,* 1.275 → flood's impact: *fragmina . . . silvarum,* 1.284; wind: *sternit,* 1.274; *stragem,* 1.280 → flood: *stragem,* 1.288) and claims that this is an instance of Lucretius' *multiple-correspondence* similes.[38] According to this technique, Lucretius draws numerous parallels between the two parts of a simile in a consistent way in order to improve the structure of the simile, firmly establish the similarities between tenor and vehicle and enforce their unity. Sedley, in turn, rightly remarks that "the multiplicity of correspondences has an argumentative motive, and not merely a descriptive one: the more correspondences there are, the more persuasive the analogy becomes."[39] More significantly, Sedley identifies Empedocles as Lucretius' predecessor in this technique.

Elsewhere, West rightly observes that in some of Lucretius' similes "the terms of the analogy are not kept systematically distinct from the terms of his literal argument." This is what West calls *transfusion of terms* between the image and the literal context.[40] A striking instance can be spotted in the simile that we have just mentioned above (1.271–297), in which the comparison of the motion of wind with that of water in a river is foreshadowed by referring to the former as "flowing" (wind: *fluunt,* 1.280 → water: *flumine,* 1.282; *fluctibus,* 1.289; *flumen,* 1.291). In more general terms, while

Lucretius metaphorically applies to the tenor language which is typical of the vehicle, he strengthens the coherence between the two, emphasizes the homogeneity between different levels of reality and prepares the pupil to envision better and more persuasively the invisible vehicle.

Taking these assertions as my starting points, in what follows I will exemplify the techniques of *multiple-correspondence* and *transfusion* within Lucretian similes by taking a closer look at three such instances.[41] I will then turn back to Empedocles' similes to verify what Sedley calls Empedocles' technique of *multiple-correspondence*. At the same time, Empedocles will be identified as the likely precursor of Lucretius for the technique of *transfusion* as well.

A characteristic example of Lucretius' transfusion technique occurs in his first explanation of how such a small sun can emit so much light; as he suggests, this is due to the fact that the sun receives a constant succession of fire, which is then distributed over the earth, sea and sky (5.592–603):[42]

> *Illud item non est mirandum, qua ratione*
> *tantulus ille queat tantum sol mittere lumen,*
> *quod maria ac terras omnis caelumque rigando*
> *compleat et calido perfundat cuncta vapore.*   595
> *nam licet hinc mundi patefactum totius unum*   597
> *largifluum fontem scatere atque erumpere lumen,*
> *ex omni mundo quia sic elementa vaporis*
> *undique conveniunt et sic coniectus eorum*   600
> *confluit, ex uno capite hic ut profluat ardor.*
> *nonne vides etiam quam late parvus aquai*
> *prata riget fons interdum campisque redundet?*

"Another thing also need not excite wonder, how it can be that so small a sun emits so much light, enough to fill with its flood seas and all lands and the heavens, and to suffuse all with warm heat. For it is possible that from this place is opened one single fountain of the whole world, to splash its generous flood and to fling forth light, because the elements of heat gather together from all parts of the world in such a manner, and their assemblage flows together in such a manner, that the heat flows out here from one single source. Do you not see also how widely a small spring of water sometimes floods the meadows and streams over the fields?"

In order to make his point effectively, he compares the sun with a spring of water, which albeit small can irrigate large tracts of land thanks to a constant supply of water. The common denominator in the two halves of the simile is the smallness of the single provider in contrast with the never-ending quantity and thus overwhelming presence of the product. Although this analogy has probably already been used by Epicurus,[43] Lucretius neatly shapes it into a systematic comparison relying on the transfusion technique; by directly calling the sun "fountain" (sun: *largifluum fontem,* 5.598 → fountain: *aquai / . . . fons,* 5.602–603) and referring to the movement of heat by verbs characteristic of flowing water already in the tenor (sun: *rigando,* 5.594; *perfundat,* 5.595; *confluit . . . profluat,* 5.601 → water: *riget . . . redundet,* 5.603), Lucretius assimilates fire with water.[44] Hence, despite the fact that he puts forward three alternative suggestions regarding the initial question (cf. 5.604–609, 5.610–613), the latter is integrated only with the tenor of the first analogy, i.e. the fountain, not only by means of transfusion, but also by forging multiple correspondences with it (sun: *tantulus,* 5.593 → water: *parvus,* 5.602; sun: *cuncta,* 5.595 → water: *late,* 5.602). In this way Lucretius creates a decrescendo in terms of the importance of the three explanations.

Besides the indisputable argumentative and rhetorical value of the assimilation of fire with water, in the case in question transfusion bears a very specific philosophical significance. Lucretius' choice of the "flowing water" pattern that induces us to perceive the unseen motion of fire particles in terms of regular fluidity discloses not only the underlying similarity between the atomic substance of light and a stream, but also the philosophical reality of incessant albeit invisible atomic movement.[45] As Clay notes, "what Lucretius is bringing home by these confused and synaesthetic metaphors is the unity of the phenomena that can move as water, fire or air and the similarity of the effluences projected from all solid bodies as they are perceived by sight and by hearing."[46]

Lucretius also applies the technique of transfusion in order to penetrate the invisible microcosmic world of atoms and establish the fundamental principles that condition it. Along these lines, he demonstrates why atoms of any given shape have to be infinite in number, otherwise they could not recombine once an atomic aggregation is dispersed (2.547–564):[47]

> *quippe etenim sumam hoc quoque uti finita per omne*
> *corpora iactari unius genitalia rei,*
> *unde, ubi, qua vi et quo pacto congressa coibunt*
> *materiae tanto in pelago turbaque aliena?*   550
> *non, ut opinor, habent rationem conciliandi;*
> *sed quasi naufragiis magnis multisque coortis*
> *disiectare solet magnum mare transtra cavernas*

> *antemnas proram malos tonsasque natantis,*
> *per terrarum omnis oras fluitantia aplustra* 555
> *ut videantur et indicium mortalibus edant,*
> *infidi maris insidias virisque dolumque*
> *ut vitare velint, neve ullo tempore credant,*
> *subdola cum ridet placidi pellacia ponti,*
> *sic tibi si finita semel primordia quaedam* 560
> *constitues, aevom debebunt sparsa per omnem*
> *disiectare aestus diversi materiai,*
> *numquam in concilium ut possint compulsa coire*
> *nec remorari in concilio nec crescere adaucta;*

"Indeed, if I should go so far as to assume that the bodies generative of this one thing were finite in number, tossed about through the universe, whence, where, by what force, in what manner will they meet and combine amidst such an ocean of matter, such an alien crowd? They have no way, I think, to combine; but as when many great shipwrecks have come about, the high sea is accustomed to toss asunder transoms, ribs yards, prow, masts, and oars all swimming, so that the poop-fittings are seen floating around all the shores, and provide a warning for mortals, that they eschew the treacherous deep, with her snares, her violence, and her fraud, and never trust her at any time when the calm sea shows her false alluring smile: so if you once lay down that certain first-beginnings are finite in number, they must be scattered through all time and tossed asunder on the sundering tides of matter, so that never can they be driven together and come into combination, nor grow by increase;"

Lucretius explores what would actually happen if this possibility were to be realized. He thus draws an analogy between an atomic cluster that is dissolved and a shipwreck. In the introductory question, he metaphorically refers to the totality of matter as an ocean; by means of this transfusion, he anticipates the comparison with the sea that follows (matter: *materiae tanto in pelago,* 2.550; *aestus diversi materiai,* 2.562 → sea: *magnum mare,* 2.553). It is also remarkable, in connection with the analogy of the sun that we have just discussed, that in this case as well Lucretius resorts to the image of water. Since the sea is considered the cause of the shipwreck, in the very same way the incessant movement of matter, which resembles tides, brings about microcosmic dissolution. Moreover, the scattered parts of the vessel are meant to be analogous to the atoms. Further verbal correspondences reinforce the analogy: both the atoms and the components of the ship are described as being tossed about (matter: *iactari,* 2.548; *disiectare,* 2.562 → sea: *disiectare,* 2.553;

fluitantia, 2.555). However, whereas the atoms can be recombined into new compounds, there is no such possibility for the remnants of the ship. At that basic level, the sameness of the substance of matter in general, which is the cause of the dissolution, and of each atomic cluster that actually springs from it, brings about a confusion in the boundaries between the tenor and the vehicle. It is this reality which overturns the validity of the analogy. That is why, Lucretius concludes, we should not think that the first beginnings are finite in number. To counterbalance the annulment of the analogy, Lucretius resumes the socio-political imagery (2.563–564: *concilium, coire, concilio,*) already used in the introductory verses (2.549–551: *congressa coibunt, turbaque aliena, conciliandi*).

Last but not least, should be cited an example that displays how multiple correspondences and especially transfusion within a simile enable Lucretius to spell out the causes of abstruse meteorological phenomena in a more comprehensible and persuasive way than his predecessors. Among other explanations of thunder, Lucretius claims that such a sound may come about when wind blows through ragged clouds (6.132–136):

> *Est etiam ratio, cum venti nubila perflant,*
> *ut sonitus faciant; etenim ramosa videmus*
> *nubila saepe modis multis atque aspera ferri;*
> *scilicet ut, crebram silvam cum flamina cauri*   135
> *perflant, dant sonitum frondes ramique fragorem.*

"There is another way whereby the clouds make a noise, that is, when the winds blow through them. For indeed we often see clouds branching in many ways, and ragged as they sweep along; just as, you may be sure, leaves rustle, and branches creak, when the blasts of the north-west wind blow through a thick forest."

At this point it is worth recalling that with reference to the very same type of thunder Theophrastus deployed the image of butchers blowing up pieces of gut (*Metars.* 1.15–17 Daiber). Lucretius replaces this rather prosaic analogy; he observes instead the action of wind and the noise thus produced in another parallel situation, that of winds blowing through the branches of trees. The similarity between the two processes is strengthened by a number of verbal correspondences between the two parts of the simile: winds are omnipresent (cloud: *venti,* 6.132 → forest: *flamina cauri,* 6.135); moreover, even when referring to thunder, Lucretius opts for the more neutral word "sound" (cloud: *sonitus,* 6.133 → forest: *sonitum,* 6.136). Finally, in both parts of the simile there is embedded the metaphor of the motion of air viewed as a stream (cloud: *perflant,* 6.132 → forest: *perflant,* 6.136). More significantly, Lucretius cunningly manipulates a subtle transfusion in order to help us perceive his analogy more easily; by means of the coined adjective "branching" (*ramosa,* 6.133), which directly points to the branches of trees in the vehicle (*ramique,* 6.136), he rhetorically assimilates the shape of certain clouds with that of trees with branches. In fact, this devised resemblance between the structure of clouds and forests is what essentially accounts for the suggested sameness in the nuance of the sound heard.[48]

As far as Empedocles is concerned, as Sedley rightly proposes, a clear instance of a multiple-correspondence simile is the lantern simile (B84):

ὡς δ' ὅτε τις πρόοδον νοέων ὡπλίσσατο λύχνον,
χειμερίην διὰ νύκτα πυρὸς σέλας αἰθομένοιο,
ἅψας παντοίων ἀνέμων λαμπτῆρας ἀμοργούς,
οἵ τ' ἀνέμων μὲν πνεῦμα διασκιδνᾶσιν ἀέντων,
φῶς δ' ἔξω διαθρῷσκον, ὅσον ταναώτερον ἦεν,   5
λάμπεσκεν κατὰ βηλὸν ἀτειρέσιν ἀκτίνεσσιν·
ὡς δὲ τότ' ἐν μήνιγξιν ἐεργμένον ὠγύγιον πῦρ
λεπτῇσιν <τ'> ὀθόνῃσι λοχάζετο κύκλοπα κούρην·
αἱ δ' ὕδατος μὲν βένθος ἀπέστεγον ἀμφινάοντος,
πῦρ δ' ἔξω διΐεσκον ὅσον ταναώτερον ἦεν.   10

"As when a man who intends to make a journey prepares a light for himself, a flame of fire burning through a wintry night; he fits linen screens against all the winds, which break the blast of the winds as they blow, but the light that is more diffuse leaps through, and shines across the threshold with unfailing beams. In the same way the elemental fire, wrapped in membranes and delicate tissues, was then concealed in the round pupil—these kept back the surrounding deep water, but let through the more diffuse light."

Straightforward links between its two halves can be easily pointed out: the light in the lantern is equated with the light within the eye (lantern: πυρὸς σέλας αἰθομένοιο, l. 2 → eye: ὠγύγιον πῦρ, l. 7). Moreover, although in both cases the fire within the container is protected (lantern: διασκιδνᾶσιν, l. 4 → eye: ἀπέστεγον, l. 9), light jumps out (lantern: φῶς δ' ἔξω διαθρῷσκον, l. 5 → eye: πῦρ δ' ἔξω διΐεσκον, l. 10) due to its identical substance (lantern: ὅσον ταναώτερον ἦεν, l. 5 → eye: ὅσον ταναώτερον ἦεν, l. 10).[49]

When it comes to the simile by means of which Empedocles strives to clarify the alternation of air and blood in our lungs, by comparing it with the interchange of water and air in a clepsydra, we can also track down some direct links between the tenor and the vehicle (B100).

ὧδε δ᾽ ἀναπνεῖ πάντα καὶ ἐκπνεῖ· πᾶσι λίφαιμοι
σαρκῶν σύριγγες πύματον κατὰ σῶμα τέτανται,
καί σφιν ἐπὶ στομίοις πυκιναῖς τέτρηνται ἄλοξιν
ῥινῶν ἔσχατα τέρθρα διαμπερές, ὥστε φόνον μὲν
κεύθειν, αἰθέρι δ᾽ εὐπορίην διόδοισι τετμῆσθαι.   5
ἔνθεν ἔπειθ᾽ ὁπόταν μὲν ἀπαΐξῃ τέρεν αἷμα,
αἰθὴρ παφλάζων καταΐσσεται οἴδματι μάργῳ,
εὖτε δ᾽ ἀναθρῴσκῃ, πάλιν ἐκπνέει, ὥσπερ ὅταν παῖς
κλεψύδρῃ παίζουσα διειπετέος χαλκοῖο·
εὖτε μὲν αὐλοῦ πορθμὸν ἐπ᾽ εὐειδεῖ χερὶ θεῖσα
εἰς ὕδατος βάπτῃσι τέρεν δέμας ἀργυφέοιο,
†οὐδετ᾽ ἐς† ἄγγοσδ᾽ ὄμβρος ἐσέρχεται, ἀλλά μιν εἴργει
ἀέρος ὄγκος ἔσωθε πεσὼν ἐπὶ τρήματα πυκνά,
εἰσόκ᾽ ἀποστεγάσῃ πυκινὸν ῥόον· αὐτὰρ ἔπειτα
πνεύματος ἐλλείποντος ἐσέρχεται αἴσιμον ὕδωρ.   15
ὣς δ᾽ αὔτως, ὅθ᾽ ὕδωρ μὲν ἔχῃ κατὰ βένθεα χαλκοῦ
πορθμοῦ χωσθέντος βροτέῳ χροΐ ἠδὲ πόροιο,
αἰθὴρ δ᾽ ἐκτὸς ἔσω λελιημένος ὄμβρον ἐρύκει
ἀμφὶ πύλας ἠθμοῖο δυσηχέος, ἄκρα κρατύνων,
εἰσόκε χειρὶ μεθῇ, τότε δ᾽ αὖ πάλιν, ἔμπαλιν ἢ πρίν,
πνεύματος ἐμπίπτοντος ὑπεκθέει αἴσιμον ὕδωρ.
ὣς δ᾽ αὔτως τέρεν αἷμα κλαδασσόμενον διὰ γυίων
ὁππότε μὲν παλίνορσον ἐπαΐξειε μυχόνδε,
αἰθέρος εὐθὺς ῥεῦμα κατέρχεται οἴδματι θῦον,
εὖτε δ᾽ ἀναθρῴσκῃ, πάλιν ἐκπνέει ἴσον ὀπίσσω.

"This is the way in which all things breathe in and out: they all have chan-
nels of flesh, which the blood leaves, stretched over the surface of the body,
and at the mouth of these the outside of the skin is pierced right through
with close-set holes, so that blood is contained, but a passage is cut for air
to pass through freely. Then, when the smooth blood rushes away from the
surface, a wild surge of blustering air rushes through, and when the blood
leaps up, the air breathes out again. It is like a girl playing with a clepsydra
of shining bronze—when she puts the mouth of the pipe against her pretty
hand and dips it into the smooth body of shining water, no liquid yet
enters the vessel, but the mass of air pressing from within against the close-
set perforations holds it back until she releases the compressed current, and
then, as the air escapes, a due amount of water enters. Similarly, when she
has water in the hollow of the bronze vessel, and the neck and passage are
closed by human hand, the air outside, pressing inward, keeps the water in
at the gates of the harsh-sounding strainer, controlling the defenses, until

> the girl releases her hand; then, the reverse of the former process—as the
> air rushes in, a due amount of water runs out before it. In the same way,
> when the smooth blood surging through the body rushes back and inward,
> a flooding stream of air at once comes pouring in, and when the blood
> leaps up, an equal amount (of air) in turn breathes back out again."

There are verbs that indicate in pairs first hindering (respiration: *κεύθειν*, l. 5; *εὐπορίην διόδοισι τετμῆσθαι*, l. 5 → clepsydra: †*οὐδετ'* . . . *ἐσέρχεται*, l. 12; *εἴργει*, l. 12), then simultaneous departure from (respiration: *ἀπαΐξη*, l. 6; *ἐπαΐξειε*, l. 23 → clepsydra: *ἐλλείποντος*, l. 15) and entrance (respiration: *καταΐσσεται*, l. 7; *κατέρχεται*, l. 24 → clepsydra: *ἐσέρχεται*, l. 15) into the vessel. Inversely, in a second stage corresponding verbs denote reinvasion (respiration: *ἀναθρώσκη*, l. 8; *ἀναθρώσκη*, l. 25 → clepsydra: *ἐμπίπτοντος*, l. 21) and going away from the container (respiration: *πάλιν ἐκπνέει*, l. 8; *πάλιν ἐκπνέει*, l. 25 → clepsydra: *ἀναθρώσκη*, l. 8; *ἀναύπεκθέει*, l. 21).[50]

Despite the identification of these multiple correspondences, the interpretation of this simile seems to still be a quite demanding undertaking, which brings about lengthy scholarly exchanges. Regarding the subjects of the verbs, scholars are split into two opposing camps: should we take the blood as corresponding to water that flows in and out of the clepsydra and accordingly air that we inhale and exhale as parallel to the air that flows in and out the clepsydra?[51] Alternatively, should we equate blood with the air of the clepsydra and air of respiration with the water of the clepsydra?[52] From this point of view, at first glance this simile does not seem to be a very successful model. However, a closer look could perhaps dispel some of the confusion.

Empedocles describes metaphorically the motion of air we breathe in twice, in wording that—literally—would characterize the boisterous motion of water. First, blustering air rushes down with an impetuous swelling surge, just like water (*αἰθὴρ παφλάζων καταΐσσεται οἴδματι μάργῳ*, l. 7); in this case, the emphasis is placed both on the force and the acoustic effect. Empedocles replicates the image towards the end of the simile, when wind is clearly equated with a stream that comes down seething in a billow (*αἰθέρος εὐθὺς ῥεῦμα κατέρχεται οἴδματι θῦον*, l. 24). In other words, already in the exposition of his tenor, Empedocles induces us to comprehend the behaviour of air in respiration in terms similar to that of water that flows in and out through the holes of the clepsydra, the phenomenon that he is about to explicate as the vehicle of the simile. Should we be blind to the significance of this metaphorical transference, the overall meaning of the analogy would be obfuscated. The table that follows shows the correspondences between tenor and vehicle and thus schematizes the suggested interpretation of the simile.

Table 3.

Process	Mechanism of Respiration (Tenor: Motion of Air-Blood)	Clepsydra (Vehicle: Motion of Water-Air)
1. Reactive substance barred outside the vessel	*Air:* δ' εὐπορίην διόδοισι τετμῆσθαι, l. 5	*Water:* †οὐδετ' . . . ἐσέρχεται, l. 12
2. Active substance in the vessel	*Blood:* κεύθειν, l. 5	*Air:* εἴργει, l. 12
3. Active substance coming out of the vessel	*Blood:* ἀπαΐξῃ, l. 6; ἐπαΐξειε, l. 23	*Air:* ἐλλείποντος, l. 15
4. Reactive substance entering the vessel	*Air:* καταΐσσεται, l. 7; κατέρχεται, l. 24	*Water:* ἐσέρχεται, l. 15
5. Active substance re-entering the vessel	*Blood:* ἀναθρῴσκῃ, l. 8; ἀναθρῴσκη, l. 25	*Air:* ἐμπίπτοντος, l. 21
6. Reactive substance coming out of the vessel	*Air:* πάλιν ἐκπνέει, l. 8; πάλιν ἐκπνέει, l. 25	*Water:* ὑπεκθέει, l. 21

Beside the illustrative power of this metaphor, we should also remark that the assimilation of air with water carries a further philosophical meaning. It actually reflects Empedocles' metaphorical conceptualization of the ubiquitous and unremitting emission of roots out of matter in terms of "flowing water," what he calls "effluences" (ἀπορροαί, B86).

We have just identified in Empedocles a metaphor similar to what West calls transfusion à propos Lucretius' similes. More importantly, the specific philosophical connotations of the image of "wind flowing like water" directly recall those underlying Lucretius' "flowing water" metaphor, as outlined in the simile about the sun's light that we have just discussed above. Since I will develop at length elsewhere Lucretius' debt to Empedocles as far as this metaphor is concerned, which also involves their shared belief in the theory of effluences, I will confine myself here to signalling the clear correspondence.[53]

It seems, therefore, very probable that Lucretius directly draws the transfusion technique from Empedocles and transplants it into his similes as a probative and illustrative device bearing philosophical implications; at the same time, he creatively expands its use for rhetorical and didactic purposes.

In brief, three main recurring techniques have been identified in Empedocles' and Lucretius' similes which have been evaluated in terms of poetic effect and scientific precision. Whereas Empedocles' *multi-dimensional similes,* although justified by the poetic form, may thwart the clarity of his arguments, on the contrary Lucretius' similes, by encompassing several vehicles, by and large augment the probative power of his analogies. At the same time, Empedocles is Lucretius' precursor in both his techniques of *multiple-correspondence* and *transfusion,* both of which bear argumentative, scientific and philosophical value. Whereas by means of the former, the philosopher emphasizes pre-existing similarities, when it comes to transfusion these are rather created and forced. At any rate, Lucretius seems to have detected both of these techniques in Empedocles in embryonic form and appropriates them into his similes in a very creative and supplementary way. He does this in order to corroborate their systematicity, lend consistency to his argument and turn them into effective mechanisms of conceptualizing the unseen and initiating into the secrets of nature. As a result, Lucretius smoothes out more successfully than Empedocles the disproportion between poetic impact and scientific credibility. Still, by no means does this entail that his similes are wanting in poetic richness and charm.

3.4 VARIOUS TYPES OF SIMILES

Empedocles strikingly alters Homeric similes from yet another different perspective. Whereas Homer generally compares events from contrasting spheres of life and is principally interested in "capturing brief manifestations of life,"[54] on the contrary, Empedocles aims at illuminating an invisible process which is permanently subject to the general natural laws that operate at every level of reality. As a result, Empedocles modifies the relationship between the tenor and the vehicle; instead of bringing into the narrative extra-textual images, he analogically projects a similar process which is perceivable by our senses. So, he blurs the Homeric contrast between tenor and vehicle and suggests that their correspondences are not devised in order to impose what lies below our ken, but rather demonstrate their objective inner similarity.

The Epicureans share with Empedocles this particular view of the world, concerning intrinsic similarities in the nature of things and isonomy. In the light of this, Lucretius found in Empedocles' similes specific argumentative methods according to which the similes are organized, in order systematically to make scientific conjectures about invisible natural phenomena and reveal the natural laws underlying them. At the same time Lucretius relieves the natural phenomena of any negative associations with supposed divine origins. More precisely, there are two types of probative mechanisms that Lucretius appropriates within his similes from Empedocles, that of describing *similar physical processes* that take place on parallel levels (Section 3.4.1) and that of observing the *consistent behaviour of an Empedoclean root* in different environments (Section 3.4.2).

3.4.1 Inferences Based on Similar Physical Processes

Lucretius embraces from Empedocles the method of making deductions about the unseen on the strength of observing the same natural mechanism taking place on a coordinated level of reality.

We have already discussed how Empedocles explains his theory of respiration by means of comparison with the workings of a clepsydra (B100).[55] More precisely, Empedocles likens the interchange of blood and air within human body (ll. 1–8, 22–25) with that of air and water within the clepsydra (ll. 8–21). As Wright aptly formulates it, "a stream of air and a stream of liquid can occupy the same amount of space and exert equivalent pressures."[56] In more general terms, in both cases a rather inert substance comes in or out of a vessel, depending on the variation of pressure exerted upon by another, more dynamic substance.

A closer look at the simile itself reveals that the legitimacy and therefore the validity of Empedocles' comparison are supported by numerous and consistent parallels between the acts and motions that are described in both parts of the simile by means of similar verbs. Let us repeat once more the suggested process: at first, the entrance of the reactive substance is hindered (respiration: εὐπορίην διόδοισι τετμῆσθαι, l. 5 → clepsydra: †οὐδετ᾽ . . . ἐσέρχεται, l. 12) by an active one, which occupies all the available space within the vessel (respiration: κεύθειν, l. 5 → clepsydra: εἴργει, l. 12). Then, the contained substance departs (respiration: ἀπαΐξῃ, l. 6; ἐπαΐξειε, l. 23 → clepsydra: ἐλλείποντος, l. 15) and simultaneously the hindered one enters into the vessel (respiration: καταΐσσεται, l. 7; κατέρχεται; l. 24 → clepsydra: ἐσέρχεται, l. 15). Finally, the substance that controls the overall motion takes advantage and re-enters (respiration: ἀναθρῴσκη, l. 8; ἀναθρῴσκη, l. 25 → clepsydra: ἐμπίπτοντος, l. 21), whereas the other substance passively surrenders (repiration: πάλιν ἐκπνέει, l. 8; πάλιν ἐκπνέει, l. 25 → clepsydra: ὑπεκθέει, l. 21). In the case in question, while blood is dynamic due to its mechanical initiation of movement, air becomes dynamic due to the deliberate unplugging of the neck of the clepsydra by the child.

This Empedoclean probative method, as attested within the clepsydra simile, can also be detected in later writers, such as the Hippocratic writers and then Aristotle and Theophrastus, who used it broadly, plausibly under Empedocles' influence.[57] Likewise, Lucretius systematically applies to a certain group of obscure physical phenomena the Empedoclean method of extracting conclusions by comparing two different manifestations of the same natural operation, yet he does so in atomic terms.[58] Moreover, going back directly to Empedocles' poem, he often fashions his explanations into multiple-correspondence similes of the epic bipartite form; while mainly placing the emphasis upon the corresponding verbal forms, he effectively accentuates the specific resemblances between the two parallel processes. Let us examine some characteristic examples in detail.[59]

One instance is the widely discussed simile—which is quoted in full above—by which Lucretius strives to demonstrate the corporeality of the invisible atoms of wind by comparing them with the similar yet visible effects of water atoms (1.265–297).[60] Lucretius creates a chain of successive analogical proofs: a visible process, i.e. the action of water, is brought in, in order to explain a similar process, the action of wind, that takes place on a coordinated level of nature; in its turn, the image of wind serves Lucretius to reach down to the subordinated level of the microcosmic atomic world and defend the Epicurean principle that atoms exist, even if they are invisible (1.265–270). Hence, wind is endowed with a dual role: it functions both as a tenor being itself invisible and thus needing explanation by a vehicle from the visible world and as a tenor to throw light upon the unseen atomic world. The common denominator in the two parts of the main comparison is that both wind and river can cause destruction by collision of their atoms with the objects which obstruct them. As Hardie puts it, "the force of the wind is the sensible result of exactly the same kind of atomic operation as underlies the force of water."[61] Phillips has plausibly suggested that we should look at the Hippocratic treatise *On Breaths* as Lucretius' source for his claim that the power of air, even if unseen, may be inferred from its visible manifestations, such as uprooted trees, sea swollen into waves and ships tossed about.[62] Not only does Lucretius embrace the Hippocratic theory, but he goes one step further by adding a visible analogy. He chooses a vehicle nearest to the nature of the tenor so as to approximate them: while wind is invisible, water is transparent; in this way, the distinction between them is elided and the argumentative force of Lucretius' image is augmented. Within this framework, in a way vividly reminiscent of Empedocles' clepsydra simile, he repeats several verbs and nouns denoting similar operations and thus forges a multiple-correspondence simile.[63] Moreover, in order to disclose the underlying sameness between the motions of wind and water, he metaphorically refers to the action of wind also as flowing; as we have already pointed out, this is an instance of Empedocles' transfusion technique, also detected in the clepsydra simile.[64] Therefore, by recontextualizing threads drawn from divergent contexts, both literary and scientific, Lucretius builds a simile in the Empedoclean style and presents the pupil with a vivid visualization of the phenomenon in question.

Another striking application of Empedocles' method occurs in two parallel explanations of lightning and thunderbolts, both of which are based on the natural law of ignition caused by rotation.[65] In Montserrat and Navarro's words, Lucretius takes it for granted that "the heat atoms a thing contains regroup owing to motion and come to constitute heat; the movement of a thing also results in its capturing of fire particles from the medium through which it travels."[66] In his clarification Lucretius opts for a prosaic manifestation of this process, the ignition of a siege missile shot from a catapult, which seems to have been a commonplace in similar contexts.[67] However, within the framework of Lucretius' philosophical mission, this particular analogy acquires an additional role, that of demythologizing supernatural celestial phenomena; a thunderbolt may be like a weapon, but by no means can it be a divine one.[68]

Lucretius suggests that lightning occurs when wind enclosed in a cloud grows hot by its circular motion (6.175–179):[69]

> *ventus ubi invasit nubem et versatus ibidem*   175
> *fecit ut ante cavam docui spissescere nubem,*
> *mobilitate sua fervescit; ut omnia motu*
> *percalefacta vides ardescere, plumbea vero*
> *glans etiam longo cursu volvenda liquescit.*

> "When wind has entered a cloud, and moving about within the same
> has made the cloud grow thick round the hollow, as I explained before,
> it becomes hot by its own quick movement; just as you see everything
> become very hot and catch fire by movement, and indeed a leaden bullet even melts when it is whirled a long distance."

In order to prove this, he makes a general statement about the natural law according to which everything grows hot and catches fire by its movement (6.177–178). Then he draws a specific analogy with a leaden bullet which melts when it is whirled a long distance. However, in a very Empedoclean way, Lucretius formulates this analogy into an extended long simile and through specific linguistic correspondences (wind: *mobilitate sua fervescit,*

6.177 → natural law: *motu / percalefacta . . . ardescere,* 6.177–178 → missile: *longo cursu volvenda liquescit,* 6.179) reinforces the coherence between the overarching natural law and its two separate manifestations, one invisible and one visible.

Lucretius picks up the same analogy with the lead projectile later on, among his explanations about the causes of thunderbolts (6.300–308):

> *Fit quoque ut interdum venti vis missa sine igni*　　　　　300
> *igniscat tamen in spatio longoque meatu,*
> *dum venit, amittens in cursu corpora quaedam*
> *grandia, quae nequeunt pariter penetrare per auras;*
> *atque alia ex ipso conradens aëre portat*
> *parvola, quae faciunt ignem commixta volando,*　　　　　305
> *non alia longe ratione ac plumbea saepe*
> *fervida fit glans in cursu, cum multa rigoris*
> *corpora dimittens ignem concepit in auris.*

"It happens also at times that a force a wind sped forth without fire, yet takes fire in its long journey through space, losing in its course as it comes on certain bodies too large to pass equally well through the air, and scraping together from the air itself and carrying with it other very small bodies, which commingled together with it produce fire during the flight; in much the same way as a leaden bullet often grows hot in its course, when casting off many bodies of coldness it catches fire in the air."

This time the explanation he proposes is set forth in atomic terms: the wind outside the cloud travelling through the air ignites not only owing to the violence of its own motion, but also because it loses its colder and denser elements and picks up from the air lighter and smaller particles, which are themselves ignited; thus, air converts itself into a thunderbolt. It is also remarkable that Lucretius differentiates himself from Theophrastus, according to whom, whereas wind catches fire while it circulates within the cloud, bullets melt away within air, after they are shot from a catapult (*Metars.* 6.18–21 Daiber). Lucretius slightly modifies the comparison by observing the process of both wind and bullets igniting within a similar environment, i.e. during their journey through the air. In this way Lucretius forges more tangible correspondences between the two parts of his analogy and thus enhances its probative force.[70]

3.4.2. Inferences Based on the Empedoclean Roots

Lucretius incorporates within his similes Empedocles' technique of inferring conclusions about a particular group of invisible physical phenomena, which involve the presence of an Empedoclean root, by observing its behaviour or action within an accessible container or environment under conditions which are similar to the visible ones.

This scientific method is inextricably related to Empedocles' philosophical belief that everything is made out of the four basic elements. Empedocles' theory of matter, although reformed and readjusted by the various philosophical schools, remained of seminal importance throughout antiquity.[71] Within this framework, later writers have also incorporated the scientific method that stems from his theory and elaborated upon it accordingly.

The writers of the Hippocratic corpus appropriated this Empedoclean method in order to derive information about the behaviour of substances within the human body. However, due to the specific nature of their inquiries, they made a rather limited use of the method, since the human body inflexibly remains the container of elements under observation. To cite just such an example, in the treatise *On Breaths* the author observes the force of wind upon visible things in order to infer the effects of the one contained within human body; he names this wind ἀήρ outside the body and φῦσα within it (Hippoc. *Flat.* 3).[72] Instances could also be detected in Aristotle's treatises about remote physical phenomena and the human body.[73] In a similar way, in Theophrastus' meteorological works we also come across a systematic use of this type of analogies. It is significant that Theophrastus had investigated the nature and properties of the elements and their different effects on things (e.g. his treatises *On Fire, On Stones*).[74] Moreover, in his account of earthquakes (*Metars.* 15 Daiber) he remarkably differentiates himself from the explanations of Aristotle on this topic, by adding next to wind other Empedoclean roots as plausible causes, and thus going back to the four elements theory turned now into a principle of organization in the order of topics as a whole.[75]

It is within this tradition that Lucretius avails himself of such analogies. Nevertheless, due to the discrepancies in Empedocles' and Epicurus' theory of matter, in manifold ways Lucretius takes pains to explain why the various manifestations of the Empedoclean elements are different from each other in their atomic structure as a result of many varieties of atomic shapes. For instance, whereas he draws analogies on the grounds of the parallel presence of fire, he first clarifies that unlike our fire which springs from wood and is made from a torch (*ignis / noster hic e lignis ortus taedaque creatus,* 2.386–387), the heavenly fire, i.e. thunder (*fulmineus . . . ignis,* 2.382; *caelestem fulminis ignem,* 2.384), is finer and made of smaller shapes and that is why it has a greater capacity for penetration (2.381–387).[76]

3.4.2.1. Various Containers of Roots

In his lantern simile (B84), while describing the structure of the human eye, Empedocles explains how it comes about that an eye may contain both fire and water without the latter extinguishing the former.[77] He compares two different containers of fire, a lantern and a human eye. Fire can be easily traced as the thread connecting the two halves of the simile (lantern: πυρὸς σέλας αἰθομένοιο, l. 2; φῶς, l. 5; λάμπεσκεν . . . ἀτειρέσιν ἀκτίνεσσιν, l. 6 → eye: ὠγύγιον πῦρ, l. 7; πῦρ, l. 10). Its nature in either case seems to differ; the traveller has lit the fire in the lantern for his intended journey, whereas fire in the eye is eternal (lantern: ὡπλίσσατο, l. 1; ἄψας, l. 3 → eye: ὠγύγιον, l. 7).[78] Yet Empedocles does not seem to take into account this discrepancy for his conclusion. On the other hand, he meticulously describes the structure of both containers. Special emphasis is placed upon the analogous function of the panes of the lantern and of the membranous tissues of the pupil, since Empedocles attempts to establish that in both cases the interaction of fire with the sides of the vessels is analogous (lantern: λαμπτῆρας ἀμοργούς, l. 3→ eye: ἐν μήνιγξιν . . . / λεπτῇσιν <τ'> ὀθόνῃσι, ll. 7–8); thanks to the nature of their respective materials, although light can get out, they both protect the fire enclosed within, in the case of the lantern by not letting the wind from without quench it, and in that of the eye by separating it from water (lantern: ἀνέμων μὲν πνεῦμα διασκιδνᾶσιν ἀέντων, l. 4 → eye: ἀπέστεγον, l. 9). In a word, Empedocles attempts to illustrate and to establish the structure of the eye through his belief in the sameness of the substance of fire at every level of its worldly manifestations.[79]

Lucretius himself applies to his similes the Empedoclean method of observing the behaviour of a root within a palpable container in order to draw conclusions about its analogous behaviour within a container into which we could not penetrate except by analogy and projection.[80] This method can be traced in several of his similes in the meteorological account. While discussing the cause of certain celestial phenomena such as thunder, lightning, thunderbolts or rain, Lucretius treats *clouds* as containers of the elements air, fire or water respectively and compares them with other accessible containers. When he comes to shed light on subterranean phenomena, it is *earth* which is now viewed as a container of elements. Lucretius modifies the analogical function of certain containers which constantly recur in Theophrastus' meteorological account (e.g. bladder, sponge, wool), adds more (e.g. furnace, human body) and repeatedly comes back to some of them both in similes and in other metaphorical contexts as if they were archetypal models.[81] As I am going to argue, these alternations arise as an immediate consequence of Lucretius' appropriation of Empedocles' scientific technique and simultaneously spring from his effort to present his pupil with the most effective explanations, so as to demythologize the phenomena in question and free his pupil from wonder and religious fear.

Lucretius sketches the texture of clouds by negation at the beginning of his meteorological account, when he sets out the causes of thunder (6.102–107):

> *praeterea neque tam condenso corpore nubes*
> *esse queunt quam sunt lapides ac ligna, neque autem*
> *tam tenues quam sunt nebulae fumique volantes;*
> *nam cadere aut bruto deberent pondere pressae*   105
> *ut lapides, aut ut fumus constare nequirent*
> *nec cohibere nives gelidas et grandinis imbris.*

> "Besides, clouds can neither be made of so dense a body as stones and wood, nor again so thin as mist and flying smoke; for then they must either fall thrust down by their dead weight, like stones, or, like smoke, be unable to hold together or to contain cold snow and showers of hail."

This picture of clouds will be used as the basis of Lucretius' arguments about the causes not only of thunder, but also of thunderbolts, strokes of lightning and rain, all of which come about within the very same container, i.e. cloud.[82]

In his account of the causes of thunder, Lucretius explains that a terrible noise comes about when whirling air invades a cloud, then hollows it and thickens its outer layer. Subsequently, when wind has weakened the cloud enough, this bursts out. In order to visualize the phenomenon, Lucretius points to the noise produced when a small bladder containing air is split open if inflated (6.121–131):[83]

> *Hoc etiam pacto tonitru concussa videntur*
> *omnia saepe gravi tremere et divolsa repente*
> *maxima dissiluisse capacis moenia mundi,*
> *cum subito validi venti conlecta procella*
> *nubibus intorsit sese, conclusaque ibidem*   125
> *turbine versanti magis ac magis undique nubem*
> *cogit uti fiat spisso cava corpore circum,*
> *post ubi conminuit vis eius et impetus acer,*
> *tum perterricrepo sonitu dat scissa fragorem.*

> *nec mirum, cum plena animae vesicula parva*   130
> *saepe ita dat magnum sonitum displosa repente.*

"In this way also all things often appear to shake and tremble with a
heavy thunderclap, and it seems that the great walls of the capacious fir-
mament suddenly torn asunder have leapt apart, when a gale of strong
wind gathered together has twisted itself all at once into the clouds, and
enclosed in that same place, whirling round and round, compels the
cloud more and more in every direction to form a hollow with a thick
crust all round; afterwards, when the wind's power and fierce impulse
have weakened it, then the cloud is torn and explodes with a most hor-
rifying crash. And not wonder, when a small bladder full of air often
makes so loud a noise as it is suddenly burst."

This analogy seems to be drawn directly from Theophrastus' account (*Met-
ars.* 1.18–20 Daiber). Nonetheless, it is striking that Lucretius differenti-
ates himself from both Epicurus and Theophrastus. In Epicurus' *Letter to
Pythocles,* when clouds abound in rotating air, which thickens their sides
and reverberates loudly, they are compared to vases (βροντὰς ἐνδέχεται
γίνεσθαι καὶ κατὰ πνεύματος ἐν τοῖς κοιλώμασι τῶν νεφῶν ἀνείλησιν,
καθάπερ ἐν τοῖς ἡμετέροις ἀγγείοις, / "Thunder may be due to the roll-
ing of wind in the hollow parts of the clouds, as it is sometimes impris-
oned in vessels which we use," *Ep. Pyth.* 100).[84] It is most probable that
Epicurus' source was Theophrastus, who had appealed to caves along with
jars with regard to the very same phenomenon (*Metars.* 1.6–8 Daiber).
However, Lucretius is more economical in his explanations; instead of set-
ting forth two models—vases and a bladder—as Theophrastus and (per-
haps) Epicurus did, he merges the two explanations into one and provides
a single illustration. Moreover, although a bladder serves Theophrastus as
a model in three more instances in connection with thunderbolts,[85] Lucre-
tius confines his use of it to the simile in question, i.e. that about thunder.
Why should Lucretius eliminate the model—or one of the models—that
his master had handed down to him, give preference to that of the bladder
and then use it only in the present context?

Following Empedocles' method of observing the same element in sim-
ilar containers, Lucretius seems to have judged that a vase could not provide
an adequate elucidation of how a cloud can be gradually blown up. On the
contrary, due to its membranous texture, a bladder is particularly appropri-
ate for such a comparison, as it has the same attribute of getting squeezed or
perforated when filled up with air. Furthermore, Lucretius opts for using a
bladder only as a container of air with the intention of making his argument

more coherent.[86] That is why, when it comes to thunderbolts, where the emphasis falls mainly on their fiery nature and not on their airy one or the agent of their expulsion out of the cloud as in Theophrastus, Lucretius does not resort to a bladder as his explanatory model.

Moreover, a cloud is viewed as a container of particles of fire twice, in the discussion about the causes of lightning and then again in that about the causes of thunderbolts. In both cases Lucretius sets forth how, when two containers of particles of fire smash together, those particles are struck out. Regarding lightning, Lucretius explains that it occurs when two clouds containing fire collide and then seeds of fire are expelled; in the same way, when stone and steel also containing fire collide, they scatter sparks of fire (6.160–163):[87]

> *Fulgit item, nubes ignis cum semina multa*   160
> *excussere suo concursu, ceu lapidem si*
> *percutiat lapis aut ferrum; nam tum quoque lumen*
> *exilit et claras scintillas dissipat ignis.*

> "It lightens also, when clouds by their collision have struck out many seeds of fire; as if stone or steel should strike stone, for then also a light leaps forth scattering abroad bright sparks of fire."

The Theophrastean account should be considered once more the ultimate source of this analogy (*Metars.* 2.2–9 Daiber). Still, Lucretius has omitted friction as a possible cause and on the whole presents us with a much more simplified explanation than the one offered by his predecessor. In addition, in the discussion of thunderbolts, both clouds and wind are considered as containers of fire which collide and generate a thunderbolt, just as when we strike stone with iron (6.309–316):[88]

> *Fit quoque ut ipsius plagae vis excitet ignem,*
> *frigida cum venti pepulit vis missa sine igni,*   310
> *nimirum quia, cum vementi perculit ictu,*
> *confluere ex ipso possunt elementa vaporis*
> *et simul ex illa quae tum res excipit ictum;*
> *ut, lapidem ferro cum caedimus, evolat ignis,*
> *nec, quod frigida vis ferrist, hoc setius illi*   315
> *semina concurrunt calidi fulgoris ad ictum.*

"It may be also that the very force of the blow produces fire, when a force of wind, sped forth cold without fire, has struck; doubtless because, when it has smitten with a violent blow, elements of heat may

> flow together from the wind itself and at the same time from that thing
> which then receives the blow; just as, when we strike stone with iron,
> out flies fire, nor do the seeds of hot fire any the less run together at the
> blow because iron is a cold thing."

Lucretius' deployment of the identical analogy in those two instances is legitimized by and at the same time demonstrates the similarity in the nature of the phenomena in question. On the other hand, in order also to establish the differences between them, Lucretius elaborates upon the second explanation; he first shapes it into an experiment, using a verb in the first person plural (*caedimus*, 6.314) and then emphasizes both the coldness of the containers and the force of the blow.

While Lucretius envisages clouds as containers of fire, he strikingly differentiates himself from Theophrastus' acccunt. In his explanations of lightning, Theophrastus uses twice the analogy of a sponge and tufts of wool containing water, first to explain how hidden fire comes out of a cloud which is compressed, squeezed or split and cut up (*Metars.* 2.13–17 Daiber), and then again how lightning may occur even without being accompanied by thunder, when the cloud is rarefied and not dense (*Metars.* 4.4–7 Daiber).[89] However, Lucretius is more cautious than Theophrastus in his choice of vehicles. According to Empedocles' probative method, the conclusion would be more valid if one were to observe the behaviour of the same element within the two containers. As a consequence, Lucretius reserves wool and a sponge to be used explicitly only when the behaviour of water—not fire—is under consideration in both parts of the analogy.[90]

At the same time, Lucretius introduces an additional image of clouds as containers of fire, one not found in Theophrastus' account, that of a furnace. First, there is a literal reference to a furnace in a simile about thunder, where it functions as the vehicle (6.145–149).[91] Then, whilst winds eddying about a flame make a fork of lightning within a cloud, this is envisaged as a hollow furnace (6.201–203).[92] In the same line, Lucretius deploys the same analogy in the forging of a thunderbolt with the whirlwind becoming the smith himself (6.274–280). What are Lucretius' reasons for such an innovation?

By means of this scientific model Lucretius exemplifies a particular function of the cloud, that of allowing lightning or a thunderbolt to be shaped within it out of the enclosed atoms of fire when wind interacts with them. Nonetheless, the furnace here embeds specific mythological allusions as a result of its associations with the forging of thunderbolts; it actually hints at the mythological workplace of the Cyclopes, where thunderbolts were said to have been forged.[93] As Hardie puts it, "a traditional locution or myth is placed before us, and we are suddenly led to realize that it has a quite different meaning from what we saw before. This is close to a certain type of allegory: we are to discard the outer husk of the traditional form of words and to retain only the *physica ratio* contained within it."[94] Thus, Lucretius rationalizes the fearful meteorological phenomenon by positing a cloud as a container instead of the mythological one and wind as an agent instead of monstrous smiths.

Moreover, bearing in mind the specific links of the Cyclopes with Etna, and that this was supposed to be their actual dwelling, when Lucretius comes to the explanation of volcanic eruptions he picks up again the image of the furnace in order to compare it with the volcano itself (6.681).[95] He clearly spells out the similarities between furnace and volcano, with the intention of further divesting his explanatory model of any disturbing connotations. As Peta Fowler notes, "air from the bellows, squeezed into the furnace, raises the temperature of the fire. The air enclosed in underground caverns has a similar effect."[96] So, not only does Lucretius reduce an awe-inspiring phenomenon to its purely physical causes, but he also suggests a plausible origin of a popular myth.

Finally, Lucretius avails himself once more of the furnace as explanatory model in a totally different context: in his account of plague, when the stomach is filled up by fiery disease (*sacer . . . ignis,* 6.1167) it is compared with a furnace (*flagrabat stomacho flamma ut fornacibus intus.* / "a flame burnt in the stomach as in a furnace," 6.1169).[97] As Peta Fowler notes, it is remarkable that whereas this image "in Stoic sources figures in contexts of sustenance or creation, in Lucretius it brings out the extreme torture of one particular mode of destruction."[98] Whilst Lucretius compares plague with erysipelas (6.1167) and the stomach with a furnace (6.1169), he counterbalances the optimistic image that was first deployed by his philosophical adversaries and unmasks nature's double face, as destroyer as well as creator. However, although this semantic inversion seems plausible, in my view its implications should not be considered so intensely negative. Lucretius rather vividly evokes the foregoing discussion about volcanic eruptions, where volcanic lava was likened to human disease and the volcano itself to a furnace, in order to illuminate the workings of the phenomenon on physical grounds (6.639–702). Bringing to mind this purely rationalistic explanation, Lucretius invites us to project it also upon the appalling image of the infected stomach and reconsider its sinister impact with mental tranquillity.

On the whole, Lucretius applies the Empedoclean method of comparing various containers (cloud, volcano, stomach) of the same primary element, i.e. fire, and assimilates them into the furnace, which now appears as an archetypal-like container of fire; in this way, he discloses by analogy the same natural law, which is active at different levels of reality, and at the same time dissociates the furnace itself from any mythical connotations.

Finally, in his description of why moisture evaporates from the sea to the clouds and thus increases the bulk of their initial formations, Lucretius compares the clouds to clothes hung up on the shore, within a simile that, as we will see, bears Empedocles' imprint in a twofold way (6.470–475):[99]

> *Praeterea permulta mari quoque tollere toto* 470
> *corpora naturam declarant litore vestes*
> *suspensae, cum concipiunt umoris adhaesum.*
> *quo magis ad nubis augendas multa videntur*
> *posse quoque e salso consurgere momine ponti;*
> *nam ratio consanguineast umoribus omnis.* 475

"Besides, that nature takes up very many bodies over the whole sea is made clear, when clothes are hung up on the shore and absorb the sticky moisture: which makes it more likely that many bodies can gather upwards to swell the clouds from the salt movement of the ocean, since there is a complete kinship between both these moistures."

Lucretius suggests that besides their similar appearance, clouds and clothes share properties in common: like sponges, they both collect the sticky marine moisture that is emitted, the behaviour of which within them should be expected to be more or less the same. At the first level, Lucretius bases his inference on the natural mechanism according to which a container already containing moisture absorbs more from without, thanks to its texture (*permulta mari . . . / corpora,* 6.470–471; *umoris adhaesum,* 6.472; *umoribus,* 6.475). To make his comparison even more persuasive, Lucretius observes both clouds and clothes under the same physical conditions; thus, he regards sea as the origin of the rainy moisture in both parts of the simile (*mari . . . toto,* 6.470; *e salso . . . momine ponti,* 6.474). The analogy conjures up the probative mechanism detected in Empedocles' lantern simile (B84), in which the similarity in the structure of the containers—eye and lantern—was particularly significant for the conclusion deduced. In the present case, the phenomenon under investigation is especially obscure, since Lucretius should also account for the automatic nature of the internal motions of water bodies. Therefore, he additionally resorts to the Empedoclean principle of "like joining its like"; according to this, moist particles that exist in the clouds are joined by others emitted by the sea because of their inherent kinship (6.475). Since the process of water evaporation appears to be so complicated and thus hard to perceive, in the following verses (6.476–482) Lucretius resorts to additional metaphors:

> *Praeterea fluviis ex omnibus et simul ipsa*
> *surgere de terra nebulas aestumque videmus,*
> *quae velut halitus hinc ita sursum expressa feruntur*
> *suffunduntque sua caelum caligine et altas*
> *sufficiunt nubis paulatim conveniundo;*   480
> *urget enim quoque signiferi super aetheris aestus*
> *et quasi densendo subtexit caerula nimbis.*

"Besides, from all rivers and also from the earth itself we see clouds and steam arising, which exhaled from these sources like breath are carried up in this way, and suffuse the sky with their blackness and bring up supplies to the clouds on high as little by little they come together; for the heat also of the starry ether presses on them from above, and by packing them close seems to weave a texture of cloud beneath the blue."

We should note here the image of exhalation (6.478) and the socio-political imagery (6.480) which are used in order to sketch water rising up from rivers and the earth.[100] Still, this passage concludes with a weaving metaphor, which keeps clear before our eyes the conceptualization of clouds as cloth-like tissue (6.482).

After suggesting that some particles come into sky from outside the world (6.483–494), Lucretius goes on to explain how some water elements, which are also emitted from all kinds of things, are not incorporated into the body of clouds, but constitute the rainy moisture within them, which is condensed to be discharged in the form of rain (6.495–507):

> *Nunc age, quo pacto pluvius concrescat in altis*   495
> *nubibus umor, et in terras demissus ut imber*
> *decidat, expediam. primum iam semina aquai*
> *multa simul vincam consurgere nubibus ipsis*
> *omnibus ex rebus, pariterque ita crescere utrumque,*
> *et nubis et aquam quaecumque in nubibus extat,*   500
> *ut pariter nobis corpus cum sanguine crescit,*
> *sudor item atque umor quicumque est denique membris.*
> *concipiunt etiam multum quoque saepe marinum*
> *umorem, veluti pendentia vellera lanae,*
> *cum supera magnum mare venti nubila portant.*   505
> *consimili ratione ex omnibus amnibus umor*
> *tollitur in nubis.*

> "Now attend, and I will explain in what manner rainy moisture grows
> together in the clouds on high, and how showers fall sent down upon
> the earth. First of all you will concede that many seeds of water rise
> upward together with the clouds themselves from things of all sorts, and
> that in this way both grow together, the clouds and whatever water is in
> the clouds, just as in ourselves body grows along with blood, sweat, also
> and in a word whatever moisture is in the frame. The clouds also often
> take up a great deal of sea-water besides, like hanging fleeces of wool,
> when the winds carry clouds above the great sea. In like fashion water is
> raised to the clouds from all rivers."

In order to illustrate this phenomenon Lucretius merges all the different
explanations about the sources of evaporated water, which contribute to the
formation of clouds (*omnibus ex rebus*, 6.499; *supera magnum mare*, 6.505; *ex
omnibus amnibus umor*, 6.506) and in a form of ring composition he resumes
the analogy with woollen garments (6.504).

Nonetheless, Lucretius has to somehow account for the binary role of
this analogy, which is simultaneously employed for both the formation of
clouds and the rain within them. Therefore, he first displays the similarity
between the two situations by a number of verbal echoes (6.472 = 6.503:
concipiunt; 6.474 = 6.498: *consurgere*; 6.470: *mari . . . toto* ≈ 6.474: *e salso
. . . momine ponti* ≈ 6.503–504: *marinum / umorem* ≈ 6.505: *supera mag-
num mare*; 6.473: *augendas* ≈ 6.495: *concrescat* ≈ 6.499: *crescere* ≈ 6.501:
crescit ≈ 6.508: *adaucta*). At the same time, he inserts a bridging simile, in
which he compares a cloud with the *human body* (6.497–502). By doing
so he inverts the method of the Hippocratic writers, who had the structure
and functions of the human body as the sole target of their investigations,
and observes the behaviour of moisture within clouds from a different per-
spective. Hence, he suggests that the emitted particles of moisture that are
entrapped within a cloud increase the bulk of both the cloud itself and of
the water particles already enclosed within it, just as our body increases
along with blood, sweat and any other moisture contained within it by the
addition of liquids.

Therefore, while radiating the image of clouds in two different direc-
tions (fleeces of wool and the human body), Lucretius creates a multi-dimen-
sional simile. The element of water is the connecting thread between the
two analogies (*pluvius . . . umor*, 6.495–496; *ut imber*, 6.496; *semina aquai*,
6.497; *aquam quaecumque*, 6.500; *sanguine*, 6.501; *sudor*, 6.502; *umor qui-
cumque*, 6.502). Even more remarkably, in a way similar to Empedocles'
practice in the lantern simile (B84: lantern: πυρὸς σέλας αἰθομένοιο, l. 2

→ eye: ὠγύγιον πῦρ, l. 7; πῦρ, l. 10), the word *umor* is used recurrently, albeit successively modified by various adjectives (*pluvius . . . umor*, 6.495–496; *umor quicumque*, 6.502; *marinum / umorem*, 6.503–504; *ex omnibus amnibus umor*, 6.506), in order to denote the ultimate sameness in its substance at every level of the world, despite its various manifestations. In brief, from a didactic point of view, the role of this two-fold simile is functional, as Lucretius invites us to constantly keep in mind both pictures in order to fully grasp the unseen workings of the element in question.

When lightning falls from a cloud onto a water-laden cloud, the latter is illustrated as a container of both fire and water; the hissing sound of thunder that is thus produced is considered to be the outcome of their interaction (6.145–149):

> *Fit quoque, ubi e nubi in nubem vis incidit ardens*
> *fulminis: haec multo si forte umore recepit*   146
> *ignem, continuo magno clamore trucidat,*
> *ut calidis candens ferrum e fornacibus olim*
> *stridit, ubi in gelidum propter demersimus imbrem.*

"Thunder occurs also when the burning force of lightning falls from a cloud upon a cloud: if this cloud chance to be soaked with water when it receives the fire, it makes a great noise in destroying it at once, just as white-hot iron from the hot furnace often hisses when we have dipped it into cold water near by."

In order to demonstrate this process persuasively, Lucretius describes the similar sound heard when a red-hot iron from a hot furnace is plunged into a vessel full of water (cloud: *incidit*, 6.145 → *demersimus*, 6.149). In both containers fire from without (cloud: *vis . . . ardens / fulminis*, 6.145–146; *ignem*, 6.147 → vessel: *calidis candens ferrum e fornacibus*, 6.148) interacts with water already contained within (cloud: *multo . . . umore*, 6.146 → vessel: *gelidum . . . imbrem*, 6.149) and together the two bring about a great noise (cloud: *continuo magno clamore*, 6.147 → vessel: *stridit*, 6.149). In this case Lucretius articulates the comparison into a multiple-correspondence simile, which carries further specifically Empedoclean resonances.

It has been repeatedly pointed out that Lucretius recontextualizes here the Homeric image of the sound heard when a blacksmith immerses an axe or an adze in cold water (*Od.* 9.391–393):[101]

ὡς δ' ὅτ' ἀνὴρ χαλκεὺς πέλεκυν μέγαν ἠὲ σκέπαρνον
εἰν ὕδατι ψυχρῷ βάπτῃ μεγάλα ἰάχοντα
φαρμάσσων· τὸ γὰρ αὖτε σιδήρου γε κράτος ἐστίν·

"[The Cyclops' eye hissed round the olive stake] in the same way that
an axe or adze hisses when a smith plunges it into cold water to quench
and strengthen the iron."

In the original context, the image was used to describe the noise made by
the glowing stake that Odysseus and his men twist into Polyphemus' eye. As
Aicher has analyzed in detail, the Homeric simile undergoes specific trans-
formations before being incorporated into the Lucretian scientific discourse.
Apart from the elimination of unessential details (e.g. the specific tool), Lucre-
tius adds the word *calidis* (6.149) to counter-correspond *gelidum* (6.149), i.e.
the Latin equivalent of the Homeric ψυχρῷ, in order to emphasize the antith-
esis between hot and cold and convey not just the sound, but more impor-
tantly the elemental cause of thunder.[102] Moreover, Lucretius changes the
verbal form from the third person singular to the first person plural and thus
the point of view in order to lend the image of an experiment that is deliber-
ately carried out.

Although the above remarks are true, if we were to trace the line
directly from Lucretius straight back to Homer, this would present us with
a narrow reading of the simile, which would obfuscate the existence and
the significance of a much broader intertextual network. On the contrary,
Lucretius should not be given the sole credit for transplanting this specific
Homeric image into his scientific context.[103] Long before him, Theophras-
tus had already robbed the Homeric image of the blacksmith throwing iron
into water out of its poetic context and reemployed the analogy twice in
his meteorological account, first in order to illustrate the very same cause of
thunder as Lucretius (*Metars.* 1.9–12 Daiber) and then again in the corre-
sponding explanation of lightning (*Metars.* 2.10–12 Daiber). In turn, Lucre-
tius has further elaborated the analogy. On the one hand, he has restored its
original epic form, by reformulating it into a simile in dactylic hexameter.
On the other, he has resorted to additional changes such as the omission of
the blacksmith and the multiple correspondences, so as to make it even more
effective within its scientific context. In any case, this is a clear instance of a
"double allusion,"[104] as Lucretius simultaneously hints at both the Homeric
and Theophrastean intertexts, which are already inextricably linked.

However, the stemma of Lucretius' intertextual relationships as
reflected in the simile in question has not been yet fully sketched. There is

still a significant detail that so far has been gone unnoticed, a detail which adds a third dimension, i.e. a subtle allusion to Empedocles. When turning the Homeric verses into Latin, Lucretius surprisingly replaces the Greek ὕδατι ψυχρῷ (cold water, *Od.* 9.392) with the phrase *gelidum imbrem* (cold rain, 6.149). By no means should this replacement of water—the word that should be normally expected here—with rain,—an instance of water's worldly manifestation—be considered coincidental.

In fact, a similar instance occurs in Empedocles' clepsydra simile (B100); the water that flows in and out of the clepsydra is referred to either as ὕδωρ (l. 11, l. 15, l. 16) or as ὄμβρος (l. 12, l. 18). This interplay of names, when referring to roots, was actually Empedocles' usual practice, which was legitimized by his belief in the overall unity in the substance of things. Sedley codifies it as "Empedocles' avoidance of terminological technicality."[105] In his *Annales 7*, Ennius has also embraced this technique and substituted the element of water with rain in a context burdened with Empedoclean echoes (*Cui par imber et ignis, spiritus et grauis terra* / "for whom water and fire and breath and heavy earth are equal," fr. 221 Skutsch).[106] Therefore, it seems most probable that in line 6.149 Lucretius directly, or indirectly, alludes to Empedocles. However, what is his purpose in this specific context? A possible answer could be that it was Empedocles who gave this explanation of thunder (A63b = Aët. 3.3.7 = *Dox. Gr.* 368):

Ἐμπεδοκλῆς ἔμπτωσιν φωτὸς εἰς νέφος ἐξείργοντος τὸν ἀνθεστῶτα ἀέρα, οὗ τὴν μὲν σβέσιν καὶ τὴν θραῦσιν κτύπον ἀπεργάζεσθαι, τὴν δὲ λάμψιν ἀστραπήν, κεραυνὸν δὲ τὸν τῆς ἀστραπῆς τόνον.

"Empedocles says it is the impact of light on a cloud, which drives out the air which resists it. Its extinguishing and breakup produce noise, and its gleam the lightning, and the tension of the lightning the thunderbolt."

Yet, in my view, this interchange has deeper implications. In fact, this is not the only instance of the replacement of water with rain in the poem. It is remarkable that in two cases Lucretius strikingly appropriates Empedocles' technique, in a context where he explicitly rejects the latter's philosophical doctrine of matter (*et qui quattuor ex rebus posse omnia rentur* / *ex igni terra atque anima procrescere et imbri.* / "and those who think that all can grow forth out of four things, from fire, earth, air, and water," 1.714–715; *hinc imbrem gigni terramque creari* / *ex imbri.* / "and from this water is produced, and earth made from water," 1.784–785).[107] Moreover, the image of moisture in the cloud-slaughtering fire (*trucidat,* 6.147) that Lucretius draws in the simile in Book 6 we are discussing implies that, since Empedoclean roots are mutually destructive, when they meet they cannot claim divinity or even eternal existence. This vividly recalls similar ideas expressed in Book 1, where rain and lightning along with wind in a storm are used to illustrate exactly the mortal nature of roots (1.759–762).[108]

Coming back to the simile in Book 6, it seems highly probable that Lucretius grasps the chance to implicitly suggest that although he extensively resorts to Empedocles' scientific technique of drawing conclusions relying on the presence of roots, still he disapproves of Empedocles' doctrine of matter.

While discussing the causes of certain subterranean phenomena such as earthquakes and volcanoes, Lucretius shifts the focus of the action and interaction of the Empedoclean roots from clouds to the earth in order to disclose by analogy her internal mechanisms. Within this framework there are two instances in which Lucretius combines the Empedoclean technique of examining the behaviour of the elements within two different containers with the device of personification. More precisely, Lucretius portrays first the earth and then our world as animate beings and simultaneously treats them as containers of elements.[109]

At first glance, the technique resembles the one also employed in the discussion of rain. Lucretius arbitrarily takes once again the Hippocratic knowledge about the human organism for granted, analogically projects it onto miraculous subterranean phenomena and thus reinforces the validity of his conclusions.[110] Yet, in the present context both personifications entail multiple corollaries. As I have already discussed at length, in the course of the poem the images of the earth visualized as mother and *mundus* as *makranthropos* are deployed as analogical tools in a variety of ways, while their functional role has been repeatedly clarified.[111] As I will try to show, in the cases in question both devices assist Lucretius in further revealing the sinister aspect of nature, pertaining not only to the destructibility of both the earth we inhabit and our world, but ultimately to our mortal existence. Despite this reality, Lucretius suggests that the Epicurean should be aware of these facts and their natural causes, but remain serene whatever happens. This frame of mind is significant, as it precedes the final account of the plague.

Among other alternative causes that Lucretius conjectures for earthquakes is the suggestion that this may be brought about when wind enclosed within the earth, but not strong enough to burst out, is disseminated through the veins of the earth and so causes a trembling (6.591–600):

> *Quod nisi prorumpit, tamen impetus ipse animai*
> *et fera vis venti per crebra foramina terrae*

> *dispertitur ut horror, et incutit inde tremorem,*
> *frigus uti nostros penitus cum venit in artus,*
> *concutit invitos cogens tremere atque movere.*   595
> *ancipiti trepidant igitur terrore per urbis:*
> *tecta superne timent, metuunt inferne cavernas*
> *terrai ne dissoluat natura repente,*
> *neu distracta suum late dispandat hiatum*
> *idque suis confusa velit complere ruinis.*   600

"But if there is no breaking forth, yet the impetuous air itself and the furious force of wind is distributed abroad through the many interstices of the earth like an ague, and thus transmits the trembling; just as, when cold penetrates deep into our limbs, it shakes them, making them tremble and quake against our will. Therefore men shiver in their cities with a twofold terror: they fear the houses above, they dread the caverns below, lest the earth's nature loosen all asunder in a moment, or torn asunder open abroad her own gaping jaws, and in confusion seek to gorge it with her own ruins."

Lucretius compares the action of wind shut in the caverns of the earth (*impetus . . . animai*, 6.591; *vis venti*, 6.592) with that of cold which provokes shuddering within the human body (*frigus*, 6.594). The foundations for this comparison were already laid in Book 3, where Lucretius explains in fully atomic terms the composition of the soul out of breath, heat, air and a fourth nameless substance and then considers their interrelations and their different proportions within the soul as the origin of permanent or temporary differences in human or animal temperaments (3.231–322). According to this account, heat is prominent in anger, cold wind in fear and air in repose (3.288–306). In particular he writes about wind (3.290–291):[112]

> *est et frigida multa comes formidinis aura,*
> *quae ciet horrorem membris et concitat artus;*

"It has also abundance of that cold wind, fear's comrade, which makes the limbs shiver and stirs the frame;"

and he then gives an example (3.299–301):

> *at ventosa magis cervorum frigida mens est*
> *et gelidas citius per viscera concitat auras,*
> *quae tremulum faciunt membris existere motum.*

> "But the cold mind of the stag has more of wind, and more speedily
> sends currents of cold breath through his flesh, which cause a tremulous
> movement to pervade the limbs."

Given, therefore, the fact that the elements of cold wind in the body produce
shuddering, it should be no wonder, if, when shut in the body of the earth, they
cause a similar trembling (earth: *tremorem*, 6.593 → man: *ut horror*, 6.593; *tre-*
mere, 6.595; *ancipiti trepidant . . . terrore*, 6.596; *timent, metuunt*, 6.597).

As commentators have already pointed out, Lucretius has probably
drawn this specific analogy between the earth and the human body from
Aristotle, who similarly explained how an earthquake may be caused due to
wind enclosed within the earth. Aristotle basically distinguishes two types of
shock, i.e. a horizontal one, like a shudder (τρόμος), and a vertical one, like
a spasm (σφυγμός).[113] By eliminating Aristotle's distinction between trem-
bling and throbbing, Lucretius presents us with a rather simplified model.
Even more significantly, Lucretius substitutes air for Aristotle's obscure humid
and dry exhalations, which were considered the main cause of earthquakes.
In this replacement, Lucretius seems to follow again Theophrastus' meteo-
rological account (*Metars.* 15.2–16 Daiber); departing from Aristotle's divi-
sion between vertical and horizontal shock, Theophrastus gives multiple
causes corresponding to the four elements and distinguishes basically between
two types of earthquakes, the "shakers" caused by earth collapse, and "lean-
ers" and "rebounders" classified by air pressure.[114] Unfortunately, the anal-
ogy that Theophrastus may have employed in his explanation involving air
is not extant (*Metars.* 15.10–12 Daiber); Whatever the case may have been
for Theophrastus, when it comes to Lucretius, his modification of Aristotle's
comparison seems to reflect his application of the Empedoclean technique,
according to which one should compare as similar substances as possible (i.e.
different sorts of wind) within the two particular containers (the earth and the
human body). So, although Lucretius maintains the vehicle of Aristotle's anal-
ogy, he fully integrates it into his poetical, didactic and philosophical system.

Lucretius introduces his explanatory analogy with a brief simile (*ut hor-*
ror, 6.593), which is then reduplicated with a general statement about fear
caused by cold penetrating into our body (6.594–595). This image is further
expanded by a more specific one, in which Lucretius calls to mind shudder-
ing in the human body, due to the trembling caused by an earthquake in
the "body" of the earth (6.596–600). Thus, he no longer describes two dis-
tinct processes, but an instance in which the same wind simultaneously brings
about both physical phenomena, and so merges the tenor with the vehicle
(earth: *incutit*, 6.593 → man: *concutit*, 6.595). Next, by means of a metaphor

that points to atomic dissolution Lucretius emphasizes that the earth's substance is a mere atomic compound, subject to death (*dissolvat,* 6.598).

The simile ends with the revelation of the two-faced identity of the earth. Although Lucretius sustains her personification, he changes the *persona* that the earth embodies by bringing into play next to the image of a mother that of a second animate being, with radically contrasting characteristics. Thus, the earth is now transformed into a wild beast, with its jaws gaping ready to engulf itself and devour its children (6.599–600).[115] By this switch in the image of the earth, which has been verbally anticipated since the beginning of the account on earthquakes, Lucretius puts forward the earth's double face, closely interrelated with that of nature, sometimes acting as creator, sometimes as destroyer and the ultimate tomb of everything, being mortal herself.[116] In this case wind is the agent of this metamorphosis. Therefore, by shedding light on earth's sinister aspect, Lucretius' analogy further demythologizes her image as mother.

Soon after his account of earthquakes, Lucretius places that of volcanic eruptions of Etna, which were also considered a marvel and were equally prone to arouse superstitious fears (6.639–702). At this point, it is important to recall how closely the figure of Empedocles was associated with Etna. According to the biographical tradition he is said to have leapt into its crater in order to prove his divinity; one of his sandals is also said to have been found as evidence of this.[117] Lucretius himself refers to this Empedoclean semi-scientific, semi-mystic approach, which aimed at releasing mankind from the shackles of conventional religion and resembled in this respect Epicurus' doctrine (1.722–725):[118]

> *hic est vasta Charybdis et hic Aetnaea minantur*
> *murmura flammarum rursum se colligere iras,*
> *faucibus eruptos iterum vis ut vomat ignis*
> *ad caelumque ferat flammai fulgura rursum.*   725

"Here is wasteful Charydis, and here Etna's rumblings threaten that the angry flames are gathering again, that once more its violence may belch fires bursting forth from its throat, and once more shoot to the sky the lightnings of its flame:"

Lucretius, on the one hand, embraces Empedocles' stance towards religious superstitions; on the other, he actually goes one step ahead and incorporates Empedocles' probative method in order to systematically rationalize the volcanic activity. Lucretius' task is a twofold one: first he has to explain the merely physical causes of a phenomenon with such overwhelming effects; at the same time, he undertakes to dissociate the volcano itself from any mythological undertones. He follows two stages in his exposition. First he accounts in general terms for the thorough impact that overflowing lava has on the world (6.655–679); then he enters into a more detailed discussion about the mechanism of lava originating within the volcano (6.680–693). At any rate, his investigation concerns a phenomenon in which the element of fire plays the focal role; a volcanic eruption appears to be an instance of partial victory of fire in the war of the elements (*dominata*, 6.642), which reveals the sinister aspect of nature and points to the destructibility of our world.[119]

At this point Lucretius reintroduces the makranthropic image of the world in order to compare both the causes and effects of a volcanic eruption with those of diseases within the human body (6.647–672):

Hisce tibi in rebus latest alteque videndum
et longe cunctas in partis dispiciendum,
ut reminiscaris summam rerum esse profundam
et videas caelum summai totius unum   650
quam sit parvula pars et quam multesima constet,
nec tota pars, homo terrai quota totius unus.
quod bene propositum si plane contueare
ac videas plane, mirari multa relinquas.
Numquis enim nostrum miratur, siquis in artus
accepit calido febrim fervore coortam   656
aut alium quemvis morbi per membra dolorem?
obturgescit enim subito pes, arripit acer
saepe dolor dentes, oculos invadit in ipsos,
existit sacer ignis et urit corpore serpens   660
quamcumque arripuit partim, repitque per artus,
nimirum quia sunt multarum semina rerum,
et satis haec tellus morbi caelumque mali fert,
unde queat vis immensi procrescere morbi.
sic igitur toti caelo terraeque putandumst   665
ex infinito satis omnia suppeditare,
unde repente queat tellus concussa moveri
perque mare ac terras rapidus percurrere turbo,
ignis abundare Aetnaeus, flammescere caelum;
id quoque enim fit et ardescunt caelestia templa,   670
et tempestates pluviae graviore coortu
sunt, ubi forte ita se tetulerunt semina aquarum.

"In considering these matters you must cast your view wide and deep, and survey all quarters far abroad, that you may remember how profound is the sum of things, and see how very small a part, how infinitesimal a fraction of the whole universe is one sky—not so large a part as one man is of the whole earth. If you should keep this steadily before your mind, comprehend it clearly, see it clearly, you would cease to wonder at many things.

For is there any of us who feels wonder, if someone has got into his limbs a fever that gathers with burning heat, or any other pain from disease throughout his body? For the foot suddenly swells, a sharp aching often seizes the teeth, or invades the eyes themselves, the accursed fire appears creeping over the body and burning each part it takes hold on, and crawls over the limbs, assuredly because there are seeds of many things, and this earth and sky produce enough noxious disease that from it may grow forth an immeasurable quantity of disease. In this way therefore we must believe that a supply of all things is brought up from the infinite to the whole heaven and earth, enough to enable the earth on a sudden to quake and move, the swift whirlwind to scour over land and sea, Etna's fires to overflow, the heaven to burst in a blaze; for that also happens, the regions of heaven burn, and rainy tempests appear with heavier increment, when by some chance the seeds of waters have gathered to that effect."

Within a similar context in Book 5 about the mortality of the world, human disease has already been used as an analogy with retrospective validity (5.338–350): as we are subject to death by diseases similar to those that brought about the death of our predecessors, in the same way the present calamities of the world reveal its mortality and its imminent destruction.[120] In the context in question, Lucretius reiterates the proportional terms of his comparison (6.647–654): as a single man is to the earth, so is a single world to the universe; hence, by no means should the relative magnitude of the phenomenon surprise us.

Lucretius subsequently establishes a synchronic comparison between diseases and a volcanic eruption which bears Empedocles' imprint: by taking for granted the fiery nature of disease, he compares the devastating action of a special kind of fire, a noxious one, within the human body and within the world. As West notes, medical and meteorological terminology should be similar, given that man and the world are subject to the same atomic principles.[121] As erysipelas (*sacer ignis*) or fever penetrates and spreads throughout the limbs of the human body, in the same way volcanic lava gradually invades and overflows onto the limbs of the world (volcanic fire: *Aetnae / . . . ignes,* 6.639–640; *flammea tempestas,* 6.642; *ignis . . . Aetnaeus,* 6.669; *incendi turbidus ardor,* 6.673; *flamma,* 6.681; *calidum flammis velocibus ignem,* 6.688; *ardorem . . . favillam,* 6.690 → fire within the human body: *calido febrim fervore,* 6.656; *sacer ignis,* 6.660).[122] As Leen points out, by means of his wording "Lucretius repeatedly stresses the visual and tactile similarity between the fevered warmth of disease and the flames of Aetna."[123]

Afterwards, Lucretius emphasizes in general why worldly upheavals should not appear miraculous to us, and discusses the origins of such deleterious atomic congregations (6.662–672). As our world supplies an immeasurable amount of atoms, the combinations of which generate diseases, in the same way the universe furnishes our world with an even greater number of atoms, which provoke endless meteorological disorders such as earthquakes, volcanic eruptions, rainstorms and the like. Therefore, it turns out that both diseases and volcanic flames ultimately share a similar atomic substance.[124]

After a digression about the amazement caused also by the novelty of the phenomenon (6.673–679), Lucretius resumes his discussion about the specific physical mechanism that begets the initial generation of lava within the volcano (6.680–693):

Nunc tamen illa modis quibus inritata repente	680
flamma foras vastis Aetnae fornacibus efflet,	
expediam. primum totius subcava montis	
est natura, fere silicum suffulta cavernis.	
omnibus est porro in speluncis ventus et aer;	
ventus enim fit, ubi est agitando percitus aer.	685
hic ubi percaluit calefecitque omnia circum	
saxa furens, qua contingit, terramque, et ab ollis	
excussit calidum flammis velocibus ignem,	
tollit se ac rectis ita faucibus eicit alte.	
fert itaque ardorem longe, longeque favillam	690
differt, et crassa volvit caligine fumum,	
extruditque simul mirando pondere saxa,	
ne dubites quin haec animai turbida sit vis.	

"Nevertheless I will now explain in what ways the flame is excited which suddenly breathes out of the vast furnaces of Etna. Firstly, the whole mountain is hollow beneath, being supported for the most part upon caverns in the basalt rock. In all the caverns, moreover, is wind and air; for wind arises when the air is excited by driving about. When this wind has grown hot, and has heated all the surrounding rocks by its fury wherever it touches, and also the earth, and from these has struck out hot fire with quick flames, it rises and throws itself upwards straight through the mountain's throat. Thus it carries its fire afar, scatters ashes far abroad, rolls the smoke all thick and black, thrusts out at the same time rocks of wonderful weight; so that you may be sure that this is the turbulent force of air."

This is due to air within the volcano which, when agitated, becomes wind and then, growing hot with motion, heats and melts the earth and rocks. I have already discussed how the description of the volcanic action helps Lucretius to demythologize its image as a gigantic furnace within which thunderbolts were forged as divine weapons.[125] Moreover, it has been already pointed out that the conventional anthropomorphic wording by means of which Lucretius sketches the parts of a volcano (*per fauces . . . / expirent,* 6.639–640; *faucibus,* 6.689; *nos quod fauces perhibemus et ora,* 6.702), points to mythological accounts of the Giant Enceladus (or Typhoeus) or the divine smiths, the Cyclopes.[126] At any rate, although up to this point the dominant analogy has explicitly been that between the world and man, we should trace here an additional analogical dimension.

The volcano is the part of the world that somehow serves as the container that first receives the contagious atoms from the universe. So it is within it that the volcanic fire will be formed and only then will it be emitted throughout the makranthropic world, as if the whole becomes infected by illness in one of its parts. Moreover, the description of the volcano's inner structure as containing caverns (*subcava,* 6.682; *suffulta cavernis,* 6.683) bears close resemblance to the description of the earth itself, as sketched in the preceding account of earthquakes (*subter item ut supera ventosis undique plenam / speluncis, multosque lacus multasque lacunas* / "[the earth] below as above to be everywhere full of windy caverns, bearing many lakes and many pools," 6.537–538). This similarity should put us on the alert, as it points to a subtle interrelation with the preceding account of earthquakes, in which the earth containing air was assimilated to a human body shaking with fear. Accordingly, while Lucretius alludes to the mythical fury of the buried monster that breaths fire so as to demythologize it (*inritata,* 6.680; *furens,* 6.687), at the same time he evokes the atomic explanation of emotions in Book 3, where he parallels the stirring of fire with wrath (3.288–289):[127]

Est etiam calor ille animo, quem sumit, in ira
cum fervescit et ex oculis micat acrius ardor;

"The mind has also that heat, which it takes on when it boils in wrath
and fire flashes more fiercely from the eyes;"

and he then gives an example (3.294–298):

sed calidi plus est illis quibus acria corda
iracundaque mens facile effervescit in ira.   295
quo genere in primis vis est violenta leonum,
pectora qui fremitu rumpunt plerumque gementes
nec capere irarum fluctus in pectore possunt.

"But there is more of the hot in those creatures whose bitter hearts and
angry minds easily boil up in wrath. A notable instance of this is the vio-
lent fury of the lion, which so often bursts his breast with roaring and
growling, nor can he find room in his heart for the storm of passion."

Therefore, by sketching the earth as an angry human being, while she con-
tains a surplus of fire, Lucretius sheds further light on the fearsome phenom-
enon of volcanic eruptions.

In sum, Lucretius follows the life-cycle of noxious fire ever since its
intrusion from the universe into our world, and provides two parallel atomic
explanations by simultaneously bringing into play two personifications, that
of the earth and of the world. He compares the volcanic flames within the
earth initially with human anger in order to illuminate their fiery substance,
and then with disease, so as to encompass the tremendous impact they have
when spread all over the world.

3.4.2.2. Roots in Action

Even when an Empedoclean root is not contained anywhere, still one may
make valid scientific deductions by means of comparing its action upon two
different material substances. By attesting the effects that it brings about upon
an accessible object, one may infer its similar action upon an inaccessible one.

Although such comparisons are not explicitly preserved among Emped-
ocles' extant fragments, according to Longrigg's plausible suggestion our tes-
timonia allow at least for one to have existed. Given the references about the
solidifying effect of fire in connection with the visible phenomenon of salt
being crystallized like ice or hail under the action of sun's heat (ἅλς ἐπάγη
ῥιπῇσιν ἐωσμένος ἠελίοιο / "salt was crystallized under pressure from the
rays of the sun," B56),[128] Empedocles could have used this phenomenon as
an analogy in order to illuminate the formation of the "crystalline" outer-
heaven during cosmogony (Ἐμπεδοκλῆς στερέμνιον εἶναι τὸν οὐρανὸν

ἐξ ἀέρος συμπαγέντος ὑπὸ πυρὸς κρυσταλλοειδῶς, τὸ πυρῶδες καὶ τὸ ἀερῶδες ἐν ἑκατέρῳ τῶν ἡμισφαιρίων περιέχοντα. / "Empedocles says that the heaven is solid, [being made] from air solidified in the manner of ice by fire, for it contains the fiery and the airy in each of its hemispheres," A51a = Aët. 2.11.2 = *Dox. Gr.* 339).[129] As Longrigg rightly notes, in both cases "fire acts upon another body [water and air accordingly], compacting it so that it forms a residue, which resembles hail or ice."[130]

Beyond this assertion, such comparisons are widely found in the philosophical tradition of writers who may have been influenced by Empedocles' analogical methods, most characteristically again in the Hippocratic writers and Aristotle. For example, Aristotle draws comparisons between the action of the "vital heat" within the organic body and the action of heat elsewhere, outside the body (*Gen. an.* 743a26ff.). According to him the embryo may become deformed through an excess or deficiency of heat, and he compares with it the way in which in cooking too much or too little heat spoils the food.[131] In his turn, Lucretius also applies this analogical method in order to elucidate the causes of certain phenomena.

In his discussion of how the sun although so small emits so much light, Lucretius proposes as a possible explanation that it may kindle the air around it, just like a spark kindles a cornfield (5.604–609):

> *Est etiam quoque uti non magno solis ab igni*
> *aera percipiat calidis fervoribus ardor,*   605
> *opportunus ita est si forte et idoneus aer,*
> *ut queat accendi parvis ardoribus ictus,*
> *quod genus interdum segetes stipulamque videmus*
> *accidere ex una scintilla incendia passim.*

> "It is possible also that, even if the sun's fire be not great, yet the glow may pervade the air with hot burnings, if by any chance the air is so fit and disposed that it can be kindled when struck by small quantities of heat, just as at times we see a wide conflagration fall upon corn and straw from one spark."

The simile is based on the natural principle that, even if fire is proportionally small in comparison with the material it acts upon (sun: *non magno solis ab igni,* 5.604; *parvis ardoribus,* 5.607 → cornfield: *una scintilla,* 5.609), still if the material it comes into contact is flammable this causes a large conflagration (sun: *calidis fervoribus aer,* 5.605; *accendi,* 5.607 → cornfield: *incendia,* 5.609). For his comparison to hold true, Lucretius changes the absolute quantity of fire, but retains the ratio with the substance on which it exerts its action in each case.

In a different context, the action of fire upon clouds is compared with that upon wax, in order to explain how clouds emit rainy moisture and drip (6.513–516):

> *praeterea cum rarescunt quoque nubila ventis*
> *aut dissolvuntur, solis super icta calore,*
> *mittunt umorem pluvium stillantque, quasi igni*   515
> *cera super calido tabescens multa liquescat.*

"Besides where the clouds are blown thin by the winds, or loosened abroad, struck from above by the sun's heat, they emit rainy moisture and drip, as wax over a hot fire melts and grows fluid apace."

While wax melts when heated over fire, in the same way the texture of clouds is blown thin or loosened abroad by wind and sun (cloud: *solis . . . calore,* 6.514 → wax: *igni / . . . calido,* 6.515–516; cloud: *dissolvuntur, . . . / mittunt umorem pluvium stillantque,* 6.514–515 → wax: *tabescens . . . liquescat,* 6.516).

Moreover, in order to explain the sound of thunder that is produced when a dry cloud receives a bolt of lightning, Lucretius relies on the physical principle that, when dry materials get burnt, then a similar sound is heard (6.150–155):

> *aridior porro si nubes accipit ignem,*   150
> *uritur ingenti sonitu succensa repente,*
> *lauricomos ut si per montis flamma vagetur*
> *turbine ventorum comburens impete magno;*
> *nec res ulla magis quam Phoebi Delphica laurus*
> *terribili sonitu flamma crepitante crematur.*   155

"If, further, the cloud be drier when it receives the lightning, it is suddenly kindled and burns up with a loud din, as if the mountains were covered with laurel, and a flame were driven over by a tempest of winds, consuming them with mighty rush; and there is no other thing that burns with more terrible sound in the crackling flames than the Delphic laurel of Phoebus."

He thus appeals once again to common experience and compares a dry cloud with mountains covered with laurel; when these get burnt up thanks to their particularly dry substance, they produce a sound similar to that of thunder. Lucretius builds a multiple-correspondence simile by using as a scaffolding mainly words denoting fire—this being the initial cause—(cloud: *ignem,*

6.150 → laurel: *flamma*, 6.152; *flamma*, 6.155), and other words for the similar sound produced (cloud: *ingenti sonitu*, 6.151 → laurel: *terribili sonitu . . . crepitante*, 6.155), as well as verbs of burning (cloud: *uritur . . . succensa*, 6.151 → laurel: *comburens*, 6.153; *crematur*, 6.155). What is more, he quite unexpectedly brings in the mythological associations of laurel with Delphic Phoebus. By means of this allusion the simile acquires a double function, for besides the rationalization of the tenor, light is shed also upon the true nature of the vehicle itself.

Conclusions may also be formed on the basis of the parallel action of the wind (5.637–649):

> *Fit quoque ut e mundi transversis partibus aer*
> *alternis certo fluere alter tempore possit,*
> *qui queat aestivis solem detrudere signis*
> *brumalis usque ad flexus gelidumque rigorem,*   640
> *et qui reiciat gelidis a frigoris umbris*
> *aestiferas usque in partis et fervida signa.*
> *et ratione pari lunam stellasque putandumst,*
> *quae volvunt magnos in magnis orbibus annos,*
> *aeribus posse alternis e partibus ire.*   645
> *nonne vides etiam diversis nubila ventis*
> *diversas ire in partis inferna supernis?*
> *qui minus illa queant per magnos aetheris orbis*
> *aestibus inter se diversis sidera ferri?*

"It is possible also that from parts of the world across the sun's path two airs may flow alternately each at its own fixed time, one strong enough to push him away from the summer signs as far as the midwinter solstice and the stiffening cold, one to throw him back from the icy shades of cold as far as the regions full of heat and the burning signs. And in like manner we must suppose that the moon, and the stars which revolve for vast years in vast orbits, may move driven by airs this way and that way. Do you not see also that clouds driven by contrary winds in contrary directions move in layers, the lower contrary to the upper? Is it not equally possible that those constellations can be carried by contrary tides through the great orbits of the ether?"

In order to visualize the courses of the sun, moon and stars caused by contrary tides, Lucretius appeals to a phenomenon in our experience, the action of contrary winds upon clouds, being the actual agents of their motions (constellations: *aeribus . . . alternis*, 5.645; *aestibus . . . diversis*, 5.649 → clouds: *diversis . . . ventis*, 5.646).

Another such example is put forward among his explanations of thunder (6.137–141):

> *Fit quoque ut interdum validi vis incita venti*
> *perscindat nubem perfringens impete recto.*
> *nam quid possit ibi flatus manifesta docet res,*
> *hic, ubi lenior est, in terra cum tamen alta*   140
> *arbusta evolvens radicibus haurit ab imis.*

"It sometimes happens also that the swift force of strong wind tears through a cloud, breaking through with a direct rush. For what the blast can do there is plain from our own experience, when here on the earth, where it is gentler, it nevertheless tears up tall trees and wretches them from their deepest roots."

According to this we may perceive why wind tearing through a cloud produces such a terrible noise, by looking at the similar effects that a more gentle wind brings upon tall trees on the earth.[132]

The final example comes from Lucretius' enumeration of the causes of earthquakes (6.552–556):

> *Fit quoque, ubi in magnas aquae vastasque lacunas*
> *gleba vetustate e terra provolvitur ingens,*
> *ut iactetur aquae fluctu quoque terra vacillans,*
> *ut vas interdum non quit constare, nisi umor*   555
> *destitit in dubio fluctu iactarier intus.*

"Sometimes also, when from lapse of time a huge mass is rolled forwards from the earth into some great and wide pool of water, the earth also is moved and shaken by the wave of water: just as a vessel sometimes cannot remain still, unless the water within it ceases to be moved about in waves to and fro."

The action of water that becomes agitated within a vase and thus transmits its agitation to the vase itself is compared to that of water shaken within the caverns of the earth, which brings about a trembling when a mass of earth falls into a subterranean lake and water communicates its vacillation to the earth (earth: *aquae fluctu,* 6.554 → vessel: *umor / . . . fluctu,* 6.555–556; earth: *iactetur . . . vacillans,* 6.554 → vessel: *iactarier,* 6.555). Here it is important to point out another subtle adjustment of Theophrastus' model, which compared the shaking of the earth by the agitation of subterranean waters with that of a ship shaken by billows on the sea (*Metars.* 15.8–9 Daiber). Whereas in Theophrastus' analogy the water in motion is not contained, but rather the container of the ship, Lucretius formulates a more effective analogy, since he observes in both parts of it the impact of oscillating water upon its container.

3.4.2.3. Roots Now and Then

Given Lucretius' belief in the principle of isonomy not only in synchronic, but also in diachronic terms, the behaviour of roots in the present can also be used as a probative tool with retrospective value in order to extract conclusions on the macroscale about their behaviour during cosmogony, when after the original chaos atoms started separating out, like joining with its like, so as to form the four great members of the world (5.436ff.). Due to the particularly obscure nature of the phenomenon in question, Lucretius embeds within his cosmogonic account a wide variety of literary means with cognitive value; even more remarkably, most of them are tinged in vivid Empedoclean colour.[133]

After generally referring to the remote origins of our world, Lucretius describes separately the process by which the light particles of air and fire flew out and rose highest in order to form aether as a kind of exhalation (5.457–470):

>   *ideo per rara foramina terrae*
> *partibus erumpens primus se sustulit aether*
> *ignifer et multos secum levis abstulit ignis,*
> *non alia longe ratione ac saepe videmus,*   460
> *aurea cum primum gemmantis rore per herbas*
> *matutina rubent radiati lumina solis*
> *exhalantque lacus nebulam fluviique perennes,*
> *ipsaque ut interdum tellus fumare videtur;*
> *omnia quae sursum cum conciliantur in alto,*
> *corpore concreto subtexunt nubila caelum.*
> *sic igitur tum se levis ac diffusilis aether*
> *corpore concreto circumdatus undique flexit*
> *et late diffusus in omnis undique partis*
> *omnia sic avido complexu cetera saepsit.*   470

"Therefore through the loose-knit interstices, breaking out from the parts of the earth, first fiery ether uplifted itself and lightly drew with it quantities of fire; in no very different way than we often see, when in the morning the golden light of the beaming sun first blushes over herbage jewelled with dew, when the lakes and the ever-flowing streams exhale a mist, and the very earth seems sometimes to smoke; then when all these exhalations come together on high above us, clouds with body now cohering weave a texture under the sky. In this way therefore at that time the light and expansive ether, with coherent body, bent around on all sides, and expanded widely on all sides in every direction, thus fenced in all the rest with greedy embrace."

Even if we have to rely again on secondary sources, we should point out here that, along with other cosmologists, both Empedocles and Epicurus may have deployed the word ἀναθυμίασις, meaning exhalation, as a technical term. As Clay rightly remarks, Lucretius seems to be aware of the metaphorical connotations of the Greek term. In order to further illuminate the phenomenon in question, while translating the term, he formulates out of it an explicit comparison with a present day phenomenon.[134] Thus, he draws an image of the daily phenomenon of dawn, when early morning mist rises; in fact this is another example of the very same process that he strives to explain.[135]

The analogy is articulated in two stages. First, Lucretius compares the rising of mist out of lakes and streams with breath (*exhalant*, 5.463) and correspondingly that of fire out of earth with smoke (*fumare*, 5.464). Then, he switches over the vehicle of his analogy to compare the interweaving of fire and air particles that form the world's boundaries, the *flammantia moenia*, with that of clouds (5.465–470). The emphasis now is shifted from the initial process of rising to the final reunion of atoms into a new cloud-like entity. This border line between the two stages is usually hardly discerned and the emphasis is laid only upon the second part.[136] However, if we were to interpret this multi-dimensional analogy on the basis of the Empedoclean principle of comparing the behaviour of like roots within different environments, its rather complicated meaning could be easily disentangled.

Although the analogy as a whole bears a close resemblance to that about the formation of clouds as expounded in Book 6 (6.476–482), there is here a significant detail that often goes unobserved. In the first part of it (5.457–464), Lucretius specifies the exact moment of the day that the analogical phenomenon takes place, "when in the morning the golden light of the beaming sun first blushes over herbage jewelled with dew" (5.462). It suffices to glance a few lines further down in order to realize that here Lucretius hints at the fixed moment of the day when fire atoms gather to form the new sun. Actually, in the latter passage he deals with this phenomenon in similar vocabulary and even brings to mind a specific instance of it as seen from Mount Ida in the Troad (5.656–665):[137]

Tempore item certo roseam Matuta per oras
aetheris auroram differt et lumina pandit,
aut quia sol idem, sub terras ille revertens,
anticipat caelum radiis accendere temptans,
aut quia conveniunt ignes et semina multa   660
confluere ardoris consuerunt tempore certo,
quae faciunt solis nova semper lumina gigni;
quod genus Idaeis fama est e montibus altis
dispersos ignis orienti lumine cerni,
inde coire globum quasi in unum et conficere orbem.

"At a fixed time also Matuta diffuses the rosy dawn through the regions of ether and spreads out her light, either because the same sun returning under the earth takes his first hold on the sky as he tries to kindle it with his rays, or because there is a gathering together of fires, and many seeds of heat are accustomed to flow together at a fixed time, which make each day the light of a new sun arise: just as it is said that from the lofty mountains of Ida at sunrise scattered fires are seen, and then as it were these gather together into one globe and together form an orb."

In the second part of the analogy (5.465–470), Lucretius compares the final formation of aether into a coherent body with that of clouds that resemble an interwoven texture. Given that other metaphors occurring in the present context, such as the image of exhalation, the socio-political imagery and the weaving metaphor are used also in the discussion about the initial formation of clouds,[138] this metaphor that approximates aether with clouds should not surprise us. Yet, one should not overlook an essential difference in their substance: unlike aether, clouds are not formed out of particles of fire or air, but mainly out of water particles. By means of uniform imagery, Lucretius somehow merges the three distinct processes, i.e. the formation of aether into the walls of the world, morning mist and clouds before rain, as ultimately they are all subject to the same natural law, that of light atoms rising up and then uniting into similar structures. At the same time, Lucretius sheds light upon the liquid nature of the particles of aether and foreshadows the analogy between them and water that he is about to draw in 5.495ff.

The passage ends with the image of aether dispersed all round and embracing the whole world (*avido complexu*, 5.470). This image vividly echoes Empedocles' B38.4 (Τιτὰν ἠδ᾽ αἰθὴρ σφίγγων περὶ κύκλον ἅπαντα / "and Titan sky, whose circle binds all things fast").[139] However in this fragment, Empedocles quite unexpectedly appears to place αἰθήρ next to the four elements. Given that in other cases this word is used as an equivalent for air, we could even go so far as to allege that Lucretius here undertakes to settle the ambiguity of the Empedoclean verse by explicitly clarifying the difference between air and aether.

3.4.3. CONCLUSIONS

To recapitulate, there are two major categories of Lucretian similes, which are modelled after two Empedoclean probative mechanisms respectively. On the one hand, following a specific Empedoclean scientific method, as exemplified in his clepsydra simile, Lucretius fashions a certain group of similes by means of which he compares similar natural processes that take place at coordinated levels of reality; given the universality of natural laws, he appeals to a visible process, in order to make a valid conjecture about an invisible one and rationalize it. On the other, one may identify three types of similes, the common denominator of which is the presence of an Empedoclean root; hence all three of them are conditioned by variant applications of a single Empedoclean principle. Within this framework, Lucretius observes either the behaviour of an element within an accessible container or its perceptible impact upon another atomic structure; in this way he speculates about the assumed analogous behaviour of this very element within a remote container, or its effect upon a structure which is situated beyond the reach of our senses. What is more, this technique serves Lucretius to create analogies not only with synchronic, but also with diachronic value, so as to extract conclusions about the behaviour of the elements in the distant past.

Nevertheless, since Epicurus vehemently rejects Empedocles' theory of matter, Lucretius takes pains to clarify his philosophical stance and refute those elements of Empedocles' doctrine with which he does not agree; as he repeatedly and variously states, although the Empedoclean roots can be considered as the most basic atomic structures, by no means are they the ultimate material units, nor are they eternal. Yet, this does not prevent him from adopting an Empedoclean technique which is so closely connected with this otherwise rival philosophical principle and turning it into an organic part of his argumentation.

Very significantly, specific Empedoclean echoes that have been detected within Lucretius' similes substantiate further my main assumption that Lucretius credited Empedocles with the fatherhood of these probative methods. At the same time, there are cases in which, regarding the same obscure phenomenon, Lucretius combines a simile with another literary device with supplementary probative and illustrative function, such as personification, in order to corroborate his argument and thus convey his liberating message more effectively.

As regards the role of Theophrastus' meteorological account in the transmission of Empedocles' analogical method, it has been pointed out that this account is full of analogies in the Empedoclean fashion, and that Lucretius probably turns to them directly regarding his own meteorological account. In this connection it has been argued that, while Lucretius appropriates from Theophrastus a considerable number of vehicles, at the same time he makes crucial modifications and substitutions; and he does so, because he applies the scientific techniques that he himself inherited from the Presocratic philosopher in a more creative and consistent way than Theophrastus.

All in all, by applying Empedocles' scientific techniques, Lucretius creates models in the form of Empedoclean similes. By appeal to visible phenomena he analogically makes compelling inferences about the unseen and hence demythologizes a wide range of obscure physical phenomena. In this way, he turns similes as well into a cogent instrument of philosophical initiation and enlightenment.

Chapter Three
Metaphors

4.1 INTRODUCTION

Empedoclean precedent showed Lucretius that metaphors could be made to serve both a poetic and a cognitive function, and suggested to him that this dual role could be exploited for the exposition of Epicurean doctrine too.[1] It also furnished Lucretius with a number of specific metaphorical fields, in which he can be seen systematically developing a metaphorical range of his own on the basis—to a greater or lesser extent in different cases—of starting-points discovered in Empedocles. Yet at the same time Lucretius remained aware of the need to purge Empedocles' original metaphors of the specific doctrinal associations he had attached to them in order to be able to use them to clarify the divergent doctrines of Epicurus.

Although Epicurus was writing in prose, his philosophical language was nevertheless imbued with metaphorical usages of words. Yet, as might be expected from a philosopher with didactic aspirations, concern about the correct use of language and the vocabulary in which he expresses his doctrine is necessarily a priority for him. Although a detailed analysis of Epicurus' theory of the use of metaphors in philosophical discourse falls beyond the scope of this book, it is necessary to refer here to certain important aspects of it.[2] As Sedley observes, "Epicurus seems in *Ep. Hdt.* 75–76 to suggest that the original natural words had a close relationship with perceptible objects, which has been somewhat obscured by the metaphorical application of some words to abstract concepts or invisible entities."[3] Bearing this in mind, we should quote an earlier passage in the same letter, where Epicurus gives his pupil the following advice (*Ep. Hdt.* 37–38):[4]

Πρῶτον μὲν οὖν τὰ ὑποτεταγμένα τοῖς φθόγγοις, ὦ Ἡρόδοτε, δεῖ εἰληφέναι, ὅπως ἂν τὰ δοξαζόμενα ἢ ζητούμενα ἢ ἀπορούμενα

ἔχωμεν εἰς ταῦτα ἀνάγοντες ἐπικρίνειν, καὶ μὴ ἄκριτα πάντα ἡμῖν
<ἴη> εἰς ἄπειρον ἀποδεικνύουσιν ἢ κενοὺς φθόγγους ἔχωμεν. ἀνάγκη
γὰρ τὸ πρῶτον ἐννόημα καθ᾽ ἕκαστον φθόγγον βλέπεσθαι καὶ μηθὲν
ἀποδείξεως προσδεῖσθαι, εἴπερ ἕξομεν τὸ ζητούμενον ἢ ἀπορούμενον
καὶ δοξαζόμενον ἐφ᾽ ὃ ἀνάξομεν.

"In the first place, Herodotus, you must understand what it is that
words denote, in order that by reference to this we may be in a position
to test opinions, inquiries, or problems, so that our proofs may not run
on untested *ad infinitum,* nor the terms we use be empty of meaning.
For the primary signification of every term employed must be clearly
seen, and ought to need no proving; this being necessary, if we are to
have something to which the point at issue or the problem or the opin-
ion before us can be referred."

According to Diogenes Laertius, Epicurus uses "ordinary language"
(λέξει κυρίᾳ, Diog. Laert. 10.13) to refer to things; and indeed Epicurus
himself can be observed defending his use of a word as being in accordance
with regular usage (κατὰ τὴν πλείστην ὁμιλίαν / "according to current usage,"
Ep. Hdt. 67; κατὰ τὴν πλείστην φοράν / "in the commonest sense," *Ep. Hdt.*
70).[5] Epicurus repeats this claim in his *On Nature* 28, in which, according
to Sedley's reconstruction of the papyrus,[6] the philosopher probably deals
among other things with the question of whether and how ordinary lan-
guage is to be used in the exposition of philosophy (οὐκ ἔξω τῶν ἰθισμένων
λέξεων ἡμῶν χρωμένων οὐδὲ μετατιθέντων ὀνόματα ἐπὶ τῶμ φανερ]ῶν /
"our own usage does not flout linguistic convention, nor do we alter names
with regard to the objects of perception," Epicur. ΠΦ 28, fr. 13 col. v 8–12
sup. Sedley). Therefore, it seems that Epicurus would encourage his pupils to
use words in their literal meaning.

However, soon after this statement in the very same book Epicurus
gives up his quest for accuracy in philosophical vocabulary and discusses
the issue of metaphors. There is even an occurrence of the word μεταφορά
in its Aristotelian sense of metaphor rather than that of "analogical infer-
ence" (ἄλλο[υς . . .] μεταφορὰς ποι[εῖν φωνῶ]ν ἐπὶ τὰ ἄγνωστα ὑ[πὸ τῶγ
γν]ωστῶν, ἀλλὰ διὰ τὰς αὐ[τ]ῶμ πλάνας / "others transfer words from
the class of that which is knowable to denote that which is unknowable,
but because of their own errors," Epicur. ΠΦ 28, fr. 13 col. v 5–7 inf. Sed-
ley).[7] Therefore, despite his alleged initial hostility to metaphors, Epicurus
concedes that a philosopher may base his usage on common conventional
use;[8] the metaphorical use of words in philosophical treatises is an inevitable
choice, albeit under certain conditions. Only if they fulfill these prerequisites

are metaphors acceptable, since otherwise they could obfuscate the philosophical concepts and fail to convey a successful preconception. As Sedley aptly summarizes: "Epicurus' conclusion that the philosopher may, for want of a better medium, use ordinary language, is therefore necessarily qualified by the demand which he was already making when he wrote the *Letter to Herodotus,* that the resulting linguistic inaccuracies and ambiguities should he evaded by always seeing beyond the present conventional meanings of words to the natural first meanings which underlie them [. . .]."[9]

By the same token, as Wigodsky persuasively argues, Philodemus does not eliminate metaphors from philosophical discourse. In his *On Rhetoric,* he writes that "καὶ πᾶσα τέχνη φων[ὴ]ν οὐ δύναται προ[ίεσ]θαι στερ[η]θεῖσα τῆς ἐκ τῶν μεταφορῶν εὐχρησ[τίας]." ("all arts cannot utter a word, if deprived of the aid of metaphors," *Rh.* 4 col. xv 15–18 vol. 1 p. 175 Sudhaus) and that "[καὶ ἐπεσκέφθαι] φιλοσ[οφήσαν]τι ποιη[τῆι ἀν]αν[καῖον, π[ῶς καὶ π[όθ]εν [τ]ρ[οπικὴ ἅμα λέξι]ς καὶ κ[α]τὰ [τί]ν[α τρόπον ἴστ]αντ[αι] φυσικοὶ [λόγοι, ἢ] μάταιον δ[ὴ] θεω[ρ]εῖν, [πῶς] τὸ μ[ὲ]ν ἐκλέγητα[ι] τ[ὸ δ' ἐ]κ[κλ]είνηι·" ("it is necessary for a poet who has studied philosophy to have considered the nature and origins of both figurative and philosophical language, or else he will choose and avoid [metaphors] at random." *Rh.* 4 col. xxi 8–15 vol. 1 p. 180 Sudhaus)[10]

Regarding Empedocles, according to Diogenes Laertius (8.57), in his now lost treatise *On Poets* Aristotle called Empedocles μεταφορητικός, pinpointing exactly his remarkable ability to manipulate metaphors. Accordingly, Aristotle, in his *Poetics,* quotes several fragments from Empedocles' poem in order to exemplify his own categories of metaphors.[11]

From a different point of view, Empedocles' practice can be seen to consist in employing a range of alternative metaphorical terms in order to highlight different aspects of one single concept. As Sedley has rightly suggested, it is because Lucretius follows this particular practice of informality and variety that he himself keeps in play a whole set of mutually complementary live metaphors, thus moving away from Epicurean-style technical terminology.[12]

Still, Empedocles' use of metaphors was not unanimously accepted within the Epicurean school; Hermarchus probably launched an attack against Empedocles' metaphorical language in connection with the gods (fr. 29 Longo Auricchio).[13] From this point of view, Lucretius' adoption of this particular poetical device was not unproblematic. But Empedocles was not oblivious to the issues underlying the use of metaphors in philosophical discourse.[14] Indeed he acknowledges more than once that he conforms to the conventional usage of words in philosophy, in spite of their lack of precision, provided that his pupil is aware of this very fact (†ἧ θέμις† καλέουσι, νόμῳ δ᾽ ἐπίφημι καὶ αὐτός. / "these terms [birth and death] are not right, but I follow the custom and use them myself," B9.5; Γηθοσύνην καλέοντες ἐπώνυμον ἠδ᾽ Ἀφροδίτην. / "giving her the name Joy, as well as Aphrodite," B17.24). Therefore, it is because he consents to do so, that he calls birth and death what in reality is just mixing and separation (φύσις δ᾽ ἐπὶ τοῖς ὀνομάζεται ἀνθρώποισιν / "and to these men give the name 'birth'," B8.4).[15] Empedocles' theoretical approach to the use of metaphors could be viewed as consonant with Epicurus' principles and could serve Lucretius as a safety valve for this aspect of his intertextual engagement with his Presocratic predecessor. In the same spirit, Lucretius explains many of his key-metaphors by juxtaposing metaphorical and literal meanings in the form of extended similes (in the tenor and vehicle correspondingly). In this way, he goes back to the first meaning of each word, τὸ πρῶτον ἐννόημα, and teaches us how the semantic stretch took place; while reading the poem, the pupil is asked to bear in mind the vehicle of these similes.[16]

However, Lucretius' debt to Empedocles' metaphors should not be confined only to these two particular aspects. There is no doubt that Empedocles' metaphors stem from and at the same time reflect his philosophical beliefs. It should be stressed once again that his pluralistic materialism and the concomitant belief that everything surrounding us is composed of the same unchangeable minor entities, i.e. "roots," allow him to describe the structure of the world at every level, from the microcosm to the macrocosm as homogeneous, conditioned by the same natural laws. Within this framework metaphors assist Empedocles in schematizing abstract philosophical notions and delineating invisible natural processes. Moreover, given his theory of language, his metaphors call for a more "literal-flavoured" reading, by means of which the materialistic aspect of his doctrine can be made to stand out.

In addition to those cases where Lucretius clearly hints at Empedocles' metaphors and the specific concepts underlying them, the Epicurean philosopher seems more generally to comprehend Empedocles' deeper motives for his particular choices of metaphor. Epicurus' belief that everything is made of atoms and void allows Lucretius to follow the same route as Empedocles when he wants to draw similar conclusions and fill in logical gaps in the picture of the microcosm that he strives to illustrate. Likewise, he works out germs of metaphorical imagery already found in Epicurus' writings as well as other philosophical writers and transforms them into fully-developed metaphors. Metaphor is yet another didactic technique that Lucretius learns from Empedocles and elaborates creatively. Nonetheless, when he comes across fundamental philosophical discrepancies between Epicurus and Empedocles, Lucretius clarifies the extent to which it is legitimate for him to appropriate

Empedocles' metaphors in his Epicurean poem. In other words, although he applies the same criteria as Empedocles, and often opts for the same source domain in the schematization of an unfamiliar concept, yet Lucretius differentiates himself from his predecessor and enriches his range of metaphors in order to convey his Epicurean message effectively. Unfortunately, due to the fragmentary state of Empedocles' poem, how much exactly Lucretius owes to him, how much he draws from Epicurus or from other sources, and how much stems from his own creative genius cannot be specified without a certain degree of speculation.

The discussion that follows will be selective in the choice of metaphors. A network of metaphorical meanings that certain words bear will be sketched by projecting them back to their literal connotations. The focus will be on four major metaphorical fields that seem to dominate Lucretius' poem and best underscore the intertextual relationship between himself and Empedocles.

> a. The metaphor of "piecing together the primary elements" [Section 4.2].
> b. The metaphor of "filling or emptying the atomic container" [Section 4.3].
> c. The metaphor of "flowing water" [Section 4.4].
> d. The metaphor of "squeezing out the sponge" [Section 4.5].

All four metaphors under study have a common denominator, i.e. *the concept of the atomic container.* This will serve throughout as the background against which to illustrate Lucretius' system of metaphors in comparison with or against those of Empedocles.

Lucretius singles out a wide range of dissimilar atomic aggregations, with both microcosmic and macrocosmic origins, and envisages them as vessels in order to draw inferences about the behaviour of an inaccessible container or its contained substance by means of observing the accessible one.[17] Thanks to his similes, Lucretius explicitly creates instantaneous models in order to compare coordinated and subordinated levels in nature and penetrate into the world of the unseen. Yet, the direct juxtaposition of tenor with vehicle within a simile as well as the multiple-correspondence technique leaves little space for creativity and schematization of the remote microcosmic and macrocosmic processes; the image is rather forced.

On the contrary, by means of his metaphors, Lucretius ultimately aims at revealing the uniform material structure of seemingly dissimilar atomic compounds and eventually grasping unseen realities in a more universal way. In tune with this, it will be explored how, by his metaphorical language, Lucretius sketches manifold processes of the temporary building up of atomic containers or their ultimate crumbling (cf. a, c), as well as processes of systematic differentiation and the subsequent departure of certain atomic groups out of containers (cf. a, b, c, d). In the latter case, the elements emerging from the container do not seem to be an integral part of it; they are rather perceived as independent atomic entities.

Epicurus' fundamental belief in the concept of void, which is absent from Empedocles' philosophical system, turns out to be the regulatory factor in Lucretius' manipulation of all these metaphors. From this point of view, the depiction of the porosity of the containers is highly significant, since it establishes the possibility of atomic motion in and out of them.[18] Yet, thanks to Empedocles' theory of pores, the role of which is similar to that of the atomic void, Lucretius perceives specific points of contact between Empedocles' and Epicurus' metaphorical language. In line with this, he uses Empedocles' metaphors as his point of departure in order to express comprehensively the Epicurean truth.[19]

However, if one bears in mind that everything can be considered a combination of atoms mingled with void, and that there exists an ultimate material similarity between container and contained substance, this kind of distinction may appear to a certain degree arbitrary. To such a possible objection one could reply that the relatively stable existence of the atomic structures that Lucretius describes as containers is sufficient to stand out against the ceaseless atomic motion, as described in the metaphorical models in question.

All these processes should be considered as worldly manifestations of creation and destruction. By highlighting these processes, the grim image of the world that certain scholars reconstruct through Lucretius' imagery will be counterbalanced and this one-sided reading will be eventually replaced with a more balanced approach.[20]

4.2 PIECING TOGETHER PRIMARY ELEMENTS: TECHNOLOGICAL METAPHORS FOR ELEMENTARY MIXTURE (FITTING TOGETHER, BINDING, WEAVING)

Lucretius uses technological images of *fitting together, binding* and *weaving*—as well as their opposites—as a cognitive tool in order to reveal and depict the initial invisible mixing together and separating of atoms and then similarly, in a broader way, to conceptualize, visualize and thus unite material substances and materialized abstract notions. Although for their provenance one should first look within the Atomic tradition, it seems that Lucretius turns directly to corresponding images in Empedocles' poem, creatively draws upon them and systematizes their usage accordingly. He is justified in doing so by specific philosophical principles and objectives that he shares in common with his predecessor; at the same time, he differentiates himself in order to clarify divergent Epicurean tenets.[21]

Although the use of these processes as vehicles in metaphors is not unique,[22] Empedocles and Lucretius are set apart in their approach, due to their thorough-going materialism. Semantic transference takes place across similar mental domains, both of them material in substance, the target domain being elementary matter and the source domain perceptible matter that is subject to piecing together or dismantling.

Both Empedocles and Lucretius illustrate the process of elementary mixture by means of personification of the primary elements as well as through corresponding long similes.[23] Whereas in the former case the philosophers aim principally at describing a dynamic process, in the latter the emphasis is placed more on the idea of the plurality of creations, despite the limited number of types of unchangeable primary elements. On the contrary, the technological metaphors under review are used to describe the temporary arrangements and rearrangements of elements in a more static way. The primary elements are now sketched more as passive elements of the elementary formations.[24]

This type of imagery inevitably entails the existence of an agent who exerts his creative power upon the elements. As it has already been discussed above in the chapter on Personification, as far as Empedocles' physiological and biological account is concerned, the dominant presence of Aphrodite as a divine artisan who brings together the elements into temporary compounds could be tentatively taken as a reflection of his teleological ideas—vague though and crude these may be—without this posing a threat to his overall philosophical doctrine. However, such metaphors could cause an alarming tension within the Epicurean mechanistic world, a tension which Lucretius is at pains to tone down.[25]

Empedocles' Metaphors

According to Empedocles, elementary mixture is feasible only thanks to microscopic passages, the pores (πόροι), which interpenetrate all roots and their compound bodies (A86, A87).[26] As the size and structure of pores differ, depending on their reciprocity, mixing between different roots or elementary structures may or may not be possible, as they might or might not admit the particles of other substances into their pores. As a consequence, the theory of pores was used to explain why some substances combine more easily than others, as it is a question of having symmetrical pores. As Williams notes, "the *poroi* might be interstices between horizontal layers of a substance, and in this case, if the interstices between the layers of substance A exactly fitted the layers of substance B, it would be possible for A and B to interpenetrate."[27] In addition, Mourelatos correctly remarks that we need not suppose that the pores are rigid.[28] For example, according to Aristotle, Empedocles bases his explanation of the sterility of the entire species of mules upon his theory of pores (B92 = Arist. *Gen. an.* 747a24-b3 = A 82 Inwood):[29]

> τὸ δὲ τῶν ἡμιόνων γένος ὅλον ἄγονόν ἐστιν. περὶ δὲ τῆς αἰτίας, ὡς μὲν λέγουσιν Ἐμπεδοκλῆς καὶ Δημόκριτος, λέγων ὁ μὲν οὐ σαφῶς Δημόκριτος δὲ γνωρίμως μᾶλλον, οὐ καλῶς εἰρήκασιν. λέγουσι γὰρ ἐπὶ πάντων ὁμοίως τὴν ἀπόδειξιν τῶν παρὰ τὴν συγγένειαν συνδυαζομένων. [. . .] Ἐμπεδοκλῆς δ᾽ αἰτιᾶται τὸ μίγμα τὸ τῶν σπερμάτων γίγνεσθαι πυκνὸν ἐκ μαλακῆς τῆς γονῆς οὔσης ἑκατέρας· συναρμόττειν γὰρ τὰ κοῖλα τοῖς πυκνοῖς ἀλλήλων, ἐκ δὲ τῶν τοιούτων γίγνεσθαι ἐκ μαλακῶν σκληρὸν ὥσπερ τῷ καττιτέρῳ μιχθέντα τὸν χαλκόν,

> "The entire species of mules is sterile. As to the reason for this, as Empedocles and Democritus give it, the one speaking unclearly and Democritus more intelligibly, they have not explained it well. For they give the demonstration similarly in the case of all animals which copulate outside their own species . . . And Empedocles alleges as cause that the mixture of the seeds becomes dense, each seed having been soft before. For their hollows fit into the dense parts of each other and by such a process it becomes hard instead of soft, like bronze mixed with tin."

Since the seeds of both the parent animals are by nature soft, they become hard and thus infertile when they unite, the densities of the one fitting into the hollows of the other. In addition, if we were to believe Alexander of Aphrodisias' testimony about Empedocles' explanation of the magnet, it appears that the effluences played a great role in the latter's mechanism of mixture (A89 = Alex. Aphrod. *Quest.* 2.23, CIAG Supp. 2.2 72.9–27):

> Περὶ τῆς Ἡρακλείας λίθου, διὰ τί ἕλκει τὸν σίδηρον. Ἐμπεδοκλῆς μὲν ταῖς ἀπορροίαις ταῖς ἀπ᾽ ἀμφοτέρων καὶ τοῖς πόροις τοῖς τῆς λίθου συμμέτροις οὖσιν ταῖς ἀπὸ τοῦ σιδήρου τὸν σίδηρον φέρεσθαι λέγει πρὸς τὴν λίθον· αἱ μὲν γὰρ ταύτης ἀπόρροιαι τὸν ἀέρα τὸν ἐπὶ τοῖς τοῦ σιδήρου πόροις ἀπωθοῦσί τε καὶ κινοῦσι τὸν ἐπιπωματίζοντα αὐτούς· τούτου δὲ χωρισθέντος ἀθρόᾳ ἀπορροίᾳ ῥεούσῃ τὸν σίδηρον ἕπεσθαι· φερομένων δὲ τῶν ἀπ᾽ αὐτοῦ ἀπορροιῶν ἐπὶ τοὺς τῆς λίθου πόρους, διὰ τὸ συμμέτρους τε αὐτοῖς εἶναι καὶ ἐναρμόζειν καὶ τὸν σίδηρον σὺν ταῖς ἀπορροίαις ἕπεσθαί

τε καὶ φέρεσθαι. ἐπιζητήσαι δ' ἄν τις, εἰ καὶ συγχωρηθείη τὸ τῶν
ἀπορροιῶν, τί δήποτε ὁ λίθος οὐχ ἕπεται ταῖς ἰδίαις ἀπορροίαις,
κινεῖται δὲ πρὸς τὸν σίδηρον. οὐδὲν γὰρ μᾶλλον ἐκ τῶν εἰρημένων
ἡ λίθος πρὸς τὸν σίδηρον ἢ ὁ σίδηρος κινηθήσεται πρὸς τὴν λίθον.
ἔτι διὰ τί οὐ καὶ χωρὶς τῆς λίθου κινηθήσεταί ποτε σίδηρος ἐπ' ἄλλο
τι τῶν ἀπ' αὐτοῦ ἀπορροιῶν ἀθρόων φερομένων. διὰ τί γὰρ μόναι
αἱ ἀπὸ τῆς λίθου ἀπόρροιαι κινεῖν δύνανται τὸν ἐπιπωματίζοντα
τοὺς τοῦ σιδήρου πόρους ἀέρα καὶ ἐπέχοντα τὰς ἀπορροίας; ἔτι
διὰ τί ἄλλο οὐδὲν πρὸς ἄλλο τι οὕτω φέρεται, καίτοι πολλὰ λέγεται
ὑπ' αὐτοῦ συμμέτρους τοὺς πόρους πρὸς ἀλλήλας ταῖς ἀπορροίαις
ἔχειν; λέγει γοῦν "ὕδωρ (B91) οἴνῳ μᾶλλον ἐνάρθμιον, αὐτὰρ
ἐλαίῳ οὐκ ἐθέλει."

"On the stone of Heracles (magnet) and why it draws iron. Empedocles
says that the iron moves toward the stone because of the effluences from
both and because the pores of the stone are symmetrical with the efflu-
ences from the iron. For the effluences from it displace and move the
air in the pores of the iron which covers them. When this is removed
the iron follows the effluences which flow all at once. And when the
effluences from the iron move to the pores of the stone, because these
effluences are symmetrical with and fit into the pores, the iron too fol-
lows along with the effluences and moves. Even if one were to concede
the point about the effluences, one might further enquire why the stone
does not follow its own effluences and move towards the iron. For on the
theory as stated, there is no more reason for the stone to move towards
the iron than for the iron to move towards the stone. Again, why will
the iron not sometimes move toward something else, even without the
stone, when the effluences from it move all at once. For why is it that
only the effluences from the stone are able to move the air which cov-
ers the pores of the iron and checks the effluences? Again, why does
nothing else move towards anything else in this fashion, although he
says that many things have pores which are mutually symmetrical with
another's effluences? At any rate he says: [Water is] more easily fitted to
wine, but with oil it does not want [to mix] [B91]."

Given that the perfect mixing occurs when the effluences of one thing are
symmetrical and fit into the pores of another, it is because the pores in the
magnet are proportionate to the emanations from the iron that the whole
iron adheres so closely to the magnet.[30] In any case, Empedoclean mixture
should not be considered a chemical process, but rather one of *interpenetra-
tion* or *adaptation*.

In order to illustrate this particular process of mixture, Empedocles portrays Aphrodite joining together roots as well as creating animal parts, such as eyes, bones and other organic structures in *technological terms*.[31] Empedocles builds his metaphors of mixture out of Homeric vocabulary.[32] He deploys words used literally in Homer to denote the matching, binding and securely fitting together of inanimate structures in contexts where he portrays the fastening together of elementary roots and the generation of animal organs. In the same spirit, in B33 (ὡς δ' ὅτ' ὀπὸς γάλα λευκὸν ἐγόμφωσεν καὶ ἔδησε / "As when the sap [of the fig tree] has riveted and set white milk") he recontextualizes a Homeric simile about fig-juice solidifying milk (*Il.* 5.902–904):[33]

> ὡς δ' ὅτ' ὀπὸς γάλα λευκὸν ἐπειγόμενος συνέπηξεν
> ὑγρὸν ἐόν, μάλα δ' ὦκα περιτρέφεται κυκόωντι,
> ὡς ἄρα καρπαλίμως ἰήσατο θοῦρον Ἄρηα.

> "As when the juice of the fig in white milk rapidly fixes
> that which was fluid before and curdles quickly for one who
> stirs it; in such speed as this he healed violent Ares."

Whereas in Homer the focus was on the swiftness of curdling, in Empedocles the emphasis has been now shifted to the process of "fastening" and "binding" of two liquids to produce a solid.[34]

There are several fragments in which creation is sketched as a process of firmly fitting together (e.g. παντοίαις ἰδέῃσιν ἀρηρότα, θαῦμα ἰδέσθαι. / "fitted with all kinds of forms, a wonder to see," B35.17; τόσσ' ὅσα νῦν γεγάασι συναρμοσθέντ' Ἀφροδίτῃ / "which have now arisen, fitted together by Aphrodite," B71.4).[35] Elsewhere, roots are compacted so as to make solid and stiff structures (e.g. τῶν δ' ὅσ' ἔσω μὲν πυκνά, τὰ δ' ἔκτοθι μανὰ πέπηγε, / "But of those which are compact within and loosely formed without," B75.1).[36] Moreover, Empedocles pictures Aphrodite as a carpenter who joins the roots together by dowels (γόμφοις ἀσκήσασα καταστόργοις Ἀφροδίτη / "Aphrodite, having fitted [them] with rivets of affection," B87).[37] These pegs are characterized by the newly-coined adjective καταστόργοις, implying thus their vital role in the process of creation; conversely, the joining is artificial, since if the nails are taken away, the compound will be dissolved into its components.[38] As Mourelatos remarks, "the reference must be to mechanical 'joints,' even to the tenon and mortise structure of dovetail joints."[39] In addition, with reference to B33 Mourelatos points out that "in the curdling of milk, Empedocles seems to be saying, we have visual and palpable evidence that even in the mixing of liquids there is an underlying process of fitting of bolt and socket."[40]

Empedocles also draws his imagery from metallurgy or even baking, when he depicts the mutual relationship between wet and dry ingredients and describes it as a gluing together (ἄλφιτον ὕδατι κολλήσας / "when he had glued barley meal with water," B34). As Mourelatos again comments, if we were to take into consideration Empedocles' theory of imperceptible elementary mixture, "κολλάω in B34 cannot mean to 'glue' or to 'cement,' as no third bonding material is involved." And he concludes that the fragment should be translated "having fastened barley meal tightly on to water."[41] Empedocles also applies the binding metaphor; very significantly, human death is equated to a mere unbinding of man's component parts (πρὶν δὲ πάγεν τε βροτοὶ καὶ <ἐπεὶ> λύθεν, οὐδὲν ἄρ᾽ εἰσιν. / "and that before they were formed, and after they have disintegrated, they do not exist at all," B15.4).[42]

Unfortunately, the fragmentary state of Empedocles' poem once more prevents us from sketching a full-scale picture of the extent to which he made use of these metaphors. Still, our belief in their dominance in Empedocles' language and thought would be strengthened if we were to take into account their reception by philosophical texts which reflect the influence of his elementary theory or explicitly refer to it. For example, Empedoclean language has been clearly incorporated into Plato's *Timaeus* (*Ti.* 43a):[43]

> πυρὸς καὶ γῆς ὕδατός τε καὶ ἀέρος ἀπὸ τοῦ κόσμου δανειζόμενοι μόρια ὡς ἀποδοθησόμενα πάλιν, εἰς ταὐτὸν τὰ λαμβανόμενα συνεκόλλων, οὐ τοῖς ἀλύτοις οἷς αὐτοὶ συνείχοντο δεσμοῖς, ἀλλὰ διὰ σμικρότητα ἀοράτοις πυκνοῖς γόμφοις συντήκοντες,

> "They borrowed from the Cosmos portions of fire and earth and water and air, as if meaning to pay them back, and the portions so taken they cemented together; but it was not with those indissoluble bonds wherewith they themselves were joined that they fastened together the portions but with numerous pegs, invisible for smallness."

Moreover, Plutarch refers to Empedocles' theory of mixture in a similar metaphorical wording (*Adv. Col.* 10.1112A):

> καίτοι ὁ μὲν Ἐμπεδοκλῆς τὰ στοιχεῖα κολλῶν καὶ συναρμόττων θερμότησι καὶ μαλακότησι καὶ ὑγρότησι μῖξιν αὐτοῖς καὶ συμφυΐαν ἐνωτικὴν ἀμωσγέπως ἐνδίδωσιν,

> "Yet, when Empedocles cements and joins the elements together by the operation of heat, softness, and moisture he somehow opens the way for them to a 'mixture' that coalesces into a natural unity;"

Lucretius' Metaphors

Among other aspects linked to elementary mixture that Epicurus shares with Empedocles is the mechanism of pores and the idea that two things are best mingled when the pores of the one are symmetrical with the effluences emitted by the other (διὰ πόρων συμμετρίας / "because the pores are symmetrical," *Ep. Pyth.* 107).[44] Yet, despite this major point of contact, the Atomists' belief in the existence of void allows for the improvement of Empedocles' theory.[45] As a result, whereas Empedocles, being a *plenum* theorist, believes that the process of mixture consists in the *interpenetration* and *adaptation* of elements, for the Atomists atoms are mutually *entangled*.[46] As has been already observed, the metaphors of binding and weaving, being closely related to the notion of mixture are dominant in the fragments of the Greek Atomists, Leucippus and Democritus, and then in Epicurus:[47]

> ταῦτα δέ ἐστιν ἄτομα καὶ ἀμετάβλητα, εἴπερ μὴ μέλλει πάντα εἰς τὸ
> μὴ ὂν φθαρήσεσθαι, ἀλλ᾽ ἰσχύοντα ὑπομένειν ἐν ταῖς διαλύσεσι τῶν
> συγκρίσεων, πλήρη τὴν φύσιν ὄντα, οἷα δὴ οὐκ ἔχοντα ὅπῃ ἢ ὅπως
> διαλυθήσεται. ὥστε τὰς ἀρχὰς ἀτόμους ἀναγκαῖον εἶναι σωμάτων
> φύσεις. (*Ep. Hdt.* 41)

> "These elements are indivisible and unchangeable, and necessarily so, if
> things are not all to be destroyed and pass into non-existence, but are to
> be strong enough to endure when the composite bodies are broken up,
> because they possess a solid nature and are incapable of being anywhere
> or anyhow dissolved."

> καὶ αἱ μὲν εἰς μακρὰν ἀπ᾽ ἀλλήλων διιστάμεναι, αἱ δὲ αὐτοῦ τὸν παλμὸν
> ἴσχουσιν, ὅταν τύχωσι τῇ περιπλοκῇ κεκλειμέναι ἢ στεγαζόμενοι παρὰ
> τῶν πλεκτικῶν. (*Ep. Hdt.* 43)

> "Some of them rebound to a considerable distance from each other, while
> others merely oscillate in one place when they chance to have got entan-
> gled or to be enclosed by a mass of other atoms shaped for entangling."

At the same time, while Epicurus refutes Plato's theory of elements, he embraces the Empedoclean wording for mixture as a process of interweaving or compacting, which had already been assimilated by Plato (*PHerc.* 1148 = Epicur. *ΠΦ* 14, fr. 60 col. xxxviii Leone = fr. 29.26 Arr.²):[48]

> τὰ αὐτῶι τρίγωνα ἐξ ὧν / καὶ τὰ λοιπὰ συμπλέκει / σχήμ[α]τα. Εἰ
> μὲν ἄτομα / ὑφείληπτο εἶνα[ι] τί οὐχὶ / ἐποιήσατό τινα ἀπόδειξιν / ὡς

ἔστιν ἄτομα [σ]ώματα; / εἰ δὲ μὴ ἄτομα τ[ί] ἄν ἐκ τού/των νομίζοι τις
συνίστα/σθαι τὰ λοιπὰ ἅ συμπηγνύ/ει ἐξ ἄλλων ὡνδήποτε;

"the triangles out of which he intertwines also the rest of the figures. On
the one hand, if he had assumed that they are indivisible, why he does
not provide a proof that they are bodies indivisible? If, on the other, he
had assumed that they are not bodies indivisible, why should he main-
tain that the rest of the figures are put together from those which he
compounds from others of whatever kind?"

It seems very plausible that Lucretius' intertextual engagement with
Empedocles' technological metaphors of mixture is direct and creative, even
if its precise extent can only be settled by conjecture. In tune with this, in
what follows it will be demonstrated how Lucretius goes back directly to
Empedocles' metaphors and seems to discern not only their expressive power,
but also Epicurus' debt to them. In a way Lucretius creatively incorporates
Empedocles' metaphors into his philosophical discussion and thus elaborates
scattered philosophical ideas into a fully-fledged metaphorical system.

By his manipulation, Lucretius appears to be conscious of Epicurus'
intrinsic philosophical alliance with his Presocratic predecessor, that is, the
affinity in their theories of mixture and the similar role of Empedoclean
pores and atomic void. In addition, given the Epicurean belief in innumer-
able atomic shapes, Lucretius partly accepts Empedocles' idea that in their
mixture the primary elements—or the effluences of the compound bod-
ies—being symmetrical, may combine with each other by their hollows fit-
ting into the dense parts of each other as in a jigsaw puzzle. Still, contrary
to Empedocles' philosophical tenets, Lucretius believes that every atomic
aggregation is a mixture of atoms and void, no matter if its atoms are mutu-
ally entangled and interlaced or adapted, depending on their shape.[49] Hence,
even when referring to an Empedoclean-like type of mixture, Lucretius defi-
nitely allows for a certain degree of porosity, albeit small.

In keeping with his theory of metaphors, Lucretius also deploys the
words for fitting together, binding and weaving in their literal meaning.
When he discusses the origins of arts and crafts in Book 5, he makes a clear
distinction between plaited (*nexilis . . . vestis,* 5.1350) and woven clothes
which are made by the loom out of finer threads and are more closely com-
pacted (*textile tegmen,* 5.1350). As far as the concept of interpenetration is
concerned, in the vehicle of a complicated comparison pertaining to the
absence of atomic colour, Lucretius presents us with a palpable example of a
thing created out of parts fitted together, that of a square within which dif-
ferent shapes and various figures fit together; this is how he eventually proves

that, if seeds were of many colours, these would be distinguishable after their intermingling (2.776–787):[50]

> sin alio atque alio sunt semina tincta colore   776
> quae maris efficiunt unum purumque nitorem,
> ut saepe ex aliis formis variisque figuris
> efficitur quiddam quadratum unaque figura,
> conveniebat, ut in quadrato cernimus esse   780
> dissimiles formas, ita cernere in aequore ponti
> aut alio in quovis uno puroque nitore
> dissimiles longe inter se variosque colores.
> praeterea nil officiunt obstantque figurae
> dissimiles quo quadratum minus omne sit extra;   785
> at varii rerum inpediunt prohibentque colores
> quominus esse uno possit res tota nitore.

"Or if different seeds that make up the sea's uniform and pure brightness are steeped in different colours, just as often from different shapes and various figures something square is composed with a uniform figure, then it were fitting that, as in the square we perceive unlike forms to be contained, so on the surface of the deep or in any other pure and uniform brightness we should perceive various colours very different from one another. Besides, there is nothing in the unlike figures to hinder and debar the whole thing from being square on the outside; but the various colours of things do thwart and forbid the whole thing to be of one brightness."

Conversely, in the vehicle of another simile, Lucretius describes literally the process of the gradual dismantling of a material texture into its atomic constituents (2.826–833):

> Quin etiam quanto in partes res quaeque minutas
> distrahitur magis, hoc magis est ut cernere possis
> evanescere paulatim stinguique colorem;
> ut fit ubi in parvas partis discerpitur austrum:
> purpura poeniceusque color clarissimu' multo,   830
> filatim cum distractum est, disperditur omnis;
> noscere ut hinc possis prius omnem efflare colorem
> particulas quam discedant ad semina rerum.

"Moreover, the more minute the particles into which anything is pulled apart, the more readily it is perceived that the colour gradually fades away and is extinguished; as happens when purple wool is torn up into small parts: the purple and the scarlet colour, brightest of all, is wholly destroyed when the wool has been pulled apart threadwise; so that you may learn from this that the particles breathe away all their colour before they are dispersed apart into the seeds of things."

In order to visualize the fundamental Epicurean precept that the atoms are colourless, Lucretius presents us with the analogy of the dissolution of purple wool, which gradually loses its colour when pulled apart thread by thread (*filatim,* 2.831). Despite the accuracy of the comparison, the atoms leave behind their colour completely only at the threshold of the ultimate level; but then they bar us from entering into their world, unless by conjecture and the projection of the mind.[51]

The study of Lucretius' metaphors of mixture should be now advanced with a close look at his account of the mechanism of the magnet (6.906–1089).[52] For his didactic purposes, Lucretius modifies the Epicurean theory of the magnet by assimilating scientific elements from other philosophers, including Empedocles.[53] This passage is highly enlightening, since it vividly echoes Empedocles at various levels. To begin with, it provides us with further evidence that Lucretius goes back directly to Empedocles' metaphorical language. On a different level, here we come across instances of the direct juxtaposition of the metaphors of fitting together and binding with that of weaving. Conclusions can be thus drawn as regards correspondences and discrepancies between Lucretius' and Empedocles' handling of them.

Lucretius wishes to discuss the phenomenon of the magnet within the more general framework that, since atoms have different shapes, the *foedera naturai* dictate that not every atomic mixture is possible. Lucretius frames his account with the theory of effluences (6.921–935), general statements about the permeability and porosity of bodies (6.936–958), the different effects of the same things on different objects (6.959–978), the availability of minute passages in things and their diversity in size and shape, which determine their cohesibility (6.979–997). I will leave aside for a moment the explanation of the magnet to focus on the coda of the passage, in which Lucretius lists other things that have affinity and thus can be indissolubly bound together; there, he puts forward two alternative possibilities of perfect mixture, both of which carry equal importance (6.1065–1089):

Nec tamen haec ita sunt aliarum rerum aliena,   1065
ut mihi multa parum genere ex hoc suppeditentur
quae memorare queam inter se singlariter apta.

saxa vides primum sola colescere calce.
glutine materies taurino iungitur una
ut vitio venae tabularum saepius hiscant   1070
quam laxare queant compages taurea vincla.
vitigeni latices aquai fontibus audent
misceri, cum pix nequeat gravis et leve olivom.
purpureusque colos conchyli iungitur una
corpore cum lanae, dirimi qui non queat usquam—   1075
non si Neptuni fluctu renovare operam des,
non mare si totum velit eluere omnibus undis.
denique non auro res aurum copulat una,
aerique aes plumbo fit uti iungatur ab albo?   1079
cetera iam quam multa licet reperire! quid ergo?
nec tibi tam longis opus est ambagibus usquam,
nec me tam multam hic operam consumere par est,
sed breviter paucis praestat comprendere multa:
quorum ita texturae ceciderunt mutua contra,
ut cava conveniant plenis haec illius illa   1085
huiusque inter se, iunctura haec optima constat.
est etiam, quasi ut anellis hamisque plicata
inter se quaedam possint coplata teneri;
quod magis in lapide hoc fieri ferroque videtur.   1089

"But yet these properties are not so alien to other things that I could not find good store of similar examples to hand which I might mention, of things that have affinity for each other and for nothing else. Firstly you see stones cemented by mortar alone. Wood is joined together with bull's glue, so that the grain of boards often gapes open with a crack before the joints of the bull's glue loosen their hold. The juice of the grape is ready to mingle with spring-water, when heavy pitch and light olive-oil cannot. The colour of the sea-purple shell unites with the substance of wool so that it can nowhere be separated, not if you do your best to restore it with Neptune's flood, not if the whole sea would wash it out with all his waters. Again, is there not only one thing that solders gold to gold, and is not bronze joined to bronze by tin? How many other examples of the same sort are to be found! But to what purpose? You do not need anywhere ways so long and so round-about, and I must not use so much labour on this point, but it is best briefly to comprise many things in a few words: when the textures of things have fallen into such a relation to each other that the empty places of this answer to the full places of that, the empty places of that to the full of this, here is the best conjunction.

> It is also possible that some pairs may be held in coupling as if they were linked with sort of rings and hooks, which seems to be rather what happens between this stone and iron."

First, Lucretius refers to examples of what he considers as the best conjunction (*iunctura . . . optima*, 6.1086; cf. *inter se singlariter apta*, 6.1067), i.e. when the pores of two atomic structures are symmetrical in such a way that the projections of one substance come into contact and exactly fit into the cavities of the other *as if* there were no void in between (6.1085). This explanation immediately rings a bell, since it echoes Empedocles' similar explanation of jigsaw puzzle-like interpenetration, as transmitted by Aristotle (συναρμόττειν γὰρ τὰ κοῖλα τοῖς πυκνοῖς ἀλλήλων / "for their hollows fit into the dense parts of each other," B92 = A82a Inwood).

The intertextual hint at Empedocles becomes even more palpable when one goes back to the list of cases of cohesion itself, since many examples directly allude to Empedocles' fragments.[54] Lucretius exemplifies various categories of things joined together either indirectly by way of a visible or an invisible joining, or directly, when it pertains to things like colour or liquid mixture. When Lucretius refers to the example of wine that easily mixes with water, while pitch and oil do not (6.1072–1073), this brings to mind Empedocles' similar statement about the interaction of water with wine and oil ([ὕδωρ] οἴνῳ μᾶλλον †ἐναρίθμιον†, αὐτὰρ ἐλαίῳ / οὐκ ἐθέλει. / "[water] combines more with wine, but refuses with oil," B91).[55] Likewise, the image of the colour of the sea-purple shell uniting so closely with the substance of wool that nothing can wash it out (6.1074–1077) hints at Empedocles' pointing to the brightness of pale saffron mixing with linen, in order to provide an example of fast union from the combination of dissimilar ingredients (βύσσῳ δὲ †γλαυκῆς κρόκου† καταμίσγεται ἀκτίς, / "And the gleam of bright saffron mixes in with the linen," B93).[56] Bronze is joined to bronze by tin (6.1078–1079) in a way similar to Empedocles' image pertaining to the sterility of mules, that of soft copper mixing with soft tin, thus producing hard bronze (ὥσπερ τῷ καττιτέρῳ μειχθέντα τὸν χαλκόν / "like bronze mixed with tin," B92).[57] Therefore, although Lucretius seems to be aware of Empedocles' theory of interpenetration, he redefines it as a special case of ideal mixture with little but certainly *not entirely without void*. What is even more remarkable is that, although the substance of things is considered a kind of texture (*texturae*, 6.1084), the description of different conjunctions of this category is imbued throughout with the metaphors both of fitting together and of binding (*inter se singlariter apta*, 6.1067; *iungitur*, 6.1069; *compages*, 6.1071; *iungitur*, 6.1074; *copulat*, 6.1078; *iungatur*, 6.1079). This should be borne in mind, since wherever used this wording should call to mind this Empedoclean-like kind of mixture.

Lucretius then adds a second possibility in the form of a simile; objects can also be bound when the particles of the one are like hooks and those of the other like rings which the hooks can grasp (6.1087). According to Lucretius this seems to be rather like what happens between stone and iron. Why does Lucretius give preference to this explanation? Even though Epicurus'—now lost—full account may have given multiple causes of this miraculous phenomenon, Lucretius plausibly evokes here his master's vocabulary of the interlacing of the effluences and the corresponding explanation, as it can be recovered from the testimonia (Epicur. fr. 293 Us. = Gal. *Nat. Fac.* I. 14 = vol. 2 p. 45 Kühn):

Ἐπίκουρος μὲν οὖν καίτοι παραπλησίοις Ἀσκληπιάδη στοιχείοις πρὸς τὴν φυσιολογίαν χρώμενος ὅμως ὁμολογεῖ, πρὸς μὲν τῆς ἡρακλείας λίθου τὸν σίδηρον ἕλκεσθαι, πρὸς δὲ τῶν ἠλέκτρων τὰ κυρήβια καὶ πειρᾶταί γε καὶ τὴν αἰτίαν ἀποδιδόναι τοῦ φαινομένου. τὰς γὰρ ἀπορρεούσας ἀτόμους ἀπὸ τῆς λίθου ταῖς ἀπορρεούσαις ἀπὸ τοῦ σιδήρου τοῖς σχήμασιν οἰκείας εἶναί φησιν, ὥστε περιπλέκεσθαι ῥᾳδίως. προσκρουούσας οὖν αὐτὰς τοῖς συγκρίμασιν ἑκατέροις τῆς τε λίθου καὶ τοῦ σιδήρου κἄπειτ' εἰς τὸ μέσον ἀποπαλλομένας οὕτως ἀλλήλαις τε περιπλέκεσθαι καὶ συνεπισπᾶσθαι τὸν σίδηρον.

"Now Epicurus, despite the fact that he employs in his *Physics* elements similar to those of Asclepiades, yet allows that iron is attracted by the lodestone, and chaff by amber. He even tries to give the cause of the phenomenon. His view is that the atoms which flow from the stone are related in shape to those flowing from the iron, and so they become easily interlocked with one another; thus it is that, after colliding with each of the two compact masses (the stone and iron) they then rebound into the middle and so become entangled with each other, and draw the iron after them."

This image is probably thought of as better illustrating the existence of void. At the same time, as Bollack rightly remarks, in this way Lucretius conjures up the image of rings hanging in a chain that he actually strives to rationalize (*quippe catenam / saepe ex anellis reddit pendentibus ex se. /* "because it often makes a chain out of little rings hanging from it," 6.910–911); once more, the invisible is illuminated by the visible phenomenon.[58]

Having established the relationship between Lucretius and Empedocles within this passage, it is time to go back to the explanation of the magnet to quote its first part (6.1002–1021):

Principio fluere e lapide hoc permulta necessest
semina, sive aestum qui discutit aera plagis
inter qui lapidem ferrumque est cumque locatus.
hoc ubi inanitur spatium multusque vacefit 1005
in medio locus, extemplo primordia ferri
in vacuum prolapsa cadunt coniuncta, fit utque
anulus ipse sequatur eatque ita corpore toto.
nec res ulla magis primoribus ex elementis
indupedita suis arte conexa cohaeret 1010
quam validi ferri natura et frigidus horror.
quo minus est mirum, quod †dicitur ex elementis†
corpora si nequeunt e ferro plura coorta
in vacuum ferri, quin anulus ipse sequatur;
quod facit, et sequitur, donec pervenit ad ipsum 1015
iam lapidem caecisque in eo compagibus haesit.
hoc fit idem cunctas in partis: unde vacefit
cumque locus, sive e transverso sive superne,
corpora continuo in vacuum vicina feruntur;
quippe agitantur enim plagis aliunde, nec ipsa 1020
sponte sua sursum possunt consurgere in auras.

"In the first place, it must be that very many seeds flow out from this stone, or, let us say, a current which by its blows beats away all the air that lies between the stone and the iron. When this space is made empty and a large place becomes vacant between, at once the first-beginnings of the iron gliding forward into the empty space fall in a body together, and the result is that the ring itself follows and passes in this way as a whole. And indeed there is nothing that has its first elements more intertwined, nothing more closely connected together and coherent, than the substance of strong iron with its chilly roughness. For this reason it is less surprising . . . if the large number of bodies emanating from the iron cannot move into the void without the ring itself following; this it does, and follows until it has reached that very stone and clung to it by unseen attachments. The same thing happens in all directions: wherever an empty space is formed, whether on the sides or above, the neighbouring bodies at once are carried into the void; for they are impelled by blows from other directions, and they cannot of their own accord rise up into the air."

In this passage the two sets of metaphors, i.e. on the one hand those of fitting together and binding, and on the other that of weaving are directly juxtaposed. When Lucretius refers to the substance of iron, he uses the weaving metaphor; the iron's first beginnings are inherently intertwined, closely connected and coherent (*indupedita suis arte conexa cohaeret,* 6.1010).[59] In the description of the connection of the ring with the magnet, when the first beginnings of iron are detached to become effluences, Lucretius follows Empedocles' vocabulary; while the two objects will be connected like a jigsaw-puzzle, he envisages the effluences emitted from iron as closely fitting together with the magnet (*coniuncta,* 6.1007). At the same time, he refers to "hidden fastenings" that hold the magnet fast with iron (*caecisque in eo compagibus haesit,* 6.1016), recalling Empedocles' nails, this time though granting them a tangible adhering function.[60] On the other hand, the interlacing of the hooked atoms of the iron is also very strong; this is actually what causes the whole ring to follow the effluences that are emitted.

It could then be observed that, although all three metaphors (fitting together, binding, weaving) had plausibly been used interchangeably by Epicurus in order to visualize Empedocles' notion of elementary mixture, in his account of the magnet Lucretius appears to employ them in a more systematic way in his attempt to grasp and convey the invisible homogeneity of the universe. On the one hand, he translates into Latin the metaphor of weaving, the kernel of which could be easily spotted within the Atomic tradition. On the other, when he alludes to Empedocles' concept of interpenetration, he resorts to the images of fitting together and binding,—which were probably used by Empedocles—not to the metaphor of weaving. However, since these two metaphors carry with them strong Empedoclean connotations of elementary mixture without void and thus could prove misleading within an Epicurean context, he redefines them as another case of atomic mixture next to that of interlacing. By so doing, Lucretius, in contrast to Empedocles, consistently emphasizes the existence of void. Hereafter, the application of the metaphors of fitting together, binding and weaving employed interchangeably so as to express various types of close relationship—even between two dissimilar, yet inextricably linked things—is taken for granted in the course of the poem, without a major semantic differentiation as to the ideas conveyed. As might be expected, preference is given to one or the other, depending on the context.

There are more passages in which Lucretius discusses Empedocles' ideas by resorting to technological metaphors. As will become clear, Lucretius keeps Epicurus' play between the metaphor of fitting together and that of weaving; still, he seems to suggest that those of fitting together and binding are more appropriate for Empedoclean and Empedoclean-like intermingling, i.e. elementary interpenetration with void.

Lucretius refutes Empedocles' theory of the four roots by describing the elementary masses of water, earth and sky as atomic compounds that each have a different "texture." In order to illustrate their mortality, he asks Memmius to recognize that "these three textures so interwoven one day shall consign to destruction" (*tria talia texta, / una dies dabit exitio,* 5.94–95); he thus suggests that the Empedoclean elements are prone to "unravelling." At the same time, Lucretius embraces Empedocles' vocabulary of "fitting together" in order to describe the articulation of the four elementary masses out of the original chaos, when like was united with like, in a context that carries clear echoes of Empedocles' cosmogony (*coniuncta,* 5.441; *paresque / cum paribus iungi res,* 5.443–444; cf. Empedocles B37).[61] In a similar way, when Lucretius gives his account of rival cosmological theories in Book 1, he creates a homogeneous imagery and refers to their teaching of elementary mixture too as a process of "fastening together" in couples of what were thought of as first beginnings of things, i.e. air to fire and earth to water (*aera iungentes igni terramque liquori, /* "joining air to fire and earth to water," 1.713).

From a different perspective, Lucretius hints at Empedocles' technological imagery in connection with similar theories about the creation and evolution of the human species. As was observed long ago, Lucretius' non-teleological theory about the survival of the fittest echoes closely Empedocles' zoogony.[62] Within this framework, it is equally remarkable that Lucretius assimilates Empedocles' metaphor of "fitting together" in order to depict how certain creatures had their limbs *fastened together* (*vinctaque,* 5.842) in such a way that they could not use or move them, and therefore were doomed to extinction, since they were practically limbless (*vinctaque membrorum per totum corpus adhaesu, /* "some bound fast with all their limbs adhering to their bodies," 5.842. Cf. εἰλίποδ' ἀκριτόχειρα [καὶ] βουγενῆ ἀνδρόπρωρα / "with twisted feet and a hundred hands" and "oxlike [animals] with human faces," B60 = Plut. *Adv. Col.* 28.1123B).[63] Lucretius may echo Empedocles' metaphor also in the next stage of evolution, that of survival of the fittest species in the struggle for life; when he refers to the "fateful chains" (*indupedita suis fatalibus omnia vinclis, /* "being all hampered by their own fateful chains," 5.876) that foreshadow the extinction of certain species, this recalls Empedocles' rivets of affection (γόμφοις . . . καταστόργοις, B87) which, however, perform exactly the opposite function, that of keeping together.[64]

Despite the correspondences between Empedocles' and Epicurus' accounts, according to Plutarch Empedocles' cross-species hybrids were harshly derided by the Epicureans. That is why at the end of the section

Lucretius cautiously distances himself from Empedocles' compound creatures and launches a polemical attack against the existence of Centaurs and double-natured creatures (5.878–924):

> *Sed neque Centauri fuerunt, nec tempore in ullo*   878
> *esse queunt duplici natura et corpore bino*
> *ex alienigenis membris compacta, potestas*   880
> *hinc illinc †parvis ut non sit pars† esse potissit.*
> *id licet hinc quamvis hebeti cognoscere corde.* (5.878–882)

"But Centaurs never existed, nor at any time can there be creatures of double nature and twofold body combined together of incompatible limbs, such that the powers of the two halves can be fairly balanced. Here is a proof that will convince the dullest wit."

> *nam quod multa fuere in terris semina rerum*   916
> *tempore quo primum tellus animalia fudit,*
> *nil tamen est signi mixtas potuisse creari*
> *inter se pecudes compactaque membra animantum,*
> *propterea quia quae de terris nunc quoque abundant—*   920
> *herbarum genera ac fruges arbustaque laeta—*
> *non tamen inter se possunt complexa creari,*
> *sed res quaeque suo ritu procedit, et omnes*
> *foedere naturae certo discrimina servant.* (5.916–924)

"For although there were many seeds of things in the soil at the time when first the earth poured forth the animals, that is nevertheless no proof that creatures of mixed growth could be made, and limbs of various creatures joined into one; because the various kinds of plants and the corn and the luxuriant trees, which even now spring in abundance from the earth, nevertheless cannot be produced interwoven together, but each thing proceeds after its own fashion, and all by fixed law of nature preserve their distinctions."

Here Lucretius applies both the "fitting together" and the "weaving" metaphor; incompatible limbs could never have been *stuck together* (*compacta*, 5.880; *compactaque*, 5.919), nor could they become *interwoven* (*complexa*, 5.922). Whereas in Book 5 Lucretius refutes the existence of Empedocles' creatures at the macroscopic level, in Book 2 he offers a similar account that relies on the fundamental Epicurean tenet, which now pertains to the microcosm, that not all atomic combinations are possible (2.700–717):

> *Nec tamen omnimodis conecti posse putandum est*   700
> *omnia; nam volgo fieri portenta videres,*
> *semiferas hominum species existere, et altos*
> *interdum ramos egigni corpore vivo,*
> *multaque conecti terrestria membra marinis,*
> *tum flammam taetro spirantis ore Chimaeras*   705
> *pascere naturam per terras omniparentis.*
> *quorum nil fieri manifestum est, omnia quando*
> *seminibus certis certa genetrice creata*
> *conservare genus crescentia posse videmus.*
> *scilicet id certa fieri ratione necessust.*   710
> *nam sua cuique cibis ex omnibus intus in artus*
> *corpora discedunt conexaque convenienti*
> *efficiunt motus; at contra aliena videmus*
> *reicere in terras naturam, multaque caecis*
> *corporibus fugiunt e corpore percita plagis,*   715
> *quae neque conecti quoquam potuere neque intus*
> *vitalis motus consentire atque imitari.*

"However, it must not be thought that all can be conjoined in all ways: for then you would commonly see monstrosities come into being, shapes of men arising that would be half beasts, lofty branches at times sprouting from a living body, parts of terrestrial creatures often conjoined with creatures of the sea, Chimaeras again, breathing flame from noisome throats, pastured by nature over the lands that produce everything. But that none of these things happen is manifest, since we see that all things bred from fixed seeds by a fixed mother are able to conserve their kind as they grow. Assuredly this must come about in a fixed way. For in each thing, its own proper bodies are spread abroad through the frame within from all its foods, and being combined produce the appropriate motions; but contrariwise we see alien elements to be thrown back by nature upon the earth, and many, beaten by blows, escape from the body with their invisible bodies, which were not able to combine with any part nor within the body to feel the life-giving motions with it and imitate them."

Depending on the different types of atoms that come into union, the atoms can or cannot perform the appropriate motions so as to *interweave* and form a compound (*conecti*, 2.700; *conecti*, 2.704; *conexaque*, 2.712; *conecti*, 2.716). As a result, monsters such as the Centaurs, tree-men, Scylla and the Chimera could never have existed, because they would have been dissolved straightaway at the atomic level.[65]

Finally, by means of the metaphor of binding, Lucretius hints at and redefines Empedocles' Aphrodite and her cohesive power synchronically as well as diachronically. As Clay rightly points out, when Venus appears in the proem as "causing to propagate" (*propagent,* 1.20) animal kind, the verb "propagate" carries a metaphor which is brought into focus by its etymology, which is apparent in the Greek πηγνύναι (to peg) and could easily allude to Empedocles' corresponding images.[66] In Book 4 Lucretius demythologizes Empedocles' Aphrodite by disclosing the material nature of love; the lovers are physically bound together as if by a bond (4.1201–1208):[67]

> *nonne vides etiam quos mutua saepe voluptas*
> *vinxit, ut in vinclis communibus excrucientur?*
> *in triviis cum saepe canes, discedere aventes,*
> *divorsi cupide summis ex viribu' tendunt,*   1204
> *quom interea validis Veneris compagibus haerent.*
> *quod facerent numquam, nisi mutua gaudia nossent*
> *quae lacere in fraudem possent vinctosque tenere.*
> *quare etiam atque etiam, ut dico, est communi' voluptas.*

"Do you not see also, when mutual pleasure has enchained a pair, how they are often tormented in their common chains? For often dogs at the crossways, desiring to part, pull hard in different directions with all their strength, when all the while they are held fast in the strong couplings of Venus. But this they would never do, unless they both felt these joys which were enough to lure them into the trap and to hold them enchained. Therefore again and again I say, the pleasure is for both."

In this context Lucretius applies the same technical word *compages* (*validis Veneris compagibus,* 4.1205) denoting close connection, that he also employs in his account of the magnet. Even more strikingly, when Lucretius refers to the compatibility of human seeds he employs the word *harmonia* (*harmoniae Veneris,* 4.1248), which carries vivid Empedoclean undertones (Ἁρμονίης κόλλησιν / "by the gluing of Harmony," B96.4).[68] Therefore, when Lucretius describes the first sexual intercourse of primitive human beings as a *fitting together* which was incited by Venus (*et Venus in silvis iungebat corpora amantum;* / "And Venus joined the bodies of lovers in the woods," 5.962), as Campbell rightly points out, this may ironically evoke the role of Empedocles' Φιλότης, who combined the roots and fashioned the human organs at the very beginning of the world (τόσσ᾽ ὅσα *νῦν γεγάασι συναρμοσθέντ᾽ Ἀφροδίτη* / "which have now arisen, fitted together by Aphrodite," B71.4).[69]

A more thorough analysis of Lucretius' technological metaphors of fitting together, binding and weaving should now be undertaken.[70] These metaphors are first applied by negation to the most fundamental level of reality, that of individual atoms. Henceforth, they radiate in several directions and to different levels of the homogeneously structured universe. Along with the process of continuous creation, the reverse process, that of destruction, equally operative and pervasive in the universe, is also described metaphorically in terms of either a gradual and partial or a more massive, thoroughgoing dissolution of the atomic formations and an unravelling of their inner texture; the atoms are always the beginning and the end of these processes, the basic material out of which everything originates and which remains intact after the various material substances have been separated.

More specifically, in laying the foundations of the atomic doctrine, contrary to Empedocles' concept (1.746–752), Lucretius puts forward the atomic principle of indivisibility.[71] Since everything that is subject to dissolution cannot be eternal and given that the atoms are eternal, despite the existence of minimal parts "these can neither be dissolved by blows, when struck from without, nor again be pierced inwardly and decomposed" (*haec neque dissolvi plagis extrinsecus icta / possunt nec porro penitus penetrata retexi,* 1.528–529).[72] In the same spirit, the atoms are also characterized with the adjectives *stipatus* and *solidus,* which denote precisely the absolute absence of void from their body (e.g. *sunt igitur solida primordia simplicitate, / quae minimis stipata cohaerent partibus arte,* / "The first-beginnings, therefore, are of solid singleness, made of these smallest parts closely packed and cohering together," 1.609–610).[73] The idea of unity is also conveyed through a more forceful metaphor, that of the impossibility of further breaking the atomic body, which underlines what would be the permanently negative result if this process were true (*Denique si nullam finem natura parasset / frangendis rebus, iam corpora materiai / usque redacta forent aevo frangente priore,* / "Moreover, if nature had provided no limit to the breaking-up of things, by this time the bodies of matter would have been reduced by the breaking of ages past," 1.551–553).[74]

When the indivisibility and the durability of the first beginnings are established, Lucretius among other alternative names calls the atoms *exordia,* thus indicating that these will be the first threads of creation (*exordia rerum / cunctarum quam sint subtilia* / "how fine are the first elements of all things," 4.114–115). In addition, he states that there is a great variety in the shapes of atoms (2.333–729). In line with this, he describes the nature of certain atomic shapes as *perplexa* or *perplicatus,* both meaning "entwined."[75] In this particular case, although he draws on the Epicurean terminology, i.e. the words πλεκτικός and περιπλεκόμενος, he slightly deviates from it. As Don Fowler rightly remarks, Lucretius changes the prefix from περι- into *per-* to stress the notion of "completely, thoroughly," using a word that had lost its literal meaning long before; still, the commoner meaning of the word, i.e. "muddled up" or "confusing" is not erased, conveying thus the notion of the fortuitous atomic motion.[76] Lucretius assigns to other atoms the characteristic of being hooked (*hamatus*).[77] These inherent attributes of specific atoms are highly significant, since they condition and foreshadow the analogous behaviour of the atoms, that is their tendency to become interwoven or bound together into atomic compounds. However, contrary to Epicurus, who had a wide range of names corresponding to the variety of the atomic shapes,[78] Lucretius confesses his lack of geometrical terminology in Latin to describe every single category (*nec reperire figurarum tot nomina quot sunt / principiis, unde haec oritur variantia rerum* / "nor find names enough to fit the shapes assumed by the first-beginnings from which arises this variety in things," 3.317–318).[79] Due to this linguistic deficiency, when Lucretius describes *interpenetration* on the atomic level, he refers again to hooked or branched atoms, as if he were talking about mixture by atomic interlacing (*Denique quae nobis durata ac spissa videntur, / haec magis hamatis inter sese esse necessest / et quasi ramosis alte compacta teneri.* / "Again, whatever seems to us hardened and close set must consist of elements more closely hooked and held knit deeply together by branch-like shapes," 2.444–446).

In any case, every atomic compound, from the very basic aggregations up to more complex structures such as our bodies, and ultimately the whole universe, is a mixture of atoms and void. The ratio of void to atoms within the atomic compositions affects their density or looseness. The diversity of the atomic structures is partly due to such variations. For that reason, through the metaphor of weaving, Lucretius describes various substances with reference to their internal texture. The words *conexus* and *nexus* thus acquire a technical value, the former expressing precisely the variety as well as the limits of possible atomic interweavings, the latter denoting the material connections themselves.[80]

In a similar way, while Lucretius uses the word *foedus* to denote the more abstract notion of law, as has been seen above in detail, at the same time, regarding Reich's identification of *foedera naturai* with the Epicurean basic compounds (συγκρίσεις) and his translation of the phrase as bond,[81] Long rightly notes that "Lucretius is playing on the meaning of *foedus* as both something concrete—a bond or union of atoms with congruent shapes—and the more abstract notion of law."[82] However, since this idea of *foedus* as bond is rather innovative, as I have argued elsewhere, it seems very plausible that in this case as well Lucretius looks back at Empedocles' metaphor of oath, the one exchanged between Love and Strife (ὅς σφιν ἀμοιβαῖος πλατέος παρ᾽ ἐλήλαται ὅρκου / "a time of exchange for them, which has been defined by a broad oath," B30.3).[33] More precisely, the word ὅρκος is etymologically connected with ἕρκος and ὁρκάνη, which means something that constrains, or an enclosure. Therefore, at some point the oath was thought of as something that literally binds and constrains;[84] however, this sense of a binding force became gradually weaker. It seems very likely that, following Epicurus' theory of language, Lucretius looks back to the first meaning of an oath (πρῶτον ἐννόημα), revives this concept of binding that was already latent in Empedocles' oath and transfers it to the *foedera* that, as it has already been argued above, he employs as the Latin equivalent to the Greek metaphor.[85] As a result, he broadens the semantic scope of *foedera* by bringing all three meanings—the political (agreement), the abstract (natural law) and the material (physical bond)—into play for his own philosophical and poetical purposes. This evoked etymological connection of *foedera* with the notion of binding will prove to be particularly important when it comes to Lucretius' intertextual dialogue with Stoic ideas which will be revisited in the end of this section.

At this point, we should turn back to another metaphor that Lucretius employs as an alternative to that of *foedera naturai* in order to convey the notion of natural law, namely the image of the deep-set stone pillar marking the boundary between properties (*alte terminus haerens*), and explore the interconnection between those two metaphors. By employing these two metaphors supplementarily, he seems to exploit the semantic association of the Greek oath with the concept of enclosure, by disclosing and unfolding this underlying meaning. In order to clarify this assertion, we should turn to a passage in which the two metaphors are used together. In Book 1 Lucretius discusses one of the main principles of Epicurean philosophy, namely that the first beginnings are solid, indestructible and unchangeable. In order to support his claim, he draws one of his proofs from the fact that living things in their species show a certain immutability from generation to generation (1.584–598):

> *Denique iam quoniam generatim reddita finis*
> *crescendi rebus constat vitamque tenendi,*   585
> *et quid quaeque queant per foedera naturai,*

> *quid porro nequeant, sancitum quandoquidem extat,*
> *nec commutatur quicquam, quin omnia constant*
> *usque adeo, variae volucres ut in ordine cunctae*
> *ostendant maculas generalis corpore inesse,*   590
> *inmutabili' materiae quoque corpus habere*
> *debent nimirum; nam si primordia rerum*
> *commutari aliqua possent ratione revicta,*
> *incertum quoque iam constet quid possit oriri,*
> *quid nequeat, finita potestas denique cuique*   595
> *quanam sit ratione atque alte terminus haerens,*
> *nec totiens possint generatim saecla referre*
> *naturam mores victum motusque parentum.*

"Again, since a limit has been fixed for the growth of things after their kind and for their tenure of life, and since it stands decreed what each can do by the ordinances of nature, and also what each cannot do, and since nothing changes, but all things are constant to such a degree that all the different birds show in succession marks upon their bodies to distinguish their kind, they must also have beyond a doubt a body of immutable matter. For if the first-beginnings of things could be changed, being in any way overmastered, it would also now remain uncertain what could arise and what could not, in a word in what way each thing has its power limited and its deep-set boundary mark, nor could the generations so often repeat after their kind the nature, manners, living, and movement of their parents."

Lucretius claims that, since nature imposes a certain limit on the growth, life and powers of things, something indestructible exists in things. Strikingly, the metaphorical phrases *foedera naturai* and *alte terminus haerens* which are employed here bearing equal semantic weight, share the same connection that we discern between ὅρκος and ἕρκος: in both cases an agreement leads to the establishment of limits. This connection helps one to further explore and define the content of *foedera:* just like the Empedoclean oath, the *foedera* are in effect a limitation of powers; they are "boundary pacts." In other words, according to Epicurean physics, atomic associations cannot go beyond a certain limit, but must stop at certain points; the *foedera naturai* crystallize the exact location of this limit.

Along the same lines, by means of the imagery of weaving Lucretius describes other atomic combinations in an even more technical context. This is the case especially in Book 4, when Lucretius describes the *simulacra,* the invisible thin films thrown off from the outermost surface of things which are responsible for vision. In order to make the transition from the visible to the invisible, Lucretius picks up various types of atomic aggregations that are discharged from the surface of things; taking for granted their ultimate material and structural similarity, he compares them on the basis of their more or less close texture (e.g. smoke and heat: *diffusa solute* / "loosely diffused abroad," 4.55; the skin of crickets and snakes, the caul of calves: *contexta magis condensaque* / "more close-knit and condensed," 4.57; films: *subtili praedita filo* / "of finest texture," 4.88; *textura praedita rara* / "with a rarefied texture," 4.196). One should just decrease the degree of rarity in these visible textures so as to perceive and firmly establish the existence of the unseen realities. Yet, once again the ultimate level of existence can be reached only by projection of the mind (4.724–731):

> *Principio hoc dico, rerum simulacra vagari*
> *multa modis multis in cunctas undique partis*   725
> *tenvia, quae facile inter se iunguntur in auris,*
> *obvia cum veniunt, ut aranea bratteaque auri.*
> *quippe etenim multo magis haec sunt tenvia textu*
> *quam quae percipiunt oculos visumque lacessunt,*   729
> *corporis haec quoniam penetrant per rara cientque*
> *tenvem animi naturam intus sensumque lacessunt.*

"In the first place I tell you that many images of things are moving about in many ways and in all directions, very thin, which easily unite in the air when they meet, being like spider's web or leaf of gold. In truth these are much more thin in texture than those which take the eyes and assail the vision, since these penetrate through the interstices of the body, and awake the thin substance of the mind within, and assail the sense."

While Lucretius compares films that unite in the air when they meet (4.726) to a spider's web or leaves of gold (4.727), one should always bear in mind that films are far thinner in their texture (4.728).

Again, when it comes to proving the atomic nature of the human soul and its close connection with our body, Lucretius describes the unique texture of the soul, which is made up out of small, fine atoms (e.g. *tenui . . . textura*, 3.209). The material substance of the spirit also becomes apparent through the process of its dissolution (e.g. *ocius et citius dissolvi in corpora prima,* / "[the spirit] is more speedily dissolved into its first bodies," 3.438). Next, although body and soul differ in their atomic structure, Lucretius, wishing to emphasize their intimate interrelation, describes the indissoluble link that unites them by envisaging the soul *interlaced* through veins, flesh and sinews (e.g. *ergo animam totam perparvis esse necessest / seminibus, nexam per venas viscera nervos, /* "Accordingly the whole spirit must consist of very small seeds, being interlaced through veins, flesh, and sinews," 3.216–217).[86] This fundamental relationship is also conveyed by the metaphor of joining together (e.g. *ut videas, quoniam coniunctast causa salutis, / coniunctam quoque naturam consistere eorum. /* "so that you may see that, since conjunction is necessary to their existence, so also theirs must be a joint nature," 3.348–349).[87] Moreover, since in this case as well Lucretius aims at elucidating the nature of an unseen phenomenon, he feels that perhaps his analogies are inadequate. That is why he does not hesitate to invite the reader to conjure up a better example of an even closer link than those he himself proposes (*sive aliud quid vis potius coniunctius ei / fingere /* "or any other similitude you may choose for a closer conjunction," 3.556–557).[88]

At this point, it would be very interesting to have a look at Diogenes' of Oinoanda fr. 37.I.7–12 Smith:

> [. . .] ἀλλ' οὖν γε
> τὸν ὅλον ἄνθρωπον δι-
> έζωσεν οὕτως καὶ ἀντέ-
> δησε δεζμουμένη ὥσ-
> περ τῶν ὀπῶν ὁ βραχύ-
> τατος ἄπλατον γάλα.

"yet it [the soul] girdles the whole man and, while being itself confined, binds him in its turn, just as the minutest quantity of acid juice binds a huge quantity of milk."

When Diogenes compares the relationship between soul and body with acid juice that binds a huge quantity of milk, he evokes Empedocles' B33 (ὡς δ' ὅτ' ὀπὸς γάλα λευκὸν ἐγόμφωσεν καὶ ἔδησε / "As when the sap [of the fig tree] has riveted and set white milk"). This could mean that Epicurus himself had already drawn the analogy from Empedocles and accordingly that Lucretius follows his master in appropriating—but at the same time also developing—Empedocles' metaphorical imagery for his own demonstrative purposes.

Along the same lines, Lucretius applies both the metaphor of binding and that of joining together in order to establish the close interdependence between spirit and mind (e.g. metaphor of binding: *hoc anima atque animus vincti sunt foedere semper. /* "Such is the alliance by which spirit and mind are for ever bound," 3.416; metaphor of fitting together: *atque animam verbi causa cum dicere pergam, / mortalem esse docens, animum quoque dicere credas, / quatenus est unum inter se coniunctaque res est. /* "and when for example I speak of spirit, showing it to be mortal, believe me to speak also of mind, inasmuch at it is one thing and a combined nature," 3.422–424). Commenting on line 3.424 West notes the syntactical play—the ambiguous *inter se* (itself? themselves?) placed between the two singular complements—which is relevant to the sense, "indeed a linguistic embodiment of it"—in his words—suggesting that soul and mind are one phenomenon, a third united *inter se*. West calls this phenomenon "syntactical onomatopoeia, being syntactical shapes which correspond to logical patterns or intellectual concepts or emotional states."[89] Similarly, we should also point out the double elisions in 3.416, which reflect and strengthen further the interpenetration of mind and soul.

This image—in turn—serves as an additional analogy when Lucretius deals with another sort of close interdependence, the connection between the earth and the atmosphere (5.550–563):[90]

> *Praeterea grandi tonitru concussa repente*   550
> *terra supra quae se sunt concutit omnia motu;*
> *quod facere haud ulla posset ratione, nisi esset*
> *partibus aeriis mundi caeloque revincta;*
> *nam communibus inter se radicibus haerent*
> *ex ineunte aevo coniuncta atque uniter apta.*   555
>   *Nonne vides etiam quam magno pondere nobis*
> *sustineat corpus tenuissima vis animai*
> *propterea quia tam coniuncta atque uniter apta est?*
> *denique iam saltu pernici tollere corpus*
> *quid potis est nisi vis animae quae membra gubernat?*
> *iamne vides quantum tenuis natura valere*   561
> *possit, ubi est coniuncta gravi cum corpore, ut aer*
> *coniunctus terris et nobis est animi vis?*

"Besides, the earth shaken suddenly with a mighty thunderclap shakes all that is above itself with its motion, which it could not by any means do, unless it were bound fast to the airy parts of the world and to the sky. For they cling together joined and knit together into one by common roots from the beginning of their existence.

Do you not see also how the most thin essence of the spirit sustains our body for all its great weight, just because it is so joined together and knit up with it into one? Again, what is able actually to lift the body in a vigorous leap, except the power of the spirit which guides the limbs? Now do you see how great can be the power of a thin nature when it is

> joined together with a heavy body, as air is joined together with earth
> and the power of mind joined together with us?"

By revealing the homogeneous structure of the natural world (earth: *coniunctam atque uniter aptam,* 5.537; *revincta,* 5.553; *coniuncta atque uniter apta,* 5.555 → human body: *coniuncta atque uniter apta,* 5.558; heavy body in general: *coniuncta,* 5.562 → human body and earth: *coniunctus,* 5.563), Lucretius is ultimately empowered to evoke other similar correlations and thus to elucidate retrospectively the obscure concept in question.

In a similar vein, Lucretius applies the "joining together" metaphor in order to translate an abstract Epicurean term into Latin, the so-called ἀΐδια συμβεβηκότα or παρακολουθοῦντα, i.e. the properties of a body, its permanent accompaniments without which it cannot be thought as such.[91] When Lucretius discusses these properties he calls them *coniuncta,* thus putting a gloss on the abstract Greek terms and commenting on their philosophical meaning (*coniunctum est id quod nusquam sine permitiali / discidio potis est seiungi seque gregari,* / "A property is that which without destructive dissolution can never be separated and disjoined," 1.451–452).[92] As Sedley remarks, in this case Lucretius coins a technical term, while Greek lacks one single word for the concept.[93] Given the function of this metaphor in other contexts, where it is employed to denote various types of *indissoluble* links, when Lucretius applies it with reference to the relationship between the atomic compound and its properties, he helps his pupil to perceive the abstract idea that a property can never be separated and disjoined from the body without destructive dissolution. Lucretius exemplifies further the sense of his metaphorical image by way of another sort of "syntactical onomatopoieia," that of tmesis (*seque gregari,* 1.452). To put it in Hinds' words "at the very point where he is writing not just of separation in a body, but of separation *and* fatal dissolution, Lucretius has produced a tmesis which, besides (like all other tmeses) enacting a separation, also gestures interestingly towards a complete dissolution of sense in a word concerned."[94]

Lastly, the conventional self-referential representation of poetic creation as weaving and of text as a web is now turned into an integral part of the cosmic order, where everything, even the poem itself, is seen as a small piece of the cosmic fabric (e.g. *pertexere dictis* / "weaving the web of this discourse," 1.418).[95] Hence, the use of this metaphor is imposed by the philosophical system and the conventional metaphor turns out to be an inevitable choice.[96]

Let us now focus on the process of the *crumbling of the atomic compound,* be it an inanimate thing, a living body or the entire world. Lucretius seems to distinguish various factors which threaten to overturn the order of the first beginnings that constitute a mortal creation, related not only to the force of the destructive blow, but also to the tightness or looseness of the creation's texture. Destruction can be due either to an external blow, which will shatter the compound at once, or—if less violent—will impinge on the knots that bind together the atoms and will untie them, or again to a disintegrating force, which will affect the atomic texture. This division is reflected in the use of the metaphors of breaking, unfastening and unravelling respectively (1.215–224):[97]

> *Huc accedit ut quidque in sua corpora rursum*   215
> *dissolvat natura neque ad nilum interemat res.*
> *nam si quid mortale e cunctis partibus esset,*
> *ex oculis res quaeque repente erepta periret;*
> *nulla vi foret usus enim quae partibus eius*
> *discidium parere et nexus exsolvere posset.*   220
> *quod nunc, aeterno quia constant semine quaeque,*
> *donec vis obiit quae res diverberet ictu*
> *aut intus penetret per inania dissolvatque,*
> *nullius exitium patitur natura videri.*

"Add to this that nature resolves everything again into its elements, and does not reduce things to nothing. For if anything were perishable in all its parts, each thing would then perish in a moment snatched away from our sight. For there would be no need of any force, to cause disruption of its parts and dissolve their connexions. But as it is, because the seed of all things is everlasting, nature allows no destruction of anything to be seen, until a force has met it, sufficient to shatter it with a blow, or to penetrate within through the void places and break it up."

Behind all these mechanical processes we may recognize as the ultimate moving power the sinister worldly metamorphosis of *Natura* (*quove eadem rursum natura perempta resolvat,* / "and into which the same nature again reduces them when dissolved," 1.57). The various agents of Lucretian Strife which are directly related to these physical phenomena should be now briefly identified.

Although all the Empedoclean roots are elsewhere depicted as fighting one another, thus undermining the universal equilibrium and ensuring the eternal cycle,[98] Lucretius singles out some of them more prominently as physical factors of dissolution. From this point of view, the action of fire is dominant, often in the form of the sun or a thunderbolt or even of disease.[99] Fire acts upon different substances and instigates their gradual decomposition, either by unravelling their texture or by dissolving their inner knots.[100]

Lucretius offers the example of vessels whose texture becomes loosened and rarefied and the particles of wine within dispersed under the impact of heat (6.231–235):

> *curat item vasis integris vina repente*   231
> *diffugiant, quia nimirum facile omnia circum*
> *conlaxat rareque facit lateramina vasi*
> *adveniens calor eius, et insinuatus in ipsum*
> *mobiliter solvens differt primordia vini.*   235

> "Also it makes wine suddenly evaporate without harming the vessels, doubtless because its heat approaching easily relaxes all the earthenware of the vessel and makes it porous, then penetrating into the vessel itself with quick movement dissolves and disperses abroad the first-beginnings of the wine."

The water of rivers evaporates as if the sun unravels it (*radiisque retexens aetherius sol,* / "as does the sun on high unravelling it with his rays," 5.267),[101] while the water in wells and springs or ice in general when shaken by the sun discharge the cold they contain and loosen their knots, thus becoming porous (*quasi saepe gelum, quod continet in se,* / *mittit et exsolvit glaciem nodosque relaxat.* / "just as water often discharges the cold which it contains, and melts the ice and loosens its knots," 6.877–878). The action of pain and disease penetrating our body and equally crumbling our mind is analogous (*quare animum quoque dissolvi fateare necessest,* / *quandoquidem penetrant in eum contagia morbi;* / "Therefore, you must confess that the mind also is dissolved, since the contagion of disease penetrates within it," 3.470–471). On the other hand, wind can act upon the texture of a cloud, causing its diffusion and a flash of lightning without noise (*nam cum ventus eas leviter diducit euntis* / *dissolvitque,* / "For when the wind gently disperses them abroad and diffuses them abroad as they pass," 6.215–216).

As far as human beings are concerned, additional causes are referred to as worldly agents of destruction. For example, old age may creep over our limbs and break down the barriers of life within us (*ut verear ne tarda prius per membra senectus* / *serpat et in nobis vitai claustra resolvat,* / " that I fear lest laggard age may creep over our limbs and break down the barriers of life within us," 1.414–415).[102] More generally, fatal blows are blamed for depriving a creature of life and sensation, by unfettering the bonds that join together soul and body (*vitalis animae nodos a corpore solvit* / "[until the shock] loosens from the body the vital knots of the soul," 2.950)[103] By calling these purely material knots "vital," Lucretius may hint at the analogous function of the Empedoclean rivets (γόμφοις . . . καταστόργοις, B87). Yet, despite their deadly impact, these threatening powers are paradoxically called "*makers* of death" (*nam dolor ac morbus leti fabricator uterquest,* / "for both pain and disease are makers of death," 3.472). By assigning to them—and retrospectively to all the other destructive powers just mentioned—the role of a craftsman, Lucretius appears to point to the simultaneous inverse process of creation. In the same way, death is elsewhere said to "conjoin others with others," being quite surprisingly responsible for creation (*inde aliis aliud coniungit,* / "then it [death] conjoins others with others," 2.1004).

In addition, fear, care, love and any other feelings which carry negative connotations are depicted as being fastened tightly to the texture of human body and soul, since they are -according to Epicurus- material in their substance.[104] In order to fight them, Lucretius arms his pupil with the insight of the metaphors in question; once we perceive the actual structure of things, we are empowered to put into action by ourselves the unbinding mechanism for therapeutic purposes. In this case, although the releasing of the bonds brings about alteration within the atomic combinations and therefore a certain atomic death, this does not entail a thorough disintegration of both parts of the atomic union. On the contrary, this kind of deliberately caused atomic dissolution simultaneously generates an enhanced creation, that is a human being enjoying a life liberated from excruciating passions.

More specifically, early in the poem Lucretius proclaims that, whilst superstition is closely tied to man's mind, the salutary effects of his poem consist exactly in the slackening of those bonds (*artis / religionum animum nodis exsolvere pergo,* / "I proceed to unloose the mind from the close knots of superstition," 1.931–932). At this point, the poet obviously hints at the etymology of the word *religio,* which is associated with the verb *religare* (meaning "to bind fast").[105] Furthermore, whereas the expression "free from care" (*curaque solutum,* 2.46) would be considered in other texts a dead metaphor, it recaptures here its latent meaning, that of literal disentanglement, once it is read according to the Epicurean doctrine for the proper use of language.[106]

Within the same framework, in contrast to Empedocles' Aphrodite, Lucretius proposes the physical nature of Epicurean love, which binds the two lovers together. Even if one gets imprisoned in Venus' nets, Lucretius admonishes his pupil that, although it is difficult, there is still hope for setting oneself free; once we realize the material basis of love, our sentimental relief is guaranteed. In order to illustrate this, Lucretius draws an elaborate image of hunting with nets, assimilating and distorting conventional erotic imagery for his didactic purposes (4.1146–1152):[107]

> *nam vitare, plagas in amoris ne laciamur,*
> *non ita difficile est quam captum retibus ipsis*
> *exire et validos Veneris perrumpere nodos.*
> *et tamen implicitus quoque possis inque peditus*
> *effugere infestum, nisi tute tibi obvius obstes*   1150
> *et praetermittas animi vitia omnia primum*
> *aut quae corpori' sunt eius, quam praepetis ac vis.*

"For to avoid being lured into the snares of love is not so difficult as, when you are caught in the toils, to get out and break through the strong knots of Venus. Yet you can escape the danger even when involved and entangled, unless you stand in you own way, and begin by overlooking all faults of mind and body in her whom you prefer and desire."

In this case, the agent (Venus) and her tool (the mesh) coincide, both standing in for atomic love. The tmesis in line 4.1149 (*inque peditus*) foreshadows and underlines this possibility for extricating oneself from Venus' snares. Retrospectively, this healing method should be equally valid for all other disturbing feelings.

Before concluding the discussion, a very significant instance should be considered, in which Lucretius finds the metaphor of weaving inadequate to be deployed in the philosophical context in question. While Lucretius introduces the idea of the swerve and of free will (2.216–293), he denies the possibility that all motion may always be like an *unbreakable long chain* (*Denique si semper motus conectitur omnis / et vetere exoritur motu novus ordine certo, /* "Again, if all motion is always one long chain, and new motion arises out of the old in order invariable," 2.251–252).

This very metaphor was also found in many Chrysippean fragments, used in order to conceptualize and visualize the operations of a continuous cosmic πνεῦμα, which pervades the whole universe and keeps it coherent. As Lapidge remarks, for the Stoics "all parts [of the universe] must be bound temporally as well as spatially, such that every event is linked to every other. The spatial bond was described as a δεσμός; by the same token, the temporal bond of fate was described as an ἐπισύνδεσις. Through this bond, all events are linked together in a cosmic chain. [. . .] Associated with the metaphor of a chain of fate went metaphors of weaving, so that fate was described variously as a 'texture' (συμπλοκή, ἐπιπλοκή) of causes and events."[108]

It would seem quite implausible to claim that a metaphor, which was found in both Stoic and Epicurean texts in similar contexts, though conveying different philosophical ideas, had simply enjoyed an independent parallel life by coincidence. Rather, Lucretius probably picks up and manipulates the cardinal Stoic metaphor of the temporal bond for the concept of fate in order to refute the cosmological doctrine of determinism.[109] While embracing their wording, Lucretius shifts its semantic focus from the continuous Stoic matter onto the atomic compounds themselves, so as make clear that there does not exist an unbreakable "chain" of fate such as the Stoics believed in. This is a clear case of Lucretius' cunning intertextual play, a creative borrowing and simultaneously a direct reply to the rival philosophical system.

In this connection, we might revisit Lucretius' metaphor of agreement (*foedera*), which is used in this context, instead of the expected Stoic metaphor of law (2.253–255):

> *nec declinando faciunt primordia motus*
> *principium quoddam quod fati foedera rumpat,*
> *ex infinito ne causam causa sequatur,*

> "and if the first-beginnings do not make by swerving a beginning of motion such as to break the decrees of fate, that cause may not follow cause from infinity,"

Since this expression, as it has been already made clear, embeds the notion of binding, it turns out that it can here function equally well as an expression for the Epicurean natural law (*foedera naturai*) as well as the Stoic ideas of cosmic binding (*fati foedera*, 2.254) and thus further buttress Lucretius' argument.[110]

4.3 THE "FILLING OR EMPTYING THE ATOMIC CONTAINER" METAPHOR

Lucretius amply uses in his poem the processes of "filling or emptying the atomic container" as a metaphor, in order to establish the cardinal atomic principle that everything is void and atoms in motion. As the processes that Empedocles personifies as Love and Strife are operating simultaneously within the Epicurean system, it should not come as a surprise that Lucretius' poem is especially abundant in verbs denoting this eternal and ubiquitous mechanism of change.[111] Yet, since full treatment of this particular aspect of Lucretius' imagery falls far beyond the scope of this study, the present discussion will be confined just to those passages which are more indicative of the focal role that this metaphor holds within the broader metaphorical network of the poem in juxtaposition with Empedocles.

As far as Empedocles is concerned, the absence of void from his philosophical system prevents him from using metaphorical concepts such as *filling or emptying*, unless unconsciously or catachrestically; instead, as has been repeatedly stressed, the elements are joined like the parts of a jigsaw puzzle. Even so, we can detect in his extant fragments expressions in which the concept of elements entering into or leaving a container lurks. For example, ready-made human beings seem to spring from the Sphairos, and their birth is described as a "pouring out" of a container (τῶν δέ τε μισγομένων χεῖτ' ἔθνεα μυρία θνητῶν· / "And as they were mixed, countless types of mortal things poured forth," B35.7 and B35.16).[112] How could one account for such a concession on Empedocles' part? The employment of such an unexpected metaphor could once again be justified by the close affinity between Empedocles' theory of pores and the atomic theory of void. That is why when in his *On the Heavens* Aristotle discusses cosmological accounts which hold that there is no real coming to be, but only rearrangement of unchangeable elements, he places Empedocles next to the Atomists and—what is most important for the present discussion—uses for both of them the "emptying the container" metaphor (Arist. *Cael.* 305b1–5; cf. Democritus DK68 A46a):

> Οἱ μὲν οὖν περὶ Ἐμπεδοκλέα καὶ Δημόκριτον λανθάνουσιν αὐτοὶ αὑτοὺς οὐ γένεσιν ἐξ ἀλλήλων ποιοῦντες, ἀλλὰ φαινομένην γένεσιν· ἐνυπάρχον γὰρ ἕκαστον ἐκκρίνεσθαί φασιν, ὥσπερ ἐξ ἀγγείου τῆς γενέσεως οὔσης, ἀλλ' οὐκ ἔκ τινος ὕλης, οὐδὲ γίγνεσθαι μεταβάλλοντος.

> "The followers of Empedocles and Democritus fail to see that their theory produces, not generation, but only the semblance of generation out of one another. They speak of each element 'inhering' and 'being separated out,' as if generation were emergence from a receptable instead of from a material, and did not involve change in anything."

Lucretius deploys first the processes of "filling or emptying" the container as a metaphor at the fundamental level of existence, with reference to the description of atoms. Before him, Epicurus had already attached to the atom among other adjectives the word πλῆρες (meaning full, filled with; e.g. *Ep. Hdt.* 41), so as to convey the absence of void and its solidity.[113] Lucretius inherited this terminology, and also suggested that an atom is an entity that cannot be filled any further; only void—specified by Lucretius as *inane, vacuum, vacans*—can be filled (e.g. *nam vacuum tum fit quod non fuit ante / et repletur item vacuum quod constitit ante; /* "for in that case a void is made which was not there before, and a void also is filled which was there before," 1.393–394).[114] Yet, as Longo observes, Lucretius does not use the adjective *plenus,* Latin equivalent to Epicurus' term, to qualify atom; he rather opts for *stipatus* and *solidus* and reserves *plenus* for use only in a periphrastic way.[115]

Within this framework, Lucretius employs the word *plenus* in order to refer to rival philosophical systems that deny the existence of void (1.370–383):

Illud in his rebus ne te deducere vero	370
possit, quod quidam fingunt, praecurrere cogor.	
cedere squamigeris latices nitentibus aiunt	372
et liquidas aperire vias, quia post loca pisces	
linquant, quo possint cedentes confluere undae;	
sic alias quoque res inter se posse moveri	375
et mutare locum, quamvis sint omnia plena.	
scilicet id falsa totum ratione receptumst.	
nam quo squamigeri poterunt procedere tandem,	
ni spatium dederint latices? concedere porro	
quo poterunt undae, cum pisces ire nequibunt?	380
aut igitur motu privandumst corpora quaeque,	
aut esse admixtum dicundumst rebus inane,	
unde initum primum capiat res quaeque movendi.	383

"And here in this matter I am driven to forestall what some imagine, lest it should lead you away from truth. They say that water yields to the pressure of scaly creatures and opens liquid ways, because fish leave room behind them for the yielding waves to run together; that so other things also are able to move in and out and to change place, although all is full. You must know that this has been accepted on reasons wholly false. For whither, I ask, will the scaly fish be able to move forward, unless the water shall give place? Into what place, again, will the water be able to move back, when the fish will be unable to go? Either then all bodies must be deprived of movement, or we must say that void is intermingled in things, as a result of which each thing may begin to move."

His Epicurean claim is that if this were true and everything were full, then the universe would be solid, and, more importantly, motion would be impossible (*omnia plena*, 1.376).[116] This refutation could easily be considered an anti-Parmenidean polemic.[117] Then, Lucretius also outlines the rival theory of ἀντιπερίστασις, which held that even without void motion was possible due to the shifting of places between things, one thing occupying immediately the space left by the other. In order to illustrate this, he gives the example of a fish, which is thought of as being able to move because the water it displaces goes into the space it leaves; but, as he objects, if there were

no void in between the two events, water could not begin to withdraw, and
no space would be left for the fish to move. As Sedley points out, what is
especially noteworthy in the present context is that when Lucretius deploys
the compound adjective *squamigeris* (1.372; cf. 1.378), he probably echoes
an Empedoclean adjective (plausibly a compound of λεπιδο-). This would
therefore mean that Empedocles is Lucretius' source for this particular the-
ory of motion.[118]

Lucretius also uses this metaphor to convey the essential attribute that
makes rough particles unpleasant; the metaphor in this case acts as an alterna-
tive to the use of the more technical term *coniuncta* (*quanto quaeque magis sunt
asperitate repleta.* / "in proportion as they are more full of roughness," 4.626).

The same metaphor is elsewhere used as a tool to conceptualize an
abstract aspect of the invisible microcosm (2.515–521):

> *Denique ab ignibus ad gelidas iter usque pruinas*   515
> *finitumst retroque pari ratione remensumst;*
> *omnis enim calor ac frigus mediique tepores*
> *interutrasque iacent explentes ordine summam.*
> *ergo finita distant ratione creata,*
> *ancipiti quoniam mucroni utrimque notantur,*   520
> *hinc flammis illinc rigidis infesta pruinis.*

"Again, limited is the path that extends from fiery heat to the icy frosts,
and it is measured backwards in the same way, for all the heat and cold
and middle warmth lies between these extremes, filling up the sum in
succession. Therefore things produced differ by limited degrees, since
they are marked at both extremes by two points, one at either end, beset
on the one side by flame, on the other by stiff frost."

While Lucretius suggests that there is a limit to the shapes of the atoms and
consequently to their effects on sensation, he presents us with the continuous
chain of the potential grades of hot and cold. First, he illustrates this scale as a
linear path (*iter,* 2.515), split into numerous small parts, all of which are filled
up in succession by different degrees of temperature (*explentes,* 2.518). Once the
qualities are endowed with material substance, Lucretius can apply the "filling
up" metaphor to the present context in order to visualize the notion that there
is absolutely no gap in the gradual differentiation between hot and cold. Only
then does the picture seem to be transferred from space onto a piece of paper, to
mark the definite extremes of the scale by the point of a *stylus* (2.520).

Moreover, when Lucretius strives to explain the undeniable materiality
of certain atomic compounds, when they are disseminated or incorporated,

he talks of their motion in terms of the filling of empty spaces. For example, he consistently uses such wording in order to establish the atomic structure of vocal sound (*ergo replentur loca vocibus abdita retro,* / "Therefore places hidden away from sight are filled with voices," 4.607).[119] In this case, once a vocal sound is emitted, the prospective containers are not so distinct, since it is dispersed in different directions; that is why the image of fire is brought in as an auxiliary example (*quasi ignis,* 4.605). Since feelings, too, are perceived as something material, the process of their invading our body or our heart is also frequently equated with the replenishment of a vessel (*pavida complebant pectora cura,* / "they filled their hearts with panic fear," 6.645).[120] Along the same lines, bodily contamination by disease is also recorded as an instance of material filling (*per fauces pectus complerat* / "when passing through the throat [the fell disease] had filled the chest," 6.1151).

Last but not least, this interplay between the processes of material filling up and the emptying of containers turns out to be the fundamental metaphor upon which Lucretius, after Epicurus' example, builds and articulates his ethical theory of pleasure. It suffices to recall here that, according to this theory, pleasure is brought about by the total absence of pain and desire; this ideal state which only the wise man enjoys is called katastematic pleasure (ἡ μὲν γὰρ ἀταραξία καὶ ἀπονία καταστηματικαί εἰσιν ἡδοναί·/ "Peace of mind and freedom from pain are pleasures which imply a state of rest," Diog. Laert. 10.136). By means of metaphorical language Lucretius explores the possibility of reaching this stage and its ultimate limits; he then endeavors to identify the likely causes that prevent man from achieving it, and proposes the one and only remedy, which is conversion to Epicureanism. What Lucretius actually does is to set forward various types of defective vessels, which he blames for our failure to reach the Epicurean τέλος. Desires are envisaged as smaller vessels embedded within the soul. The soul, too, is construed as a vessel.

This imagery, which is not found in Epicurus' writings, undoubtedly carries an intertextual allusion to Plato's *Gorgias* (493a–494c). When referring to undisciplined and thoughtless people, Plato calls the part of their soul where the desires are found and which is easily persuaded a "leaky jar" (τετρημένον πίθον, 493b) because it is so insatiate; their soul is then compared to a sieve, since it is perforated and unable to hold anything (τὴν δὲ ψυχὴν κοσκίνῳ ἀπήκασεν τὴν τῶν ἀνοήτων ὡς τετρημένην, 493c). Desires themselves are also compared to a number of jars (493d πίθοι), those of the licentious men being leaky and decayed (τὰ δ᾽ ἀγγεῖα τετρημένα καὶ σαθρά, 493e), contrary to those of the wise, which being sound, can be permanently filled up with wine, honey and milk.[21] Yet, bearing in mind the various Lucretian deployments of the "filling and emptying the container" metaphor in different contexts and with different objectives, the seemingly conventional Platonic image becomes creatively appropriated into the atomic context and turns out to be an integral part of Lucretius' poetic imagery.

Following the Epicurean distinction between necessary or unnecessary natural desires and the so-called empty ones, which are both unnatural and unnecessary and arise from "empty," i.e. illusory opinion (Τῶν ἐπιθυμιῶν αἱ μέν εἰσι φυσικαὶ καὶ <ἀναγκαῖαι· αἱ δὲ φυσικαὶ καὶ> οὐκ ἀναγκαῖαι· αἱ δὲ οὔτε φυσικαὶ οὔτε ἀναγκαῖαι ἀλλὰ παρὰ κενὴν δόξαν γινόμεναι. / "Of our desires some are natural and necessary; others are natural, but not necessary; others, again, are neither natural nor necessary, but are due to illusory opinion," *ΚΔ* 29).[122] Lucretius compares our needs with smaller jars that we ceaselessly strive to fill up. Although, in general, filling entails pleasure, depending on the nature of the needs, some of them can be easily satisfied and others cannot, notwithstanding our vain efforts.[123] Only natural and necessary desires, such as hunger and thirst, belong to the first category (*sic igitur tibi anhela sitis de corpore nostro / abluitur, sic expletur ieiuna cupido. /* "Thus then your panting thirst is swilled away out of the body, thus your starved craving is filled up," 4.875–876; *nam cibus atque umor membris adsumitur intus; / quae quoniam certas possunt obsidere partis, / hoc facile expletur laticum frugumque cupido. /* "For food and liquid are absorbed into the body, and since these can possess certain fixed parts, thereby the desire of water or bread is easily fulfilled," 4.1091–1093). On the contrary, by no means can sexual passion, being a natural but unnecessary desire, be sated (*nec satiare queunt spectando corpora coram, /* "nor can bodies even in real presence satisfy lovers with looking," 4.1102). Lucretius warns us that we should not even try to replenish such types of "vessels." As Brown correctly remarks, in the case of hunger and thirst, the metaphorical filling of a desire coincides with the literal filling of corporeal spaces, since food and water are taken in to restore the loss of bodily particles through exercise and exhalation, and this is exactly what makes our efforts successful. On the contrary, when it comes to sexual desire, *simulacra* are the only things that enter our body; the material description of love in terms of food and drink should not mislead us (*pabula amoris /* "what feeds love," 4.1063).[124] It is exactly due to this fallacy about the exact nature of our needs or—in metaphorical terms—the type of the vessel we are dealing with, that prevents us from experiencing true happiness. Yet, in respect of the satisfaction of necessary and natural desires, there is a certain limit to the quantity that every vessel can hold so as to remove pain, a limit which is established by nature. If we surpass it, the result is again painful loss of pleasure (*et finem statuit cuppedinis atque timoris /* "he put a limit to desire and fear," 6.25).[125]

In more general terms, a possible cause of unhappiness is considered to be a mind which, being unable to retain its contents, behaves like a cracked or leaky vessel.[126] This is the reproach that personified Nature fires against those miserable people who are incapable of storing up the memories of past pleasures and are thus reluctant to die, still craving for more (3.931–951). Lucretius counter-proposes the ideal image of a banqueter who departs from a feast having attained both material and mental replenishment (3.935–943):

> *nam si grata fuit tibi vita anteacta priorque*   935
> *et non omnia pertusum congesta quasi in vas*
> *commoda perfluxere atque ingrata interiere,*
> *cur non ut plenus vitae conviva recedis*
> *aequo animoque capis securam, stulte, quietem?*
> *sin ea quae fructus cumque es periere profusa*   940
> *vitaque in offensost, cur amplius addere quaeris,*
> *rursum quod pereat male et ingratum occidat omne,*
> *non potius vitae finem facis atque laboris?*

"For if your former life now past has been to your liking, if it is not true that all your blessings have been gathered as it were into a riddled jar, and have run through and been lost without gratification, why not, like a banqueter fed full of life, withdraw with contentment and rest in peace, you fool? But if all that you have enjoyed has been spilt out and lost, and if you have a grudge at life, why seek to add more, only to be miserably lost again and to perish wholly without gratification? Why not rather make an end of life and trouble?"

Since this image hints at the account of the fulfillment of necessary desires in Book 4, the comparison here acquires a literal value. The vessel image is resumed shortly after with a clear allusion to the myth of the Danaids, who carried water in vain, an allegory which was first used as a psychological interpretation of insatiable desires (3.1003–1010):[127]

> *Deinde animi ingratam naturam pascere semper*
> *atque explere bonis rebus satiareque numquam—*
> *quod faciunt nobis annorum tempora, circum*   1005
> *cum redeunt fetusque ferunt variosque lepores,*
> *nec tamen explemur vitai fructibus umquam—*
> *hoc, ut opinor, id est, aevo florente puellas*
> *quod memorant laticem pertusum congerere in vas,*
> *quod tamen expleri nulla ratione potestur.*   1010

"Then to be always feeding an ungrateful mind, yet never able to fill and satisfy it with good things—as the seasons of the year do for us when they come round bringing their fruits and manifold charms, yet we are never filled with the fruits of life—this, I think, is meant by the tale of the damsels in the flower of their age pouring water into a riddled urn, which, for all their trying, can never be filled."

In this way, Lucretius remarkably integrates mythological material into the imagery of his philosophical account.

Lucretius picks up the container metaphor once more in his third hymn to Epicurus, where he underscores his master's catalytic impact upon the human mind and soul (6.9–28):

> *Nam cum vidit hic ad victum quae flagitat usus*
> *omnia iam ferme mortalibus esse parata,*   10
> *et, proquam possent, vitam consistere tutam,*
> *divitiis homines et honore et laude potentis*
> *affluere atque bona gnatorum excellere fama,*
> *nec minus esse domi cuiquam tamen anxia corda,*
> *atque animi ingratis vitam vexare sine ulla*   15
> *pausa atque infestis cogi saevire querellis,*
> *intellegit ibi vitium vas efficere ipsum,*
> *omniaque illius vitio corrumpier intus*
> *quae conlata foris et commoda cumque venirent,*
> *partim quod fluxum pertusumque esse videbat,*   20
> *ut nulla posset ratione explerier umquam;*
> *partim quod taetro quasi conspurcare sapore*
> *omnia cernebat, quaecumque receperat, intus.*
> *veridicis igitur purgavit pectora dictis*
> *et finem statuit cuppedinis atque timoris*   25
> *exposuitque bonum summum quo tendimus omnes*
> *quid foret, atque viam monstravit, tramite parvo*
> *qua possemus ad id recto contendere cursu,*

"For when he saw how mortals had ready for them nearly all that need demands for living, and that, as far as they could, their life was established safe; saw how men were rolling in riches, mighty in honour and fame, proud in the good repute of their sons, while at home nevertheless each had an anxious heart; saw how they tormented their life in their own despite without any pause, and were compelled to wax furious with racking lamentations:—then he understood that the pot itself made the flaw, and that by this flaw an inward corruption tainted all that came in from without though it were a blessing; partly because he saw it to be leaking and riddled, so that nothing ever sufficed to fill it; partly because he perceived that it befouled, as one may say, with a noisome flavour everything that it received, as soon as it came in. Therefore with truth–telling words he scoured the heart, he put a limit to desire and fear, he showed what was that chief good to which we all move, and pointed the way, that strait and narrow path by which we might run thither without turning."

In this context, along with the perforated jar-like minds, he adds a new dimension and refers to another principal sort of flawed vessel, that which is filthy due to its contents, i.e. false ideas. These do not allow man to absorb any new sound ideas without being contaminated first by pre-existing ones. In this case Epicurus' achievement consists exactly in restoring those vessels, first by purging them and then by constructively filling them up. Lucretius proposes his poem to Memmius as an effective surgical tool fit for this purpose.[128]

4.4 "THE FLOWING WATER" METAPHOR

There are three main concepts that Lucretius envisages analogically with reference to the conceptual model of *water flowing in or out of atomic containers*:[129] a *regular flow of water* is used to describe either (i) in epistemological contexts, the constant emission of atoms out of everything, the so-called *effluences;* or (ii) in cosmological contexts, the *ceaseless atomic motion* and the ensuing cycle of life and death. The *irregular flowing* of water in the form of waves (iii) is used to describe *disturbed psychological states* in atomic terms.

Lucretius takes over from Epicurus a metaphor which retains traces of its Empedoclean and also Heraclitean origins, consciously keeps it in his Latin version of the Epicurean doctrine, and breathes new life into it. Yet, at the same time, he clearly subordinates all these influences to his own atomic theory. Due to the composite nature of the metaphor, it will be neutrally labelled the "flowing water" metaphor, instead of using its conventional name "flux metaphor," in order to strip it of its strong Heraclitean connotations and thus avoid erroneous conclusions.

Regular Flowing of Water in Epistemological Contexts

Empedocles argues for the omnipresence of *effluences,* which are given off not only by the elementary roots but also by compounds ([γνούς, ὅτι] πάντων εἰσὶν ἀπορροαί, ὅσσ' ἐγένοντο / "There are effluences from all things in existence," B89).[130] Therefore, he introduces the model of flowing water so as to describe a specific microcosmic process, that of the ceaseless, yet systematic coming out of root-aggregations from the surface or the inside of all "elementary containers." By talking of "effluences," Empedocles baptizes a new abstract idea and presents us with an effective depiction of it, simultaneously imposing the way in which we should mentally conceive it.

Despite the fact that there is only one occurrence of the word among Empedocles' extant fragments, thanks to secondary sources we can infer that, in his epistemological account, Empedocles associates his theory of effluences mainly with the senses and perception, in particular with reference to the reception of effluences by pores. For example, in Plato's *Meno* (A 92 = Pl. *Men.* 76 c-d) we read:[131]

–ΣΩ. Βούλει οὖν σοι κατὰ Γοργίαν ἀποκρίνωμαι, ᾗ ἂν σὺ μάλιστα ἀκολουθήσαις;
–ΜΕΝ. Βούλομαι· πῶς γὰρ οὔ;
–ΣΩ. Οὐκοῦν λέγετε ἀπορροάς τινας τῶν ὄντων κατὰ Ἐμπεδοκλέα;
–ΜΕΝ. Σφόδρα γε.
–ΣΩ. Καὶ πόρους εἰς οὓς καὶ δι' ὧν αἱ ἀπορροαὶ πορεύονται;
–ΜΕΝ. Πάνυ γε.
–ΣΩ. Καὶ τῶν ἀπορροῶν τὰς μὲν ἁρμόττειν ἐνίοις τῶν πόρων, τὰς δὲ ἐλάττους ἢ μείζους εἶναι;
–ΜΕΝ. Ἔστι ταῦτα.
–ΣΩ. Οὐκοῦν καὶ ὄψιν καλεῖς τι;
–ΜΕΝ. Ἔγωγε.
–ΣΩ. Ἐκ τούτων δὴ "σύνες ὅ τοι λέγω," ἔφη Πίνδαρος. ἔστιν γὰρ χρόα ἀπορροὴ σχημάτων ὄψει σύμμετρος καὶ αἰσθητός.

-"Do you want me to answer you in the manner of Gorgias, which would enable you most easily to follow?
-Yes, I do. Of course.
-You say, then, following Empedocles, that there are certain effluences from things?
-I certainly do.
-And pores into which and through which the effluences move?
-Certainly.
-And that some of the effluences fit into some of the pores and others are too small or too large?
-That is right.
-You also say, then, that there is such a thing as [the organ of] vision?

-I do indeed.

-'Grasp what I tell you,' as Pindar said, on the basis of these points.
For colour is an effluence from things symmetrical with [the organ of]
vision and perceptible."

He also employs this theory for various explanations, such as the reflection of
mirrors and the attraction of magnets.[132]

Empedocles' theory of effluences, the details of which remain rather
obscure to us, proved to be highly influential upon later authors. Likewise,
the word ἀπορροαί was destined to become standardized as a technical term.
In addition, several other words related to the process of flowing reached an
analogous technical status. In line with this, the Atomists and subsequently
Epicurus embraced the theory of effluences when clarifying similar physi-
cal phenomena to those explained by Empedocles (e.g. οὔτε ἀπόρροιαι τὴν
ἐξῆς θέσιν καὶ βάσιν διατηροῦσαι, ἥνπερ καὶ ἐν τοῖς στερεμνίοις εἶχον·
τούτους δὲ τοὺς τύπους εἴδωλα προσαγορεύομεν. / "[it is not impossible
that there should be found] effluxes [sic] preserving the same relative position
and motion which they had in the solid objects from which they come. To
these films we give the name of 'images' or 'idols,'" *Ep. Hdt.* 46).[133] Yet, due
to their belief in the existence of the void, although they retained the termi-
nology, they had to adjust the content of the theory.[134] The extant fragments
let us tentatively delineate, to a certain extent, the explanation of the Atomic
theory of effluences. In Rosenmeyer's words, "atoms are in constant motion
within bodies, but if bodies are to have any relation with one another as
bodies, there must be atomic motion outside the bodies as well, and some of
this external atomic motion, Epicurus' ἔξωσις, originating from the motion
within, πάλσις, will replicate the structure of bodies as effluences."[135]

While the effluences are portrayed as separate elementary entities, the
way in which they are envisaged as "flowing water" induces us to perceive
the precarious existence of the atomic compound from which the efflu-
ences emerge and warns us of its ultimate decomposition. Still, according to
Epicurus, whereas compound bodies incessantly emit atoms in the form of
effluences, at the same time they receive others from without. That is why
the size of the object does not diminish, up to the moment when the bal-
ance between incoming and out-going atoms is overturned (*Ep. Hdt.* 48):

καὶ γὰρ ῥεῦσις ἀπὸ τῶν σωμάτων τοῦ ἐπιπολῆς συνεχής, οὐκ
ἐπίδηλος τῇ μειώσει διὰ τὴν ἀνταναπλήρωσιν, σῴζουσα τὴν ἐπὶ τοῦ
στερεμνίου θέσιν καὶ τάξιν τῶν ἀτόμων ἐπὶ πολὺν χρόνον, εἰ καὶ
ἐνίοτε συγχεομένη ὑπάρχει,

> "For particles are continually streaming off from the surface of bodies, though no diminution of the bodies is observed, because other particles take their place. And those given off for a long time retain the position and arrangement which their atoms had when they formed part of the solid bodies, although occasionally they are thrown into confusion."

At any rate, from a certain point of view, the constant emission of effluences could be considered as a process of continuous destruction.

Regular Flowing of Water in Cosmological Contexts

Epicurus resorts again to the image of flowing water in his account of the formation of worlds, where he depicts the motion of atoms as seeds which *flow* from different directions and produce *irrigations* of appropriate matter for creation to each part of the world (*Ep. Pyth.* 89):

> ἐπιτηδείων τινῶν σπερμάτων ῥυέντων ἀφ᾽ ἑνὸς κόσμου ἢ μετακοσμίου ἢ ἀπὸ πλειόνων κατὰ μικρὸν προσθέσεις τε καὶ διαρθρώσεις καὶ μεταστάσεις ποιούντων ἐπ᾽ ἄλλον τόπον, ἐὰν οὕτω τύχῃ, καὶ ἐπαρδεύσεις ἐκ τῶν ἐχόντων ἐπιτηδείως ἕως τελειώσεως καὶ διαμονῆς ἐφ᾽ ὅσον τὰ ὑποβληθέντα θεμέλια τὴν προσδοχὴν δύναται ποιεῖσθαι.

> "It arises when certain suitable seeds rush in from a single world, or *intermundium,* or from several, and undergo gradual additions or articulations or changes of place, it may be, and waterings from appropriate sources, until they are matured and firmly settled in so far as the foundations laid can receive them."

According to Plutarch, the Epicureans also applied a similar metaphorical vocabulary of flowing water in connection with the reverse process, that of atomic decomposition (Epicur. fr. 282 Us. = Plut. *Adv. Col.* 16.1116C):

> τὰ δὲ συγκρίματα πάντα ῥευστὰ καὶ μεταβλητὰ καὶ γινόμενα καὶ ἀπολλύμενα εἶναι, μυρίων μὲν εἰδώλων ἀπερχομένων ἀεὶ καὶ ῥεόντων, μυρίων δὲ ὡς εἰκὸς ἑτέρων ἐκ τοῦ περιέχοντος ἐπιρρεόντων καὶ ἀναπληρούντων τὸ ἄθροισμα, ποικιλλόμενον ὑπὸ τῆς ἐξαλλαγῆς ταύτης καὶ μετακεραννύμενον,

> "While all aggregates of atoms are subject to flux and change and come into being and pass out of it, as innumerable films leave them in a constant stream, and innumerable others, it is inferred, flow in from

the surroundings and replenish the mass, which is varied by this interchange and altered in its composition"

With reference to these passages, scholars record an echo of Heraclitus' metaphor of flux, by means of which he was the first to convey the idea of eternal universal change in terms of flowing water.[136] This metaphor survived, in an altered or even subverted form, in Plato. Although it goes beyond the scope of this study to investigate the thorny problem of the Platonic or Aristotelian reception of Heraclitean flux, it should be noted that scholars find it difficult to achieve a consensus on the authenticity of passages which were initially thought to be extant fragments of Heraclitus' lost work.[137] This uncertainty plays a negative role in the endless debate about the precise content of the Heraclitean "flux" concept, as it makes it more difficult to detect the degree to which Plato has modified his predecessor's ideas. It seems quite clear, at any rate, that by assigning to Heraclitus a chaotic view of the world, in which everything changes all the time in every respect, the Platonic *Cratylus* misrepresented the idea for his own purposes and therefore obfuscated our overall picture of the Presocratic philosopher.[138]

Whatever the Platonic reception of Heraclitus was, when it comes to Epicurus, the question of the nature of the flux that he found in the Presocratic arises anew.[139] Unfortunately, there is only scanty evidence about his attitude towards Heraclitus. According to Diogenes Laertius (10.8), he seems to have called Heraclitus κυκητής, the Stirrer, encapsulating the latter's focal cosmological idea of universal flux.[140] Even if this nickname alone does not clarify the exact nature of the flux that Epicurus read in the Presocratic philosopher, it does not convey the image of a world dominated by natural law and regular changes, but, on the contrary, the negative implications of a chaotic process.[141] From this point of view, Heraclitus' metaphor of flux could not illustrate effectively Epicurus' vision of the world, within which, although things are in constant change, they are subject to unalterable regular patterns and are conditioned by a fixed underlying stability. In fact, as we have seen, Epicurus accepts a chaotic state for the atomic world only at the most fundamental level, the one that precedes the primary creation.[142] Moreover, contrary to the Platonic Heraclitus, Epicurus' epistemological doctrine advocates that the eternal exchange is not a reason to downgrade or disdain the world of senses. Therefore, it seems that Epicurus' use of the flowing water metaphor in cosmological contexts could reflect an endorsement of Heraclitus' metaphor of flux in order to criticize it.

We should now turn again to Empedocles' poem, within which the notion of fluidity and universal change also dominates. Although we have to rely again on scanty evidence, we should not overlook here instances of the flowing water metaphor employed in a cosmological context as well. Empedocles describes the generation and growth of dense and solid things through the pores of the earth as a kind of flowing (ἐκ δ' αἴης προρέουσι †θέλημα† τε καὶ στερεωπά. / "and from earth issue firmly rooted solids," B21.6).[143] Similarly, this notion of flowing water is probably used with reference to the destructive impact of some deeds (αὐχμηραί τε νόσοι καὶ σήψιες ἔργα τε ῥευστά / "and parching diseases and rots and deeds of flux[?]," B121.3).[144] Moreover, as Campbell rightly points out, although the Empedoclean universe, like the Epicurean one, is fluid at the level of phenomena, exactly like the atoms, the four Empedoclean roots are eternal and unchangeable.[145] Therefore, Empedocles' pluralistic materialism and his concept of elementary streams which besides their indisputable material fabric display a certain regularity in their motion, enabled him to illustrate universal fluidity effectively. In this respect, Empedocles would appear as another possible candidate for Epicurus' source of the imagery of flowing in a cosmological context.

Lucretius' Metaphor of Flowing Water

Following in Epicurus' footprints, Lucretius applies the metaphor of "flowing water" both in epistemological and cosmological contexts.[146] Whereas direct knowledge of Empedocles' poem should be taken for granted, it is difficult to prove direct knowledge of Heraclitus' works on the part of Lucretius, as it is on the part of Epicurus.[147] It is probable, however, that Lucretius did not have direct access to Heraclitus' work, but became acquainted with his philosophical thought both via Epicurus' works, and through doxographical writings, such as Theophrastus' *Physical Opinions* or a later Epicurean critical text.[148] Only in his refutation of other cosmologists does Lucretius attack several points of Heraclitus' monism and his ambiguous style; not a word though about his theory of flux (1.635–704).[149]

It will be suggested that Lucretius inherited from Epicurus the "flowing water" metaphor with both Heraclitean and Empedoclean connotations embedded in it and likewise appropriated it not only in connection with the theory of perception but with kinetics as well. Moreover, there is substantial evidence for claiming that Lucretius perceives the potential force and the implications of the Epicurean conflation. At this point, one should bear in mind that, when in Book 5 Lucretius explains the everlasting changing nature of earth, he clearly alludes to Empedocles (5.826–836):[150]

Sed quia finem aliquam pariendi debet habere,
destitit, ut mulier spatio defessa vetusto.

> *mutat enim mundi naturam totius aetas,*
> *ex alioque alius status excipere omnia debet,*
> *nec manet ulla sui similis res: omnia migrant,*   830
> *omnia commutat natura et vertere cogit.*
> *namque aliud putrescit et aevo debile languet,*
> *porro aliud concrescit et e contemptibus exit.*
> *sic igitur mundi naturam totius aetas*
> *mutat, et ex alio terram status excipit alter,*   835
> *quo tulit ut nequeat, possit quod non tulit ante.*

"But because she must have some limit to her bearing, she ceased, like a woman worn out by old age. For time changes the nature of the whole world, and one state of things must pass into another, and nothing remains as it was: all things move, all are changed by nature and compelled to alter. For one thing crumbles and grows faint and weak with age, another grows up and comes forth from contempt. So therefore time changes the nature of the whole world, and one state of the earth gives place to another, so that what she bore she cannot, but can bear what she did not bear before."

Within this general framework, it will be claimed that Empedocles' use of the flowing water metaphor exerts a catalytic influence upon Lucretius' version of the Heraclitean flux, and turns out to be his guidebook for elaborating upon the latter in material terms and freeing it from its negative connotations.

Lucretius' creativity, which consists in the enhancement and clarification of the Greek metaphor, becomes apparent from a striking adjustment. On the one hand, in his Latin version of the flowing water metaphor pertaining to effluences, the allusion to Empedocles' theory seems pretty clear; that is why, as it will be seen below in more detail, Lucretius does not take pains to elaborate his terminology. On the contrary, as regards the discussion of cosmological issues, Lucretius does not limit himself only to the use of the verb *fluere,* the obvious equivalent of the Greek verb ῥεῖν, but also introduces the compound verb *confluere,* equivalent to συρρεῖν, which is found only in the Atomists' *testimonia.*[151] What was it exactly that prompted Lucretius to this slight, yet significant differentiation from his original or even its systematization, if we were to accept the occurence of this verb among Epicurus' now lost writings? It seems pretty plausible that he discerns the vagueness inherent in the Greek verb ῥεῖν, which was used by Epicurus for both creation and decay and could thus carry misleadingly Heraclitean connotations of chaos. So, in his effort to put into words a comprehensive image of the atomic world, he thought it necessary to clarify the double meaning of the Greek verb by dividing it into two different Latin verbs; he opts for *fluere* mainly in cases of disintegration, while he consistently uses *confluere* to describe the omnipresent reverse process, that of creation. By means of his version of the "flowing water" metaphor, Lucretius manages to tone down pre-existing connotations of absolute disorder—in case we accept that the Platonic distortion became a *locus communis*—in order to rehabilitate or to correct Heraclitus and to establish the image of an invisible world in ceaseless movement, yet dominated by regular change and subordinated to fixed *foedera naturai*. Empedocles' eternal cycle of growth and decay serves him as a compass as he moves in this direction.

The positive aspect of the "flowing water" metaphor seems to bear a close relationship with the socio-political imagery which is also used to describe the coming together of atoms—or Empedoclean roots—into aggregations:[152] that is why the two metaphors are occasionally found side by side (e.g. *undique conveniunt et sic coniectus eorum / confluit,* / "[the elements of heat] gather together from all parts of the world, and their assemblage flows together in such a manner," 5.600–601). Yet their role does not fully overlap, but should rather be considered complementary. While the socio-political imagery illustrates both the *process* of creation and the *balance* maintained between this process and the equilibrium thus achieved, the "flowing water" metaphor is particularly appropriate in order to emphasize the *ceaseless motion* of the invisible atoms, a process which becomes visible within our world by simultaneous and ubiquitous birth and decay. In any case, the use of the compound verb *confluere* seems to imply the overlapping function of the two metaphors.[153]

In order to respect the basic Epicurean tenet about the literal use of language and the correct use of metaphors, Lucretius gives a thorough explanation of the conceptual model in question, on several occasions also juxtaposing the source and target domains in the form of a simile. He thus blurs the borderline between similes and metaphors. We have already discussed above, in connection with the technique of transfusion, how the action of wind being compared to that of water is presented in terms of flowing (1.271–297: wind: *fluunt,* 1.280 → water: *flumine,* 1.282; *fluctibus,* 1.289; *flumen,* 1.291).[154] Apart from the coherence between the two parts of the simile, which such a foreshadowing of the vehicle by the tenor brings about, the choice of the vehicle itself should not be overlooked. For, if we look at other such similes, in which Lucretius opts for the very same vehicle, we may consider them as an explicit comment on his conscious use of the "flowing water" model. For example, when Lucretius puts forward the principle of the infinite number of the first beginnings, while the dissolution of the atomic cluster is compared to a shipwreck, in a very Heraclitean manner matter is compared to an ocean (2.547–564: *materiae tanto in pelago*, 2.550; *aestus diversi materiai*, 2.562).[155] In another more explicit comparison, the sun and its ceaseless emission of light is compared to and explained by the action of a small fountain, which despite its size can bring about a deluge (5.592–603: sun: *largifluum fontem*, 5.598 → fountain: *aquai / . . . fons*, 5.602–603; sun: *rigando*, 5.594; *perfundat*, 5.595; *confluit*, . . . *profluat*, 5.601 → water: *riget . . . redundet*, 5.603).[156] Lastly, when Lucretius describes the sky and its motion, in one of the multiple plausible explanations he proposes, he assimilates the phenomenon of the sky going around with its stars as moved by the air, to the image of an irrigation wheel with its buckets, which are moved by the river (5.509–516: air: *fluere*, 5.513 → water: *fluvios*, 5.516). Subsequently, when the vehicle "flowing water" is projected outside the limited textual space of the simile and is widely used as a metaphor with notable philosophical implications, these extended similes should be kept in mind, because they shed light upon the metaphorical image in question.

Lucretius can also base his comparison of the behaviour of certain atomic compounds with that of flowing water on simple atomic grounds (2.451–455):[157]

> *illa quidem debent e levibus atque rutundis*
> *esse magis, fluvido quae corpore liquida constant;*
> *namque papaveris haustus itemst facilis quod aquarum:*
> *nec retinentur enim inter se glomeramina quaeque,*
> *et perculsus item proclive volubilis exstat.*　　　　　　　　455

"Those others, the fluids which consist of liquid body, must be of elements smoother and rounder. Indeed you may scoop up poppy seed as easily as water, for the individual round particles are no hindrance to each other; and when poppy seed is knocked over, it runs downhill just as readily."

Since water is formed out of smooth and round particles, anything composed of atoms similar to those that form the substance of a liquid will certainly behave like a liquid. As a palpable example of this, Lucretius puts forward the image of poppy seeds: since their motion and velocity are similar to those of water (poppy seeds: *papaveris haustus*, 2.453 → water: *aquarum*, 2.453), he goes on to infer that their ultimate constituents should be accordingly smooth and round.[158]

Lucretius applies the flowing water metaphor on the fundamental level in order to describe the formation of the atomic aggregations (*si non, certa suo quia tempore semina rerum / cum confluxerunt, patefit quodcumque creatur,* / "unless because each created thing discloses itself when at their own time the fixed seeds of things have streamed together," 1.176–177). Later in the same book the image of elements flowing together is used in order to be refuted (1.984–997):

> *Praeterea spatium summai totius omne*
> *undique si inclusum certis consisteret oris*   985
> *finitumque foret, iam copia materiai*
> *undique ponderibus solidis confluxet ad imum,*
> *nec res ulla geri sub caeli tegmine posset,*
> *nec foret omnino caelum neque lumina solis,*
> *quippe ubi materies omnis cumulata iaceret*   990
> *ex infinito iam tempore subsidendo.*
> *at nunc nimirum requies data principiorum*
> *corporibus nullast, quia nil est funditus imum,*
> *quo quasi confluere et sedes ubi ponere possint.*
> *semper in adsiduo motu res quaeque geruntur*   995
> *partibus e cunctis infernaque suppeditantur*
> *ex infinito cita corpora materiai.*

"Besides, if all the space in the universe stood contained within fixed boundaries on all sides and were limited, by this time the store of matter would by its solid weight have run together form all sides to the bottom, nor could anything be done under the canopy of heaven, nor would heaven exist at all or the sun's light, because assuredly all matter would be lying in a heap from sinking down through infinite ages past. But as it is, sure enough no rest is given to the bodies of the first-beginnings, because there is no bottom whatsoever, for them to run together as it were into it and fix their abode there. Always the business of the universe is going on with incessant motion in every part, and the elements of matter are being supplied from beneath, rushing from infinite space."

In spite of the unchangeable nature of atomic motion, the total extent of the entire universe is not finite and thus does not have a bottom. If it were finite, the store of matter would have accumulated at the bottom because of its weight, and there would be no creation whatsoever. The use of *quasi* in this context (1.994) is significant, as it points precisely to the impossibility of the fulfilling of the process, despite its being foreshadowed by the prefix *con-*.

Lucretius talks about the creation of the Empedoclean roots also in terms of atomic flowing. In fact, we can track down cases of the metaphor, drawn from one of the elements (water), being applied to each of the other three (fire, air, earth).

The picture of the creation of the four Empedoclean roots at the very beginning of the world condenses multiple applications of the "flowing water" metaphor and thus unifies the different natural processes (5.495–508):

> *Sic igitur terrae concreto corpore pondus*   495
> *constitit, atque omnis mundi quasi limus in imum*
> *confluxit gravis et subsedit funditus ut faex;*
> *inde mare, inde aer, inde aether ignifer ipse*
> *corporibus liquidis sunt omnia pura relicta,*
> *et leviora aliis alia, et liquidissimus aether*   500
> *atque levissimus aerias super influit auras,*
> *nec liquidum corpus turbantibus aeris auris*
> *commiscet: sinit haec violentis omnia verti*
> *turbinibus, sinit incertis turbare procellis,*
> *ipse suos ignis certo fert impete labens*   505
> *nam modice fluere atque uno posse aethera nisu*
> *significat Pontos, mare certo quod fluit aestu,*
> *unum labendi conservans usque tenorem.*

"In this way, therefore, the heavy earth became solid with compact body, and all the mud of creation, so to speak, flowed together by its weight and settled to the bottom like dregs; then sea, then air, then the fiery ether itself, being made of fluid particles, were all left pure, some lighter than others, and ether, lightest and most fluid, floats above the airy breezes, and does not mingle its fluid consistency with the stormy breezes of air: it leaves all things below to be turned upside down by violent tempests, leaves them to be disturbed with wayward storms, while itself bearing its own fires it glides with unchanging sweep. For that the ether may flow gently along with one sole movement is proved by the Pontus, a sea which flows with unchanging current and keeps ever one course of gliding movement."

Lucretius bases his reconstruction of the remote past on the physical explanation of a metaphorical image, i.e. by observing that the behaviour of atoms is conditioned by both their weight and their fluidity (*corporibus liquidis . . . / et leviora*, 5.499–500). Not only sea, air and ether but even the atoms of the earth, despite their heaviness, are depicted as having flowed together (5.497 *confluxit*). Yet, in order to clarify the idiosyncrasy of these specific atoms within the homogeneous frame of the "flowing water" imagery, Lucretius adds here two short similes, comparing the formation of the earth first with mud (*quasi limus,* 5.496) and then with dregs (*ut faex,* 5.497). Then the focus shifts to the actual movement of ether, which is similarly justified by its atomic substance (5.500–501). The section concludes with a simile which equates the unaltered flowing of ether with that of Pontus (5.506–508: ether: *fluere,* 5.506 → Pontus: *fluit,* 5.507). Thus, Lucretius once more unites cosmos and macrocosm synchronically, the former providing a sign for the workings of the latter (*significat,* 5.507).

The same metaphor is also used to describe the formation and motion of Empedoclean roots in synchronic terms. The motion of air is almost conventionally assimilated to that of water (e.g. *aeris in magnum . . . mare* / "into the great ocean of air," 5.276; *sive aliunde fluens alicunde extrinsecus aer* / "or some air flowing from some outside place," 5.522). As far as fire is concerned, we have already discussed a comparison of the sun with a water spring (5.592–603).[159] Apart from the actual correspondence in the action of sun and water after their emission from their source (5.592–598), Lucretius also sketches the initial formation of the sun itself in terms of flowing water, since it is made out of elements of heat, already formed, which gather together from all parts of the world (5.599–601). This image points back to the analogous illustration of the process of dawn at a fixed time in similar metaphorical wording (*aut quia conveniunt ignes et semina multa / confluere ardoris consuerunt tempore certo,* / "or because there is a gathering together of fires, and many seeds of heat are accustomed to flow together at a fixed time," 5.660–661).[160] In a similar way, Lucretius describes the process of the formation of thunderbolts (*confluere . . . elementa vaporis,* 6.312) and fire in general (*verum semina sunt ardoris multa, terendo / quae cum confluxere, creant incendia silvis.* / "but there are many seeds of heat which stream together by rubbing and make a conflagration among the forests," 1.902–903), as well as the behaviour of thunderbolts (*liquidus . . . ignis* / "fire being fluid," 6.349) and lightning after being forged (*quare fulmineus multo penetralior ignis / quam noster fluat e taedis terrestribus ortus;* / "why the fire of lightning has a far more penetrating flow than our fire that arises from terrestrial torches," 2.382–383).

Before completing the discussion about the image of creation that Lucretius conveys through the use of the verb *confluere,* a peculiar application of this image should be considered with reference to the action of the plague, which is said to have flowed together into the mind of its victim (*morbida vis in cor maestum confluxerat aegris,* / "the fell disease had flooded into the sorrowful mind of the sufferer," 6.1152).[161] Although the context is on the whole grim, the presence of the verb itself, which is regularly used in the poem with positive connotations, allows us to discern a hint of optimism. Despite the immediate sinister implications of this sort of creation of fire, Lucretius seems to suggest that this process heralds in the long term a new cycle of birth guaranteed by the present decay. In other words, by paradoxically injecting this gloomy passage with undertones suggestive of generation, he facilitates the reader to view both the processes of creation and destruction as morally neutral.

As regards the reverse process, i.e. the *universal incessant decay*, Lucretius assimilates under the single verb *fluere* both the Empedoclean effluences and the Heraclitean-Empedoclean concept of universal fluidity. Lucretius considers atomic decomposition a gradual process which takes place on several levels, and, depending on its intensity and systematicity, does not always lead to irreversible effects.

Atomic effluences are a first instance of the regular departure of atoms in terms of streaming water. As has already been mentioned above, the vocabulary of flowing, employed to refer to the phenomenon, had a technical value in Greek. Accordingly, Lucretius retains it in his Latin translation. In particular Book 4, in which Lucretius expounds Epicurus' theory of the senses, abounds with instances of atomic emanations which are depicted in such metaphorical wording. For example, we read (4.225–229):[162]

> *usque adeo omnibus ab rebus res quaeque fluenter*   225
> *fertur et in cunctas dimittitur undique partis,*
> *nec mora nec requies interdatur ulla fluendi,*
> *perpetuo quoniam sentimus, et omnia semper*
> *cernere odorari licet et sentire sonare.*

"So true it is that from all things the different qualities pass off in a flow, and disperse in every direction around; there is no delay, no rest to interrupt the flow, since we constantly feel it, and we can at all times see all things, smell them, and perceive their sound."

At this point a closer look should be taken at the vocabulary that Lucretius employs in order to render the Greek terms into Latin. Although he expresses the process of flowing in Latin with the verb *fluere,* he seems to encounter considerable difficulty when it comes to finding a word corresponding to the Greek nouns.[163] Lucretius applies only once the word *flumen* (*flumine,* 6.1064), denoting effluences. Another alternative is the word *aestus,* which is used especially with the effluences of the magnet (*lapidis . . . aestus,* 6.1051).[164] However, this term could be considered rather inappropriate for the Empedoclean concept that Lucretius strives to put forward, since it carries "Heraclitizing" connotations of water in agitation, rather than in regular flow. In fact, Lucretius elsewhere uses the very same word with reference to the chaotic state of matter in general (*aestus diversi materiai,* 2.562). The same difficulty could also be raised by the word *fluctus* (*fluctus odorum,* 4.675. Cf. 6.1053). Due to this ambiguity underlying these words, Lucretius' choice of words could be judged ineffective. That is probably why none of them could become crystallized as the standard Latin term.[165]

Lucretius also applies the metaphor of flowing water more broadly by including descriptions of decay.[166] In this case the container is decomposed and the atomic matter gets partly or totally liquidized.

In a clearly cosmological context Lucretius explicitly uses the metaphor with negative connotations. More precisely, when he launches into his account of atomic motion, he envisages things in the universe "as if they were ebbing," thus changing in terms of "flowing water" (*fluere,* 2.69). The subtle addition of the conjunction *quasi* reveals another conscious use of the image.

Lucretius talks about the destructibility of the Empedoclean elements as a process of liquefaction (5.273–280):[167]

> *Aera nunc igitur dicam qui corpore toto*
> *innumerabiliter privas mutatur in horas.*
> *semper enim, quodcumque fluit de rebus, id omne*   275
> *aeris in magnum fertur mare; qui nisi contra*
> *corpora retribuat rebus recreetque fluentis,*
> *omnia iam resoluta forent et in aera versa.*
> *haud igitur cessat gigni de rebus et in res*
> *reccidere, adsidue quoniam fluere omnia constat.*   280

"Next then I will speak of the air, which throughout its whole body changes in numberless ways every single hour. For always whatever flows off from things is all carried into the great ocean of air; and if this contrariwise did not return back particles to the things again, and renew them as they flow away, all would by now be dissolved and changed into air. Therefore air never ceases to be produced from things and to fall back into things again, since it is certain that all things are in a constant flow."

By means of this metaphorical wording Lucretius also builds up the correspondences in the analogy he draws between *anthropos* and *makranthropos* that we have already discussed above. In this way, while he reduces both to the same natural laws, he establishes the mortality of the latter: a gradual decrease in the matter taken in results in the total "liquidation" or "dissolution" of the human body and foreshadows ultimate universal decomposition (2.1105–1174: human body: *ut fit ubi nilo iam plus est quod datur intra / vitalis venas quam quod fluit atque recedit. /* "as happens when no more is now given into the arteries of life than what flows out and passes away," 2.1118–1119 → things: *nam certe fluere atque recedere corpora rebus / multa manus dandum est; /* "For certainly we must own ourselves convinced that many elements flow out and pass away from things," 2.1128–1129; *iure igitur pereunt, cum rarefacta fluendo / sunt /* "With good reason therefore the things pass away, when by the flowing off they have become thinned," 2.1139–1140).[168] This specific image of decay is maintained also in relation to the crumbling of various atomic structures, such as visual images (*nec speciem mutare suam liquentia cessant /* "they never cease to dissolve and change their shapes," 4.141) or even a rotten jar (*partim quod fluxum pertusumque esse videbat, /* "partly because he saw it to be leaking and riddled," 6.20).[169]

In sum, by means of the "flowing water" metaphor Lucretius sketches and explains a world image subordinated to a relentless, yet regular "flux," more in tune with Epicurus and Empedocles than Heraclitus.

Irregular Flowing of Water with Ethical Implications

Lucretius inherited from Epicurus a further set of metaphors, which is drawn from the same metaphorical field, that of "*water in motion.*" On the one hand, the image of the storm-tossed sea serves to describe the cognitive state of complete mental disturbance which people endure due to their ignorance about the true nature of things. On the other, absolute happiness (ἀταραξία) is metaphorically called "calming" (γαληνισμός).[170] The description of human anxieties in terms of a tempest is not an Epicurean invention.[171] Still, its application in this particular philosophical context, along with the image of certain negative feelings such as anxiety or anger, materialized as waves, obtains additional semantic weight (e.g. *volvere curarum tristis in pectore fluctus. /* "to roll the sad waves of trouble within their breasts," 6.34; *magnos irarum . . . fluctus /* "great billows of wrath," 6.74).[172] Epicurus insists that, despite the seemingly confused state of the external world, precisely the insight of its fixed regularity should not only not negatively affect our mind, but rather result in our inner tranquility; the opposite condition apparently goes against the true workings of nature. As Lucretius explicitly states in the proem to Book 5, by unveiling nature's secrets Epicurus succeeded in saving us from those tempestuous billows and bringing us into harmony with Nature (*fluctibus e tantis,* 5.11).[173] Lucretius' primary aim, in turn, consists in bringing our mental anxieties to an end by bringing invisible atomic motion before our eyes.[174]

4.5 "SQUEEZING OUT THE SPONGE" METAPHOR

By means of the "squeezing out the sponge" metaphor Lucretius describes a rather forceful way of emptying certain atomic containers by comparing the whole process to the *squeezing out of a soaked sponge*. Whereas Epicurus vaguely described various phenomena as a "squeezing out" process (ἔκθλιψις), Lucretius makes a significant modification: he combines this process with objects viewed as sponges due to their behaviour, and in so doing shapes it into a more effective cognitive tool.

Although in this case Empedocles is not Lucretius' apparent forerunner, a close look at the metaphor will complete our picture of Lucretius' poetic mentality, which is influenced by his intertextual relationship with Empedocles. Within this framework, this will amount to a further example of the way in which Lucretius applies the Empedoclean method of elucidating complicated physical tenets by observing the behaviour of an analogous object drawn from common experience—a soaked sponge—in order to demonstrate its structural similarity with an inaccessible natural mechanism and thus infer valid conclusions about the mechanism itself. As it has been already suggested above, this method is based on scientific principles similar to those of Empedocles, but is modified according to Epicurus' teachings.

As Konstan remarks "the Atomists had recourse to a theory of displacement or extrusion called ἔκθλιψις, according to which heavier or denser objects had the capacity to drive lighter ones out and upward. [. . .] This power of atoms to jostle their lighter neighbours out of the way was precisely the property to which Democritus attached the name weight."[175] The concept of "squeezing out" was used to illuminate obscure phenomena not only synchronically, but also diachronically. For example, within Epicurus' writings, phenomena such as the production of vocal sound as well as the formation of ice are considered to be brought about by a certain "squeezing out" process (ἔκθλιψις). As far as freezing is concerned, Epicurus specifies the shape of the atoms that are involved in the process; round particles are squeezed out when triangular and acute-angled ones are driven together (*Ep. Pyth.* 109):[176]

> Κρύσταλλος συντελεῖται καὶ κατ᾽ ἔκθλιψιν μὲν τοῦ περιφεροῦς σχηματισμοῦ ἐκ τοῦ ὕδατος, σύνωσιν δὲ τῶν σκαληνῶν καὶ ὀξυγωνίων τῶν ἐν τῷ ὕδατι ὑπαρχόντων. καὶ κατὰ τὴν ἔξωθεν δὲ τῶν τοιούτων πρόσκρισιν, ἃ συνελασθέντα πῆξιν τῷ ὕδατι παρεσκεύασε, ποσὰ τῶν περιφερῶν ἐκθλίψαντα.

"Ice is formed by the expulsion from the water of the circular, and the compression of the scalene and acute-angled atoms contained in it; further by the accretion of such atoms from without, which being driven together cause the water to solidify after the expulsion of a certain number of round atoms."

On the other hand, according to Pseudo-Plutarch's account, Epicurus described the distribution of the elements and the creation of the four elementary masses at the beginning of the world in a rather vague way as the outcome of "squeezing out."[177] Within the atomic tradition, in particular, the word ἔκθλιψις was crystallized as the technical term mainly for the extrusion of fire particles.

Before turning to Lucretius, it should be pointed out that it is perhaps significant to the present discussion the fact that Empedocles himself is said to have envisaged the initial formation of stars as a process of squeezing out (A53 = Aët. 2.13.2 = *Dox. Gr.* 341):[178]

> Ἐμπεδοκλῆς πύρινα [sc. εἶναι τὰ ἄστρα] ἐκ τοῦ πυρώδους, ὅπερ ὁ ἀὴρ ἐν ἑαυτῷ περιέχων ἐξανέθλιψε κατὰ τὴν πρώτην διάκρισιν.
>
> "Empedocles says that [the stars are] fiery from the fire-like element which air contained in itself and squeezed out during the initial separation."

At first glance, it seems that Lucretius conforms to the traditional technical terminology about extrusion (ἔκθλιψις) and maintains it in his Latin translation (*exprimere*). Still, Lucretius seems to judge this term, used alone, inadequate to convey properly all the different factors involved in the preconception of the "squeezing out" process. In order to improve upon it he combines two distinct models, i.e. objects viewed as sponges due to their behaviour, and the squeezing out process. In this way he introduces a specific conceptual model, that of "squeezing out the sponge," thanks to which he explicitly or implicitly elucidates several obscure processes. Although, as we have already discussed, the sponge had been used in the physical tradition as an analogy,[179] it seems highly probable that it was Theophrastus' *Metarsiologica* or *Physical Opinions* that provided Lucretius with it, either directly or indirectly.[180] Here, I will explore the extent to which Lucretius elaborates his model and how this facilitates for him the illustration of complicated Epicurean physical doctrines.

In connection with the present discussion, the long simile in Book 4 pertaining to taste should be considered the key passage (4.617–621):

> *Principio sucum sentimus in ore, cibum cum*
> *mandendo exprimimus, ceu plenam spongiam aquai*
> *siquis forte manu premere ac siccare coepit.*

> *inde quod exprimimus per caulas omne palati*   620
> *diditur et rarae per flexa foramina linguae.*

> "In the first place, we perceive flavour in the mouth while we squeeze it
> out in munching the food, as if one by chance takes in hand a sponge
> full of water and begins to press it dry. Then that which we squeeze out
> is distributed abroad through all the pores of the palate and the tortuous
> passages of the spongy tongue."

Here Lucretius presents us with a comprehensive demonstration of the
model in question, since he juxtaposes the metaphorical usage with the lit-
eral. What he seeks to explain is what happens when we chew food. Taste is
due to particles of food *squeezed out* in the mouth and distributed through
the pores of the palate and the tortuous passages of the spongy tongue.[181]
The model proposed is a damp sponge taken in hand and pressed dry. Three
crucial components of the source domain are specified, i.e. the sponge, a
force, in this case exerted by the hand, and the water pressed out, which
directly correspond to food with a spongy texture, our teeth chewing and fla-
vour (spongy container: *cibum,* 4.617 → *spongiam,* 4.618; force: *mandendo
exprimimus,* 4.618; *exprimimus,* 4.620 → *manu premere,* 4.619; liquid con-
tent: *sucum,* 4.617 → *aquai,* 4.618).

Since Lucretius observes here a liquid within a visible container in order
to prove its analogous behaviour within another container that displays the
same structural characteristics, this simile belongs to the group labelled above
"various containers of roots" (3.4.2.1). As it has been argued there, this cat-
egory vividly bears the Empedoclean imprint of the lantern simile (B84).[182]

Let us now look at specific implications that Lucretius' choice of sponge
as vehicle in this particular simile inevitably entails. First, Lucretius suggests
that a body that can be squeezed must have a spongy texture. It also implies
that the atoms are not drawn automatically out of the atomic container, but
that this occurs as a result of a certain external force that is exerted intention-
ally upon the container in order to extract the contained substance. Con-
sequently, the tiny detachable particles inside the spongy object, although
they are incorporated within it, are eventually induced to emerge through
the pores of the object. In addition, this model effectively illustrates the cor-
porality of the particles squeezed out. The product of the squeezing is a cer-
tain category of atoms, which due to their resemblance can perform certain
motions after their emission, aggregate into a new perceptible atomic com-
pound and exist independently. Finally, their removal does not usually bring
about the immediate decomposition of the container.

When Lucretius applies the vehicle of "squeezing out a sponge" as a metaphor in other contexts and envisages several atomic compounds as sponges, he denotes the sameness in the *atomic behaviour* of both the containers and the particles squeezed out and therefore discloses the similarity between seemingly dissimilar natural mechanisms.[183] Moreover, when he describes an instance of "squeezing out," he expects his pupil to bring to mind all the parameters involved in the archetypal model as expounded in Book 4, and, when one of them is omitted, to infer it in one way or another. In this way, he manages to demystify a certain group of unfamiliar phenomena by presenting us with atomic explanations valid at every level of the world. At the same time, he takes pains to explain his conceptual tool on other occasions by means of short similes and thus merge its different applications.

This metaphor could be placed within the more general category of those used to describe the "emptying the atomic container" metaphor (Section 4.3). More specifically, it could easily be compared to the "water flowing out" metaphor (Section 4.4), as in both cases the product of the emptying process is similarly recognizable. Yet, they should not be considered interchangeable, because, while in the former metaphor the out-going atoms are moving *spontaneously,* in the "squeezing out the sponge" metaphor the emphasis is placed upon their *enforced* emergence. Moreover, due to the "flowing water" the container may eventually decompose.

Let us now look at different applications of this metaphorical image. To begin with, clouds are thought of as possessing a spongy texture. Lucretius himself compares them to woollen clothes (*vestes,* 6.471; *vellera lanae,* 6.504); within these comparisons, the emphasis is placed upon their ability to absorb external moisture.[184] In the same spirit, they can also be considered squeezable. This is actually the case when Lucretius enumerates the causes and types of rain, where he suggests that this may happen when wind presses the bulk of a cloud containing particles of moisture or when clouds are piled up (6.507–523: *premit,* 6.512; *premuntur,* 6.518).[185] On the other hand, as has already been mentioned above, Theophrastus had used the sponge and tufts of wool containing water as models of clouds in connection with his explanations of lightning (*Metars.* 2.13–17 and 4.4–7 Daiber).[186] Nonetheless, it may come as a surprise that nowhere in the meteorological explanation of lightning does Lucretius opt *explicitly* for the Theophrastean analogy. Such a modification seems to suggest that, as a sponge contains water particles, it cannot present us with an appropriate preconception of the extrusion of fire particles. As a consequence, Lucretius gives precedence to comparisons of the behaviour only of the same Empedoclean root in different media in order to make his scientific similes more coherent.

Still, Lucretius does not completely eliminate the traditional terminology of ἔκθλιψις in connection with the forced extrusion of fire. When Lucretius describes lightning as a sudden expulsion of fire particles by burning wind, he resorts to the same terminology (*dissipat ardoris quasi per vim expressa repente / semina /* "by violent pressure it seems suddenly to squeeze out and scatter abroad seeds of fire," 6.181–182). Likewise, lightning, which is caused when clouds are crowded or crushed together by wind, is said to get squeezed out (*hasce igitur cum ventus agens contrusit in unum / compressitque locum cogens, expressa profundunt / semina /* "When therefore the wind driving these has crushed them together and crowded them up together in a confined space, they squeeze out and pour forth seeds," 6.211–213). This is also the case in contexts in which some squeezing out of fire, always driven by some force, is implied. For example, when Lucretius explains how fire first originated from the friction between trees (5.1096–1101), the branches are envisaged as having a spongy texture; the force is also mentioned (*exprimitur validis extritus viribus ignis, /* "fire is pressed out by the great force of the friction," 5.1098).[187] It seems, therefore, that Lucretius only partly assimilates Theophrastus' model in order to put a gloss on the inherited atomic terminology. By displacing the depiction of the mechanism of the sponge to Book 4, he lessens its probative force in the present context and—unlike Theophrastus—chooses other containers of fire for comparison with clouds. Still, whilst he keeps the atomic terminology and the concomitant reference to the "squeezing out the sponge" metaphor, he inevitably evokes the conceptual model that this metaphor visualizes and thus may offer his pupil an illumination of the phenomena in question from a different, yet more demanding, perspective as well.

In a similar way, especially in Book 2, Lucretius asserts that nothing possesses a natural upward motion, unless it is driven by some force (2.184–215). More specifically, although flames may deceive us, he claims that fire does not naturally travel upwards; on the contrary, due to their weight fire atoms must somehow be *squeezed out* in order to move upwards (*sic igitur debent quoque flammae posse per auras / aeris expressae sursum succedere, quamquam / pondera, quantum in sest, deorsum deducere pugnent. /* "In this way, therefore, flames also must be able to rise up, squeezed out upwards through the breezes of air, although, as far as lies in them, their weights fight to draw them down," 2.203–205).[188] Lucretius goes on by pointing to several such examples, like shooting stars and the sun's heat, lightning and thunderbolts (2.206–215). As Fowler rightly remarks, here Lucretius is probably arguing against Aristotle's theory about the physical place of the elements and more specifically his claim that all heat naturally tends to rise upwards.[189] Phenomena such as burning flames and shooting stars that Lucretius also refers to contradict this Aristotelian theory. It is noteworthy that, while Aristotle explains in his *Meteorology* that, when air condenses owing to cold, pressure forcibly ejects heat downwards, he uses the image of fruit stones jumping out from between our fingers when they are squeezed (Arist. *Mete.* 342a8–11). Still, in Aristotle's analogical model the emphasis is placed more on the process, i.e. the pressure exerted and the direction of the movement, and less on the substance of the container from which the fire particles are squeezed out.[190]

For another example of this metaphor we should turn to Lucretius' explanation in atomic terms of the changes in temperature of subterranean water in wells during summer (6.840–847):

> *Frigidior porro in puteis aestate fit umor,*   840
> *rarescit quia terra calore et, semina si qua*
> *forte vaporis habet proprie, dimittit in auras.*
> *quo magis est igitur tellus effeta calore,*
> *fit quoque frigidior qui in terrast abditus umor.*
> *frigore cum premitur porro omnis terra coitque*   845
> *et quasi concrescit, fit scilicet ut coeundo*
> *exprimat in puteos si quem gerit ipsa calorem.*

"Furthermore, water grows colder in wells when it is summer, because the earth is rarefied by the heat and sends abroad into the air any seeds of heat which it has of its own. The more therefore the earth is exhausted of its heat, the colder becomes that water which is hidden in the earth. When again all the earth is crushed by cold and congeals and, as it were, grows together, the result naturally is that by congealing it presses out into the wells any heat it has in itself."

He also provides us with a parallel explanation about a similar phenomenon associated with the spring of Hammon, the so-called "water of the sun" which is cold in the daylight and hot during the night (6.848–878). In this case, he gives first the erroneous explanation of the miraculous phenomenon, which is believed to be due to the sun passing under the earth (6.850–860) and then he proceeds to expound his case in atomic terms (6.861–878):[191]

> *Quae ratiost igitur? nimirum terra magis quod*
> *rara tenet circum fontem quam cetera tellus,*
> *multaque sunt ignis prope semina corpus aquai.*
> *hoc ubi roriferis terram nox obruit undis,*
> *extemplo penitus frigescit terra coitque.*   865

> *hac ratione fit ut, tamquam compressa manu sit,*
> *exprimat in fontem quae semina cumque habet ignis,*
> *quae calidum faciunt laticis tactum atque vaporem.*
> *inde ubi sol radiis terram dimovit obortus*
> *et rarefecit calido miscente vapore,*　　　　　　　　　　870
> *rursus in antiquas redeunt primordia sedes*
> *ignis, et in terram cedit calor omnis aquai.*
> *frigidus hanc ob rem fit fons in luce diurna.*
> 　*Praeterea solis radiis iactatur aquai*
> *umor et in lucem tremulo rarescit ab aestu;*　　　　　875
> *propterea fit uti quae semina cumque habet ignis*
> *dimittat, quasi saepe gelum, quod continet in se,*
> *mittit et exsolvit glaciem nodosque relaxat.*

"How comes it then? Assuredly because the ground keeps more porous about the spring than the rest of the earth, and there are many seeds of fire near the body of water. Therefore when night has overwhelmed the earth with its dewy waves, the earth suddenly grows cold to the heart and contracts; in this fashion, as though compressed by a hand, it presses out into the spring whatever seeds of fire it has, which cause the warm touch and heat of the water. Next when the sun rising has stirred apart the earth with his rays and made it porous as his warming heat mingles with it, the first-beginnings of fire return to their ancient places, and all the warmth of the water passes into the earth. For this reason the spring becomes cold in the daylight."

Besides, the fluid of the water is tossed about by the sun's rays, and the quivering heat makes it porous at the coming of light; for which reason it discharges all its seeds of fire, just as water often discharges the cold which it contains, and melts the ice and loosens its knots.

In both cases Lucretius emphasizes the porous texture of the earth, the sun's rays being the cause of this (*rarescit,* 6.841; *rara . . . circum fontem,* 6.862). In this way, he posits the sponge-like behaviour of the earth, upon which he builds his overall atomic explanation. Water is cold either because during the summer the earth emits into the air any heat particles that it has (6.842–844), or because during the daytime it keeps them within (6.861–863). Lucretius goes on to describe two processes of extrusion: in winter in the case of wells and at night for Hammon's spring the earth is contracted and the particles of fire, which are contained in the earth, are "squeezed out" towards the water. In connection with the wells, Lucretius explicitly specifies cold as the agent causing the earth to freeze and the subsequent "squeezing out process" (wells:

frigore cum premitur, 6.845; *exprimat . . . calorem,* 6.847; spring of Hammon: *frigescit,* 6.865; *exprimat,* 6.867). Still, when it comes to the spring of Hammon, as a counterpart to the sun's action in the reverse process Lucretius adds a short simile, "as if compressed by hand" (*tamquam compressa manu,* 6.866), in order to account for the otherwise automatic freezing of the earth and the extrusion of fire particles into water (*extemplo,* 6.865). Lucretius thus imposes the rationalization of a complicated physical phenomenon by bringing to mind the articulate "squeezing out the sponge" model and filling in logical gaps. Moreover, also concerning the spring of Hammon, Lucretius points out as a complementary cause for the change in the water's temperature the fact that during the daytime, apart from the earth, the sun also makes the substance of water porous. Yet, contrary to the behaviour of the spongy earth that retains the seeds of fire, porous water discharges those that it receives during the night (*rarescit ab aestu,* 6.875).[192]

We turn now to Lucretius' manipulation of the role of ἔκθλιψις with reference to the creation of the world and the articulation of the four elementary masses (5.452–454):[193]

> *quae quanto magis inter se perplexa coibant,*
> *tam magis expressere ea quae mare sidera solem*
> *lunamque efficerent et magni moenia mundi;*

> "and the more entangled they [the bodies of earth] came together, the more they squeezed out those particles which could make sea, stars, sun, and moon and the walls of the great world;"

As we have mentioned above, in this case the Atomists had granted the analogy a retrospective value and used it as a tool to reconstruct the remote past. More precisely, they claimed that at the very beginning of the world the particles of earth, being larger and more irregular, came together and squeezed out those of water, air and fire, which were smaller, smoother and rounder; that is actually how the great parts of the world, the *membra mundi,* came into being.

Without any doubt, this particular case of "squeezing out" is exceptionally perplexing, not only because of the temporal projection that its comprehension requires, but also due to its mechanistic nature. Whereas in his account of wells and springs Lucretius enhanced the passage with a short simile, the cosmological process in question, during which like moved towards its like, is explicitly said to be spontaneous (5.419–421).[194] Moreover, although in Pseudo-Plutarch's account a force that presses out of the earth the atoms of water, air and fire is vaguely mentioned (πληκτικὴ δύναμις μετεωρίζουσα, Epicur. fr. 308 Us.), in the present context this crucial factor is missing; actually there is no apparent cause to account for this particular mechanical movement of the atoms. It is then tempting to suggest that the pupil is here expected to recall the different aspects of the "squeezing out the sponge" metaphor, as articulated throughout the poem. However, the application of this model in this particular context could be judged something of a misuse, since this type of explanation presupposes that a superior force exerts the force, and thus carries teleological implications. It is very interesting to see how Lucretius attempts to overcome this deficiency of the model by calling upon supplementary means. In fact, several alternative metaphors are condensed within this passage, probably echoing Epicurus' own vocabulary.[195] In this way, Lucretius uses different explanatory models in combination as cognitive tools, thus shedding light upon different aspects of the phenomenon and eventually imposing his otherwise obscure explanation.

The image of the "squeezing out the sponge" model is also kept at the next stage of the creation of the world, in which the analogy between *anthropos* and *makranthropos* dominates (5.480–494). Here the use of the model is more appropriate, since all three facets of the metaphor are present. Earth is porous like a sponge (*per rara foramina* / "through the loose-knit interstices," 5.457). Moreover, two external forces, i.e. the tide of ether and the sun's rays, induce the earth to be compressed into compactness as if "pressed by hand" (*inque dies quanto circum magis aetheris aestus / et radii solis cogebant undique terram / verberibus crebris extrema ad limina in artum,* / "And day by day, the more the tide of ether and the sun's rays compressed the earth into compactness with frequent blows from all sides upon its outermost confines," 5.483–485). The product is seawater, which is depicted as sweat (*tam magis expressus salsus de corpore sudor* / "so much the more did the salt sweat, squeezed out of its body," 5.487).[196] By conflating these two major analogical models, Lucretius presents us with a coherent account of the creation of the world.

In the same spirit, Lucretius sketches the formation of clouds as a process of water particles being squeezed out of rivers and the earth like breath (6.476–482: *quae velut halitus hinc ita sursum expressa feruntur* / "which exhaled from these sources like breath are carried up in this way," 6.478).[197] Since water particles are pressed out, we could record here another instance of the "squeezing out the sponge" metaphor. At this point we should turn to Book 4, where Lucretius explains how animals lose substance by sweating and exhalation, and thus come to desire food, by means of the similar vocabulary of squeezing out and breathing out, this time used in a literal way (4.862–866):[198]

> *quae quia sunt exercita motu,*
> *multaque per sudorem ex alto pressa feruntur,*
> *multa per os exhalantur, cum languida anhelant,*
> *his igitur rebus rarescit corpus et omnis*
> *subruitur natura;*

"for since these [bodies] are always in quick movement, and since many bodies are pressed out from their depths in sweat, many are exhaled through the mouth when they pant from exhaustion, by these means therefore the body becomes rarefied and its whole nature is undermined;"

Therefore, while Lucretius likens here the mechanism of the formation of clouds to that of breathing, he introduces once more the makranthropic image of the earth. This addition in connection with rivers is probably necessitated partly by the sameness in the material substance of the object being compressed and the aggregation squeezed out (i.e. water particles), but mainly by the absence of an obvious motive force that would account for the mechanical phenomenon.

4.6 CONCLUSIONS

In the field of metaphor Empedocles armed Lucretius with an exemplar of how to employ yet another poetic device with analogical and cognitive power so as to shape difficult philosophical ideas for his didactic purposes. At the same time, Lucretius was well aware that, as well as sharing specific doctrinal precepts with Empedocles, Epicurus was also indebted to his metaphorical language to the extent that he expressed parallel ideas in similar terms. It has been argued that Lucretius himself appears to be turning directly to Empedocles' poem, from which he borrows specific metaphors; in this way he also develops corresponding ones already found in the Atomistic tradition. From this point of view, in the case of metaphors he finds himself more firmly on Epicurean ground than with his use of personifications. As might be expected, Lucretius' engagement with Empedocles' philosophical language clearly points to awareness of the concepts underlying it. In this connection, several passages have been pinpointed in which Lucretius establishes a direct intertextual dialogue with Empedocles' figurative wording in order to clarify his own philosophical stance.

Within this general framework, two main metaphorical fields, which bear a vivid Empedoclean stamp have been identified, i.e. three variant technological metaphors of mixture (fitting together, binding, weaving) and the "flowing water" metaphor. Two focal principles of Epicurus' philosophy, which are at variance with Empedocles' philosophy, play a regulatory role in Lucretius' reception and manipulation of these Empedoclean metaphors: the belief in the existence of void, and the theory of pores and effluences. Lucretius thus expands and systematizes the Empedoclean hints, while at the same time he clarifies his disagreement and his own use of the recontexualized metaphors. What is more, these actual Epicurean tenets enable Lucretius to build up two further conceptual models, i.e. the metaphor of "filling and emptying the container" and that of "squeezing out the sponge." Although both these concepts can be detected already in Epicurus' writings, still it is Lucretius who develops them into elaborate metaphorical fields, by applying the method that he has learnt from Empedocles and at the same time by further clarifying his philosophical discrepancy with his Presocratic predecessor. All in all, following Empedocles' example, and at times intentionally distancing himself from it, Lucretius pervasively employs a broad spectrum of metaphors to convey the Epicurean vision of reality, elucidate obscure phenomena, and intensify the ultimate sameness of physical phenomena, which are all conditioned by the universal natural laws.

The development of such a network of metaphors, which operates in several different contexts within the poem, has two important results: what might otherwise seem dissimilar concepts and processes are brought together and the homogeneity of the universe is further exemplified. While the first meaning of the word is always evoked, each instance of that metaphor sheds light upon other occurrences of it and simultaneously is illuminated by them. Conventional metaphors are incorporated into the Epicurean philosophical system, and others, which might have been thought of as dead are brought back to life. By the same token, Lucretius resorts to metaphors when translating abstract Epicurean terms. Last but not least, he picks up metaphors widely used by rival philosophical schools such as the Stoics and initiates an intertextual dialogue; by speaking in the same language and fighting them on their own ground with their own weapons, Lucretius strives to establish Epicurean truth against other rival doctrines.

Epilogue

This study has approached Lucretius' intertextual relationship with Emped-
ocles through a very specific prism: Lucretius' use of three major categories
of literary devices, namely personification, similes and metaphors, has been
explored and it has been shown that they are all used as analogical tools
with both demonstrative and probative force. Further, it has been argued
that Empedocles should be considered Lucretius' main intertext in this
area. In the course of this analysis I have shown that Lucretius' meticulous
engagement with Empedocles' poem not only should not be restricted to
the poetic level, but it is particularly intensive at the philosophical one as
well. Since Epicurean philosophy shares in common many doctrinal ele-
ments with that of Empedocles, Lucretius could turn back to the latter
and borrow a wide range of analogical means of thought and techniques
closely associated with them. Lucretius then improved them and used them
in order to better communicate his intricate philosophical message to his
Roman addressee, convert him to Epicureanism and thus liberate him from
superstitious fears about death and terrifying physical phenomena. Never-
theless, given specific discrepancies between Epicurus' and Empedocles'
philosophical systems, Lucretius had to clarify his Epicurean stance and
modify the corresponding literary devices before recontextualizing them
into his didactic philosophical poem.

These conclusions are important in two respects. In the first instance,
they let us reconsider and eventually redefine Lucretius' relationship
with his master, who is often thought of as his only Muse of knowledge.
Although Lucretius' intertextual relationship with Empedocles' poem does
not necessarily jeopardize his faith to Epicurus, certainly his choice to draw
so extensively from Empedocles deserves special attention. As our analysis
has shown, Lucretius' creation of his Latin version of Epicurean philosophy
was not just a mechanical process, sterilized by other influences, but rather a

multifaceted and dynamic one. At the same time, it turns out that Lucretius is of pivotal importance for the transmission of Empedoclean philosophical poetry to later Latin literature. From this point of view, this study could be considered as the starting point for study of Empedocles' presence in Augustan literature.

Notes

NOTES TO THE INTRODUCTION

1. There is a major disagreement as to whether Empedocles' fragments belong only to one poem (*Περὶ φύσεως*) or also to a second one (*Καθαρμοί*). However, I do not intend to get into the discussion about the number of Empedocles' poems here. For a recent discussion see Trépanier (2004) 1–30 with further bibliography. For practical reasons I will always refer to Empedocles' corpus in the singular, without necessarily implying that I prefer one view over the other.
2. Sedley (1998) 142–143 argues that this passage is modelled on a similar mixture of praise and criticism in Epicurus' *On Nature* Book 25, which is plausibly also directed against Empedocles.
3. Kollmann (1971) 89 n. 46; Gale (1994a) 59.
4. For a recent discussion concerning the division between the genres and the specific categorization of Lucretius' poem see Volk (2002) 25–68.
5. In this passage Cicero also attests the—plausibly simultaneous—publication of an *Empedoclea* by someone called Sallustius, which was probably a Latin translation or imitation of Empedocles and inferior to Lucretius' poem. Cf. also Cic. *De. or.* 1.217, *Acad.* 2.74, *Lael.* 24, *Re publ.* 3.19. See Bardon (1952) 335; Préaux (1964); Sedley (1998) 1–2.
6. According to Sedley (1998) 23–34, Empedocles' proem would consist of the following parts: a hymn to Aphrodite (cf. *DRN* 1.1–43), followed by an address to Pausanias (imitated in Lucretius' mention of Memmius in 1.25–43), a passage in which Pythagoras is praised (B129), a diatribe against the evils of blood sacrifice, a passage on metempsychosis and last a passage on the misleading language with which men describe the gathering and dispersal of matter as "birth" and "death" (B8 and B9). For objections about this reconstruction see e.g. Gale (1994a) 210; O'Brien (2001) 117–124; Trépanier (2004) 38–44. Nevertheless, Gale (1994a) 60 acknowledges that Empedocles' poem may have had a structural progression very similar to that of *DRN* 1 (cf. B6, B8–12, B15, B21 and B23). Cf. also further discussion on 37ff.

7. Tatum (1984). Cf. also Kollmann (1971) 89: "The climax of Empedocles' feat are his *carmina*, which are mentioned almost against the uses of syntax at the beginning of 731." I will not discuss here the highly intriguing issue of Lucretius' choice to write poetry. For this issue see Asmis (1995); Sider (1995); Wigodsky (1995).

8. For Empedocles' Muse (B3, B131, B4 and B23.9–11) see Trépanier (2004) 52–65. For Lucretius' allusions to Empedocles' Muse (especially in 1.1–49, 1.921–930, 6.47, 6.92–95) see Jobst (1907) 14; Waszink (1954) 254–255 n. 37; Clay (1983) 251–257; Gale (1994a) 68–69, 136–137. As I have recently argued (Garani forthcoming), it seems highly plausible that Empedocles' Calliope in Book 6 embeds Pythagorean connotations and may be read as an allegory of harmony, corresponding to Aphrodite in the proem to Book 1.

9. For Empedocles' Pausanias see B1 with Obbink (1993) 80–89. Regarding Memmius' identity we cannot be sure whether he was an aristocrat of his era, praetor and perhaps Lucretius' patron, or the tribune of 54 B.C. Cf. Hutchinson (2001). For Lucretius' addressee see Farrington (1965); Lenagham (1967); Classen (1968); Townend (1978); Clay (1983) 212–225; Keen (1985); Mitsis (1993); Volk (2002) 73–83 with further bibliography. For correspondences in the way both poets address their pupils see Jobst (1907) 11–14; Gale (1994a) 65. Gale notes the parallel didactic function of the frequent exhortations to their pupil: they are both encouraged to pay attention (e.g. Empedocles B17.14 and B17.26; *DRN* 1.331–333, 2.66), warned against rival theories (e.g. Empedocles B23.9; *DRN* 1.370, 1.1052), imagined as formulating objections (e.g. Empedocles B71.1; *DRN* 1.267) and assured of the value of the teaching they are receiving (e.g. Empedocles B23.11, B62.3; *DRN* 1.62–79 and the proems).

10. In Empedocles e.g. ἄλλο δέ τοι ἐρέω, B8.1; ἀλλ᾽ ἄγε μύθων κλῦθι, B17.14; ἄγε, B38.1. In *DRN* cf. e.g. *passim*: *nunc age, nonne vides, sed quoniam docui, illud in his rebus longe fuge credere*. See Gale (1994a) 63–64.

11. For theoretical claims about the use of repetition in Empedocles see B25, B35.1–2 with Hershbell (1968); DeRubeis (1991). Cf. examples of striking repetitions in Lucretius: 3.784–797 = (with slight alterations) 5.128–141, 1.670–671 = 1.792–793 = 2.753–754 = 3.519–520. For the association of Lucretius' practice of repetitions with the Epicurean practice of memorization (Epicur. *Ep. Hdt.* 35–36, 84–85; *DRN* 2.90, 2.581–582, 2.891, 4.643) see Ingalls (1971); Clay (1983) 176–186; Gale (1994a) 116–117; Schiesaro (1994) 98–104. For Lucretius' debt to Empedocles see Gale (1994a) 64. For more on their parallel use of repetition in connection with the cycle of growth and decay see below 11ff.

12. For Empedocles' use of compound adjectives as a didactic tool, which bring out essential qualities of the objects to which they are attached see Plut. *Quaest. Conv.* 683E with Gemelli Marciano (1990); Gale (1994a) 63 n. 236. For Lucretius' use of Empedoclean compound adjectives see Sedley (2003) and further discussion below.

13. Cf. also A2.
14. Hardie (1986) 16–22; Conte (1994); Schiesaro (forthcoming).
15. Gale (1994a) 191–192.
16. Hardie (1986) 209–213.
17. Furley (1970) 61–62.
18. Hardie (1986) 20.
19. Clay (1983) 49–52; Castner (1987). For the strong Empedoclean connotations see further discussion on 20ff. For Epicurus' viewing philosophy as prophecy see Epicurus *SV* 29; Diog. Laert. 10.12. Cf. Phld. *De Piet.* 2044–2045 Obbink; Cic. *Fin.* 2.20; Metrodorus fr. 37 Körte (*GV* 10) which quotes the oracle of Homer's prophet (*Il.* 1.70).
20. Sedley (1998) especially 11–34 and 44–46 has profoundly deepened our knowledge about Lucretius' poetical debt to Empedocles.
21. On the contrary Edwards (1989) believes that Lucretius' reference to Empedocles is completely ironical. According to him, despite the ostensive praise, the repetition of verbs meaning "it seems" undermines Lucretius' praise; probably Empedocles was not such an important figure as people thought. Similarly Edwards interprets the allusion to Empedocles' legendary death by leaping into Etna in order to be taken for a god (Diog. Laert. 8.70) as an indirect negative reference to his predecessor's personality, since, if this were true, it would constitute a disgrace to his fame (Cf. Hor. *Ars P.* 464–466).
22. Sedley (1998) 21.
23. Sedley (1998) 23. Cf. also ibid. 22 with particular reference to the Empedoclean colouring of Lucretius' proem: "Lucretius' purpose is to establish from the outset the precise Greek literary mantle he is assuming." This dichotomy regarding Empedocles' poetry and philosophy is also found in Aristotle, who claims that Homer and Empedocles have nothing in common but the metre (*Poet.* 1447b17–20).
24. Hallier (1857); Bästlein (1874–75); Jobst (1907); Kranz (1943); Niccolini (1955); J. Bollack (1959); Furley (1970); Gale (1994a) 59; Clay (1983) 22–23, 82–110, 253–257 and (2000); Campbell (2003) *passim.* Cf. also Roller (1988) 53, who goes so far so as to allege that Lucretius may have been Empedocles' devotee before becoming an Epicurean.
25. Sedley (1998) 18.
26. Campbell (2003) 167–168. Cf. Sedley (1976); Kleve (1978).
27. Westman (1955).
28. On uncertainty about the title see Obbink (1988). On Hermarchus against Empedocles see also Gallo (1985); Longo Auricchio (1988) 66–73, 92–99 and 125–150; Vander Waerdt (1988) 89–90; Obbink (1996) *passim.*
29. Gallavotti (1975–77); Casanova (1984); Smith (1992) 491–493 *ad loc.*
30. Sedley (1998) 18.
31. Sedley (1998) 20 n. 75 argues that Lucretius echoes Epicurus' own criticism in his *On Nature* Books 14 and 15, which in turn heavily rely upon

Theophrastus' *Physical Opinions*. Rösler (1973) claims that Lucretius here
relies exclusively on Peripatetic doxography, since his treatment of the three
Presocratics reiterates misunderstandings that were first introduced by
this tradition. Montarese (2005) 53–87 believes that Lucretius follows an
Epicurean text which was reviewing and criticizing earlier theories of mat-
ter. According to this view, this Epicurean author composed a text which
refuted fire monism (and with it monism generally), limited pluralism and
unlimited pluralism and was somehow dependent on the Peripatetic doxog-
raphy. See Clay (1983) 22 who rightly remarks that "a doxographic presen-
tation does not necessarily mean that Lucretius knew Empedocles through
a doxographic source. [. . .] He calls him *Acragantinus* (1.716). [. . .] It is
noteworthy too that, whereas Epicurus and Diogenes of Oinoanda speak of
Empedocles' elements as air, earth, fire and water, Lucretius speaks of them
as Empedocles did himself: *aera solem imbrem terras* (1.744)."

32. In this particular passage Empedocles is not the sole target of Lucretius'
     criticism; quite the opposite, his arguments attack any variety of the four-
     element theory (1.735–736). This multiplicity of rival theories (including
     probably the Peripatetics, the Stoics, even Heraclitus) that Lucretius tackles
     here could account for any divergences from the canonical—so to speak—
     Empedoclean theory of matter that he mainly attacks. This passage deserves
     further investigation and reconsideration of Lucretius' possible targets; such
     an analysis, however, falls beyond the scope of this study. Cf. e.g. Lenagham
     (1967) 232 n. 37. See now Piazzi (2005); Montarese (2005).

33. Cf. B14. Thanks to Empedocles' belief in the mechanism of pores and efflu-
     ences, his roots were able to intermingle with one another. We will come
     back to this issue in Section 4.2. On the Epicurean conception of void see
     DRN 1.329–397. Cf. also Inwood (1981); Sedley (1982b).

34. On divisibility in Empedocles see Macció (1980); Gemelli Marciano
     (1991). For the notion of indivisibility in the Atomic tradition see Konstan
     (1982); Bodnár (1998); Taylor (1999) 294 with further bibliography. Yet,
     Empedocles would not endorse Lucretius' conclusion that the roots' unlim-
     ited division would bring about their annihilation (cf. Cic. *Acad.* 1.27).

35. Montarese (2005) 72 rightly suggests that, since Empedocles nowhere holds
     the alternation in the nature of the four elements, Lucretius following his
     source launches an attack against quadruple pluralists.

36. Sedley (1998) 21.

37. Yet, it is probable that the title was not fixed. See Clay (1983) 82–83;
     Volk (2002) 84 n. 43. Three shadowy contemporaries of Lucretius, i.e.
     Catius, Egnatius and Varro Reatinus, are also said to have written *de
     rerum natura,* possibly following the title of Lucretius' poem. For these
     authors see Sallmann (1962) 239–240; Rawson (1985) 282–285. For
     more on Varro Reatinus and Empedocles see Deschamps (1986); on
     Empedocles, Varro and Lucretius see Deschamps (1997).

38. Cf. Melissus *On nature, or on what there is* (Περὶ φύσεως ἢ περὶ τοῦ ὄντος). See. Sedley (1998) 21–22.
39. Furley (1970) 60.
40. Sedley (1998) 28–29.
41. Leonard and Smith (1942) 219 *ad* 1.146–328; Hallier (1857) 15; Kranz (1943) 83 (who disregards Epicurus)
42. It is very tempting to point out that Epicurus' language itself in *Ep. Hdt.* 39 sounds very Empedoclean, given the unusual stylish repetition. Cf. Empedocles B16. For Lucretius' relationship with Parmenides see Rumpf (2005).
43. Kyllo (1994) 192.
44. Hallier (1857) 16–17; Jobst (1907) 24; Kranz (1943) 89; J. Bollack (1959) 674. Cf. also *DRN* 3.806–818, 5.351–363.
45. Gale (1994a) 61 n. 225. Cf. also 2.296 *adaugescit* with B17.32 ἐπαυξήσειε.
46. Cox (1986) 224–227.
47. Trépanier (2003a) 8.
48. For a recent discussion of the cycle see the collection of essays in Pierris ed. (2005).
49. E.g. B17.1 = (A) → B17.2 = (B); B17.4 = (A) → B17.5 = (B); B17.7 = (A) → B17.8 = (B); B17.9 = (A) → B17.10 = (B); B17.16 = (A) → B17.17 = (B). Cf. also B20.2–3 = (A) → B20.4–5 = (B); B22.4–5 = (A) → B22.6–9 = (B); B26.5 = A → B26.6 = (B). See exception in B21: B21.8 (B) → B21.9 (A); See Graham (1988); Trépanier (1999).
50. See Clay (1983) 85–87. As Clay points out, the words *exortum* (1.5) and *exoritur* (1.23) represent common Latin equivalents for γένεσις and γίγνεται.
51. Plut. *Adv. Col.* 10.1111F-12.1113E. Cf. Westman (1955) 57.
52. Cf. discussion in the chapter on Personification 43.
53. In the course of the study I will identify several examples of Lucretius' cycle of growth and decay. See Liebeschuetz (1967–68); Minadeo (1965) and (1969).
54. For further discussion of this issue see the chapter on Personification 40ff.
55. Schiesaro (1994) 100. Schiesaro also quotes Dionigi's argument (1988 11ff.) that certain expressions that Lucretius employs to describe the behaviour of the atoms (2.1021 *concursus motus ordo positura figura*) are derived from grammatical terminology and concludes (p. 85) that "it is reasonable to suggest that a great number of stylistic and rhetorical features of the poem are actually devised to reflect a set of underlying atomic phenomena." See also Thury (1987) 284–287.
56. Gale (1994a) 71.
57. Empedocles' cosmic cycle has been used to explain Lucretius' so-called "pessimism." See Gale (1994a) 71 n. 264. Cf. 2.1105–1174 and 5.91–415. Cf. especially 5.222–227 with Empedocles B118.
58. Giussani (1898) 77; Bailey (1947) 1355 *ad* 5.235–323. Sedley (1998) 174 argues that it is from Theophrastus (fr. 184 FHS&G) that Lucretius got the order earth–water–air–fire which describes the cosmic strata outwards from the earth to the heavens in 5.235–323 (cf. 5.449–459, 5.495–498).

On this basis, Montarese (2005) 337 concludes that the emphasis on the four elements derives from Theophrastus and not from Empedocles. However, Sedley (1998) 74 notes that elsewhere in the poem a different order of the elements occurs (1.567, 1.715, 5.142–143, 5.248–249). Therefore, although Theophrastus could be bestowed with the elaboration of the four-element theory that Lucretius draws upon, to which Sedley points, still Empedocles could be considered the ultimate source. Cf. the similar Theophrastean intermediary regarding Empedoclean elements in the case of Lucretius' meteorological account below in the chapter on Similes 130ff.

59. Jobst (1907) 25.

60. Empedocles repeats these verses in a formulaic way in B21.10–13 and fr. a (i) 9–fr. a (ii) 2 M&P, this time though used not in a simile but straightforwardly for the description of the creation of the world. For more on similes in Empedocles and Lucretius see chapter 2.

61. Cf. 1.196–198, 1.907–914, 2.688–699, 2.1013–1018. The fact that *elementa* was used in Latin also with reference to the four Empedoclean elements (Lucilius 789–795 Krenkel) could point to this phenomenon of unified imagery. What is more, *elementa* translates the Greek word στοιχεῖα, which was used by Epicurus also for Empedocles' roots (Epicur. *ΠΦ* Book 14, fr. 60 col. xxxiv Leone = fr. 29.22 Arr.², fr. 60 col. xxxvi Leone = fr. 29.24 Arr.²). Although the analogy with the letters of the alphabet had already been used by Plato, it seems to go back to Leucippus and Democritus (Cf. Arist. *Metaph.* 985b16–19, *Gen. corr.* 315b6ff.). For the history of the analogy see Diels (1899); Snyder (1980) 31–52; Volk (2002) 100–105.

62. For Lucretius' practice of following Empedocles' technique of using a range of alternative terms see Sedley (1998) 44–46.

63. We should note the identification of sky (οὐρανός) with the element of air also in Empedocles B22.2. See Furley (1970) 55 with further bibliography; Sedley (1998) 16–19, who, however, does not fully endorse Furley's conclusions. See also Schmidt (1975); Hardie (1986) 168–172.

64. Snyder (1972). Snyder also notes Lucretius' typical pairing of the two "heavier" elements, water and earth, and the two "lighter" elements, fire and air. See also Mackay (1955); Sedley (1998) 14–15.

65. Cf. especially Section 3.4.2.

66. See chapter on Personification 35ff.

67. Furley (1970) 61. Cf. also Sedley (2003) 2–4; Campbell (2003) 98–138 *ad* 5.837–877.

68. Campbell (2003) 107. See also Sedley (1998) 19–20; Campbell (2003) 109–111 *ad* 5.837.

69. Sedley (1998) 120–123.

70. Campbell (2000) and (2003) *passim*.

71. Simplicius (*In Phys.* CIAG 9, 371.33–372.14) acknowledges the affinity between the doctrine of Empedocles and the Epicureans in this issue. This

affinity with Empedocles' zoogony has been noted down already by Jobst (1907) 38. Cf. also Furley (1970) 60–61 with n. 15 who points out the close similarity between B57 and 5.837–841. Campbell (2003) 102 *ad* 5.837–854, records the main similarities with Empedocles in this section at 5.839 (cf. B61.3–4 about the existence of hermaphrodites), 5.842 (cf. B60 about creatures practically limbless), 5.845 and 5.847 (cf. B71 about the role of Aphrodite), 5.864–867. Regarding the last passage, Campbell follows Sedley (2003) 10–11, who rightly suggests that, when Lucretius pairs two compound adjectives (5.864: *levisomna*, 5.866: *lanigeraeque*), he unmistakably echoes Empedocles, with whom he agrees on the account about the survival of the fittest, in this case thanks to their usefulness to mankind. Sedley accepts that the echo here bears philosophical value, and underlines the explanatory value of the adjectives. In line with this Sedley ibid. 6–9 adds another echo from Empedocles' zoogony (2.1081–1083 = fr. a (ii) 26–28 M&P).

72. See Campbell (2003) 139–179 *ad* 5.878–924.

73. Campbell (2003) 102. For Sedley's arguments against Furley's thesis see chapter on Personification 41ff.

74. Campbell (1999). Cf. also Clay (2000) 265: "Lucretius is quite capable of situating Empedocles in a meaningful context in place and he is as capable of understanding Epicurus' place in the history of philosophy as he is of making himself a part of that history."

75. Campbell (2003) 181–182, quoting Hardie (1986) 11. See also especially D. Fowler (2000b) 138–155.

76. Lyne (1994) 194. Cf. also ibid. 196: "This is one of those many occasions where the text of the *Aeneid* is in dialogue, one might say in conflict, with itself." Ibid. 198: "Poetic creativity works at such incalculably multiple and profound levels, poetic genius is so rich, that the poet may pack his text with meaning and effects way beyond what his immediate audience can grasp, way beyond indeed what he himself may be consciously aware of."

77. Hardie (1995). For Vergil's *Eclogue* 6 see Stewart (1959), Spoerri (1970), Farrell (1991) 253–272 and 291–324. For Vergil's *Georgics* see Nelis (2004); for Vergil's *Aeneid* see Nelis (2000) and (2001) 96–112, 289, 345–359. For Ovid's *Metamorphoses* see Hardie (1995) and Wheeler (2000) 12–23; for Ovid's *Fasti* see Pfligersdorffer (1973), Hardie (1991).

78. Cf. 1.146–148, 3.91–93, 6.39–41.

79. Clay (1983) 105–108. Clay mentions Cicero's corresponding—though semantically different—collocation *naturae ratio* (e.g. *ND* 1.20). Cf. Sedley (1998) 37–38; D. Fowler (2002) 141–143 *ad* 2.61.

80. Diog. Laert. 10.31–32; Epicur. *Ep. Hdt.* 38, *KΔ* 23–24.

81. Long (1971); Long and Sedley (1987) 78–97 with further bibliography.

82. Cf. B2.1. For Empedocles' theory of sensory perception see also A86–94. See also Beare (1906) *passim;* Long (1966); Andriopoulos (1972).

83. Schiesaro (1985).

84. Cf. Section 4.4.

85. For the place of touch in Lucretius see Schoenheim (1966).

86. For the "psychagogic" function of this metaphor see Schrijvers (1969); P. Fowler (1984) 162–163 *ad* 6.68.

87. Kranz (1943) 77 and 104 compares these verses with B110 and B111. See also Bignone (1916) 481. For objections see J. Bollack (1960).

88. Cf. 1.324, 1.599–600, 6.187ff.

89. Cf. in *DRN obscura reperta,* 1.136; *res . . . occultas,* 1.145. Lucretius also employs as equivalent of ἄδηλον the words *caecus* (e.g. 1.277, 1.295, 1.1110), *naturam clandestinam* (1.779). Cf. Cic. *De or.* 1.68 *in naturae obscuritatem.* See Kleve (1963) 28–31; Clay (1983) 107.

90. Cf. Sextus Empiricus' categorization of the imperceptible things, which may reflect an Epicurean scheme (*Pyr.* 2.97–99, *Adv. Math.* 8.145–156): 1. Things that are absolutely and forever beyond the ken of human understanding, called καθάπαξ ἄδηλα (e.g. the number of the grains of sand). 2. Things which naturally cannot be grasped by means of direct investigation, but only by means of inference, called ἄδηλα φύσει (e.g. the pores in the body). 3. Things which are temporarily non-evident due to particular circumstances, called πρὸς καιρὸν ἄδηλα (e.g. the city of Athens, when I am not there). Temporarily non-evident matters can be revealed by commemorative signs, whereas naturally non-evident matters can be revealed by indicative ones. See Schiesaro (1990) 95–101; Allen (2001) 108–109; D. Fowler (2002) 190ff.

91. See Ernout and Robin (1928 III) 17 *ad* 5.102; Kranz (1943); Clay (1983) 50–51; Castner (1987). Cf. *DRN* 5.97 with Empedocles B114 and Ernout and Robin (1928 III) 16 *ad loc.* Cf. also *DRN* 5.148–151 with Empedocles B133 and *DRN* 5.155 with Empedocles B131, which reveals a similarity in their theology. Jobst (1907) 46. Cf. also n. 19 above for the prophetic imagery that follows again in connection with Empedocles.

92. As D. Fowler (2002) 385–386 *ad* 2.308 remarks, the doctrine of *nil admirari* goes back to Democritus, whose ἀθαμβίη (DK68 A169) had much of the breadth of meaning of Epicurus' ἀταραξία. Cf. Conte (1994); Warren (2002) 29–71.

93. Diller (1932); Lloyd (1966) 337–341 and 353–355, (1979) 129–138.

94. Cf. Epicur. *Ep. Hdt.* 38, 39; *Ep. Pyth.* 87, 97, 104; fr. 137.10–15 Arr.[2] (= fr. 212 Us.). Cf. also Epicur. fr. 263 Us. (Plut. *Adv. Col.* 29.1124B); Phld. *De Sign.* vi, xv, xxvii De Lacy. See Furley (1971); Wasserstein (1978); Sedley (1982a); Asmis (1984) 175–224; Barnes (1988); Allen (2001) 194–223; D. Fowler (2002) 186–195.

95. Cf. debates in Phld. *De Signis* with De Lacy and De Lacy (1978). Cf. also Asmis (1984) especially 197–211; Allen (2001).

96. Schrijvers (1999) 183–213; Schiesaro (1990) *passim;* D. Fowler (2002) 186–208 *ad* 2.112–141. Cf. *significant,* 2.128; *significat,* 4.696 corresponding to

the Greek technical term σημεῖα. Cf. also *simulacrum et imago,* 2.112; *exemplare . . . vestigia notitiai,* 2.124.

97. Schiesaro (forthcoming).
98. This formula recurs in 2.565, 3.690, 6.139, 6.249. Cf. also 1.188. 1.803, 1.855, 2.149, 2.246, 2.707, 2.867, 3.30, 3.353, 4.504. Leonard and Smith (1942) 569 *ad* 4.504 suggest that Lucretius intended the literal force of "grasped by the hand." Cf. Epicur. fr. 247 Us. πάντων δὲ κρηπὶς καὶ θεμέλιος ἡ ἐνάργεια.
99. Clay (1983) 48. Cf. *perspicis,* 1.949; *pervideamus,* 1.956; *pernosces,* 1.1114; *pervideas,* 1.1117; *pervideas,* 2.90; *pernoscere,* 3.181; *persentis,* 4.25; *perspicere,* 6.380. We should note that Empedocles also appeals to Pausanias, employing verbs with intellectual meaning, and encourages him to make use of his mental powers (e.g. νόει, B3.8; γνῶθι, B4.3; νόῳ δέρκευ, B17.21; ἴσθι, B110.10; cf. especially B23.11 (ἀλλὰ τορῶς ταῦτ᾽ ἴσθι,) with *DRN* 1.921 (*Nunc age quod superest cognosce et clarius audi.* / "Come now, mark and learn what remains, and hear a clearer strain"). See Schiesaro (1985) 157.
100. Cf. *spectare,* 2.2; *cernere,* 2.4; *tueri,* 2.5; *despicere* 2.9 which correspond to Epicurean terms for cognition (e.g. συνθεωρεῖν, συνορᾶν). For Lucretius' philosophical use of the religious imagery of initiation into mystery cults, the important role of the revelation of light involved in this process and the μακαρισμός for those who gained true knowledge of the natural world see Gale (1994a) 193–195; D. Fowler (2000c) 213–215; D. Fowler (2002) 25–28 *ad* 2.1ff. and 131–143 *ad* 2.54–61. For similar imagery in Empedocles see B110.1–2, B129.4–6, B132.
101. Gentner (1982) 108. Cf. Lakoff (1993) 202–251.
102. Hardie (1986) 221.
103. Schiesaro (1990) 32–34 and *passim.* Relevant here is the notion of ἐπιλογισμός and the Epicurean principle of ἐπιβολὴ τῆς διανοίας (cf. in *DRN animum . . . advertere,* 2.125; *inice mentem,* 2.1080; *conicere ut possis ex hoc,* 2.121). See also Bailey (1928) 559–576.
104. Hardie (1986) 222.
105. Hardie (1986) 221–222. See also Hardie's remark that "the awareness of the real analogy between the two things compared sets up a two-way movement within the simile: in the Lucretian simile the access of fresh vision or understanding works in both directions; as well as illustrating the less clear by the more clear, the simile also adjusts our perception of its own content."
106. For the terms tenor and vehicle see Silk (1974) 8–15, who elaborates on terminology first used by Richards (1936) 94. See also Silk (2003); Innes (2003). In particular for Empedocles see now Rosenfeld-Löffler (2006) especially 11–33.
107. See the correspondences between the two parts of the simile: man: *vestigia parva,* 1.402 → dogs: *vestigia certa,* 1.406; man: *caecasque latebras / insinuare,* 1.408–409 → dogs: *naribus inveniunt intectas fronde quietes,* 1.405.
108. Cf. also Phld. *De Sign.* xxi.20 De Lacy with Clay (1998) 167–168.
109. See West (1969) 75; Leen (1984) 111–112; Thury (1987) 276–280.

110. D. Fowler (2000c) 210. We should distinguish between different catego-
ries of *vestigia* within the didactic context. The footprints that the pupil is
asked to trace down and follow are different from Epicurus' *vestigia* (3.3–4),
which Lucretius intends to follow, since the latter do not leave any space
for creation. Moreover, πρόληψις is physically a footprint on the mind. See
D. Fowler (2002) 203–204 *ad* 2.124; Schiesaro (forthcoming). Kennedy
(2000) 211–212 rightly draws attention to the fact that Lucretius' scientific
venture can be well described both by means of the metaphor of discovery
and that of invention. According to him, "the metaphor of discovery sug-
gests that the laws of nature are immanent in the physical world, written,
if you like in the Book of Nature. [. . .] On the other hand, the metaphor
of invention implies that investigators of the natural world create linguistic
constructs, invent descriptions of the world which are more or less useful
for predicting and controlling its phenomena."
111. Ernout and Robin (1925 I) 100 *ad* 1.404. Jobst (1907) 49 compares
Empedocles B101 also with *DRN* 4.680–682. Lucretius' simile bears also
features of Empedocles' similes, such as the multiple-correspondence tech-
nique, that we will discuss in the chapter on Similes.
112. Martin and Primavesi (1998) 232; Sedley (2003) 7–8 especially n. 20. Cf.
2.597, 2.1081.
113. D. Fowler (2000b) 154.
114. I will limit myself here to Rome. For Apollonius Rhodius' reception of
Empedocles see Kyriakou (1994), Nelis (2000); for Aratus' reception of
Empedocles see Traglia (1963).
115. Bignone (1916) 271–272, 490 *ad* B117. Cf. Skutsch (1985) 166 n. 18 for
objections.
116. Norden (1915) 10–30. The historical setting is probably the revolt of Fale-
rii, in 241 BC, provoking the re-opening of the *Ianus Geminus,* which had
been closed at the end of the First Punic War. See also Skutsch (1985) 394–
396 and 403–405.
117. Bignone (1929) 22–25.
118. Hardie (1986) 78–79.
119. Hardie (1986) 78–83 *passim.*
120. Courtney (1993) 30–38 *ad* frs. 35–41; Hardie (1986) 81.
121. Merrill (1918); Harrison (2002).
122. Lucretius describes himself in similar language (1.25) and also Epicurus (5.54).
123. Gale (1994a) 108; ibid. 107 also notes that apart from Empedocles, Ennius
and Homer are the only two poets to whom Lucretius refers by name.
124. Cf. also 6.95.
125. Hardie (1986) 79–80. As Gale (2001) 170 remarks, Lucretius comes back
to Homer's mortality in 3.1025–1044, where poetry is subordinated to
mortality.
126. Sedley (1998) 31.

127. Friedländer (1941) 20; Snyder (1980) 31 and 107.
128. I follow Inwood's translation (CTXT-69b).
129. Gale (2001) 168–169. For Empedocles' pun in B77–78 see Wright (1995a) 224 *ad loc.*
130. Sedley (1998) 31–32.
131. Hardie (1986) 18.

NOTES TO CHAPTER ONE

1. For a modern discussion on personification see Lakoff and Turner (1989) especially 72–80; Paxson (1994) especially 8–62. Specifically for the use of personification in Greek thought see Webster (1954).
2. Cf. e.g. Cic. *ND* 2.63ff. with Pease (1958) *ad loc.* for the Stoic view of *Terra* as an actual God suffused by the *anima mundi*. The *Magna Mater* is also interpreted allegorically by Varro (in August. *De civ. D.* 7.24b-c) and the Stoic Cornutus *Theol. Gr.* 6 pp. 5–6 Lang.
3. E.g. Cic. *ND* 1.18, *Div.* 2.40; Epicur. fr. 359 Us. = Hipp. Philos. 22.3 = *Dox. Graec.* 572.
4. E.g. Epicur. *Ep. Hdt.* 76–77, *Ep. Men.* 123–124; *DRN* 5.1161–1240.
5. *DRN* 5.1161–1240; Phld. *De Piet.* 1176–1217 Obbink with Campbell (2003) 164 *ad* 5.908.
6. Epicur. frs. 568–569 Us. = Diog. Laert. 10.120; fr. 43 and fr. 89 Arr.[2]; Phld. *De Piet.* 225–231 and 2480–2509 Obbink; *De Poem.* 5 cols. 1–6 Mangoni, as quoted by Campbell (2003) 102 *ad* 5.837–854. Cf. also the condemnation of Stoic allegory by Phld. *De Piet.* pt 2. cols. 123ff. (Obbink forthcoming) = *P. Herc.* 1428 cols. 1ff. (Henrichs 1974), as quoted also by Campbell (2003) 60 *ad* 5.795–796. See further discussion by Clay (1995); Obbink (1995b). In this section I will not discuss the distinctions between personification, allegory, symbolism and allegorical exegesis. For a comprehensive discussion see Gale (1994a) especially 19–26, 39–45. As Gale (1994a) 19 notes, personification may be defined as the attribution of a personality to an abstraction or to a concrete but inanimate entity, while allegory is essentially narrative in form, though often (but not necessarily) involving personified abstracts.
7. Obbink (1994) 111. See also Henrichs (1974); Obbink (2002). Cf. Cic. *ND* 1.36–41.
8. Whitman (1987) 271.
9. A thorough discussion of Lucretius' ideas about myth and gods is well beyond the scope of this study. For this see Ackermann (1979); Gale (1994a).
10. Gale (1994a) 26–32.
11. Lines 2.644–651 are repeated in 1.44–49, just after the invocation to Venus where Lucretius defines the essence of divine. For problems with this

passage see Sedley (1998) 27. In 5.110–234 Lucretius embarks on more detailed refutation of the theological view of the world. In the same book (5.1161–1240), he gives the historical account of the origins of the false concepts about gods.

12. Campbell (2003) 60–61 *ad loc.*

13. See chapter on Metaphors 153ff.

14. Gale (1994a) 70.

15. E.g. the word *coetus* which is used both for sexual intercourse and social coming together (*TLL* iii, 1439, 47ff.). In my reading of the words, I will give preference to their meaning of socio-political gathering, rather than the underlying meaning of sexual intercourse, because we are dealing with coming together of more than just two atoms or atomic compounds. However, this does not prevent the other meaning from standing out, depending on the context. For the words *coeo, coetus, coniungo* etc. used with sexual connotations in Latin see Adams (1982) 178–180. Cf. also the word *condicio,* which can mean both agreement and marriage (see below 59). I will refrain from dealing here with the verb *coniungere:* although it can also mean "to get married," I will give preference here to its primary meaning "to join together," without excluding the possibility of vague metaphorical hints in its use by Lucretius (see Section 4.2).

16. For the role of Empedocles' forces see Section 1.1.

17. Ἀφροδίτη: B17.24, B22.5, B66, B71.4, B86, B87, B151; Κύπρις: B73.1, B75.2, B95, B98.3, B128.3.

18. Cf. also B17.21–26, B29; a similar attitude is expressed by Xenophanes (e.g. DK21 B15).

19. Menander Rhetor I.333.12–15 (A23), I.337.1–13 ; Ammonius *In Int.* CIAG 4.5, 249.1–21. See Wright (1995a) 22.

20. Gale (1994a) 65–66. Cf. also B21.12 in which the gods are said to be mortal, even if long lived (θεοὶ δολιχαίωνες).

21. In the third stage whole-natured beings were created (B62). The present generation of men and women belong to the fourth stage. There is a major argument over Empedocles' cosmogony, especially whether he has only one cosmogony and zoogony or a double one, which takes place in the other half of the cosmic cycle. For a recent discussion see Trépanier (2003a); Sedley (2005).

22. See Arist. *Cael.* 300b25–31; Simpl. *In Cael.* CIAG 7, 586.5–587.26, *In Phys.* CIAG 9, 371.33ff. Cf. Arist. *De An.* 430a27–30, *Gen. an.* 722b3–28.

23. Sedley (2005) 339. He also adds to this list B96 and B98 in which Love figures as preparing her materials, such as flesh, bone and blood, by mixing the four roots in a variety of proportions. Simplicius (*In Cael.* CIAG 7, 528.3–530.26) adds B71, B73, B75, which refer to Aphrodite's role today.

24. In B19 Aphrodite is called σχεδύνην. Cf. also the use of the word ἁρμονία both as a proper name (B122.2, perhaps B27.2) and meaning "the sort of

mechanism that reconciles unlikes, cohesive structure" (B23.4, B96.4). Plato's Craftsman in the *Timaeus* and Aristotle's Nature in his *Physics* are striking examples of philosophical usages of personification in order to illustrate the teleological workings of Nature.

25. Arist. *Phys.* 198b29–32, 199b10–12, *Part. an.* 640a18–25; Simp. *in Phys.* CIAG 9, 371.33–372.11. Cf. Furley (1987) 177–200; Furth (1987); Johnson (2005) 95–104.

26. Furley (1970) 60. See further discussion in 15ff.

27. See Trépanier (2003a) 52–54; Campbell (2003) 103–109 *ad* 5.837–844; Sedley (1998) 20. For the opposite idea see Mourelatos (1986) 167; Solmsen (1968) 336.

28. See Section 2.1.

29. As far as the exact symbolism of Aphrodite's figure is concerned, there are numerous alternative possibilities, which are not mutually exclusive; e.g. spring, peace, poetic *lepos, voluptas,* katastematic pleasure etc. For the proem see the excellent discussion by Gale (1994a) 208–224 with bibliography cited there, from which I amply draw for my discussion. Cf. also Sedley (1998) 10–34; Giancotti (1959); Kleve (1966); Kenney (1977) 13–17; Clay (1983) 82–110; Catto (1988–9); Nugent (1994); D. Fowler (2002) 444–452.

30. For the Muse see Section 1.1.

31. Obbink (1995) 208–209; Sider (1997) 187–190.

32. Gale (1994a) 219, who points out the existing similarities between *Venus genetrix* and *natura creatrix.* For Parmenides' Goddess see DK28 B8.3–6 with Clay (1983) 87; Gale (1994a) 51. For a possible connection with Stoic Zeus see Asmis (1982). Especially for Empedocles see Munro (1893) 328; Jobst (1907) 56. More recently see Furley (1970) 55–57; Gale (1994a) 71–72, 219–220.

33. Sedley (1998) 24.

34. Sedley (1998) 24–25. See further Sedley (2003) for more instances of the same phenomenon of pairing compound adjectives. For this aspect of Empedocles' poetic technique see also Gemelli Marciano (1990) 83–144. For other such instances in Lucretius see also 25, 47, 84–85, 190, 224.

35. Gale (1994a) 219.

36. Hom. *Od.* 8.266–369. Cf. e.g. Heraclitus Ponticus *Quaest. Hom.* 69.1–6. Cf. Pl. *Rep.* 3.390c; Scholion T *ad Od.* 8.332, reporting the opinion of Zoilus (p. 386 Dindorf). Gale (1994a) 41–42, 71–72; O'Brien (2001) 119–123.

37. Gale (1994a) 83. See also Edmunds (2002).

38. Sedley (1998) 17–28, especially 27.

39. Gale (1994a) 72. On the contrary Sedley (1998) 27 actually believes in the existence of such a scene in Empedocles' proem. Along the same line as Gale, Campbell (1999) comments on lines 1.56–57 in which Lucretius

states that all things are created out of atoms and are again dissolved into them: while Sedley (1998) 28–29 supports a strongly Empedoclean reading of this passage comparing the idea of cyclical creation and destruction with that in Empedocles' B17, Campbell rightly suggests that Lucretius seems to implicitly argue against Empedocles' cosmic forces, Love and Strife, since nature is in charge of both creative and destructive processes.

40. Gale (1994a) 41–42. Cf. Sedley (1998) 27, who sees in Empedocles "a moral use of myth and prayer."
41. See p. 223 n. 6.
42. Sedley (1998) 27 n. 98.
43. Cf. also Philodemus' hostile reference to the Stoic allegoresis of Aphrodite: *PHerc.* 1428 col. i 1–4 Henrichs = Phld. *De Piet.* pt. 2 col. 123 Obbink (forthcoming) Ἀφρο-] | δείτην δύναμιν | οὖσαν συναπτικὴν | οἰκείως τῶν μερῶ[ν] πρὸς ἄλληλα / "that Aprhodite is a force joining the parts fittingly to one another;" *PHerc.* 1428 col. iv 32—col. v 8 Henrichs = Phld. *De Piet.* pt. 2 cols. 127 Obbink (forthcoming) καὶ Εὐνομίαν καὶ Δί- | κην καὶ Ὁμόνοιαν [καὶ] | Ἰρήνην καὶ Ἀφροδ[εί-] | την παρ[α]πλή- | σιον πᾶν. / "And that Eunomia and Dike and Homonoia and Eirene and Aphrodite and everything of this sort are all the same thing."
44. See Introduction 1.1.
45. Sedley (1998) 20.
46. Sedley (1998) 27.
47. See Section 2.1.
48. For the notion of nature in Lucretius see Merrill (1891); Heidel (1910); Sallmann (1962); Pellicer (1966); Clay (1983) 89; Gigandet (1996); and D. Fowler (2002) 243 *ad* 2.168.
49. D. Fowler (2002) 243 *ad* 2.168 ascribes to Nature 7 functions in *DRN: creatrix / daedala,* provider, permitter / forbidder, demander, forcer, governor (*gubernans*), destroyer.
50. For the relationship of this monologue with Bion's Hellenistic diatribe see Wallach (1976); Reinhardt (2002).
51. For the language of Empedocles see Traglia (1952) especially 11–40, 117–160 and *passim;* Gerke (1953) 7–57; Capizzi (1987); Gemelli Marciano (1990).
52. Cf. also B17, B53, B100, B115, fr. a (ii) 3 M&P, A30. See Capizzi (1987) 115–117.
53. See Gemelli Marciano (1990) 141, 151 and *passim.*
54. In B27 Diels–Kranz unnecessarily conflate two Empedoclean fragments; hence, modern editors make two fragments out of it: B27.1 = Simpl. CIAG *In Phys.* 10, 1183.30 = 21.1 Wright = 33.1 Inwood; B27.2 = Plut. *De fac.* 926E7 = 19.2 Wright = 31.2 Inwood; as Wright (1995a) 187 remarks, Simplicius' passage refers to the complete mixture of the elements under the reign of Love, whereas Plutarch writes about the four elements completely unmixed under the power of Strife.

55. See Gemelli Marciano (1990) 51. About the sun see also B44.
56. As Lloyd (1966) 233 notes, each of the Milesians held that the primary substance of things is alive and divine. For a different interpretation of B59 see O'Brien (1969) 325–336. Cf. also A40 = Arist. *Gen. corr.* 333b19–22.
57. Cf. also B38, B96, B98.
58. Gemelli Marciano (1990) 49; Wright (1995a) 204 *ad loc.*
59. Cf. Velleius' criticism against Empedocles' ascription of divinity to his 4 elements (Cic. *ND* 1.29).
60. Sedley (1998) 44.
61. Keen (1979) 64–65.
62. Keen (1979) 65.
63. Cf. also 1.240, 2.459, 4.70, 5.876, 6.453, 6.1010 with D. Fowler (2002) 181 *ad* 2.102.
64. Cf. also 2.1114–1115 with Empedocles B37, both discussed in 73 Cf. also 2.197 (*respuat umor aquae*) with Empedocles B115.10 (ἀπέπτυσε).
65. See the accumulation of compound adjectives: 2.1081: *montivagum genus,* 2.1082: *geminam prolem,* 2.1083: *squamigerum pecudes et corpora cuncta volantum.* Sedley (2003) 6–9 comments on the similarity between 2.1081–1083 and fr. a (ii) 26–28 M&P. Empedocles speaks of mountain-wandering beasts (θηρῶν ὀριπλάγκτων), the twin race of humans (δίδυμον φῦμα), root-bearing fields (ῥιζοφόρων γέννημα), and a vine-climbing grape-cluster (ἀμπελοβάμονα βότρυν), while Lucretius replaces the last two items with scale-bearing herds and birds. Given the differences between the two passages, probably Lucretius translates a lost part of Empedocles' zoogony, repeated with variations from fr. a (ii) 26–28 M&P. At any rate, Lucretius' linguistic debt does not seem to conceal any philosophical resonance. For Lucretius' pairing of compound adjectives as an Empedoclean fingerprint-test see 25, 40, 84–85, 190, 224.
66. Cf. *ignea corpora,* 1.679; *corpus aquae,* 2.232.
67. Cf. also the personification of *diffusilis aether* (*avido complexu,* 5.470) which seems to echo directly Empedocles' B38.4 quoted in 148.
68. Cabisius (1984–85). See also Masson (1907) 26; Davies (1931–32); Pope (1949); Kenney (1977) 33; D. Fowler (1989) and (2002); Schiesaro (forthcoming). As Schiesaro (forthcoming) remarks, this kind of analysis does not aim at a new politicization of the *DRN* as Farrington (1939) 172–216 claims.
69. D. Fowler (1989) 145 and (2002) 379 *ad* 2.302.
70. Cf. Aristotle's grouping together of Parmenides' and Hesiod's Eros in the *Theogony* as being both rudimentary efficient causes (*Metaph.* 984b23ff.). Aristotle attributes this use of analogy to Empedocles, who saw Love and Strife in operation among men and extrapolated these forces to the cosmos (*Phys.* 252a27–31). For the model of sexual attraction see Lloyd (1966) 242.
71. For Love: Φιλότης: B17.7, B17.20, B20.2, B21.8, B26.5, B35.4, B35.13; Στοργή: B109.3; Ἁρμονία: B27.3; Γηθοσύνη: B17.24. For the Homeric precedence see Capizzi (1987) 113–115.

72. There are more fragments in which the presence of Aphrodite and the
     context point to sexual allusions. Cf. B27.2, B66, B98.3. See Mourelatos
     (1986) 175–176. Cf. also the literal use of the word "desire" in B64.

73. Cf. Plut. *De fac.* 926D-927A *ad* B27.

74. That is why Aristotle (*Gen. corr.* 333b27–33) suggests that the κατὰ φύσιν
     motion of the elements is νεῖκος and not φιλότης, as Empedocles thinks,
     which makes the elements tend to their opposites, a particularly παρὰ φύσιν
     course. Furthermore, that is why there is a zoogony under Strife. For this
     intriguing matter see O'Brien (2000), Trépanier (2003a) 36.

75. Cf. also B90, B91, B110.9.

76. 37ff.

77. Furley (1970) 59–60. Furley ibid. also notes that when Lucretius warns the
     reader that the cosmos will perish one day (5.91–109) he does not mention
     Strife. However, cf. 6.646 in which the role of Strife as instigator of warfare
     has been assumed by Nature. See below 65. Cf. also Clay (1983) 95.

78. Cf. Epicur. *Ep. Hdt.* 48, 50, 52, 53, 64 with Lee (1978) especially 28.
     The vocabulary cannot but bring to mind the homonymous Stoic theory
     according to which every part of the cosmos transmits its movements to
     all the others; this could be considered as an instance in which Epicurus
     refutes a rival theory by appropriating its formal name into a new context.
     For συμπάθεια in the Stoics see Lapidge (1989) 1383. For Lucretius' imag-
     ery in the account of hearing see *DRN* 4.557–562.

79. Vlastos (1947); Lloyd (1966) 224. Cf. also Kahn (1974), who discusses
     Anaximander's use of the terms δίκη, ἀδικία, τίσις, τάξις (DK12 B1) which
     are transferred from the field where they were first used—human society—
     to describe the whole universe. Cf. Vernant (1983) 176–211. For objections
     see Gagarin (2002). For the ancient notion of natural law see Kullmann
     (1995). For political imagery in the Hippocratic corpus see Vegetti (1983);
     Cambiano (1983); Langholf (1989).

80. See LSJ s.v. σύνοδος (B) I, s.v. συνέρχομαι II.

81. See also B26.5, B35.5, fr. a (i) 6, fr. a (ii) 20, fr. a (ii) 30 M&P. Cf. also
     Plut. *Adv. Col.* 10.1112B. Cf. metaphorical sense in B20.2–3 (cf. fr. c 3
     M&P).

82. These congregations could be thought of as microscopic κόσμοι. Cf. the
     ambiguous use of the word κόσμος in Empedocles (B26.5, B134.5), which
     could mean both a well-ordered constitution of things, including society
     and macrocosm or the Sphere. For the relevant discussion see Kranz (1939)
     and (1958); Kerschensteiner (1962); Finkelberg (1998).

83. Cf. e.g. Leucippus DK67 A24; Democritus DK68 A49, A75, A93. Cf. also
     Plut. *Adv. Col.* 10.1112B *ad* B8; Epicur. fr. 308 Us.

84. Cf. also Epicur. *Ep. Pyth.* 115. Diogenes of Oinoanda's uses similar word-
     ing in order to convey what would happen if the atoms were to lack socia-
     bility among themselves (ἀσυνέλευστοι, fr. 67.II.2 Smith; συνελθεῖν, fr.

67.II.14 Smith). Cf. also the phrasing of the 3rd cent. A.D. anti-Epicurean Dionysius of Alexandria (*ap. Euseb. PE.* 14.25.9)—as cited by D. Fowler (2002) 185 *ad* 2.110—which gives further evidence for the indubitable existence of such democratic metaphors in Epicurus' writings.

85. Keen (1974) 67. For σύγκρισις see e.g. Epicur. *Ep. Hdt.* 40, 41. For ἄθροισμα see e.g. *Ep. Hdt.* 63, 64.

86. Cabisius (1984–85) 111.

87. Cf. also 3.808–810.

88. Cf. also 1.185, 1.484, 1.517, 1.1017, 1.1026, 1.1048, 2.563–564, 2.1003, 4.948, 5.190, 6.452.

89. Because of the fragmentary state of Heraclitus' and Anaxagoras' doctrine we cannot be sure whether they used such wording or more importantly such images. It seems, however, probable that their primary terms of mixing and separating were different. Cf. the terms σύμμιξις (DK59 B4), σύγκρισις (DK59 B9) which may have been used by Anaxagoras.

90. One could tentatively agrue that Empedocles' fire-root is implied by the mention of the creation of men, who are said in Empedocles to have been made by κρινόμενον πῦρ (B62.2). Cf. also e.g. 5.450, 5.452, 5.486.

91. Cf. e.g. 4.1259, 5.600, 5.665, 6.508, 6.897.

92. Vlastos (1947) 158–161 notes that the principles of *isonomia* and *isomoiria* pervade the whole Empedoclean cosmos. Their subversion will result in disturbance e.g. in health and wisdom (A78, A86, B98).

93. Lloyd (1966) 213, 217–219.

94. Cf. also Arist. *Phys.* 252a5–19; Simp. *In Phys.* CIAG 10, 1183.19–1185.15. Laks (2005); O'Brien (2001) especially 84–87.

95. For the practice of oaths in ancient Greece see now Hirzel (1902) and Plescia (1970). For the specific background of Empedocles' oath see also J. Bollack (1958), although I do not agree with the conclusion of this article. For more on problems involved in Empedocles' use of the imagery of oaths see Garani (2007).

96. For the notion of Ἀνάγκη in Empedocles see Schreckenberg (1964) 110–113. Cf. also J. Bollack (1969 I) 127–162 and his frs. 100–116. Cf. also B139 (cf. fr. d 1–4 M&P). See also Laks (2005). For a more general use of law in Empedocles see B135.

97. Wright (1995a) 22.

98. Vlastos (1947) 160.

99. Jobst (1907) 16–17. See also Ernout and Robin (1925.I) 128. Generally on *foedera naturai* see D. Fowler (2002) 376–381 *ad* 2.302; Droz-Vincent (1996); Campbell (2003) 178–179 *ad* 5.923–924. See also De Lacy (1969) and Long (1977). For the choice of the word *foedera* instead of *ius iurandum* we should note that there is an etymological connection of *foedera* with *fides* (Enn. *ap. Varro LL* 5.86; Cic. *ap. Serv. auct. Aen.* 8.641; Paul. Fest. 84 p. 74 Lindsay; Isid. *Orig.* 8.2.4, 18.1.11), a word that is often matched with *ius*

iurandum (e.g. Caes. *Gal.* 1.3.8 *inter se fidem et ius iurandum dant*). Cf. the corresponding Greek phrases ὅρκους καὶ πίστιν ἀλλήλοις δότε (e.g. Ar. *Lys.* 1185), πίστιν καὶ ὅρκια ποιέεσθαι (e.g. Hdt. 9.92). The discussion that follows reproduces by and large the arguments developed in Garani (2007). Cf. the literal use of the words *foedus* and *pacta* in 3.781, 5.1155, 5.1443. For more on the actual institution of *foedus* see *OCD s.v.*

100. Cf. 2.1116–1121.
101. For more on the notion of Nature in Lucretius see Section 2.2.1.
102. Cabisius (1984–85) 113 sees between Nature and the atoms an agreement similar to the relationship between Rome and her *foederatae civitates,* with *Natura* like *Roma* being superior and the allied states (the atoms) still retaining internal independence. In that case this parallelism and the ensuing deification of Nature would facilitate a teleological interpretation of natural laws, which Epicurus would not approve of.
103. Schiesaro (forthcoming).
104. This topic is not within the scope of this study. Cf. Schiesaro (1990) 141–143 and (forthcoming).
105. D. Fowler (2002) 378 makes the following distinction: 5.306–310, 5.56–61: duration, the agreement is for how long the compound is to last; 1.584–592, 5.916–924, 6.906–907: properties of compounds, in particular those which form the basis of the classification into natural kinds.
106. See also 5.309–310, where Lucretius, trying to prove that every world is mortal, points to its mortal parts and in particular the gods' temples and their images that wear out and crack according to nature's laws. Cf. also 5.57, where the phrase is used in general terms and 6.906, where Lucretius discusses by which specific law of nature it comes about that iron can be attracted by a magnet. For more on the use of *foedera naturai* in 1.584–598 in connection with the metaphor *alte terminus haerens* see now Section 4.2.
107. Cf. Cic. *Cael.* 14, *Lael.* 34. Cf. *TLL* iv. 127.83ff.
108. E.g. Smith (1992) 119. Conversely, see D. Fowler (2002) 375 *ad* 2.301.
109. For *aevum* see Berns (1976) and Luciani (2000) 120–126 with further bibliography.
110. E.g. Chrysippus *SVF* III.314–326. Cf. D. Fowler (2002) 379 *ad* 2.302; Watson (1971); Striker (1986); and Inwood (1986). Due to these correspondences in Stoic and Epicurean ideas on natural law, later Latin Stoic poets incorporated—and redefined—in their wording Lucretius' metaphor of *foedera.* Cf. e.g. Manilius *Astron.* 2.271, 3.55; Luc. *Phars.* 1.80 with Lapidge (1989) 1393–1397, 1405–1409. See also below the discussion on *foedera fati* (2.254). For another occurrence of the law metaphor see *DRN* 2.719.
111. For many more examples see Wacht (1991) s.v. *pactum.*
112. D. Fowler (2002) 342 *ad* 2.254 and his remark that "*foedera* may suggest the concrete *concilia* in the *animus* which the *clinamen* disrupts." Cf. on

the contrary Long (1977) 86: "the *foedera naturai* are probably identical to the *foedera fati* except in the case of *libera voluntas*." Cf. here Russell (2000) 229–230 on the distinction between the "cosmological role" of the swerve (it ensures that atoms have sufficient internal principles of motion to account for collision between them) and what we may call the swerve's "psychological" role, "in which it is (somehow) relevant to the ability of sentient creatures to initiate their own motion." In the same context (2.251) cf. Lucretius' play also with the Stoic metaphor of weaving (for discussion see below in Section 4.2).

113. Cf. 238 for the problems involved in the meaning of the word κόσμος.

114. Gale (1994a) 123 n. 95 remarks that natural processes are described in terms of *res gestae* in 1.442, 1.634, 2.1069, 3.27, 5.1439.

115. Cf. 1.336–338.

116. For *coniuncta* see also Section 4.2.

117. Cf. 1.792–793, 3.519–520.

118. Cabisius (1984–85) 112.

119. For the use of this metaphor see also 1.76–77, 1.594–596, 2.1087, 5.88–90, 6.64–66. See further discussion in 176–178. For the role of *terminus* in Rome see *OCD s. v.*

120. Cabisius (1984–85) 113. Cf. also 1.595, 5.89, 6.65. For the concepts of limit and variation in the Epicurean philosophy see De Lacy (1969). See also Schiesaro (forthcoming).

121. Davies (1931–32) 36–37 who remarks that whereas in Ciceronian Latin —expect for Lucretius—the word was used in its legal meaning, denoting the relationship between debtor and creditor, slave and master in connection with loan transaction (e.g. Cic. *Mur.* 3.14; Livy 7.19.5), it was used by later authors in its material meaning, denoting physical bond (e.g. Ov. *Met.* 6.242; Tac. *Ann.* 4.62). Cf. also *OCD s.v. nexus*.

122. D. Fowler (1989) 147.

123. D. Fowler (2002) 202 *ad* 2.120.

124. Cf. D. Fowler (1989) 148–149, who rather refers to the *foedera naturai* as "more precarious and less perfect than immutable divine decrees. [. . .] No pact is truly eternal." That is true, but Lucretius emphatically disregards it. See also discussion in Section 4.2.

125. Νεῖκος: B17.8, B17.19, B22.9, B26.6, B30.1, B35.3, B35.9, B36, B109.3, B115.14.

126. However, cf. images of sexual desire which are used in a supplementary way, in order to account for the principle of "like joining with it like." See 49ff.

127. Cf. Bollack 158 (Scholion B to *Iliad* Υ 67, p. 231, 12ff. Dindorf). For other accounts of a storm of elements in the formation of the world see O'Brien (1969) 268–273.

128. For a rather brief discussion on war images in Lucretius see Gale (2000) 232–240.

129. σύγκρουσις (*concursio*): Leucippus DK67 A14; Democritus DK68 A50, A56; Epicur. *Ep. Hdt.* 44; στασιάζειν: Democritus DK68 A37; συμπλέκειν: Leucippus DK67 A1, A10, A23; Democritus DK68 A43, A93a; συμπλοκή: Leucippus DK67 A1, A15; Democritus DK68 A135; Epicur. fr. 35.12.6 Arr.². For συμπλοκή, συμπλέκειν see also Usener (1977) *ad loc.* and D. Fowler (2002) 225 *ad* 2.154. Cf. also Plut. *Adv. Col.* 10.1112B; Diogenes of Oinoanda fr. 54.II.9 Smith.

130. Cf. also affinities with Heraclitus' War (DK22 B53) and Hesiod's *Eris* (*Theog.* 225–226 and especially *Op.* 11–26).

131. 1.384, 1.685, 2.727, 2.1021, 5.439, 6.161, 6.172. Cf. also the use of the verb *concursare* in 3.395 and *concurrere* in 6.97, 6.116, 6.316, 6.363. Cf. *conflixere*, 2.86. Cf. Cic. *ND* 1.66: *concursu . . . fortuito;* 1.91 and 2.94: *concursus atomorum.* As Reinhardt (2005) 152 remarks, Cicero's language should be studied only in parallel with Lucretius, since there is little evidence for direct interaction between the two authors.

132. Cf. also 2.549–550.

133. For Lucretius' source see above 225–226, n. 31.

134. On Empedocles' storm see above 62. Cf. also the literal use of the word *discordia* in 5.1305.

135. Cabisius (1984–85) 115. Cf. also 4.528–534.

136. Cabisius (1984–85) 116 and especially D. Fowler (2002) 186–208 *ad* 2.112–141.

137. E.g. *Il.* 2.386. See Murley (1947); Gale (1994a) 106.

138. Cf. e.g. Empedocles B22.6–9.

139. Cabisius (1984–85) 112.

140. Cf. 6.871–872 quoted in 216

141. Cf. also 2.956, 5.894.

142. Cf. Lucretius' rebuke of Empedocles' theory on the possibility of cosmogony through union of the roots (1.759–762), quoted in full in 64. Cf. also 6.357–378.

143. Lloyd (1966) 222–228; and especially Capizzi (1990) 323–332 for a full account of Empedocles' hypothetical political activities. However, I do not agree with all the parallels the latter draws between macrocosmic and secular order. I think that he overstates his case. See also Bidez (1894) 46–49 and 125–133.

144. Diog. Laert. 8.63–66 and 72. For Diogenes Laertius see Fairweather (1974) and Meijer (1978).

145. Capizzi (1990) 329.

146. For more on the intertextual relationship between Empedocles and Ennius see Section 1.3.

147. Anderson (1960); Cabisius (1984–85).

148. Hutchinson (2001) 150–153. Cf. Cabisius (1984–85) 118 who compares the destruction of Athenian society because of the plague with the dissolution of an atomic *concilium.*

149. Cf. Diogenes of Oinoanda fr. 56 Smith, in which he envisages the arrival of a Golden Age when human beings will have attained wisdom and will live like gods on earth.

150. Anaximenes saw an analogy between the human soul, which is air, and the air of the cosmos (DK13 B2). For the Pythagoreans (DK58 B30), the cosmos was a living animal that breathes in the void outside it. Leucippus (DK67 A1.32) called the outer shell of the cosmos ὑμήν, a word that generally is used as a technical term for the amnion enclosing the foetus in the womb. See Baldry (1932); Kranz (1938); Lloyd (1966) 232–241; Hahm (1977) 63. Especially for Empedocles see Wilford's (1968) very speculative article.

151. Anaxagoras DK59 B4: σπερμάτων ἀπείρων πλῆθος; Leucippus DK67 A15, A28: πανσπερμία; Epicur. *Ep. Pyth.* 89: ἐπιτηδείων σπερμάτων. Cf. in the Stoics: σπέρμα (Zeno *SVF* I.98), σπερματικοί λόγοι (Chrysippus *SVF* II.580, II.1074). See Hahm (1977) 57–90 and *passim;* Schrijvers (1999) 185–88; Schiesaro (1990) 83–85. On seeds in Lucretius see also Sedley (1998) 193–198.

152. For the *Cosmos* as a living being see e.g. Hippoc. *Hebd.* 6, *Vict.* I.10; Sen. *Q Nat.* III.15; Pl. *Ti.* See Lloyd (1966) 252–267; especially for the Stoics see Hahm (1977) 136–184 and Lapidge (1989) 1381–1385.

153. See Bailey (1947) 975.

154. Cf. also e.g. *DRN* 2.1122–1127 with Pl. *Ti.* 81b4–5; cf. *DRN* 2.1139–1141 with Pl. *Ti.* 81d2–4; *DRN* 2.1142–1143 with Pl. *Ti.* 81a4ff. See Solmsen (1953); Schiesaro (1990) 75–78.

155. See Jobst (1907) 46; Bailey (1947) 975–976. Cf. B22, B90, B109.

156. In this description note the dominance of the "flowing water" metaphor. See more below on 208.

157. Schiesaro (1990) 79–83.

158. Cf. Epicur. fr. 308 Us. (Ps.-Plut. *Plac. Philos.* 1.4 = *Dox. Gr.* 289).

159. Jobst (1907) 58; Bailey (1947) 1355 *ad* 5.237 quoting Giussani (1896–98) *ad loc.* and 1382 *ad* 5.432–448; J. Bollack (1965 I) 175–177.

160. About the relationship of Lucretius with the Stoics see Furley (1966); Kleve (1978); Schmidt (1990) especially 170–181; Sedley (1998) 73–82; D. Fowler (2000b) 140.

161. O'Brien (1969) 274–275 sees it more likely that the limbs are in fact the limbs of Strife.

162. The cosmic articulation is also suggested by an analogous image of limbs (γυῖα) on a shorter scale, an image which is probably drawn from men's life (B20; cf. fr. c M&P).

163. See J. Bollack (1969 III.1) 202 *ad* B35; Wright (1995a) 208 *ad* B35.11, 191 *ad* B30.1 and 192 *ad* B31.

164. E.g. Chrysippus *SVF* II.633.

165. For corresponding vocabulary used by the Stoics see e.g. Chrysippus *SVF* II.441, II.465, II.528, II.534 with Lapidge (1989) 1381–1383 and bibliography cited there.

166. See Wheeler (2000) 12 n. 25 for further bibliography. For allusions to Empedocles in Ovid's creation story see Pascal (1905). The primordial strife (*discordia, Met.* 1.9) of these elements is reminiscent of Empedoclean Strife. See further examples: cf. *Met.* 1.10–14 with B27; cf. *Met.* 1.24–25 with B35; cf. *Met.* 1.26–27 with B51.

167. Pfligersdorffer (1973); Hardie (1991).

168. Regarding Ovid's *Metamorphoses* see e.g. the following correspondences: cf. *Met.* 1.9 with *DRN* 5.436–442; cf. *Met.* 1.10–14 with *DRN* 5.432–435; cf. *Met.* 1.22–23 with *DRN* 5.446–448; concering the sea and winds: *Met.* 1.36–37 with *DRN* 5.503–504; the making of hills and plains: *Met.* 1.43–44, *DRN* 5.492–493; cf. also *Met.* 1.68 (of the ether) with *DRN* 5.497 (of the earth); concerning the distribution of the parts of the universe: fire rose (*Met.* 1.26–27; *DRN* 5.458–459) and took the highest place (*Met.* 1.27; *DRN* 5.470, 5.500–501); air is next lower (*Met.* 1.28; *DRN* 5.501; cf. 5.472, 5.490); earth is heavy (*Met.* 1.29–30; *DRN* 5.429) and in the middle (*Met.* 1.31; *DRN* 5.451); water surrounds the earth (*Met.* 1.31; *DRN* 5.498). See Robbins (1913) 403–406 who however does not place great importance on these parallels; Wheeler (2000) 14–16. For Ovid's *Fasti:* cf. *Fast.* 1.107 with Lucr 5.432ff., especially 5.440–442; for the distribution of elements cf. *Fast.* 1.109–110 with *DRN* 5.449–470, 5.495–505; for fire cf. *Fast.* 1.109 with *DRN* 5.457–459; for the earth cf. *Fast.* 1.110 with *DRN* 5.449–451; cf. Ov. *Fast.* 1.111 with *DRN* 5.436. For further analysis see Green (2004) 76–78 *ad* 1.105–110.

169. See Hardie (1995) 208 for the Pythagoras' passage in Ov. *Met.* 15.75–478.

170. E.g. Ovid's *deus* is vividly reminiscent of the Stoic one; cf. also Ov. *Met.* 1.26–31 with Cic. *Tusc. disp.* 1.40, *ND* 2.91; cf. Ov. *Met.* 1.84–86 with Cic. *ND* 2.140, *Leg.* 1. 26–27. For more on Stoic echoes in Ovid's creation story in *Met.* 1 see Robbins (1913) especially 407–414. Similar imagery is used by the later Stoic poet Manilius (e.g. *Astron.* 1.137–138, 1.247–249, 2.66, 2.67, 3.50). For further relationship between Lucretius and Manilius see Rösch (1911); Flores (1996); Abry (1999); and Section 2.2.3.2.

171. Schrijvers (1999) 200–201; Schiesaro (1990) 80–81.

172. Chrysippus *SVF* II.441: συμφυῖα, *SVF* II.550: συμφυής; cf. the Latin translation of these terms as *cognatus, cognatio* with Lapidge (1989) *passim.* We should note here that Epicurus himself had used the same metaphor of "growing together" with the Stoics, though in a different context. Cf. Epicur. *Ep. Hdt.* 54: ὅσα ἐξ ἀνάγκης σχήματος συμφυῆ ἐστι; fr. 16 Arr.[2] (Plut. *Adv. Col.* 7.1110C = fr. 30 Us.): οὐκ εἶναι λέγων τὰ χρώματα συμφυῆ τοῖς σώμασιν.

173. This passage is quoted in full below in Section 4.2.

174. Chrysippus *SVF* II.475. Cf. Epicurus' use of the term συμπάθεια in Section 2.2.3.1.

175. For possible allusion here to Empedocles' botanical analogies see more in the next section.

176. Lück (1932) 30–33, as quoted by Schrijvers (1999) 201. Cf. πνεῦμα: e.g. Chrysippus *SVF* II.911; σύμπνοια: e.g. Chrysippus *SVF* II.543. Cf. in Latin *conspiro, spiritus unus* (e.g. Manilius *Astron.* 1.251) with Lapidge (1989) *passim.*

177. Cf. Hippoc. *Hebd.* 6 and 11 with Mansfeld (1971) 103–107.

178. For metaphors of the female body see DuBois (1988).

179. I will not discuss here the two similes in which both Earth's and man's bodies are treated as containers of Empedocles' roots, in order to infer the behaviour of an element in a different environment, by observing its behaviour within a human body (6.591–600 about earthquakes, 6.655–670 about disease and volcanic eruptions). In this case Lucretius' debt to Empedocles is not directly related to the device of personification, as the strength of Lucretius' proof depends mostly on the notion of "container." Cf. Section 3.4.2.1.

180. West (1969) 103–104; Duban (1982); Catto (1988–89); Schiesaro (1990) 102–122; Gale (1994a) 27–32; D. Fowler (2000b) 141–148; Campbell (2003) 60–61 *ad* 5.795–796. For supposed Stoic influences in the allegory see Boyancé (1941) and (1963) 123.

181. Cf. 2.655–660, 5.795–796. See discussion in Introduction 2.1. Lucretius uses also the opposite image, that of Earth being the tomb of all things (e.g. 1.135, 5.259).

182. Barigazzi (1950); Arrighetti (1973) 595.

183. As far as Earth's external appearance is concerned, Empedocles probably envisaged it as endowed with human features. This description is in consistence with Empedocles' personification of all four roots along with their basic manifestations in the world. See Section 2.2.2.

184. For Empedocles see Guthrie (1957) 60; Gale (1994a) 61–62; Campbell (2003) 75 *ad* 5.807–815 and 98–138 *passim ad* 5.837–877. For Epicurus and Lucretius see Schrijvers (1999) 1–15; Schiesaro (1990) 102–122; Campbell (2003) 75–85 *ad* 5.807–815. In general see Campbell (2003) 330–335 very useful table of themes in accounts of creation, zoogony and anthropogony.

185. Cf. e.g. B6, B54, B70, B99. More analogies will be cited below. Cf. Alcmaeon DK24 A5, A16, A17 with Lloyd (1966) 322–325; Aristotelian analogies (*Hist. an.* 539a18ff., *Gen. an.* 745b24ff.) with Schrijvers (1999) 11–13. Cf. also the botanical excursus in the Hippocratic treatise *On the Nature of the Child* with Lonie (1969) and (1981) 211–244.

186. Cf. Empedocles' abhorrence for animal sacrifice (B128.8 when Cypris was queen during Golden Age, B137 about the father sacrificing the animal which was once his son), which stems from the very same belief in reincarnation. Lucretius shares this revulsion for sacrifices (especially Iphigenia's myth in 1.80–101; cf. also 2.352–365, 5.1201–1202), without endorsing Empedocles' doctrine of transmigration. See Furley (1970) 62; Gale (1994a) 72.

187. Cf. 225 n. 28 above.

188. Cf. αὐτὰρ ἐχίνοις / ὀξυβελεῖς χαῖται νώτοις ἐπιπεφρίκασι. / "but for hedge-hogs sharp-pointed hairs bristle on their backs.," B83. See Jobst (1907) 36–37. Cf. also the epithets' transference from human beings into plants (e.g. B127.2).

189. Sedley (2003) 9.

190. As Campbell (2003) 52 *ad* 5.787 notes, this agrees with Hippocratic think-ing, in which children leave the womb by their own efforts, rather than being forced out by the mother's contractions (Hippoc. *Epid.* V.103, *Mul.* I.68).

191. See Sedley (2003) 9 *ad* 5.788–791.

192. Sedley (2003) 10–11. Cf. also the discussion above in 228 about more echoes with philosophical value *ad* 5.837–877 with Furley (1970) 60–61; Campbell (2003) 98–138 *ad loc.;* and Sedley's objections (2003) 2–5. How-ever, in this case we do not have a clear instance of pairing compound adjec-tives, but a looser linguistic overlap.

193. Cf. also in 5.866 the phrase *bucera saecla.* As Campbell (2003) 134 *ad loc.* remarks, *bucera* is from the Greek βούκερως and it may point to an Emped-oclean origin of the phrase.

194. Cf. 2.871–873, 2.898–901, 2.926–929, 3.719–721.

195. Campbell (2003) 66 *ad loc.* points out that in this way Lucretius also intro-duces the four Empedoclean elements.

196. Cf. 1.250–264 and 2.991–1003 with Campbell (2003) 65–68 *ad* 5.800.

197. For more on the comparison of eggs and birds with chrysalizes and cicadas see Campbell (2003) 68–74 *ad loc.* Campbell compares Empedocles' B79, in which Empedocles uses an analogy between eggs and olives, and suggests that although the original context of this is lost, it would be a useful way of accounting for the birth of the first eggs.

198. For Empedocles see mainly B35, B57, B59, B61, B62, B96. Cf. A72b (Cen-sorinus *DN* 4.7–8): *Empedocles autem egregio suo carmine, [. . .] tale quid-dam confirmat: primo membra singula ex terra quasi praegnate passim edita, deinde coisse et effecisse solidi hominis materiam igni simul et umori permix-tam. /* "Empedocles states in his splendid poem [. . .] something like this. First single limbs issued from everywhere in the earth—as though it were pregnant—and then came together and produced the stuff of a solid man, being mixed out of fire and water together."

199. I think that Empedocles' usage of the womb as a vehicle to depict plants being part of the earth (A70a) is not directly relevant to the present instance. In any case, after him the Hippocratic writers inverted the analogy by trans-ferring wombs from the source to the target domain. For the opposite view see Campbell (2003) 78 *ad* 5.808.

200. A similar idea is also used by Diod. Sic. 1.7. If we were to trust Diogenes of Oinoanda fr. 11 Smith, this would mean that Epicurus himself may have

accepted the theory of wombs. However, this fragment is highly problematic and it should hardly be used as evidence. For discussion see Schiesaro (1990) 103–108; Spoerri (1997) with further bibliography; Campbell (2003) 75–85 *ad* 5.807–817.

201. Campbell (2003) 76 *ad* 5.807–817.
202. Cf. also Philolaus DK44 B13; Hippoc. *Nat. Puer.* 22.1–5. Aristotle also draws parallels between the life of plants and animals (*Hist. an.* 539a18ff.), and compares the functions of the umbilical cord and of the roots of plants (*Gen. an.* 739b33–740b10 and 745b24ff.), as does e.g. Galen *De Ut. Diss.* 10 (2.906.10ff. Kühn), *De Foet. Form.* 2 (4.656.11–657 Kühn). See Lonie (1969); Schrijvers (1999) 11–13; Campbell (2003) 78 *ad* 5.808.
203. Cf. the metaphor of "roots" used elsewhere in Lucretius: 3.325, 3.563, 5.554. For other botanical analogies see also 1.774, 3.404, 6.133, 6.152.
204. Censorinus *DN* 4.9 (Epicur. fr. 333 Us.) attributes this detail of a milk-like juice to Epicurus, but probably takes it directly from Lucretius. Cf. Waszink (1964) 51–56; Campbell (2003) 80–84 *ad* 5.811–815.
205. Empedocles himself identified milk with a form of blood (B68).
206. E.g. Verg. *A.* 12.419; Cic. *ND* 2.120.
207. Arist. *De Plant.* 829a7ff.; Theophr. *Hist. Plant.* 1.7.2, *CP* 6.4.1 and 6.9.2; Ov. *Met.* 11.606; Verg. *A.* 4.514; Hippoc. *Nat. Puer.* 21.31–35 and 26.16–18. Cf. Schrijvers (1999) 13–14; Campbell (2003) 82–84 *ad* 5.812–813. See also Waszink (1964) 55–56.
208. See Schrijvers (1999) 14.
209. Schiesaro (1990) 149–151.
210. Campbell (2003) 93–98 *ad* 5.828–836, who rightly notes that the repetitions in the passage reflect the similar Empedoclean technique.

NOTES TO CHAPTER TWO

1. Diller (1932); Kranz (1938); Snell (1953) 191–226; Lloyd (1966) 304–383.
2. E.g. when Empedocles draws the image of a girl playing with a clepsydra (B100), he does not suggest that the apparatus was constructed just for the sake of his experimental observation; yet the process is one that can be repeated. On experiments see Lloyd (1979) 126–225, (1991) 70–99.
3. On Empedocles' similes in general see Kranz (1938); Gerke (1953) 63–69. On Lucretius' similes see Hohler (1925–26); Bardon (1964) 16–17; Maguinness (1965) 86–89; Townend (1965); West (1969) and (1970); Pasoli (1970); Battisti (1976); Schrijvers (1999) 183–213; Hardie (1986) 219–223; Leen (1984); Schiesaro (1990) *passim;* Schindler (2000) 72–149.
4. Kranz (1943) 80–3; Wöhrle (1991); Conte (1994) 10–17; Gale (1994a) 63–64; Sedley (1998) 11.
5. Wright (1995a) 9–14.

6. Jouanna (1961) 457 and *passim;* Longrigg (1985) 99–100. For more on Hippocratic analogies see also Regenbogen (1961); Lloyd (1966) 345–360; Lonie (1981) 77–86.

7. See Segal (1970) for similarities between *DRN* 3.492–494 and Hippoc. *Flat.* 14.39–46 regarding the arrangement of arguments, the phraseology and the use of the sea simile. See also Sinclair (1981) about Hippocratic echoes in the account of plague with more bibliography; Phillips (1984) for similarities between *DRN* 1.271–277 and Hippoc. *Flat.* 3.7–11 about the description of the wind's unseen power, and between *DRN* 3.463–509 and Hippoc. *Flat* 1.26–28 about the action of *medicina.*

8. Lloyd (1966) 362–380.

9. Theophrastus' *Metarsiologica* (or *Meteorology*), a two-book work, is lost in Greek but known in three translated versions: 1. an Arabic summary of a Syriac version, 2. a fragmentary copy of the Syriac version and 3. a fuller Arabic version, still an abridgement. For the text see Daiber (1992). See also Kidd (1992); Mansfeld (1992).

10. See Kidd (1992) 303–304 for different attitudes among the philosophers regarding this principle. See also Section 1.2.

11. For further correspondences between Lucretius and Theophrastus see Sedley (1998) 166–186. See also Reitzenstein (1924); Mansfeld (1992) and (1994); Runia (1997).

12. Sedley (1998) 182.

13. See discussion below 122ff.

14. In the following discussion the focus will be mainly on B84 and B100, since in B23 we have only the vehicle. For intertextual relationship between Lucretius and Empedocles regarding B23 see the discussion in Section 1.1.

15. ὡς δ' ὁπόταν, B23.1; ὡς δ' ὅτε, B84.1; ὡς δὲ τότ᾽, B84.7; ὥσπερ ὅταν, B100.8; ὡς δ' αὔτως, B100.22.

16. Wright (1998) 22 notes the Homeric echoes in the lantern simile (B84): the traveller prepares a light for himself (B84.1), as Polyphemus "prepared a meal for himself" (*Od.* 2.20); "of fire burning" (B84.2) is from *Il.* 8.563; "through a wintry night" (B84.2) recalls "through an ambrosial night" (*Il.* 2.57); the vocabulary of the winds in the fragment (B84.3–4) combines that of *Il.* 2.397 and 5.525, while the "linen screens" of the lantern and the "delicate tissues" of the membranes (B84.8) is the phrase used for the fine linen of the dresses worn by the dancing girls depicted by Hephaestus on the shield of Achilles (*Il.* 18.595). For the Homeric phrasing in the clepsydra simile (B100) cf. B100.23 with the suitors retreating before Odysseus (*Od.* 22.270).

17. Murley (1947) 339; Mayer (1990) 40–41.

18. Similes are introduced by several oblique connecting words (e.g. *ut, saepe itaque, quod genus, quin etiam, et merito, nonne vides*).

19. Townend (1965) 102–103. Cf. Schindler (2000) 74 for objections about associations with Homer.

20. E.g. Mayer (1990) 40–41; Kyllo (1994) 86 and *passim;* Schindler (2000) *passim.*
21. Schiesaro (1990) 35–38. See also De Lacy (1964–65); D. Fowler (2002) 384–406 *ad loc.*
22. See D. Fowler (2002) 389–406 whc notes the Homeric reminiscences *ad* 2.317–322 (*Od.* 10.410–414; *Il.* 2.474–475) and *ad* 2.323–332 (*Il.* 2.455–458, 4.450–456, 19.357–364; *Od.* 14.267–268).
23. For further examples cf. also *DRN* 1.271–297 with *Il.* 5.87–92 and 11.492–495; *DRN* 6.256–261 with *Il.* 4.275–279; *DRN* 6.145–149 with *Od.* 9.391–393.
24. As Gale (1994a) 114 notes, "following Empedocles, Lucretius developed the Homeric simile into a tool of 'scientific' argument." See also Leen (1984).
25. O'Brien (1970) 155.
26. E.g. Ar. *Vesp.* 7; Eur. *Ion* 876, *Hec.* 972. Sedley (1992) 22 plausibly argues for the meaning "eye" instead of "pupil."
27. There is a textual uncertainty in B84.8, with three alternative solutions as far as the verb is concerned and consequently an ambiguity regarding its subject. Some scholars accept the reading λοχάζετο, either as an active verbal form meaning "Aphrodite entrapped the fire," or in its middle sense, implying that "the fire kept itself concealed"; in this case, the eye would be formed as an ambush. See Wright (1995a) 241 *ad* B84, with a brief overview of the problem. Another suggestion is the reading λοχεύσατο, which would then mean that "Aphrodite brought to birth." See O'Brien (1970) 156; Sedley (1992) 22.
28. See above 248 n. 16 for the Homeric resonances. Cf. Parmenides DK28 B10.4 κύκλωπος . . . σελήνης.
29. O'Brien (1970) 156.
30. Cf. e.g. similar exaggeration in B15.1 with Sedley (1992) 23 n. 10.
31. Cf. two similar instances in B100.12 and B100.18, where the word ὄμβρον is used instead of ὕδωρ. For further discussion of B84 see Section 3.4.2.1.
32. The bibliography for the fragment is extensive. See Powell (1923); Last (1924); Cardini (1957); Furley (1957); Booth (1960); Lloyd (1966) 328–333; Seeck (1967); Worthen (1970); O'Brien (1970) with further bibliography; Wright (1995a) 244–248. For this simile see below 111ff. and Section 3.4.1.
33. O'Brien (1970) 155 .
34. O'Brien (1970) 156; Wright (1995a) 249.
35. For more on this simile see below 118ff. Cf. also the discussion of 6.181 in Section 4.5.
36. Shea (1977) makes the interesting suggestion that Lucretius' juxtaposition of caves and furnaces may be legitimized due to the association, both thematic and geographic, between the caves of Aeolus, the king of the winds and the lightning-forge of Vulcan, the divine creator of lightning and the thunderbolt. For the demythologizing function of this image see also Gale (1994a) 188.
37. For more on this simile see 117ff.
38. West (1970). For more correspondences see West (1970) 273–274.

39. Sedley (1998) 11.

40. West (1969) 43–48 comments on the transfusions spotted in 6.895–896, 6.903–905, 3.1042–1044, 3.1017–1019, 1.974–983.

41. For more examples of the transfusion technique see Section 4.4. For examples of multiple-correspondence in Lucretius' similes see below *passim*.

42. See Pope (1949) 74; Schrijvers (1970) 242–244; Schiesaro (1990) 69.

43. Diogenes of Oinoanda fr. 13.III.13-IV.12 Smith ἐνδέχεται τοιγα- / ροῦν τὸν ἥλιον ἀνθρακώ- / δη τινὰ κύκλον [εἶναι καὶ] / λεπτὸν ἄκρως, [ὑπό τε τῶν] / πνευμάτων αἰω[ρούμενον] / πηγῆς τε ἐπέχ[οντα τρό]- / πον, ν τοῦ μὲν ἀ[πορέοντος] / ἐξ αὐτοῦ πυρό[ς, τοῦ δ᾽ εἰσ]- / ρέοντος ἐκ τοῦ [περιέχον]- / τος κατὰ μεικρ[ομερεῖς] / συνκρίσεις διὰ [τὴν τούτου] / πολυμιγ[είαν. οὕτω δ᾽ ἐ]- / παρκεῖν αὐ[τομάτως πέφυ]- / κε τῷ κόσμῳ. / "It is therefore possible that the sun [is] a disc resembling red hot charcoal [and] of an extremely fine texture, [lifted up by the] winds and [functioning like] a spring, in that some fire [flows away] from it, while other fire flows [into] it from the [surroundings], on account of their multifarious [mixture], in aggregations of small [parts]. Thus it is [of itself naturally] sufficient for the world . . ."

44. Cf. 5.281–282 where the same analogy is used without any explanation.

45. For more examples of transfusion see Section 4.4.

46. Clay (1998) 165 also notes that "as the same letters of the Latin alphabet transform themselves from one element to another in different combinations, Lucretius' language itself illustrates the fundamental similarities between the motion of water, fire and air."

47. Schrijvers (1970) 270–271; Battisti (1976) 83–85; Leen (1984) 122; Schindler (2000) 101–105.

48. For the adjective *ramosus* see also 5.1096, where it is used in its literal sense referring to a tree and 2.446 in the description of an atomic type. See Battisti (1976) 87; Schiesaro (1990) 71.

49. Sedley (1998) 11. See more about the function of these correspondences in Section 3.4.2.1.

50. See also the detailed table 3 and further discussion in Section 3.4.1.

51. Lloyd (1966) 328–333; Booth (1960); Wright (1995a) 240–243.

52. O'Brien (1970); Worthen (1970).

53. See further in Section 4.4.

54. Snell (1953) 215. See J. Bollack (1965 I) 277–327; Lyne (1989) 66–68 and 135–143; Gale (1994a) 63.

55. See the discussion and the table above 3. Another such an example is A67 (Arist. *Cael.* 295a13–21), in which, in response to the question why the earth itself does not fall downwards, Empedocles explains that as water remains in a vessel which is swung around, the earth does not drop into space because of the quick rotation of the celestial orb. See Tigner (1974); Rossetti (2004) 151–161. Empedocles also likens the moon to a chariot on account of the closeness of its rotation round the earth (B46).

56. Wright (1995a) 248.

57. For such an example in Aristotle see below n. 67. For more examples see Lloyd (1966) 345–383 *passim;* Lonie (1981) 77–86 *passim.*

58. Gale (1994a) 64.

59. For more examples of such similes see the chapter on Metaphors. Cf. e.g. 4.617–620 discussed in 211ff.

60. See above 105–106. See especially West (1970); Battisti (1976) 81–83.

61. Hardie (1986) 231.

62. Hippoc. *Flat.* 3.7–11: ὅταν οὖν πολὺς ἀὴρ ἰσχυρὸν τὸ ῥεῦμα ποιήσῃ, τά τε δένδρα ἀνασπαστὰ πρόρριζα γίνεται διὰ τὴν βίην τοῦ πνεύματος, τό τε πέλαγος κυμαίνεται, ὁλκάδες τε ἄπειροι τῷ μεγέθει ἐς ὕψος διαρριπτεῦνται. τοιαύτην μὲν οὖν ἐν τούτοις ἔχει δύναμιν· ἀλλὰ μήν ἐστί γε τῇ μὲν ὄψει ἀφανής, τῷ δὲ λογισμῷ φανερός· / "When therefore much air flows violently, tress are torn up by the roots through the force of the wind, the sea swells into waves, and vessels of vast bulk are tossed about. Such then is the power that it has in these things, but it is invisible to sight, though visible to reason." See Phillips (1984). See also above 249 n. 23 for Homeric reminiscences.

63. See above 106.

64. See above 113–114.

65. Epicur. *Ep. Pyth.* 103: κεραυνοὺς ἐνδέχεται γίνεσθαι καὶ κατὰ πλείονας πνευμάτων συλλογὰς καὶ κατείλησιν ἰσχυράν τε ἐκπύρωσιν· / "A thunderbolt is caused when winds are repeatedly collected, imprisoned, and violently ignited."

66. Montserrat and Navarro (2000) 7–8. This principle was also used by Leucippus in order to explain how stars caught fire in the beginning of the world (DK67 A1) and by the Epicureans regarding the nature of the *flammantia moenia mundi,* whirling around on the periphery of the world (*DRN* 1.73).

67. See Theophr. *Metars.* 6.18–21 Daiber. Cf. also *DRN* 6.323–329; Arist. *Cael.* 289a19–32, *Mete.* 341a12–31.

68. Hardie (1986) 178; Gale (1994a) 137.

69. Cf. Epicur. *Ep. Pyth.* 101: καὶ κατὰ τὴν τοῦ πνεύματος ἐκπύρωσιν τὴν γινομένην διά τε συντονίαν φορᾶς καὶ διὰ σφοδρὰν κατείλησιν. / "Or it may arise from the combustion of wind brought about by the violence of its motion and the intensity of its compression."

70. Cf. the multiple correspondences: wind: *missa sine igne / igniscat tamen in spatio longoque meatu,* 6.300–301 → missile: *fervida fit . . . in cursu,* 6.307; wind: *amittens in cursu corpora quaedam / grandia,* 6.302–303 → missile: *rigoris / corpora dimittens,* 6.307–308; wind: *conradens . . . / parvola, quae faciunt ignem,* 6.304–305 → missile: *ignem concepit in auris,* 6.308.

71. Longrigg (1975); Wright (1995b) 93–108.

72. Especially the writer of the three Hippocratic treatises *On Generation, On the Nature of the Child* and *Diseases IV* makes wide use of such analogies. For

example the author puts forward the natural law according to which all fluids produce foam when they are agitated, and infers that this is why fluid within the body produces foam when stirred up (Hippoc. *Genit.* 1.8–13). For further examples see Lonie (1981) 75–86 and *passim*. See further Regenbogen (1961); Lloyd (1966) 345–360 *passim* and (1991) 96.

73. For examples in Aristotle see Lloyd (1966) 367–380 *passim;* Lloyd (1991) 91.

74. Lloyd (1991) 91–92. See also Longrigg (1975) especially 219–221; Bodnár (2002).

75. See Daiber (1992) 281–281 and 290–292; Kidd (1992) 298–300.

76. About similar distinctions see Theophr. *Metars.* 6.2–16 Daiber.

77. For further correspondences see Section 3.3.

78. Cf. Wright's translation (1981) *ad loc.* as "elemental fire." This would be the case if we were to follow the view that Aphrodite is the subject here as the divine creator. See Sedley (1992) 22.

79. Seneca reports another such an Empedoclean analogy according to which, as water that runs across heated pipes becomes warm itself, some springs are hot because they have run over the fiery parts of the earth's core (Sen. *Nat. quaest.* III.24.1–2 = A68). See Rossetti (2004) 144–147. In his physiological inquiries Empedocles plausibly compares the function of our ear with that of a ringing bell on the basis of vibrating air (A86). See Baltussen (2006).

80. For further discussion of the concept of "container" in Lucretius see Sections 4.1 and 4.3.

81. For the furnace see below 125ff., for the sponge see Section 4.5.

82. Cf. 6.451–494 for the description of the formation of clouds.

83. Cloud: *validi venti . . . procella,* 6.124 → bladder: *plena animae vesicula parva,* 6.130. Cf. the multiple correspondences: cloud: *perterricrepo sonitu,* 6.129 → bladder: *magnum sonitum,* 6.131; cloud: *subito,* 6.124 → bladder: *repente,* 6.131; cloud: *scissa,* 6.129 → bladder: *displosa,* 6.131.

84. This is the only analogy preserved in Epicurus' *Letter to Pythocles.* Bailey (1947) 1572 *ad* 6.121–131 wrongly notes that Lucretius uses the very same analogy as Epicurus.

85. Theophr. *Metars.* 6.29–36, 6.37–41, 6.64–67 Daiber.

86. Such a usage of the bladder seems to have been a commonplace. For an example in connection with lightning see Ar. *Nub.* 404–405; Anaxagoras DK59 A68 uses a bladder as a model in an experiment in order to prove that air is a material body.

87. Clouds: *ignis . . . semina,* 6.160 → stone and steel: *claras scintillas . . . ignis,* 6.163. Cf. further correspondences: clouds: *suo concursu,* 6.161 → stone and steel: *percutiat,* 6.162; clouds: *fulgit,* 6.160 → stone and steel: *lumen / exilit,* 6.162–163; clouds: *excussere,* 6.161 → stone and steel: *dissipat,* 6.163.

88. Clouds and wind: *ignem,* 6.309; *elementa vaporis,* 6.312 → stone and iron: *ignis,* 6.314; *semina . . . calidi fulgoris,* 6.316. Cf. further correspondences: clouds and wind: *ipsius plagae vis,* 6.309; *pepulit,* 6.310; *vementi perculit ictu,*

6.311; *excipit ictum*, 6.313 → iron and stone: *caedimus*, 6.314; *ad ictum*, 6.316; clouds and wind: *frigida . . . venti . . . vis*, 6.310 → stone and iron: *frigida vis ferrist*, 6.315; clouds and wind: *confluere*, 6.312 → stone and iron: *concurrunt*, 6.316.

89. Theophrastus had already depicted clouds as a woollen-like tissue (*Metars.* 1.24–38 Daiber).

90. Lucretius purposely sustains the allusion to Theophrastus' model of a sponge when he refers to the expulsion of fire out of a cloud as a process of "squeezing out" (6.181, 6.211–212, 6.275). For full discussion of this issue see Section 4.5.

91. For full discussion of this simile see below 130ff.

92. See also the discussion above 103–104.

93. Schrijvers (1970) 247; Hardie (1986) 185–187; Gale (1994a) 187.

94. Hardie (1986) 185–186.

95. See the discussion of volcanic eruptions below 126.

96. P. Fowler (1984) 416 *ad* 6.1169.

97. In 4.870–876 Lucretius depicts again the stomach as a container of fire, when thirst is explained as an accumulation of heat within our stomach; when we drink water this fire is extinguished, just like a flame.

98. Chrysippus *SVF* II.804–808 with P. Fowler (1984) 418 *ad loc.* Cf. Kohnke (1965).

99. The analogy of the clouds with wool in general is also found in Arat. *Phaen.* 938–939, in Varro Atacinus fr. 13 Courtney, in Verg. *G.* 1.393–397, in Plin. *NH* 18.356. Cf. Theophrastus' use of wool in meteorological analogies and the discussion above 125. For Lucretius' simile and the full water cycle see Montserrat and Navarro (1991) 297–299 and *passim.* For an interesting parallel use of wool as vehicle in a Hippocratic analogy see Hippocr. *Mul.* I.1.25–37.

100. See further discussion below 147ff. Cf the image of smoke in 6.523.

101. Most recently see Aicher (1992) 142–144; Schindler (2000) 113.

102. Aicher (1992) 143.

103. For later usages of the analogy in other natural philosophical treatises see Hardie (1986) 186 n. 80.

104. Hardie (1995) 208.

105. Sedley (1998) 44–45. Cf. Empedocles B73.1, B98.2.

106. Cf. Skutsch (1985) 397 *ad loc.* For Ennius' reception of Empedocles see 26ff.

107. Cf. also 6.1177. Cf. in Section 2.4 a similar technique employed by Lucretius in connection with Empedocles' compound adjectives used in pairs; in that case as well, whereas Lucretius appropriates the technique, he rejects Empedocles' philosophical principle.

108. This passage is quoted in full above 64.

109. Lucretius calls the inner structure of the earth, which is a labyrinth of caverns and chasms, a bosom (*gremio*, 6.539); the earth has also a back (*sub tergo*, 6.540).

110. Cf. 129 for a similar method in the comparison of clouds with the human body.

111. See Sections 2.1, 2.3 and 2.4.

112. Bailey (1947) 1034 *ad* 3.258–322 notes that although the connection of warmth and anger, cold and fear etc. was not an original Epicurean idea, yet Epicurus was the first to relate this physical theory with the structure of soul. For anger as warmth see e.g. Arist. *De An.* 403a26-b9.

113. Arist. *Mete.* 366b14ff., 368a6ff., 368b23ff. See Ernout and Robin (1928 III) 270–283 *ad* 6.536–607; Lloyd (1966) 362.

114. Kidd (1992) 298–300. See also Daiber (1992) 290–292.

115. For the image of engulfment by fierce jaws see Segal (1990) 136.

116. Cf. 1.135, 5.259, 6.572.

117. According to Heraclides Ponticus, Hermippus, Hippobotus, Diodorus of Ephesus (Diog. Laert. 8.67–72), despite Timaeus' objections (Diog. Laert. 8.71) which point to the untrustworthiness of the other sources. See Wright (1995a) 15–17; Chitwood (2004) 48–58. In any case this anecdote became later the standard version of Empedocles' death. Cf. e.g. Hor. *Ars P.* 464–466 with Brink (1971) *ad loc.;* Ov. *Ib.* 597–598; Lucian *Dial. Mort.* 77.6.4.; and Christian Fathers as quoted by Bidez (1894) 96.

118. Hardie (1986) 211–213.

119. Cf. the myth of Phaethon (5.396–410), which exemplifies the total victory of fire that brings about the total destruction of our world with Gale (1994a) 33–34. Cf. verbal correspondences with 6.642: *superavit,* 5.396; *superare,* 5.407. For the disintegrating effect of fire see also Section 4.2. Cf. in 6.646 the political metaphor about civil strife and discussion above in 65.

120. In more general terms, see in 1.1038–1041, 2.1105–1174 for similar comparisons between the world and human beings, in order to demonstrate world's growth, decay and mortality. For further discussion see 72ff.

121. West (1969) 75–78.

122. Cf. verbs denoting the action of fire: volcanic fire: *scintillare,* 6.644; *flammescere,* 6.669; *ardescunt,* 6.670; *percaluit calefecitque,* 6.686 → fire within the human body: *urit,* 6.660. Cf. further verbal correspondences: human body: *vis immensi . . . morbi,* 6.664 → volcano: *animai turbida . . . vis,* 6.693; human body: *coortam,* 6.656 → volcano: *coorta,* 6.641; human body: *subito,* 6.658 → in general natural upheavals: *repente,* 6.667 → volcano: *repente,* 6.680; human body: *per artus,* 6.661 → volcano: *perque mare ac terras . . . percurrere,* 6.668.

123. Leen (1984) 112–113. Cf. West (1969) 75–78.

124. It is noteworthy that Lucretius employs similar vocabulary in the account of the plague, which he also parallels with erysipelas (6.1167–1169): e.g. *mortiferam . . . cladem conflare coorta,* 6.1091; *forte coorta,* 6.1096; *coorta,* 6.1100; *aer inimicus serpere coepit,* 6.1120; *repit,* 6.1121; *subito clades,* 6.1125; *mortifer aestus,* 6.1138; *incensum fervore,* 6.1145; *morbida vis,* 6.1092; *vis . . . morborum,* 6.1098.

125. Cf. above 125–126.
126. Godwin (1991) 141 *ad* 6.680.
127. Cf. also *flammarum . . . iras,* 1.723; *irai fax,* 3.303 . For the Epicurean conception of anger see D. Fowler (1997).
128. Philo records as well that Empedocles had likened the salt formed on the sea-shore to hail (A66a = Armenian translation of Philo *De Prov.* 2.61). Cf. also A51b (Achilles *Introduction to Aratus* 5, p. 34.29–30), A51c (Scholia *on Basil* 22 Pasquali), A51d (Lactant. *De Opif. Dei* 17.6). According to Empedocles (A30 = Pseudo-Plutarch *Stromateis* [in Euseb. *Praep. Evang.* 1.8.10] = *Dox. Gr.* 582) the moon was similarly composed of air cut off by fire and then frozen or solidified "just like hail." See Longrigg (1965) 250.
129. For a plausible echo of this specific theory of Empedocles in *DRN* 1.493 *glacies aeris* see Longrigg (1970).
130. Longrigg (1965) 250–251.
131. Lloyd (1966) 368.
132. Cf. multiple correspondences: cloud: *validi vis . . . venti / . . . impete recto,* 6.137–138 → trees: *flatus,* 6.139; cloud: *perscindat . . . perfringens,* 6.138 → trees: *evolvens radicibus haurit ab imis,* 6.141. Cf. also the comparison of waves in the clouds giving a sound similar to that of waves that break in the sea with a roaring noise (6.142–144): cloud: *fluctus,* 6.142 → river-sea: *aestus,* 6.144; cloud: *in frangendo,* 6.143 → river-sea: *frangitur,* 6.144.
133. In the chapter on Personification above see the discussion of socio-political imagery 239 n. 90, of the war imagery 242 n. 131, of the *Makranthropos* image 74ff. In the chapter on Metaphor below see the discussion of the "Flowing Water" metaphor 205ff., and of the "Squeezing out the Sponge" metaphor 217ff.
134. Epicur. fr. 308 Us.: τῶν ἀναθυμιασμένων σωμάτων ἔπληττε τὸν ἀέρα; Empedocles A49b (Aët. 2.6.3 = *Dox. Gr.* 334): ἐξ οὗ θυμιαθῆναι τὸν ἀέρα. See Clay (1998) 167–169. Cf. also the parallel use of the word ἐξατμίζειν with Clay (1998) 169 n. 21.
135. See also Townend (1965) 100–101; Gale (1994a) 115–116.
136. As it will turn out, the use of the word "light", which can be understood either in terms of weight or in terms of a fiery substance, could turn out quite misleading. Although, when it comes to atoms of fire, it carries both meanings, it can still refer to atoms of moisture only with reference to their relative weight.
137. Keyser (1992). Cf. *aetherius sol,* 3.1044.
138. Image of exhalation: cf. *exhalantque,* 5.463 with *velut halitus,* 6.478; socio-political imagery: cf. *conciliantur,* 5.465 with *conveniundo,* 6.480; the weaving metaphor: cf. *subtexunt,* 5.466 with *subtexit,* 6.482. See the discussion about the formation of clouds above 127ff.
139. Jobst (1907) 31. See Kingsley (1995) 15–23 for difficulties in the interpretation of αἰθήρ in this fragment. On the contrary see Wright (1995a) 196–197 *ad loc.* See also O'Brien (1969) 291–292.

NOTES TO CHAPTER THREE

1. Silk (1974); Lloyd (1987) 172–214.
2. See especially Long (1971); Sedley (1973), on whom I draw extensively. See also De Lacy (1939); Dalzell (1987); D. Fowler (2002) 186–195 *ad* 2.112–141.
3. Sedley (1973) 20. For Epicurus' theory on the origin of language see Sedley (1973); Snyder (1980) 11–30; Schrijvers (1999) 55–80; Campbell (2003) 285–323 *ad* 5.1028–90 with full bibliography on the issue; Holmes (2005); Atherton (2005).
4. Sedley (1973) 20–21 also remarks that "the first meanings are those which even after conventional usages were fixed continued to be current until 'men in the know' gave certain words metaphorical meanings. For up to this stage every name could be said to correspond with a particular kind of perceptible objects."
5. Cf. Plut. *Adv. Col.* 10.1111Fff. Epicurus was very much concerned with ambiguity; he even wrote a treatise entitled Περὶ ἀμφιβολίας (cf. Epicur. ΠΦ 28, fr.13 col. v 8 inf.–vi 1 sup. Sedley).
6. Sedley (1973) 21.
7. Sedley (1973) 64.
8. Sedley (1973) 21 *ad* Epicur. ΠΦ 28, fr.13 col. iv 3 sup.–v 12 sup. Sedley. Cf. also Sedley (1973) 22: "he seems to say that a philosopher may use words from ordinary language provided that he always keeps in view the distinguishing characteristics from which they draw their meanings, so as to avoid the pitfalls involved in completely changing the class of object referred to. A word is only useful insofar as its underlying meaning is kept in view."
9. Sedley (1973) 23. Epicurus himself has some witty usages. Cf. e.g. Epicur. 163 Us. (Diog. Laert. 10.6): παιδείαν δὲ πᾶσαν, μακάριε, φεῦγε τἀκάτιον ἀράμενος / "avoid every education, my blessed man, hoisting the sails of your ship." As Obbink (1995) 193 remarks, this is an echo of Circe's instructions to Odysseus to flee the Sirens.
10. See Wigodsky (1995) 62–63; Guidorizzi and Beta (2000) 179–188.
11. Arist. *Poet.* 1457b13–16 (citing B138 and B143), *Poet.* 1457b22–25 (citing B152). On the contrary see Aristotle's criticism of Empedocles' use of metaphor in *Gen. an.* 777a7–12 *ad* B68, *Mete.* 357a24–28 *ad* B55. However, Aristotle's criticism does not concern their poetic value, but rather their scientific validity and clarity. For condemnation of Empedocles' ambiguity see Arist. *Rhet.* 1407a31-b6.
12. Sedley (1998) 45. Of course, as he adds (ibid. n. 32), "the variety of vocabulary in philosophical verse is partly dictated by metrical constraints: a word which works well in one place may be inadmissible in another grammatical case or at another point in the hexameter."
13. Cf. also Phld. *De Piet.* 546–547 Obbink with Obbink (1996) 363–364.

14. Sedley (1998) 32.
15. Sedley (1998) 45. Cf. Sedley (1998) 32, where he claims that Lucretius' part of the proem (1.136–145) about the deficiencies of his own language echoes exactly these fragments. Cf. similar remarks in Parmenides DK28 B8.38, Anaxagoras DK59 B17.
16. D. Fowler (2002) 189: "Lucretius does not provide a historical account of the words he uses, but he does as a poet recall his readers to their primary, most literal sense and to the τò πρῶτον ἐννόημα attached to each word. The precise, live metaphors of the poetry thus encourage clear philosophical thinking." See also Battisti (1976).
17. Section 3.4.2.1
18. Cf. 1.340–357, 4.650, 6.936–958. Cf. the use of *foramina* in connection with different containers: e.g. 2.386, 4.599, 4.621, 5.811, 6.1031. Cf. also the use of *via, cavea, caula passim.*
19. Aristotle (*Gen. corr.* 325b1ff.) had already discerned the binary role assigned to the Empedoclean pores and the philosophical affinity with the Atomic void. See Mugler (1967).
20. For the contrary view see e.g. Segal (1990) especially 94–170.
21. The key article for the issue in question is by Mourelatos (1986), to which I am much indebted.
22. Parmenides seems to have been the first to adopt vocabulary for binding in a metaphorical way, to conceptualize abstract logical Necessity. For the Eleatic philosopher, Being is not subject to either generation or destruction; rather it is an indivisible unity without past or future, *bound fast* and *chained* by Necessity (DK28 B8). See Coxon (1986) 200; Wright (1998) 18. For further use of the metaphors see Snyder (1981) on the web of song; Onians (1954) 349–351 on the weaving of Fate, 434–466 on the bond of sin, of debt, on binding in mysteries etc. Cf. also similar contemporary use of the "binding metaphor" in Turner and Fauconnier (2000).
23. For the socio-political imagery see Section 2.2.3.2. For the similes (Empedocles' painters simile B23, Lucretius' similes with the letters of the alphabet 1.196–198, 1.820–829, 1.907–914, 2.688–699, 2.1013–1022) see 13–14.
24. One should not disregard the sexual connotations of these metaphors. Cf. Solmsen (1963); Sider (1984); Mourelatos (1986) 175–176.
25. See discussion in 36ff.
26. Cf. also B3.12, B35.1. The pores had already been used by Alcmaeon (DK24 A5).
27. Williams (1982) 125 *ad* Arist. *Gen. corr.* 324b25.
28. Mourelatos (1986) 168 and *passim.* Cf. also Long (1966) 260. For Empedocles' theory of pores in connection with that of colours see Ierodiakonou (2005).
29. I follow Inwood's translation. Cf. also Philoponus *In Gen. anim.* CIAG 14.3, 123.16–21.

30. For more on Empedocles' theory of effluences see below 195ff.
31. Solmsen (1963) 476–478; Lloyd (1966) 274–275.
32. For the Homeric vocabulary see Wright (1998) 17–19.
33. For plausible reception of this simile by Epicurus see below 180.
34. Wright (1998) 19.
35. Cf. also ἀραρίσκω in B96; ἁρμόττω in A92, B107; συναρμόσσω in A92; ἐναρμόττειν in A86, A92.
36. Cf. B86, B107.1.
37. Cf. also B33. Cf. Anaximenes DK13 A14.
38. Gemelli Marciano (1990) 140.
39. Mourelatos (1986) 175.
40. Mourelatos (1986) 174.
41. Mourelatos (1986) 174: "In Homer κολλήεις and κολλητὸς are used of structures that derive their strength from close overlapping." In a similar way we should interpret B96.4 Ἁρμονίης κόλλησιν ἀρηρότα θεσπεσίῃσιν. / "held together by the marvelous gluing of Harmony." For the reading of this line see Sider (1984) whom I follow. I therefore modify Wright's translation.
42. Cf. B33. Cf. also A54 (Aёt. 2.13.11 = *Dox. Gr.* 342): Ἐμπεδοκλῆς τοὺς μὲν ἀπλανεῖς ἀστέρας συνδεδέσθαι τῷ κρυστάλλῳ, τοὺς δὲ πλανήτας ἀνεῖσθαι. / "Empedocles says that the fixed stars are fastened to the ice and that the planets are free."
43. For Empedocles' influence on Plato's *Timaeus* see Bignone (1916) 613–623; Hershbell (1974). Cf. also the vocabulary in other authors with Empedoclean echoes (e.g. Ap. Rhod. *Argon.* 1.496–498).
44. Cf. Epicur. fr. 250 Us. (Plut. *Adv. Col.* 5.1109C).
45. Mourelatos (1986) 191–192: "Instead of explaining aggregations in terms of entanglement of mostly convex structures, Empedocles explains such aggregations in terms of reciprocity of deeply concave structures, the poroi; instead of supposing one factor, the void, to provide room for the motions that lead to aggregation, the geometry of atomic shapes to provide the actual nexus, the poroi of Empedocles serve both as grooves for the motion and as binding network."
46. Mourelatos (1986) 135.
47. Cf. also. Epicur. *Ep. Hdt.* 65–66, *Ep. Pyth.* 88, ΚΔ 2; Epicur. fr. 308 Us. Cf. Leucippus DK67 A1, A10, A14; Democritus DK68 A37, A43, A49; Diogenes of Oinoanda fr. 37.III.7 Smith.
48. Schmid (1937) 48–49; Arrighetti (1973) 608–609; Leone (1984) 94–97. For serious doubts about Epicurus' confutation of Empedocles in his Book 14 see now Montarese (2005) 120–128. Cf. however, the mention of Empedocles' name in Epicur. ΠΦ 14, fr. 60 col. xl Leone = fr. 29.28 Arr.[2].
49. 1.329ff., 1.742ff.
50. Rose (1956) has plausibly argued that the *stomachion* or Chinese puzzle lies beneath this illustration.

51. Schiesaro (1990) 45–46.
52. M. Bollack (1963) and (1978) 394–415. Cf. also Wallace (1996).
53. M. Bollack (1963) discusses as well the relationship with Democritus and Plato. For Empedocles' theory of the magnet see above 158–159.
54. Jobst (1907) 35–36; M. Bollack (1978) 414.
55. Bästlein (1875) 10.
56. I adopt the reading of Wright (1995a) *ad loc.*
57. Cf. 4.1259.
58. M. Bollack (1978) 414.
59. *ferrea texta,* 6.1054; *texturae,* 6.1084. Cf. 2.102–103.
60. Cf. 6.915. See Mourelatos (1986) 174 on the role of Empedocles' nails.
61. Cf. 2.1115. Cf. also προσθέσεις, Epicur. *Ep. Pyth.* 89. Conversely, as Campbell (2003) 224 *ad* 5.962–963 rightly notes, "the analogy between the combining of the atoms and the coupling of primeval humans is in tune with the traditional analogy between cosmogony, and human sex, especially in the *hieros gamos* of earth and sky." For another possible hint at Empedocles' vocabulary cf. *DRN* 5.1205 with Empedocles A54 quoted above in full 258 n. 42. See Cazzaniga (1971); Ciappi (1999).
62. Cf. discussion in Section 1.1. For objections see Schrijvers (1999) 24–39.
63. Campbell (2003) 114 *ad loc.* I follow Inwood's translation (CTXT-51). On the contary see Sedley (2003) 5 n. 13.
64. Cf. also Empedocles' echo in 5.864–867 with Sedley (2003) 10–11 and discussion above in 228–229 n. 71.
65. Cf. 4.722–748 where Lucretius takes pains to explain the existence of mental pictures of such creatures, resorting to his physical theory of films; their *simulacra* are formed in the air of their own accord, or the *simulacra* of two or more real things, such as a man and a horse, are closely *fitted together* (*inter se iunguntur in auris,* 4.726; *haerescit,* 4.742) thanks to their thin texture and consequently form the image of a compound creature.
66. Clay (1998) 127. Cf. 5.850, 5.856.
67. See Brown (1987) 318 *ad* 1205. Cf. also 4.1113 with Brown (1987) 244 *ad loc.* Cf. conventional usages of the word in 5.853, 5.1019.
68. Brown (1987) 352 *ad loc.* rightly observes that the use of the word *harmonia* in this context "exemplifies Lucretius' feeling for the original, concrete meanings of words." About *harmonia* cf. also 3.131.
69. Campbell (2003) 224 *ad loc.* Cf. also 5.848 with Campbell (2003) 115 *ad loc.* See also D. Fowler (2002) 254–255 *ad* 2.173 who evokes Varro's etymological link between *Venus* and *vincire* (*LL* 5.61–62).
70. Von Raumer (1893) 23, 59–60, 92, 101 and 105; Pope (1949) 77–78; Snyder (1983) for a rather brief analysis of the weaving metaphor in Lucretius.
71. See Introduction 1.1.
72. Cf. Epicur. *Ep. Hdt.* 54.

73. Cf. Longo (1964–1965) especially for the Greek equivalents of Lucretius' terms; D. Fowler (2002) 152 *ad* 2.67 who also notes the possible polemical nature of Lucretius' argument.

74. Cf. 1.561–562. Cf. Epicur. *Ep. Hdt.* 56, fr. 267 Us.

75. *perplexus:* 2.102, 2.459, 2.463, 5.450, 5.452; *perplicatus:* 2.394.

76. D. Fowler (2002) 181 *ad* 2.102.

77. *hamatus:* 2.394, 2.405, 2.445, 2.468, 4.662.

78. Cf. e.g. Epicur. *Ep. Pyth.* 109: σύνωσιν δὲ τῶν σκαληνῶν καὶ ὀξυγωνίων τῶν ἐν τῇ ὕδατι ὑπαρχόντων / "and the compression of the scalene and acute-angled atoms contained in it." Cf. also Epicur. fr. 270 Us. (Ps.-Plut. *Plac. Philos.* 1.3.18 = *Dox. Gr.* 286): εἶναι δὲ τὰ σχήματα τῶν ἀτόμων ἀπερίληπτα, οὐκ ἄπειρα. μὴ γὰρ εἶναι μήτ' ἀγκιστροειδεῖς μήτε τριαινοειδεῖς μήτε κρικοειδεῖς· ταῦτα γὰρ τὰ σχήματα εὔθραυστά ἐστιν, αἱ δ' ἄτομοι ἀπαθεῖς ἄθραυστοι. ἴδια δ' ἔχειν σχήματα λόγῳ θεωρητά. / "The figures of atoms cannot be incomprehensible, but they are not infinite. These figures are neither hooked nor trident-shaped nor ring-shaped, such figures as these being unbreakable; but the atoms are impassible, impenetrable; they have indeed figures of their own, which are conceived only by reason." Cf. also Epicurus' treatment of Plato's use of Empedocles' four elements in Epicur. *ΠΦ* 14, fr. 60 col. xxxiv-xxxviii Leone (*PHerc.* 1148 = fr. 29.22–26 Arr.²), where he lists the geometrical solids of the *Timaeus.* Cf. Leucippus DK67 A23; Democritus DK68 A37, A135.

79. Clay (1983) 322 n. 76. For Lucretius' difficulties with the language of Greek geometry see McDiarmid (1959).

80. *conexus:* 1.633, 2.726, 3.557, 5.438; *nexus:* 1.220, 1.240, 1.244.

81. Reich (1958) 125.

82. Long (1977) 81.

83. Garani (2007).

84. Boisacq (1950) s.v. ὅρκος. Cf. Frisk (1954) 418–419; Luther (1954) 86 who likens this idea of enclosure to the oath-taker bringing a magic ἕρκος down around himself through a self-curse; Hiersche (1958); Callaway (1993) 18. For objections see Benveniste (1948); Leumann (1950) 91–92; Chantraine (1980). For ancient etymologies of oath see Hirzel (1902) 3 n. 5. With particular reference to Empedocles see J. Bollack (1958); and Schreckenberg (1964) 110–113. Bollack refers to a gloss in Hesychius: ὅρκοι: δεσμοὶ σφραγίδος. However, his overall interpretation especially of B30 is rather unconvincing.

85. See discussion in 55ff. For another striking example of this Lucretian technique of "vivification" see Clay (1998) 121–137 with particular reference to Empedocles and more generally Clay (1998) 161–173.

86. Cf. 3.331, 3.557, 3.688, 3.691, 3.695–696.

87. Cf. 3.558–559, 3.578–579, 3.800, 3.805.

88. For the possible Pythagorean origin of the metaphor see Pythagorean School DK58 B1a (Diog. Laert. 8.31), Philolaus DK44 B14. Cf. also

Plato's corresponding metaphors of binding regarding the relationship between soul and body, with Pender (2000) 165–170.

89. West (1975) 96. Cf. 3.136–137, 3.159, 4.889.

90. Note the use of double elisions in 5.537, 5.555, 5.558, which again illustrate the notion of close interdependence. This simile could be also classified with those discussed in Section 3.4.2.2 entitled "Roots in action."

91. Long and Sedley (1987) 32–37.

92. Cf. 1.449, 2.743, 4.493.

93. Sedley (1998) 46.

94. Hinds (1987) especially 451. See also Sedley (1998) 47–48.

95. Cf. 2.478, 5.1202. See Snyder (1981).

96. Cf. also P. Fowler (1984) 103–105 *ad* 6.42: "the weaving metaphor is apt for the composition of a philosophical poem, which has to lay out the interconnected propositions in an orderly manner, exhibiting its own system or ratio, in a way that reflects the ratio of nature, just as Epicurus' philosophy does. [. . .] Weaving as patterning is a way of beautifying or ornamenting something. [. . .] Thus, it belongs to the group of concepts in Lucretius expressing the aesthetic power of poetry."

97. For the metaphor of breaking see 1.551–553 quoted above 175. Cf. also 1.546, 1.556–557, 1.559, 1.1040, 5.278.

98. Cf. imagery of war above 67.

99. This privileged role of fire evokes and may be conditioned by the similar power that Empedocles assigned to it. See Wright (1995a) 24–25.

100. Montserrat and Navarro (2000) 8–9: "Heat often penetrates a thing as if invading it. The effect produced in the corpuscular fabric of the thing invaded: particles of heat or fire, introducing themselves into the interstices of the body, slacken *vincla* (bonds) and loose *nodi* (knots) existing between its particles. [. . .] The loosening of bonds and the increasing of separation between the particles of a body can be so great that those particles separate completely and disperse. The body is then destroyed."

101. Montserrat and Navarro (1991) 298: "Lucretius explains water evaporation by its disintegration into tiny invisible parts. The solar particles get into the water body and unbind its interior." Cf. also West (1969) 81–82: "In weaving *radii* are shuttles (5.1353), *tela* is the loom (5.1351), or what is woven upon it or strictly the vertical threads through which the *radii* fly. And the *exordium* is literally the same as the last definition of *tela*." Cf. 1.492 for the hardness of the gold; 6.514 for the melting clouds becoming thin and emitting rainy moisture.

102. Cf. aslo 6.1153 with P. Fowler (1984) 373–375 *ad loc.*

103. Cf. 3.594, 3.599, 3.602.

104. On materialized feelings see also Section 4.3.

105. Springer (1977) 57.

106. Cf. also 3.903. See D. Fowler (2002) 126 *ad* 2.46: "Philosophers always claim that they are liberators (Pl. *Phd.* 83a ἡ φιλοσοφία . . . τὴν ψυχὴν

λύειν ἐπιχειρεῖ). Epicurus in particular was seen as ἐλευθερωτὴς καὶ σωτήρ (Lucian *Alex.* 61)."

107. Brown (1987) 273–275 *ad* 4.1146–1150, commenting also on Lucretius' distortion of the conventional erotic imagery.

108. Lapidge (1980) and (1989) 1384 and *passim*. Cf. also the use of the verb ἀναλύω (*solvo*) to describe the Stoic cosmic destruction.

109. D. Fowler (2002) 340. For the *clinamen* see D. Fowler (2002) 407–427. For Epicurus and the Stoics see above 243 n. 160.

110. Cf. also *fatalibus . . . vinclis,* 5.876. See further discussion of this passage above in 60. One could perhaps think of a possible connection with Empedocles A66a (Armenian translation of Philo *De Prov.* 2.61 = fr. 60 Inwood): "Its [the sea's] ferocious edge keeps swelling, as when swamps absorb the floating hail. For all the moisture on earth tends to be driven into its hollows, being forced by the constant whirls of the wind, by the strongest bonds as it were." These allusions to Stoic ideas become even more striking if we have a look at usages of similar metaphors, transplanted into later Latin texts which more clearly embrace Stoic allusions and show also intertextual engagement with Lucretius' poem. E.g. Ov. *Met.* 1.9 *non bene iunctarum discordia semina rerum,* 1.25 *dissociata locis concordi pace ligavit;* Manilius *Astron.* e.g. 2.803 *aeternis . . . compagibus* (cf. also 1.719, 1.725, 3.55); Luc. *Phars.* 1.72 *conpage solula.* See Lapidge (1979), (1980) and (1989). Note that Lapidge (1979) 356 claims that Manilius was the first to translate Stoic "physical bonds" between various parts of the universe with *foedus.*

111. *compleo, oppleo, expleo, erumpo, dissipo, insinuo, perscindo, dispergo, labefacio, penetro, diddo, permano, perscindo, prorumpo, repleo.* Cf. also verbs suggestive specifically of an image of liquids poured in or out: *fundere, perfundere, profundere, circumfundere, effundere, suffundere.*

112. Cf. Campbell (2003) 88 *ad* 5.823 for another plausible Empedoclean echo in Lucretius, comparing B35.7 and B35.16 with *fudit.* Cf. 5.917. Cf. also the metaphor of irrigation in connection with the flowing of words in B3.2, B35.2, B39.3.

113. Longo (1964–65) 421–434.

114. For Epicurus' use of the corresponding terms ἀναφὴς φύσις, κενόν, τόπος, χώρα denoting the notion of void see Reiley (1909) 67–91.

115. Longo (1964–65) 437. Cf. ibid. 434–437. Cf. also Section 2.2.

116. Cf. 1.522, 1.525, 1.527.

117. Kleve (1978) 64.

118. Sedley (2003) 8 n. 21. For Empedocles' denial of void see B13 and B14 with 226 n. 33 above. Cf. also A35. For the use of *plenus* in *DRN* 6.1085 cf. Empedocles B92. See Longo (1964–65) 435 and further discussion in the section on magnet above 165ff.

119. Cf. 2.146, 2.358, 4.532, 4.1017, 5.226, 5.992, 5.1066. Cf. Democritus DK68 A126a. The same vocabulary is used also for light: 4.372, 4.378.

120. Cf. also in the Section 4.2.

121. Görler (1997); Reinhardt (2002). Cf. Diogenes of Oinoanda fr. 108 Smith. Cf. also Empedocles' theory of pleasure (A95b = Aët. 4.9.15 = *Dox. Gr.* 398): Ἐμπεδοκλῆς τὰς ἡδονὰς γίνεσθαι τοῖς μὲν ὁμοίοις <ἐκ> τῶν ὁμοίων, κατὰ δὲ τὸ ἐλλεῖπον πρὸς τὴν ἀναπλήρωσιν, ὥστε τῷ ἐλλείποντι ἡ ὄρεξις τοῦ ὁμοίου. τὰς δ᾽ ἀλγηδόνας τοῖς ἐναντίοις, ἠλλοτριῶσθαι γὰρ πρὸς ἄλληλα ὅσα διαφέρει κατά τε τὴν σύγκρισιν καὶ τὴν τῶν στοιχείων κρᾶσιν. / "Empedocles says that things have pleasures because of things similar to themselves, and that [they aim] at a refilling in accordance with the deficiency; so that the desire for what is similar is caused by the deficiency. And pains occur by means of opposites. For things which are different in the combination and the blend of the elements are hostile to one another." Cf. also A95a = Aët. 4.9.14 = *Dox. Gr.* 398, A95c = Aët. 5.28 = *Dox. Gr.* 440. The Empedoclean precedent is noted by Dodds (1959) 304.

122. Cf. Epicur. *Ep. Men.* 127; fr. 202, fr. 456, fr. 471 Us.; Diogenes of Oinoanda fr. 153, fr. 155 Smith.

123. Cf. τὸ μὲν φυσικὸν πᾶν εὐπόριστόν ἐστι, τὸ δὲ κενὸν δυσπόριστον. / "whatever is natural is easy procured and only the vain and worthless hard to win," Epicur. *Ep. Men.* 130; τὸ μὲν τῶν ἀγαθῶν πέρας ὡς ἔστιν εὐσυμπλήρωτόν τε καὶ εὐπόριστον διαλαμβάνοντος; / "he understands how easily the limit of good things can be reached and attained," Epicur. *Ep. Men.* 133. Cf. Epicur. *KΔ* 15.

124. Brown (1987) 216–233 *ad* 4.1073–1120.

125. P. Fowler (1984) 72 *ad loc.* Epicur. *KΔ* 3, 18, 20; fr. 417 Us. Cf. Diogenes of Oinoanda fr. 108 Smith: *[οὐ χρησιμώτερον τὸν παρὰ]* / φύσιν πλοῦτο[ν ἢ ὕδωρ ἂν]- / γείῳ τινὶ πλήρει, [ὥστε] / περιρεῖν ἔξωθεν, [ὑπολημ]- / πτέον [. . .] / "[One] must [regard] wealth [beyond] what is natural [as of no more use than water] to a container that is full [to] overflowing."

126. See also Görler (1997) 194, who draws our attention to the fact that in 3.870–873 Lucretius says that those who cannot bear the idea of what will happen to their body after death "do not ring true" (*non sincerum sonere,* 3.873), as cracked jars do not "ring true." Cf. Pl. *Phlb.* 55c.

127. Gale (1994a) 37–38.

128. Epicur. fr. 221 Us. Cf. P. Fowler (1984) 63–72. Görler (1997) quotes in this connection also Plut. *De liberis educandis* 12F.

129. Gentner (1983) discusses how people use this metaphor as a mental model in the domain of electronic circuitry.

130. Gemelli Marciano (1990) 178 remarks that probably Empedocles builds the term ἀπορροή upon its Aeschylean antonym ἐπιρροή, used there for blood (*Ag.* 1510).

131. Cf. also A86 (Theophr. *Sens.* 7–24), B101. See Beare (1906) 14–25 and *passim;* Wright (1995a) 229–230 *ad* B89.

132. For mirrors see A88 (Aët. 4.14.1). Cf. also B109a = *Pap. Oxyrh.* 1609 XIII 94. For magnets see A89 (Alex. Aphrod. *Quest.* 2.23, CIAG Supp. 2.2 72.9–27) quoted above 158–159.

133. E.g. ῥεῦσις in *Ep. Hdt.* 48; ῥεῦμα in *Ep. Hdt.* 49, 52; εἰσρέω in *ΠΦ* fr. 34.26.12 Arr.²; ἐκρέω in *ΠΦ* fr. 34.32.20 Arr.²; ἐπίρρυσις in *SV* 1. Cf. also Leucippus DK67 A29; Democritus DK68 A135, A165, B123; Epicur. fr. 319, fr. 321 Us. Epicurus' vocabulary is again echoed in later Epicurean writers. Cf. e.g. Diogenes of Oinoanda fr. 5.II.6, fr. 9, fr. 43.I.7, fr. 69.II.11 Smith.

134. Cf. Epicur. *ΠΦ* fr. 36.21–23 Arr.², in which, as Arrighetti (1973) 646 notes, Epicurus criticizes the theory of vision probably against Empedocles and Timaeus referring to the symmetry of pores.

135. Rosenmeyer (1996) 136.

136. For Heraclitus' theory of flux see Wiggins (1982); Hussey (1999) 99; Adomenas (2002).

137. Heraclitus DK22 B12 (= 40 Marcovich). Cf. Pl. *Cra.* 440c; Arist. *Metaph.* 987a32ff. Cf. Marcovich (2001) 194–214; Taran (1999) with further bibliography and recapitulation of the puzzle.

138. Adomenas (2002) 420.

139. D. Fowler (2002) 153 *ad* 2.69.

140. I agree with those who interpret the nickname as referring to the Heraclitean doctrine of eternal flux. Cf. Sedley (1976) 133, who also rightly notes that Epicurus seems to be punning on Heraclitus' metaphor of the κυκεών or barley drink (DK22 B125), which in the words of Heraclitus, separates if you do not stir it. Sedley points out as well (n. 53) that in antiquity the κυκεών was regularly understood as a symbol of universal flux (Chrysippus *SVF* II.937). For the opposing view see Leone (1984) 101.

141. Diogenes of Oinoanda fr. 5 Smith could perhaps offer elucidation on this intriguing matter. This highly problematic fragment attributes to Aristotle the view that nothing can be scientifically known because things are continually in flux and, on account of the rapidity of the flux, evade our apprehension. Probably Diogenes' disagreement is about the speed of the flux, which in his opinion is not so rapid so as to annihilate the validity of sensory evidence. See Smith (1993) 128–130 and 441.

142. According to our extant fragments, Epicurus deploys war imagery in order to describe this state. However see below 203 Lucretius' comparison of matter with an ocean, which could echo Epicurus' similar imagery. Cf. further discussion in Section 2.2.3.3.

143. Mourelatos (1986) 190.

144. For B121.3 I follow Inwood's translation (his fr. 117). Cf. Wright (1995a) 279 *ad loc.* for suspicions about the authenticity of the line.

145. Campbell (2003) 95 *ad* 5.828–836. Cf. also Long (1977).

146. Von Raumer (1893) 26–28; Schrijvers (1970) 270–272; D. Fowler (2002) 153 *ad* 2.69.

147. Kollman (1971); Pizzani (1983); Tatum (1984); Rösler (1973). See now Piazzi (2005) 25–42. Cf. Diogenes of Oinoanda fr. 6 Smith.

148. Rösler (1973); Sedley (1998) 20. Montarese (2005) 32–87, who explains in detail why in his *critique* (1.635–920) Lucretius appears to rely on information handed down by the Theophrastean doxographical tradition and suggests that Lucretius plausibly uses an earlier Epicurean author.

149. Unless we accept the assumption that in refuting the "transformationist" theory, next to the Stoics and the Peripatetics Lucretius returns to Heraclitus and his followers (1.782–800. Cf. especially 1.790–791). For discussion of Lucretius' possible targets in these lines see Ernout and Robin (1924) 155; M. Bollack (1969) 386–387; Montarese (2005) 73–77; Piazzi (2005) 196–207 *ad loc.*

150. Campbell (2003) 93–97 *ad* 5.828–836. Cf. also Ov. *Met.* 15.252–258 with Hardie (1995). For the contrary view see Galinsky (1998).

151. Leucippus DK67 A1, A10; Democritus DK68 A135. Even if we accept that Epicurus also used this vocabulary, it would seem difficult to believe that this was done in such a systematic way.

152. Cf. metaphorical uses of the Greek verb with reference to people. Cf. LSJ s.v. συρρέω I; e.g. Hdt. 5.101.

153. Due to their static nature the technological metaphors stand at the other end of the metaphorical spectrum.

154. For further discussion of this simile see now 117. Cf. similarly αἰθέρος . . . ῥεῦμα, Empedocles B100.24 with discussion above 105–106.

155. Cf. discussion in 108ff.

156. Cf. 5.281–282 where the comparison has been suppressed by the asyndeton.

157. Cf. 3.189–190.

158. Cf. 3.177–205 about the similar atomic composition of the soul. See Townend (1965) 100; Leen (1984) 114.

159. 203.

160. Cf. 5.668, 5.702.

161. Cf. also 6.1260.

162. Cf. 4.144, 4.157, 4.218, 4.260, 4.334, 4.675–676, 4.695, 4.860. Cf. in Book 6 the repetition of the theory in relation with a magnet: 6.922, 6.924, 6.931, 6.933, 6.993, 6.1002, 6.1053.

163. Reiley (1909) 17; Rosenmeyer (1996) 140–141.

164. Cf. 6.925, 6.1003, 6.1049, 6.1056.

165. Cf. Cic. *ND* 1.105 *accessio,* 1.109 *transitio.*

166. As D. Fowler (2002) 155 *ad* 2.69 points out, the word *fluo* was also used to describe putrefaction, especially that of corpses (*TLL* vi/i. 972. 22ff.).

167. Clay (1998) 164. Cf. 5.260.

168. Cf. 1.1038–1039, 4.919, 6.1204. This analogy bears vivid Platonic and ultimately Empedoclean influence. Cf. ἐπίρρυτον σῶμα καὶ ἀπόρρυτον. / "body subject to inflow and outflow," Pl. *Ti.* 43a; ὅταν μὲν δὴ πλέον τοῦ ἐπιρρέοντος

ἀπίῃ, φθίνει πᾶν, ὅταν δὲ ἔλαττον, αὐξάνεται / "and when what passes out is more than the inflow every creature decays, but when less, it increases" Pl. *Ti.* 81b4–5. See Solmsen (1953). Cf. also Klinger (1952); Müller (1978); Segal (1990) 94–114 and further discussion above in Section 2.3.

169. P. Fowler (1984) 60 *ad* 6.20.

170. Cf. Epicur. *Ep. Hdt.* 37, 83. See Smith (1966); Schrijvers (1970) 271–272.

171. For the use of this imagery elsewhere in literature see P. Fowler (1984) 89 *ad* 6.34.

172. See Brown (1987) 221–222 *ad* 4.1077.

173. Cf. parallels in the "unbinding" metaphor 185ff. and the "emptying the atomic container" metaphor 193ff.

174. It would be interesting to look at the term which was used by the Stoics as an equivalent to the Epicurean ἀταραξία, the εὔροια βίου, meaning good flow of life, i.e. happy life (Zeno Citieus *SVF* I.184; Cleanthes *SVF* I.554; Chrysippus *SVF* III.4, III.16). Cf. Long and Sedley (1987) 394–401. Although there are only speculations about the origins and the exact meaning of the phrase, the striking coincidence in the broader metaphorical field from which both rival schools draw their metaphor should be pointed out, although they opt for its two opposite poles. Whereas the Epicureans represent an ideal state of life through the image of absolutely *calm waters*, the Stoics seem to support a more energetic *modus vivendi*, which is expressed by the metaphor of a *good flow of water* (εὔροια). This direct contrast seems so obvious to me that it would be tempting to take the one metaphor as a direct reply to the other. For the related image in Plato see a full analysis in Adomenas (2002) especially 421–432.

175. Konstan (1979) 410. Cf. Epicur. fr. 276 Us. For more on ἔκθλιψις in Presocratic and Atomic philosophy see Konstan (1979) 410–412. See also Montserrat and Navarro (2000) 11–12 and especially (1991) 293: "the origin of world and of water consists in the concentration of particles whose size and shape best favours their interlacing, together with the squeezing out of smaller, smoother and rounder ones; this is how solid material is formed or contracted and how fluids detach."

176. Cf. Leucippus DK67 A28; Democritus DK68 A60, A61. For the production of voice see Epicur. *Ep. Hdt.* 53.

177. Epicur. fr. 308 Us. (Ps.-Plut. *Plac. Philos.* 1.4.2–4 = *Dox. Gr.* 290–291): ὅσα δὲ μικρὰ καὶ περιφερῆ καὶ λεῖα καὶ εὐόλισθα, ταῦτα καὶ ἐξεθλίβετο κατὰ τὴν σύνοδον τῶν σωμάτων εἴς τε τὸ μετέωρον ἀνεφέρετο. [...] τὸ δὲ πλῆθος τῶν ἀναθυμιωμένων σωμάτων ἐπέληττε τὸν ἀέρα καὶ τοῦτον ἐξέθλιβε· [...] πολλῆς δὲ ὕλης ἔτι περιειλημμένης ἐν τῇ γῇ, πυκνουμένης τε ταύτης κατὰ τὰς ἀπὸ τῶν πνευμάτων πληγὰς καὶ τὰς ἀπὸ τῶν ἀστέρων αὔρας, προσεθλίβετο πᾶς ὁ μικρομερὴς σχηματισμὸς ταύτης καὶ τὴν ὑγρὰν φύσιν ἐγέννα· / "Those bodies that were of a lesser magnitude, being round, smooth, and slippery, these meeting with those

heavier bodies were easily squeezed out, and were carried into higher places. [. . .] The multitude of these exhaled bodies, having struck and broken the air in shivers, forced a passage through it. [. . .] But a great deal of matter remaining in the earth, this being condensed by the driving of the winds and the air from the stars, every little part and form of it was compressed, which created the element of water."

178. J. Bollack (1969 III.1) 253 *ad* A53.

179. Epicur. fr. 343 Us. (Aët. 2.20.14 = *Dox. Gr.* 350–351): Ἐπίκουρος γήινον πύκνωμα τὸν ἥλιόν φησιν εἶναι ⸎κισηροειδῶς καὶ σπογγοειδῶς* ταῖς κατατρήσεσιν ὑπὸ πυρὸς ἀνημμένον. "Epicurus (says) that it is an earthy bulk well compacted, with holes like a pumice-stone or a sponge, kindled by fire." Diogenes of Apollonia had used the sponge as conceptual model to depict the stars, the sun and the moon (DK64 A12, A13, A14). The writers of the Hippocratic corpus had derived from the word sponge the adjective σπογγοειδές, in order to describe metaphorically certain human organs (e.g. Hippoc. *VM* 22.27). See Lonie (1981) 344. Cf. also Alcmaeon DK24 A17. Cf. Arist. *Mete.* 350a7–8 for the comparison of mountains and high places with a thick sponge; *Mete.* 386a20-b11 for the account on the squeezability of things.

180. Cf. discussion in the chapter on Similes 96–97, 120.

181. Cf. Rosenmayer (1996) for an interesting analysis of taste in Lucretius. This simile could also bear an echo of Diogenes of Apollonia DK64 A22 in which he explains how tastes are diffused by the tongue thanks to its softness and sponginess and because the veins are joined in it. However, although Diogenes uses also sponge as a vehicle, he refers to the spongy texture of the tongue, not of food. There is also in this case a force operating, i.e. the sensorium and the intelligent governing power. Cf. *DRN* 4.621.

182. See above chapter on Similes 121.

183. Cf. corresponding similes in Section 3.4.1.

184. Cf. discussion in the chapter on Similes 127ff.

185. Cf. Epicur. *Ep. Pyth.* 99–100; Anaximenes DK13 A17.

186. Cf. also Theophr. *Metars.* 1.24–38 Daiber.

187. Cf. 6.275, 6.328.

188. D. Fowler (2002) 262–269 *ad* 2.184–215, 289 *ad* 2.204, 297–298 *ad* 2.213–215.

189. D. Fowler (2002) 262–269 *ad* 2.184–215. Cf. Furley (1966).

190. Cf. also Arist. *Mete.* 369a20ff. The fruit stone analogy recurs at Arist. *Phys.* 214a33-b3. As D. Fowler (2002) 298 suggests, perhaps Aristotle is turning a Democritean analogy to his own purposes. It is remarkable that Philoponus (*In Phys.* CIAG 16, 88.16–23) uses this analogy with reference to Empedocles and Anaxagoras.

191. Montserrat and Navarro (2000) 12 call them secondary loops of the heat cycle, one yearly and one daily. For further details see ibid. 12–13. Cf. also Gottschalk (1966); J. Bollack (1978) 360–376.

192. As Gottschalk (1966) 313 notes, whereas in the Peripatetic tradition, cold particles are said to be responsible for the squeezing out of the hot ones, what is called ἀντιπερίστασις (e.g. Arist. *Mete.* 348b2), in Lucretius hot and cold act on each other indirectly.

193. Cf. Bignone (1920) 258–261 who cites Epiph. *Adv. haeres.* I.7.8 (*Dox. Gr.* 589).

194. Cf. Epicur. fr. 308 Us. ἀπρονόητον καὶ τυχαίαν ἐχόντων τὴν κίνησιν. For the contary view see Empedocles A49a (Armenian translation of Philo *De Prov.* 2.60 = fr. 40 Inwood): "Earth solidified by necessity emerged and settled in the middle."

195. As we have already discussed on several occasions, most of these metaphors are also present in Aëtius' account and probably echo Epicurus' own vocabulary. Cf. socio-political imagery 54ff., metaphor of fitting together 171, simile with exhalation 3.4.2.3, flowing water metaphor 205ff.

196. Cf. Empedocles B55: γῆς ἱδρῶτα θάλασσαν / "sea, sweat of earth." Cf. also Empedocles A66a (Armenian translation of Philo *De Prov.* 2.61 = fr. 60 Inwood).

197. Cf. similar usage of the verb *exhalare* e.g. in 5.463. Cf. also Democritus DK68 A106. Cf. Section 3.4.2.1.

198. Cf. also 4.550 for similar vocabulary about the emission of sound and voice.

List of Translations

Aristotle, *On the Heavens:* W. K. C. Guthrie (1953; Loeb 338).

Archelaus (in Diogenes Laertius): R. D. Hicks, *Diogenes Laertius: Lives of eminent philosophers Books 1–5,* vol. 1. (1925; Loeb 184).

Cicero, *De Natura Deorum:* Rackham, H.: *Cicero vol. XIX* (1933, revised and reprinted 1951; Loeb 268).

Diogenes Laertius: R. D. Hicks, *Diogenes Laertius: Lives of eminent philosophers* vols. 2 (1925, revised and reprinted 1931; Loeb 184–185).

Diogenes of Oinoanda: Smith, M. F. (1993), *Diogenes of Oenoanda, the Epicurean inscription* (with translation) (Naples).

Empedocles, fragments (unless otherwise indicated): Wright, M. R. (1981, 1995), *Empedocles: the Extant Fragments* (London / New Haven).

Empedocles, *testimonia:* Inwood, B. (2001), *The Poem of Empedocles* 2nd ed. (Toronto).

Ennius, *Annales:* E. H. Warmington, *Remains of Old Latin, vol. I Ennius and Caecilius* (1935, revised and reprinted 1956; Loeb 294).

Epicurus, *Letter to Herodotus, Letter to Pythocles, Letter to Menoeceus, Principal Sayings:* R. D. Hicks, *Diogenes Laertius: Lives of eminent philosophers* vol. 2 (1925, revised and reprinted 1931; Loeb185).

Epicurus, *On Nature* Book 28: Sedley, D. (1973), "Epicurus, on Nature Book XXVIII," *Cron. Erc.* 3: 5–83.

Epicurus, fr. 29.26 Arr.^{2} = fr. 60 col. xxxviii Leone: my translation.

Epicurus, fr. 343 Us. (Aëtius 2.20.14 = *Dox. Gr.* 350–351): my translation.

Epicurus, fr. 469 Us. (Stobaeus, *Anthology*): Bailey, C. (1926), *Epicurus: The Extant Remains* (Oxford).

Galen, *On the Natural Faculties:* A. J. Brock (1916; Loeb 71).

Homer, *Iliad:* Lattimore, R. (1951), *The Iliad of Homer / translated with an introduction* (Chicago).

Homer, *Odyssey:* Translated by E. V. Rieu, revised by D. C. H. Rieu in consultation with P. V. Jones (London 1991).

Hippocrates, *On Breaths:* W. H. S. Jones, *Hippocates vol. II: Prognostic, Regimen in Acute Diseases, the Sacred Disease, the Art, Breaths, Law, Decorum, Physician (Ch. 1), Dentition* (1923; Loeb 148).

Lucretius, *De Rerum Natura:* M. F. Smith, *Lucretius: De rerum natura* with an English translation by W. H. D. Rouse; revised with new text, introduction, notes, and index by Martin Ferguson Smith. 2nd. ed., revised reprint. (1992; *Loeb* 181)

Ovid, *Fasti:* Sir J. G. Frazer, *Ovid Fasti* with an English translation by James George Frazer, revised by G. P. Goold (first published 1931, reprinted with corrections 1996; Loeb 253).

Ovid, *Metamorphoses:* F. J. Miller, *Ovid, Metamorphoses in two volumes (Books I-VIII and Books IX-XV)* with an English translation by Frank Justus Miller, revised by G. P. Goold (1916, revised 1984; Loeb 42–43).

Philodemus, *On Rhetoric:* Wigodsky, M. (1995), "The Alleged Impossibility of Philosophical Poetry," in D. Obbink (ed.) (1995), *Philodemus and Poetry: Poetic Theory and Practice in Lucretius, Philodemus and Horace* (Oxford), 58–68

Philodemus, *On Piety* (Part 2): my translation.

Plato, *Timaeus:* R. G. Bury, *Timaeus, Critias, Cleitophon, Menexenus, Epistles* (1952, Loeb 234).

Plutarch, *Reply to Colotes:* B. Einarson and P. H. De Lacy, *Plutarch Moralia XIV* (1967; *Loeb* 428).

Plutarch, *Life of Demetrius:* B. Perrin, *Plutarch Lives IX Demetrius and Antony, Pyrrhus and Gaius Marius* (1914–26; Loeb 101).

Pseudo-Plutarch, *Placita Philosophorum* (fr. 308 Us., fr. 270 Us.): my translation.

Bibliography

Abry, J.-H. (1999), "Présence de Lucrèce: Les astronomiques de Manilius," in R. Poignault (ed.), *Présence de Lucrèce: Actes du colloque tenu à Tours 3–5 Décembre 1998* (Tours, Centre de Recherches A. Piganiol), 111–128.

Ackermann, E. (1979), *Lukrez und der Mythos* (Wiesbaden).

Adams, J. N. (1982), *The Latin Sexual Vocabulary* (London).

Adomenas, M. (2002), "The fluctuating Fortunes of Heraclitus in Plato," in A. Laks and C. Louguet (eds.), *Qu'est-ce que la philosophie présocratique? What is the Presocratic philosophy?* (*Cahiers de philology* Apparat Critique 20; Lille III), 419–447.

Aicher, P. J. (1992), "Lucretian Revision of Homer," *CJ* 87: 139–158.

Algra, K. A., Koenen, M. H., and Schrijvers P. H. (eds.) (1997), *Lucretius and his Intellectual Background* (Amsterdam and Oxford).

Allen, J. (2001), *Inference from Signs: Ancient Debates About the Nature of Evidence* (Oxford).

Anderson, W. S. (1960), "Discontinuity in Lucretian Symbolism," *TAPhA* 91: 1–29.

Andriopoulos, D. Z. (1972), "Empedocles' theory of perception," *Πλάτων* 24: 290–298.

Arnim, H. von (1903–5), *Stoicorum Veterum Fragmenta*, 3 vols., with indexes in vol. iv (1924) by M. Adler (Leipzig).

Arrighetti, G. (1973), *Epicuro, opere:* 2nd ed. (Turin).

Asmis, E. (1982), "Lucretius' Venus and Stoic Zeus," *Hermes* 110: 458–470.

———. (1984), *Epicurus' Scientific Method* (Ithaca and London).

———. (1995), "Epicurean Poetics," in Obbink (ed.) (1995a), 15–34.

Atherton, C. (ed.) (1998), *Form and Content in Didactic Poetry* (Nottingham and Bari).

———. (2005), "Lucretius on what Language is Not," in D. Frede and B. Inwood (eds.): *Language and Learning: Philosophy of Language in the Hellenistic Age* (Proceedings of the Ninth Symposium Hellenisticum, Cambridge), 101–138.

Bailey, C. (1926), *Epicurus: The Extant Remains* (Oxford).

———. (1928), *The Greek Atomists and Epicurus* (Oxford).

———. (1947), *Titi Lucreti Cari De rerum natura Libri Sex*, 3 vv. (Oxford).

Baldry, H. C. (1932), "Embryological Analogies in Presocratic Cosmogony," *CQ* 26: 27–34.

Baltussen, H. (2000), *Theophrastus against the Presocratics and Plato: peripatetic dialectic in the De sensibus* (Leiden, Boston and Köln).

———. (2006), "An Empedoclean 'Hearing Aid'? Fragment B99 Revisited," *Methexis* 19: 7–20.

Bardon, H. (1952), *La littérature latine inconnue I* (Paris).

———. (1964), "L'obstacle. Métaphore et Comparaison en Latin," *Latomus* 23: 3–20.

Barigazzi, A. (1950), "La μονή della Terra nei Frammenti Ercolanesi," *SIFC* 24: 3–19.

Barnes, J. (1988), "Epicurean Signs," *Oxford Studies in Ancient Philosophy* (suppl. vol.), 91–133.

Bästlein, A. (1874–75), "Quid Lucretius debuerit Empedocli Agrigentino," in G. Weicker (ed.), *Jahresbericht des K. Preuss. Hennebergischen Gymnasiums Schleusingen*, 1–21.

Battisti, M. (1976), "Metafore e similitudi in Lucrezio: funzione e rapporti reciproci," *Quaderni dell'Instituto di Filologia Latina di Padova* 6: 75–91.

Beare, J. I. (1906): *Greek Theories of Elementary Cognition* (Oxford).

Benveniste, E. (1948), "L'expression du serment dans la Grèce ancienne," *RHR* 134: 81–94.

Bergsträsser, G. (1918), *Neue meteorologische Fragmente des Theophrast arabisch und deutsch* (Heidelberg).

Bernabè, A. (1979), "Los filosofos presocráticos como autores literários," *Emerita* 47: 357–394.

Berns, G. (1976), "Time and Nature in Lucretius' De Rerum Natura," *Hermes* 104: 477–492.

Bidez, J. (1894), *La biographie d'Empédocle* (Gand).

Bignone, E. (1916), *Empedocle* (Turin).

———. (1920), *Epicuro: Opere, frammenti, testimonianze sulla sua vita* (Bari).

———. (1929), "Ennio ed Empedocle," *RFIC* 57: 10–30.

Black, M. (1962), *Models and metaphors: studies in language and philosophy* (Ithaca, Cornell).

Bodéüs, R. (1974), "De la poésie à la métaphysique: regards sur un terme d'Empédocle," *RBPhH* 52: 35–58.

Bodnár, I. M. (1998), "Atomic Independence and Indivisibility," *OSAPh* 16: 35–61.

———. (2002), "Theophrastus' De Igne: Orthodoxy, Reform and Readjustment in the doctrine of elements," in W. W. Fortenbaugh and G. Wohrle (eds.), *On the Opuscula of Theophrastus: Akten der 3. Tagung der Karl-und-Gertrud-Abel-Stiftung vom 19.-23. Juli 1999 in Trier* (Stuttgart), 75–90.

Boisacq, E. (1950), *Dictionnaire étymologique de la langue Grecque* (Paris).

Bollack, J. (1958), "Styx and Serments," *REG* 71: 1–35.

———. (1959), "Lukrez und Empedocles," *Die Neue Rundschau* 70: 656–686.

———. (1960), "Lukrez 1.1114–17 und Empedocles fr. 110," *Philologus* 104: 295–298.

———. (1965–69), *Empédocle* (Paris).

———. (1969), "Deux figures principales de l'atomisme d'après Aristote: l'entrecroisement des atomes et la sphère du feu," in I. Düring (ed.),

Naturphilophie bei Aristoteles une Theophrast; Symposium Aristotelicum IV (Heidelberg), 32–50.

———. (1980), "La cosmogonie des anciens Atomistes," in F. Romano (ed.) *Democrito e l'atomismo antico* (*Siculorum Gymnasium* 33.1; Atti del convengo internazionale, Catania 18–21 Aprile 1979), 11–59.

———. (1996), "Le langage philosophique d'Épicure." in Giannantoni and Gigante (eds.) (1996), 169–195.

———. (2003), *Empédocle: Les purifications* (Seuil).

Bollack, M. (1963), "La chaîne aimantine: Lucrèce et ses modèles grecs," *REL* 41: 165–185.

———. (1969), "Un désaccord de forme: Lucrèce et Héraclite," in *Actes du VIIIe Congrès Association Guillaume Budé* (Paris): 383–392.

———. (1978), *La raison de Lucrèce* (Paris).

Booth, N. B. (1960), "Empedocles' Account of Breathing," *JHS* 80: 10–15.

Boussoulas, N. (1958), "Éssai sur la structure du mélange dans la pensée présocratique: Émpedocle," *Revue de Metaphysique et de Morale* 63: 135–148.

Boyancé, P. (1941), "Une Exegèse Stoiciene chez Lucrèce," *REL* 19: 147–166.

———. (1962), "Épicure, la Poésie et la Vénus de Lucrèce," *REA* 64: 404–410.

———. (1963), *Lucrèce et l'épicurisme* (Paris).

Boyd, R. (1993), "Metaphor and Theory change: what is 'metaphor' a metaphor for?," in Ortony (ed.) (1993), 481–532.

Bremer, D. (1980), "Aristoteles, Empedocles und die Erkenntnisleistung der Metapher," *Poetica* 12: 350–376.

Brink, C. O. (1971), "Horace and Empedocles' Temperature: a Rejected Fragment of Empedocles," *Phoenix* 23: 138–142.

Brown, R. D. (1983), "Lucretian Ridicule of Anaxagoras," *CQ* n.s. 33: 146–160.

———. (1987), *Lucretius on Love and Sex: A Commentary on De Rerum Natura IV, 1030–1287 with Prolegomena, Text and Translation* (*Columbia Studies in the Classical Tradition* 15; Leiden).

Buhl, M. S. (1956), *Untersuchungen zu Sprache und Stil des Empedokles* (Diss., Heidelberg).

Cabisius, G. (1984–85), "Social Metaphor and the atomic cycle in Lucretius," *CJ* 80: 109–120.

Callaway, C. (1993), "Perjury and the Unsworn Oath," *TAPhA* 123: 15–25.

Cambiano, G. (1983), "Pathologie et Analogie Politique," in F. Lasserre and P. Mudry, *Formes de Pensée dans la Collection Hippocratique. Actes du IV Colloque International Hippocratique:* Lausanne, 21–26 Septembre 1981 (Genève: Droz), 441–458

Campbell, G. L. (1999), review of Sedley (1998), in *Bryn Mawr Classical Review* 29.10.99.

———. (2000), "Zoogony and Evolution in *Timaeus,* The Presocratics, Lucretius and Darwin," in M. R. Wright (ed.), *Reason and Necessity: Essays on Plato's Timaeus* (London and Swansea), 145–180.

————. (2003), *Lucretius on Creation and Evolution: a commentary on Lucretius, De rerum natura 5.772–1104* (Oxford).

Capasso, M. (1983), "Epicureismo e Eraclito," in L. Rossetti (ed.), *Atti del Symposium Heracliteum 1981;* Chieti, Italy (Rome), 423–457.

Capizzi, A. (1987), "Trasposizioni del lessico omerico in Parmenide ed Empedocle. Osservazioni su un problema di metodo," *QUCC* n.s. 25: 107–118.

————. (1990), *The Cosmic Republic: Notes for a non-Peripatetic History of the birth of Philosophy in Greece* (Amsterdam).

Caranci, A. (1988), *Il mondo animato di Lucrezio* (Napoli).

Cardini, M. T. (1957), "Respirazione e clessidra (Empedocle fr. 100)," *La Parola del Passato* 12: 250–270.

Casanova, A. (1984), "La critica di Diogene di Enoanda alla metempsicosi empedoclea (NF 2 + FR. 34 Ch.)," *Studi in onore di Adelmo Barigazzi I* (*Sileno* Anno 10, IV 1–4): 119–130.

Castner, C. J. (1987), "*De Rerum Natura* 5.101–103: Lucretius' Application of Empedoclean Language to Epicurean Doctrine," *Phoenix* 41: 40–49.

Catto, B. A. (1988–89), "*Venus* and *Natura* in Lucretius' *De rerum natura* 1.1–23 and 2.167–74," *CJ* 84: 97–104.

Cazzaniga, I. (1971), "Le Metafore Enniane relative a cielo e stelle ed alcuni placita di tradizione Anassimeno-Empedoclea," *La Parola del Passato* 26: 102–119.

Chandler, C. (2006), *Philodemus On Rhetoric Books 1 and 2: Introduction, Translation and Exegetical Essays* (New York and London).

Chantraine, P. (1980), *Dictionnaire étymologique de la langue Grecque* (Paris).

Chitwood, A. (2004), *Death by Philosophy: the biographical tradition in the life and death of the archaic philosophers Empedocles, Heraclitus, and Democritus* (Ann Arbor).

Ciappi, M. (1999), "*Super stellisque micantibus aethera fixum* per l' interpretazione di universo di Lucrezio (V 1205)," *Maia* 51 (1): 33–40.

Classen, C. J. (1968), "Poetry and Rhetoric in Lucretius," *TAPhA* 99: 77–118; repr. in Classen (1986), 331–373.

————. (ed.) (1986), *Probleme der Lukrezforschung* (Hildesheim, Zurich, and New York).

Clay, D. (1969), "*De Rerum Natura:* Greek *Physis* and Epicurean *Physiologia* (Lucretius 1.1–148)," *TAPhA* 100: 31–47; repr. in Clay (1998), 121–137.

Clay, D. (1976), "The sources of Lucretius' Inspiration" in J. Bollack and A. Laks (eds.), *Études sur l'épicurisme antique* (*Cahiers de Philologie* 1. Lille), 205–227; repr. in Clay (1998), 138–160.

————. (1983), *Lucretius and Epicurus* (Ithaca, NY).

————. (1995), "Framing the Margins of Philodemus and Poetry," in Obbink (ed.) (1995), 3–14.

————. (1996), "An anatomy of Lucretian Metaphor," in Giannantoni and Gigante (eds.) (1996), 779–793; repr. in Clay (1998), 161–173.

————. (1998), *Paradosis and survival: three chapters in the history of Epicurean philosophy* (Ann Arbor, MI).

———. (2000), "Recovering Originals: *Peri Physeos* and *De Rerum Natura*," *Apeiron* 33 (3): 259–271.

Conte, G. B. ([1991] 1994), "Instructions for a Sublime Reader: Form of the Text and Form of Addressee in Lucretius' *De Rerum Natura*," in G. B. Conte, *Genres and readers: Lucretius, love elegy, Pliny's Encyclopedia* trans. by G. W. Most (Baltimore MD), with reference made to the original 1991 Italian version, *Generi e lettori* (Milan), 1–34.

Corte, F. Della (1985), "Gli Empedoclea e Ovidio," *Maia* 37: 3–12.

Courtès, J. M. (1968), "La dialectique du réel et du possible dans le *De Rerum Natura*," *REL* 46: 170–179.

Courtney, E. (1993), *The Fragmentary Latin Poets* (Oxford).

Cox, W. (1969), "Didactic Poetry: Lucretius," in J. Higginbotham (ed.), *Greek and Latin Literature: A Comparative Study* (London), 134–145; repr. in Classen (1986), 221–235.

Coxon, A. H. (1986), *The fragments of Parmenides: a critical text with introduction and translation, the ancient testimony and a commentary* (Assen, Netherlands).

Craik, E. M. (1998), *Hippocrates 'Places in Man': edited and translated with introduction and commentary* (Oxford).

Daiber, H. (1992), "The Meteorology of Theophrastus in Syriac and Arabic Translation," in W. W. Fortenbaugh, and D. Gutas (eds.), *Theophrastus: his Psychological, Doxographical, and Scientific Writings* (Rutgers University Studies in Classical Humanities 5; New Brunswick): 166–293.

Dalzell, A. (1987), "Language and atomic theory in Lucretius," *Hermathena* 143: 19–28.

Davies, H. S. (1931–32), "Notes on Lucretius," *Criterion* 11: 25–42; repr. in Classen (1986), 272–290.

De Falco, V. (1923), *L'Epicureo Demetrio Lacone* (Naples).

De Lacy, P. H. (1939), "The Epicurean Analysis of Language," *AJPh* 60: 85–92.

———. (1964–65), "Distant views: The Imagery of Lucretius 2," *CJ* 60: 49–55.

———. (1969), "Limit and Variation in the Epicurean Philosophy," *Phoenix* 23: 104–113.

———. and De Lacy, E. A. (1978), *Philodemus On Methods of Inference²* (Naples).

De Rubeis, Gr. M. (1991), "Ripetizione nel Περὶ Φύσεως di Empedocle," *Studi Clasici e Orientali* 41: 87–93.

Demont, P. (1978), "Remarques sur le sens de ΤΡΕΦΩ," *REG* 91: 358–384.

Deschamps, L. (1986), "*Victrix Venus:* Varron et la cosmologie empédocléenne," in R. Altheim-Stiehl and M. Rosenbach (eds.), *Beiträge zur altitalischen Geistesgeschichte:* Festschrift Gerhard Radke (Munster), 51–72.

———. (1997), "Lucrèce and Varron," in Algra, Koenen, and Schrijvers (eds.) (1997), 105–114.

Diels, H. (1899), *Elementum* (Leipzig).

———. and Kranz, W. (1951–52), *Die Fragmente der Vorsokratiker⁶*, 3 vols. (Berlin).

Diller, H. (1932), "*ΟΨΙΣ ΑΔΗΛΩΝ ΤΑ ΦΑΙΝΟΜΕΝΑ*," *Hermes* 67: 14–42; repr. in H. Diller (1971), *Kleine Schriften zur antiken Literatur* (Munich), 119–143.

Dionigi, I. (1988), *Lucrezio, le parole et le cose* (Bologna).

Dodds, E. R. (1959), *Plato: Gorgias: a Revised Text with Introduction and Commentary* (Oxford).

Droz-Vincent, G. (1996), "Les *foedera naturae* chez Lucrèce," in Lévy (ed.) (1996), 191–211.

Duban, J. (1982), "Venus, Epicurus and *naturae species ratioque,*" *AJPh* 103: 165–177.

Dubois, P. (1988), *Sowing the Body: Psychoanalysis and the Ancient Representation of Women* (Chicago and London).

Dudley, D. R. (ed.) (1965), *Lucretius: Studies in Latin Literature and its Influence* (London).

Edelstein, L. (1940), "*Primum Graius Homo* (Lucretius 1.1.-149)," *TAPhA* 71: 78–90.

Edmunds, L. (2002), "Mars as Hellenistic Lover: Lucretius, *De Rerum Natura* 1.29–40 and its Subtexts," *International Journal of the Classical Tradition* 8: 343–358.

Edwards, M. J. (1989), "Lucretius, Empedocles and Epicurean Polemics," *Antike und Abendland* 35: 104–115.

————. (1990), "Treading the aether: Lucretius De Rerum Natura 1.62–79," *CQ* n.s. 40.2: 465–469.

Einarson, B. and De Lacy, P. H. (1967), *Plutarch Moralia XIV* with and English translation (*The Loeb classical library* 428; London, Cambridge Mass.).

Ernout, A. and Robin, L. (1925–28), *Lucrèce, De Rerum Natura: commentaire exégétique et critique* (Paris).

Everson, S. (1994), "Epicurus on Mind and Language," in S. Everson (ed.), *Language* (Cambridge), 74–108.

Fairweather, J. A. (1974), "Fiction in the Biographies of Ancient Writers," *Ancient Society* 5: 231–275.

Farrell, J. (1991), *Vergil's Georgics and the Traditions of Ancient Epic* (New York and Oxford).

Farrington, B. (1939), *Science and Philosophy in the Ancient World* (London).

————. (1965), "Form and Purpose in the *De Rerum Natura,*" in Dudley (ed.) (1965), *Lucretius* (London), 19–34.

Ferguson, J. (1971), "DINOS," *Phronesis* 16: 97–115.

Finkelberg, A. (1998), "On the History of the Greek kosmos," *HSCPh* 98: 103–136.

Flores, E. (1996), "Gli *Astronomica* di Manilio e l'Epicureismo," in Giannantoni and Gigante (eds.) (1996), 895–908.

Fortenbaugh, W. W., Huby, P. M., Sharples, R. W. and Gutas, D. (1992): *Theophrastus of Eresus: Sources for his Life, Writings, Thought ad Influence* (Leiden, New York, and Cologne).

Fowler, D. P. (1989), "Lucretius and Politics," in M. T. Griffin and J. Barnes (eds.) (1989), *Philosophia Togata: Essays on philosophy and Roman Society* (Oxford): 120–50.

————. (1997), "Epicurean Anger," in S. M. Braund and C. Gill (eds.), *The Passions in Roman Thought and Literature* (Cambridge), 16–35.

————. (2000a), *Roman Constructions: Readings in Postmodern Latin* (Oxford).

———. (2000b), "Philosophy and Literature in Lucretian Intertextuality," in Fowler (2000a), 138–155.

———. (2000c), "The Didactic Plot," in M. Depew and D. Obbink (eds.), *Matrices of Genre: Authors, Canons, and Society* (Cambridge Mass. and London), 205–219.

———. (2002), *Lucretius on Atomic Motion: A Commentary on Lucretius De rerum natura 2.1–332* (Oxford).

Fowler, P. G. (1984), *A commentary on Part of Book six of Lucretius De Rerum Natura* (6.1–95, 1090–1286) (Diss., Oxford).

Frede, M. (1987), "Philosophy and Medicine in Antiquity," in M. Frede, *Essays in Ancient Philosophy* (Oxford): 225–242.

Friedländer, P. (1939), "The Epicurean Theology in Lucretius' First Prooemium (Lucr. 1.44–49)," *TAPhA* 70: 368–379.

———. (1941), "Pattern of Sound and Atomistic Theory in Lucretius," *AJPh* 62: 16–34; repr. in Classen (1986), 291–307.

Frisk, H. (1954), *Griechisches etymologisches Wörterbuch* (Heidelberg).

Furley, D. J. (1957), "Empedocles and the clepsydra," *JHS* 77: 31–34

———. (1966), "Lucretius and the Stoics," *BICS* 13: 13–33; repr. in Classen (1986), 75–94; and in Furley (1989), 183–205.

———. (1967), *Two Studies in the Greek atomists* (Princeton).

———. (1970), "Variations on Themes from Empedocles in Lucretius' Proem," *BICS* 17: 55–64.

———. (1971), "Knowledge of Atoms and Void in Epicureanism," in J. P. Anton and G. L. Kustas (eds.), *Essays in Ancient Greek Philosophy* (Albany), 607–619.

———. (1987), *The Greek Cosmologists*, I (Cambridge).

———. (1989), *Cosmic Problems* (Cambridge).

Furth, M. (1987), "Aristotle's Biological Universe: an Overview," in A. Gotthelf and J. G. Lennox (eds.), *Philosophical Issues in Aristotle's Biology* (Cambridge), 21–52.

Fyntikoglou, V. (2004), "*Expedire:* From the Lucretian to the Vergilian instruction" [in Greek: *Expedire: από τη Λουκρητιανή στη Βιργιλιανή Δίδαξιν*"], in A. Vasileiades, P. Kotzia, Ai. D. Mavroudes, and D. A. Christides (eds.), *Δημητρίω στέφανος. Τιμητικός τόμος για τον καθηγητή Δημήτρη Λυπουρλή* (Thessalonike), 275–304.

Gagarin, M. (2002), "Greek Law and the Presocratics," in V. Caston, and D. W. Graham (eds.), *Presocratic Philosophy: Essays in Honour of Alexander Mourelatos* (London), 19–24.

Gale, M. (1994a), *Myth and Poetry in Lucretius* (Cambridge).

———. (1994b), "Lucretius 4.1–25 and the Proems of the *De Rerum Natura*," *PCPhS* 40: 1–17.

———. (2000), *Virgil on the Nature of Things* (Oxford).

———. (2001), "Etymological Word-Play and Poetic Succession in Lucretius," *CPh* 96: 168–172.

———. (2004), "The Story of Us: a Narratological Analysis of Lucretius' *De Rerum Natura*," in M. R. Gale (ed.), *Roman Epic and Didactic: Genre, Tradition and Individuality* (Classical Press of Wales), 49–71.

Galinsky, K. (1998), "The Speech of Pythagoras at Ovid *Metamorphoses* 15.75–478," *PLLS* 10: 313–336.

Gallavotti, C. (1975–77), "La critica di Empedocle in Diogene di Enoanda," *MCr* 10–12: 243–249.

Gallo I. (1985), "Ermarco e la polemica epicurea contro Empedocle," in P. Cosenza (ed.), *Esistenza e destino nel pensiero Greco antico* (Naples), 33–50.

Garani, M. (2007), "Cosmological oaths in Empedocles and Lucretius," in A. H. Sommerstein and J. Fletcher (eds.), *Horkos* (Nottingham), 189–202, 264–267.

————. (2007 forthcoming b), "The *Palingenesis* of Empedocles' Calliope in Lucretius," in E. Cingano and L. Milano (eds.), *Quaderni del Dipartimento di Scienze dell'Antichità e del Vicino Oriente dell'Università Ca' Foscari* (Monograph series).

Gemelli Marciano, M. L. (1990), *Le Metamorfosi della Tradizione. Mutamenti di significato e neologismi nel Peri Physeos di Empedocle* (Bari).

————. (1991), "L'atomismo e il corpuscolarismo Empedocleo: frammenti di interpretazioni nel mondo antico," *Elenchos* 12: 5–37.

Gentner, D. (1982), "Are Scientific Analogies Metaphors?," in D. S. Miall (ed.), *Metaphor: Problems and Perspectives* (Sussex and New Jersey), 106–132.

————. and Gentner, D. R. (1983), "Flowing Waters or Teeming Crowds: Mental Models of Electricity," in D. Gentner and A. L. Stevens (eds.), *Mental Models* (New Jersey and London), 99–129.

Gerke, H. (1953), *Sprache und Stil des Empedocles* (Diss., Göttingen).

Giancotti, F. (1959), *Il preludio di Lucrezio* (Messina-Firenze).

————. (1989), *Religio, Natura, Voluptas: Studi su Lucrezio* (Bologna).

Giannantoni, G. and Gigante, M. (eds.) (1996), *Epicureismo greco e romano: Atti del Congresso internazionale, Napoli 19–26 maggio 1993* (3 vols.; *Elenchos* 25; Naples).

Gigandet, A. (1996), "*Natura gubernans* (Lucrèce, v, 77)," in Lévy (ed.) (1996), *Le concept de nature à Rome* (Actes du séminaire de philosophie romaine de l'université de Paris XII-Val de Marne 1992–3) (Paris), 213–225.

Gigon, O. (ed.) (1978), *Lucrèce. huit exposés suivis de discussions* (*Entretiens sur l'antiquité classique* 24; Geneva).

Giussani, C. (1896–98), *Titi Lucreti Cari De rerum natura libri sex,* 4 vols. (Turin).

Glidden, D. K. (1983), "Epicurean Semantics," in Συζήτησις: *Studi sull' epicureismo greco e romano offerti a Marcello Gigante* (Naples), 185–226.

————. (1985), "Epicurean Prolepsis," *OSCPh* 3: 175–217.

Godwin, J. (1986), *Lucretius De rerum natura IV* (Warminster).

————. (1991), *Lucretius: De Rerum Natura VI* (Warminster).

Görler, W. (1997), "Storing up Past Pleasures: the Soul-Vessel-Metaphor in Lucretius and his Greek Models," in Algra, Koenen, and Schrijvers (eds.) (1997), 193–207.

Gottschalk, H. B. (1966), "Lucretius and the 'Water of the Sun'," *Philologus* 110: 311–315.

Gould, J. B. (1970), *The philosophy of Chrysippus* (Leiden).

Graham, D. W. (1988), "Symmetry in the Empedoclean Cycle," *CQ* n.s. 38: 297–312.

Green, S. J. (2004), *Ovid, Fasti 1. A Commentary* (*Mnemosyne* suppl. 251; Leiden).

Grilli, A. (1979), "Lucrezio e la Forza Invisibile del Vento," in *Studi di Poesia Latina in Onore di Antonio Traglia I* (Roma), 217–227.

Guidorizzi, G. and Beta, S. (2000), *La metafora: testi greci e latini* (Pisa).

Guthrie, W. K. C. (1957), *In the Beginning* (London).

Hahm, D. E. (1977), *The Origins of Stoic Cosmology* (Ohio).

Hallier, E. (1857), *Lucreti carmina e fragmentis Empedoclis adumbrata* (Diss., Iena).

Hardie, P. (1986), *Virgil's Aeneid: Cosmos and Imperium* (Oxford).

———. (1991), "The Janus Episode in Ovid's *Fasti*," *MD* 26: 47–64.

———. (1995), "The Speech of Pythagoras in Ovid's *Metamorphoses* 15: Empedoclean Epos," *CQ* n.s. 45: 204–214.

———. (1997), "Questions of Authority: the Invention of Tradition in Ovid Metamorphoses 15," in T. Habinek and A. Schiesaro (eds.), *The Roman Cultural Revolution* (Cambridge), 182–198.

———. (2004), "Approximative Similes in Ovid. Incest and Doubling," *Dictynna* 1: on line at http://halma-ipel.recherche.univ-lille3.fr/Dictynna/DictynnaNumero1.html.

Harrisson, S. (2002), "Ennius and the Prologue to Lucretius *DRN* 1 (1.1–148)," *LICS* 1.4: online at http://www.leeds.ac.uk/classics/lics/volumes.html.

Heidel, W. A. (1910), "Περὶ Φύσεως: a study of the Conception of Nature among the Pre-Socratics," *Proceedings of the American Academy of Arts and Sciences* 45.4: 79–133.

Helzle, M. (1992), "Ovid's Cosmogony (*Met.* 1.5–88) and the Traditions of Ancient Poetry," *PLLS* 7: 123–134.

Henrichs, A. (1974), "Die Kritik der Stoischen Theologie im P.Herc. 1428," *Cron. Erc.* 4: 5–32.

Hershbell, J. P. (1968), "Empedocles' Oral style," *CJ* 63: 352–357.

———. (1971), "Plutarch as a Source for Empedocles re-examined," *AJPh* 92: 156–184.

———. (1974), "Empedoclean Influences on the *Timaeus*," *Phoenix* 28: 145–166.

Hesse, M. (1965), "The Explanatory Function of Metaphor," in Y. Bar-Hillel (ed.), *Logic, Methodology and Philosophy of Science. Proceedings of the 1964 International Cogress* (Amsterdam), 249–259.

Hiersche, R. R. (1958), "Note additionelle relative à l'étymologie d' ὅρκος et d' ὀμνύναι," *REG* 71: 35–41.

Hinds, S. (1987), "Language at the Breaking Point: Lucretius 1.452," *CQ* n.s. 37.2: 450–453.

Hirzel, R. (1902), *Der Eid: Ein Beitrag zu seiner Geschichte* (Leipzig).

Hohler, R. C. (1925–26), "Lucretius' Use of the Simile," *CJ* 21: 281–285.

Holmes, B. (2005), "Daedala Lingua: Crafted Speech in De rerum natura," *AJPh* 126: 527–585.

Hussey, E. (1999), "Heraclitus," in A. A. Long (ed.), *The Cambridge Companion to Early Greek Philosophy* (Cambridge), 88–112.

Hutchinson, G. O. (2001), "The Date of *De Rerum Natura*," *CQ* NS 51.1: 150–162.

Ierodiakonou, K. (2005), "Empedocles on Colour and Colour Vision," *OSCPh* 29: 1–38.

Ingalls, W. B. (1971), "Repetition in Lucretius," *Phoenix* 25: 227–236.

Innes, D. (2003), "Metaphor, Simile and Allegory as Ornaments of Style," in G. R. Boys-Stones (ed.), *Metaphor, Analogy and the Classical Tradition—Ancient Thought and Modern Revisions* (Oxford), 7–27.

Inwood, B. (1981), "The Origin of Epicurus' Concept of Void," *CPh* 76: 273–285.

———. (1986), "Commentary on Striker," *Proceedings of the Boston Colloquium on Ancient Philosophy* 2: 95–101.

———. (2001), *The Poem of Empedocles* 2nd ed. (Toronto).

Jacobson, H. (1999), "Lucretius' Hunting Souls (3.726–728)," *MH* 56(1): 33.

Janko, R. (2000), *Philodemus On Poems Book One* (Oxford).

———. (2004), "Empedocles, *On Nature* I 233–364: a New Reconstruction of *P. Strasb. gr.* Inv. 1665–6," *ZPE* 150: 1–26.

Jobst, F. (1907), *Über das Verhältnis zwischen Lukretius und Empedokles* (Diss., Münich).

Johnson, M. (1990), *The Body in the Mind: the Bodily Basis of Meaning, Imagination, and Reason* (Chicago).

Johnson, M. R. (2005), *Aristotle on Teleology* (Oxford).

Jope, J. (1985), "Lucretius, Cybele and Religion," *Phoenix* 39: 250–262.

Jouanna, J. (1961), "Présence d'Empédocle dans la Collection Hippocratique," *Bulletin Budé de l'Association Guillaume Budé* 20: 452–463.

Kahn, C. H. (1974), "Anaximander's Fragment: the Universe Governed by Law," in A. P. D. Mourelatos (ed.), *The Presocratics: a Collection of Critical Essays* (New York), 99–117.

Keen, R. (1979), "Notes on Epicurean Terminology and Lucretius," *Apeiron* 13: 63–69.

———. (1985), "Lucretius and his Reader," *Apeiron* 19: 1–10.

Kennedy, D. (2000), "Making a Text of the Universe: Perspectives on Discursive Order in the De Rerum Natura of Lucretius," in A. Sharrock and H. Morales (eds.), *Intratextuality: Greek and Roman Textual Relations* (Oxford), 205–225.

Kenney, E. J. (1971), *Lucretius De rerum natura Book 3* (Cambridge).

———. (1977), *Lucretius* (*Greece and Rome* New Surveys in the Classics 11; Oxford).

Kerschensteiner, J. (1962), *Kosmos: Quellenkritische Untersuchungen zu den Vorsokratikern* (*Zetemata* 30, München).

Keyser, P. (1992), "Xenophanes' Sun (frr. A 32, 33.3, 40 DK⁶) on Trojan Ida (Lucr. 5.660–5, D.S. 17.7.5–7, Mela 1.94–5)," *Mnemosyne* 45: 299–311.

Kidd, I. G. (1992), "Theophrastus' Meteorology, Aristotle and Posidonius," in W. W. Fortenbaugh and D. Gutas (eds.), *Theophrastus: his Psychological, Doxographical, and Scientific Writings* (London), 295–306.

Kingsley, P. (1994): "Empedocles and his Interpreters: the Four-Element Doxography," *Phronesis* 39: 235–254.

———. (1995), "Notes on Air: Four Questions of Meaning in Empedocles and Anaxagoras," *CQ* n.s. 45: 26–29.

Kleve, K. (1963), "Zur Epikureischen Terminologie," *SO* 38: 25–31.

———. (1966), "Lukrez und Venus (*De rerum natura* 1, 1–49)," *SO* 41: 86–94.

———. (1978), "The Philosophical Polemics in Lucretius: A Study in the History of Epicurean Criticism," in Gigon (ed.) (1978), 39–71 (+72–75).

Klinger, F. (1952), "Philosophie und Dichtkunst am Ende des zweiten Buches des Lucrez," *Hermes* 80: 3–31.

Koenen, M. H. (1999), "Lucretius' Explanation of Hearing in *De Rerum Natura* IV 524–562," *Mnemosyne* 52: 434–463.

Kohnke, F. W. (1965), "*ΓΑΣΤΗΡ ΕΡΓΑΣΤΗΡΙΟΝ ΦΥΣΕΩΣ* ein Chrysippzitat," *Hermes* 93: 383–384.

Kollmann, E. D. (1971), "Lucretius' Criticism of the Early Greek Philosophers," *Studii Clasice* 13: 79–93.

Konstan, D. (1979), "Problems in Epicurean Physics," *Isis* 70: 394–418.

———. (1982), "Ancient Atomism and its Heritage: Minimal Parts," *Ancient Philosophy* 11: 60–75.

Körte, A. (1890), "Metrodori Epicurei fragmenta," *Jahrbücher für Classische Philologie* suppl. 17: 531–597.

Kranz, W. (1912), "Empedocles and die Atomistik," *Hermes* 47: 18–42.

———. (1938), "Gleichnis und Vergleich in der frühgriechischen Philosophie," *Hermes* 73: 99–122.

———. (1939), "Kosmos als Philosophischer Begriff frügriechisher Zeit," *Philologus* 93: 430–448.

———. (1943), "Lukrez und Empedocles," *Philologus* 96: 68–107.

———. (1958), "Kosmos," *Archiv für Begriffsgeschichte* 2: 3–282.

Kullman, W. (1980), "Zu den historischen Voraussetzungen der Beweismethoden des Lucrez," *RhM* 123: 97–125.

———. (1995), "Antike Vorstufen des modernen Begriffs des Naturgesetzes," in O. Behrends and W. Sellert (eds.), *Nomos und Gesezt: Ursprünge und Wirkungen des griechischen Gesetzesdenkens: 6. Symposion der Kommission "Die Funktion des Gesetzes in Geschichte und Gegenwart"* (Göttingen), 36–116.

Kyllo, E. A. (1994), *'Heliconiadum Comites': the 'De Rerum Natura' and Epic Tradition (Lucretius, Homer, Ennius, Empedocles)* (Diss., Pennsylvania).

———. (1997): "Two Allusions to the Song of Demodocus in Lucretius' De Rerum Natura," *CB* 73: 31–37

Kyriakidis, S. (2004), "Middles in Lucretius' *DRN:* the poet and his work" in S. Kyriakidis and F. De Martino (eds.), *Middles in Latin poetry* (Bari), 27–49.

———. (2007a), "Lucretius' *DRN* 1.926–50 and the Proem to Book 4," *CQ* n.s. 56: 606–610.

———. (2007b) *Catalogues of Proper Names* (Cambridge).

Kyriakou, P. (1994), "Empedoclean Echoes in Apollonius Rhodius' *Argonautica*," *Hermes* 122: 309–319.

Lachenaud, G. (1993), *Plutarque Oeuvres Morales Tome XII², Opinions des philosophes* (Paris).

Lakoff, G. (1993), "The contemporary theory of metaphor," in Ortony (ed.) (1993), 202–251.

———. and Johnson, M. (1980), *Metaphors We Live By* (Chicago IL).

———. and Turner, M. (1989), *More than Cool Reason: a Field Guide to Poetic Metaphor* (Chicago and London).

Laks, A. (2005), "Some thoughts about Empedoclean cosmic and demonic cycles," in Pierris (ed.) (2005), 265–282.

Langholf, V. (1989), "Frühe Fälle der Verwendung von Analogien in der altgriechischen Medizin," *BWG* 12: 7–18.

Langslow, D. R. (1999), "The Language of Poetry and the Language of Science: The Latin Poets and 'Medical Latin'," in J. N. Adams and R. G. Mayer (eds.), *Aspects of the language of Latin Poetry* (*Proceedings of the British Academy* 93; Oxford), 183–225.

Lapidge, M. (1979), "Lucan's Imagery of Cosmic Dissolution," *Hermes* 107.3: 344–370.

———. (1980), "A Stoic Metaphor in Late Latin Poetry: The Binding of the Cosmos," *Latomus* 39: 817–837.

———. (1989), "Stoic Cosmology and Roman Literature, First to Third Centuries A. D.," *ANRW* II.36.3: 1379–1429.

Last, H. (1924), "Empedocles and his Klepsydra again," *CQ* 18: 169–173.

Lee, E. N. (1978), "The sense of an object: Epicurus on seeing and hearing," in P. K. Machamer and R. G. Turnbull (eds.), *Studies in Perception: interrelations in the history of philosophy and science* (Columbus and Ohio), 27–59.

Leen, A. (1984), "The Rhetorical Value of the similes in Lucretius," in D. F. Bright and E. S. Ramage (eds.), *Classical Texts and Their Traditions, Studies in Honor of C. R. Trahman* (Chico, CA), 107–123.

Lenagham, L. (1967), "Lucretius 1.921–50," *TAPhA* 98: 221–250.

Leonard, W. E. and Smith, S. B. (1942), *Titi Lucreti Cari De Rerum Natura libri sex; edited with introduction and commentary* (Madison, Wis.).

Leone, G. (1984), "Epicuro, *Della natura*, libro xiv," *Cron. Erc.* 14: 17–107.

Leumann, M. (1950), *Homerische Wörter* (Basel).

Lévy C. (ed.) (1996), *Le concept de nature à Rome* (Paris).

Liebeschuetz, W. (1967/68), "The Cycle of Growth and Decay in Lucretius and Virgil," *PVS* 7: 30–40.

Lloyd, G. E. R. (1966), *Polarity and Analogy. Two Types of Argumentation in Early Greek Thought* (Cambridge).

———. (1979), *Magic, Reason and Experience* (Cambridge).

———. (1987), *The Revolutions of Wisdom: Studies in the claims and practice of ancient Greek Science* (Berkeley CA).

———. (1991), *Methods and Problems in Greek Science* (Cambridge).

———. (1996), *Aristotelian explorations* (Cambridge).

Long, A. A. (1966), "Thinking and sense-perception in Empedocles: Mysticism or Materialism?," *CQ* n.s. 16: 256–276.

————. (1971), "Aisthesis, Prolepsis and Linguistic Theory in Epicurus," *BICS* 18: 114–133.

————. (1977), "Chance and natural law in Epicureanism," *Phronesis* 22: 63–88.

————. and Sedley, D. N. (1987), *The Hellenistic Philosophers* (Cambridge).

Longo Auricchio, F. (1988), *Ermarco: Frammenti* (Naples).

Longo, O. (1964–65), "Ricerche sulla terminologia filosofica Lucreziana: *plenus, stipatus, solidus,*" *AIV* 123: 421–477.

Longrigg, J. (1965), "Κρυσταλλοειδῶς," *CQ* n.s. 15: 249–251.

————. (1967), "Roots," *CR* 17: 1–4.

————. (1970), "Ice of Bronze Lucretius I. 493," *CR* 20: 8–9.

————. (1975), "Elementary Physics in the Lyceum and Stoa," *Isis* 66: 211–229.

————. (1976), "The Roots of All Things," *Isis* 67: 420–438.

————. (1985), "Elements and after: a study in Presocratic physics of the second half of the fifth century," *Apeiron* 19: 93–115.

————. (1989), "Presocratic Philosophy and Hippocratic Medicine," *History of Science* 27: 1–39.

Lonie, I. M. (1969), "On the Botanical Excursus in *De Natura Pueri* 22–27," *Hermes* 97: 391–411

————. (1981), *The Hippocratic treatises, "On generation", "On the nature of the child", "Diseases IV": a commentary* (Berlin and New York).

Lovejoy, A. O. (1909), "The meaning of φύσις in the Greek Physiologers" *Philosophical Review* 18: 369–383.

Luciani, S. (2000), *L'éclair immobile dans la plaine. Philosophie et Poétique du Temps chez Lucrèce* (*Bibliotheque d'études classiques* 21; Leuven and Paris).

Lück, W. (1932), *Die Quellenfrage im 5. und 6. Buch des Lukrez* (Diss. Breslau).

Luther, W. (1954), *Weltansicht und Geistesleben* (Göttingen).

Lyne, R. O. A. M. (1989), *Words and the Poet: Characteristic Techniques of Style in Vergil's Aeneid* (Oxford).

————. (1994), "Vergil's Aeneid: Subversion by Intertextuality Catullus 66.39–40 and Other Examples," *G&R* 2nd ser. 41: 187–204.

Macciò, M. C. D. (1980), "I 'Corpuscoli' nel pensiero presocratico," in F. Romano (ed.), *Democrito e l'atomismo antico* (Catania), 311–323.

Mackay, L. (1955), "*De rerum natura* 1.717sqq.," *Latinitas* 3: 210.

Maguiness, W. S. (1965), "The language of Lucretius," in Dudley (ed.) (1965), 69–93.

Mansfeld, J. (1971), *The Pseudo-Hippocratic tract Περὶ Ἑβδομάδων ch. 1–11 and Greek Philosophy* (Assen).

————. (1981): "Bad World and Demiurge: a 'Gnostic' Motif: From Parmenides and Empedocles to Lucretius and Philo," in R. Van den Broek and M. J. Vermaseren (eds.), *Studies in Gnosticism and Hellenistic Religions presented to Gilles Quispel on the occasion of his 65th Birthday* (Leiden), 261–314.

————. (1992), "A Theophrastean Excursus on God and Nature and its Aftermath in Hellenistic Thought," *Phronesis* 37: 314–335.

————. (1994), "Epicurus Peripateticus," in A. Alberti (ed.), *Realtà e Ragione* (Florence), 29–47.

Marcovich, M. (2001), *Heraclitus: Greek text with a short commentary* 2nd ed. (International Pre-Platonic Studies 2).

Martin, A. and Primavesi, O. (1998), *L'Empédocle de Strasbourg: (P. Strasb. gr. Inv. 1665–1666). Introduction, edition et commentaire* (Berlin, New York, Strasbourg).

Masson, J. (1907–9), *Lucretius: Epicurean and Poet* (2 vols.) (London).

Mayer, R. (1990), "The Epic of Lucretius," *Papers of the Leeds International Seminar* 6: 35–43.

McDiarmid, J. B. (1959), "Theophrastus, *De Sensibus* 66: Democritus' Explanation of Salinity," *AJPh* 80: 56–66.

Mejer, J. (1978), *Diogenes Laertius and his Hellenistic Background* (*Hermes* Einzelschriften 40; Wiesbaden).

Merrill, W. A. (1891), "The Significance and Use of the Word *natura* by Lucretius," *TAPhA* 22: 32–35.

————. (1918), "Parallelisms and Coincidences in Lucretius and Ennius," *UCPCPh* 3: 249–264.

Mesturini, A. M. (1989), "L' eclissi di sole in Empedocle e in Lucrezio," *SIFC* 5: 173–180.

Minadeo, R. (1965), "The Formal Design of the *De Rerum Natura*," *Arion* 4: 444–461.

————. (1969), *The Lyre of Science: Form and Meaning in Lucretius' De Rerum Natura* (Detroit).

Mitsis, P. (1993), "Committing Philosophy on the Reader: Didactic Coercion and Reader's Autonomy in *De Rerum Natura*," in Schiesaro, Mitsis, and Strauss Clay (eds.) (1993), 111–128.

Monet, A. (2003), *Le jardin romain. Épicurisme et poésie à Rome. Mélanges offerts à Mayotte Bollack* (Lille).

Montarese, F. (2005), *A study of Lucretius, De Rerum Natura I, 635–920: Lucretius and his sources* (Diss., London).

Montserrat, J. M. and Navarro, L. (1991), "The water cycle in Lucretius," *Centaurus* 34: 289–308.

————. (2000), The atomistic view of heat in Lucretius," *Centaurus* 42 (1): 1–20.

Mourelatos, A. P. D. (1986), "Quality, Structure and Emergence in Later Pre-Socratic Philosophy," *Proceedings of the Boston Area Colloquium in Ancient Philosophy* 2: 127–194.

Mugler, Ch. (1967), "Le vide des atomistes et les pores d'Empédocle: à propos d'un passage d'Aristote," *Revue de Philologie, de Littérature et d'Histoire anciennes* Série 3.41: 217–224.

Müller, G. (1978), "Die Finalia der sechs Bücher des Lucrez," in Gigon (ed.) (1978), 197–231.

Munro, H. A. J. (1893), *T. Lucreti Cari De Rerum Natura Libri Sex*, 4th edition revised, 2 vols. (London and Cambridge).

Murley, C. (1947), "Lucretius, *De Rerum Natura*, Viewed as Epic," *TAPhA* 78: 336–346.

Nelis, D. P. (2000), "Apollonius Rhodius and the traditions of Latin Epic Poetry," in M. A. Harder, R. F. Regtuit, and G. C. Wakker (eds.), *Apollonius Rhodius* (*Hellenistica Groningana* 4; Leuven), 85–103.

———. (2001), *Vergil's Aeneid and the Argonautica of Appolonius Rhodius* (*Arca* 39; Leeds).

———. (2004), "Vergil's on nature: *Georgics* 2.458–542: Vergil, Aratus and Empedocles," *Dictynna* 1: on line at http://halma-ipel.recherche.univ-lille3.fr/Dictynna/DictynnaNumero1.html.

Niccolini, O. B. (1955), "De T. Lucretio Caro," *Latinitas* 3: 280–286.

Nikolaidis, A. (1996), "Homer and Lucretius" [in Greek: "Ὅμηρος καὶ Λουκρήτιος"] in *Η μίμηση στη λατινική λογοτεχνία* Athens (=5th Panhellenic Symposium of Latin Studies, 1993), 137–162.

Norden, E. (1915), *Ennius und Vergilius* (Leipzig).

Nugent, G. (1994), "Mater Matters: The Female in Lucretius' *De rerum natura*," *Colby Quarterly* 30: 179–205.

O'Brien, D. (1969), *Empedocles' Cosmic Cycle* (Cambridge).

———. (1970), "The effect of a simile: Empedocles' Theories of Seeing and Breathing," *JHS* 90: 140–179.

———. (1982), "La Taille et la Forme des Atomes dans les Systèmes de Démocrite et d'Epicure," *Revue philosophique de la France et de l'Entranger* 2: 187–203.

———. (2000), "Hermann Diels on the Presocratics: Empedocles' Double Destruction of the Cosmos (Aetius II 4.8)," *Phronesis* 45: 1–18.

———. (2001), "Empedocles: the Wandering Daimon and the Two Poems," *Aevum Antiquum* n.s. 1: 79–179.

O'Keefe, T. (2005), *Epicurus on Freedom* (Cambridge).

Obbink, D. (1988), "Hermachus, *Against Empedocles*," *CQ* n.s. 38: 428–435.

———. (1993), "The Addressee of Empedocles," in Schiesaro, Mitsis, and Strauss Clay (eds.) (1993), 51–98.

———. (1994), "A Quotation of the Derveni Papyrus in Philodemus' On Piety," *Cron. Erc.* 24: 111–135.

———. (ed.) (1995a), *Philodemus and Poetry: Poetic Theory and Practice in Lucretius, Philodemus and Horace* (Oxford).

———. (1995b), "How to Read Poetry about Gods," in Obbink (1995a), 189–209.

———. (1996), *Philodemus On Piety: Critical text with commentary, Part 1* (Oxford).

———. (2002), "All Gods are True in Epicurus," in D. Frede and A. Laks (eds.), *Traditions of Theology* (Leiden), 183–221.

Onians, R. B. (1954), *The origins of European Thought about the Body, the Mind, the Soul, the World, Time and Fate*[2] (Cambridge).

Ortony, A. (1993), *Metaphor and Thought,* 2nd ed. (Cambridge).

Pascal, C. (1905), "L' imitazione di Empedocle nelle Metamorfosi di Ovidio" in C. Pascal, *Graecia Capta* (Florence), 129–151.

Paschalis, M. (2001), "*Semina ignis:* The interplay of science and myth in the song of Silenus," *AJPh* 122: 201–222.

Pasoli, E. (1970), "Ideologia nella poesia: lo stilo di Lucrezio," *L&S* 5: 367–386; repr. in Classen (1986), 309–328.

Paxton, J. J. (1994): *The Poetics of Personification* (Cambridge).

Pease, A. S. (1955–58), *M. Tulli Cicero. De Natura Deorum libri III* (2 vols.) (Cambridge, Mass.).

Pellicer, A. (1966), *Natura: Étude sémantique et histoire du mot latin* (Diss., Paris).

Pender, E. E. (2000), *Images of Persons Unseen: Plato's Metaphors for the Gods and the Soul* (*International Plato Studies* 11).

Perutelli, A. (1985), "I 'bracchia' delgi alberi. Designazione tecnica e immagine poetica," *MD* 15: 9–48.

Peters, F. (1926), *T. Lucretius et M. Cicero Quo Modo Vocabula Graece Epicuri Disciplinae Propria Latine Verterint* (Diss., Münster).

Pfligersdorffer, G. (1973), "Ovidius Empedocleus: Zu Ovids Ianus-Deuting," *Gräzer Beiträge* 1: 177–209

Phillips, J. H. (1984), "Lucretius and the (Hippocratic) *on Breaths:* Addenda," in G. Sabbah (ed.): *Textes Médicaux Latins Antiques* (*Mémoires* 5; Saint Étienne), 83–85.

Piazzi, L. (2005), *Lucrezio e i Presocratici: un commento a De rerum natura 1, 635–920* (Pisa).

Pierris, A. (ed.) (2005), *The Empedoclean Cosmos: Structure, Process and the Question of Cyclicity. Proceedings of the Symposium Philosophiae Antiquae Tertium Myconense, 6–13 July 2003, Part 1: Papers = Publications of the Institute for Philosophical Research, Conference Series* 3 (Patras).

Pizzani, U. (1983), "Valore documentario della testimonianza Lucreziana su Eraclito," in L. Rossetti (ed.), *Atti del Symposium Heracliteum* 1981; Chieti, Italy (Rome), 459–475.

Plescia, J. (1970), *The oath and perjury in Ancient Greece* (Tallahassee FL.).

Pope, S. R. (1949), "The Imagery of Lucretius," *G&R* 18: 70–79.

Powell, J. U. (1923), "The Simile of the Clepsydra in Empedocles," *CQ* 17: 172–174.

Préaux, J. (1964), "Le jugement de Cicéron sur Lucrèce et sur Salluste," *RBPh* 42: 57–73.

Pucci, G. C. (1964), "Note di Terminologia Lucreziana," *SIFC* 36: 90–116.

Purinton, J. S. (1994), "Magnifying Epicurean *Minima*," *Ancient Philosophy* 14: 115–146.

Rangos. S. I. (2006): "Hesiod and Philosophy: The Mythopoetic Origins of the Truth of Reason in Archaic Greece" [in Greek: "Ησίοδος και Φιλοσοφία: η Μυθοποιητική Καταγωγή της Αλήθειας του Λόγου στην Αρχαϊκή Ελλάδα"] in N. P. Bezantakos, and C. C. Tsagalis (eds.): *Μουσάων αρχώμεθα: ο Ησίοδος και η αρχαϊκή επική ποίηση* (Athens), 395–540.

Raubitschek, A. E. (1938), "Zu Einigen Wiederholugen bei Lukrez," *AJPh* 59: 218–223.

Raumer, S. von (1893), *Die Metapher bei Lukrez* (Erlangen).

Rawson, E. (1985), *Intellectual Life in the Late Roman Republic* (London).

Regenbogen, O. (1961), "Eine Forschungmethode antiker Naturwissenschaft," in O. Regenbogen, *Kleine Schriften* (München), 141–194.

Reich, K. (1958), "Der historische Ursprung des Naturgesetzbegriffs," in *Festschrift Ernst Kapp zum 70 Geburtstag am 21 Januar 1958* (Hamburg), 121–134.

Reichenhart, E. (1891), "Tamquam und Quasi bei Lucretius," in *Abhandlungen aus dem Gebiet der klassischen Altertums-wissenschaft W. von Christ zum sechzigsten Geburtstag* (München), 399–404.

Reiley, K. C. (1909), *Studies in the Philosophical Terminology of Lucretius and Cicero* (New York).

Reinhardt, T. (2002), "The speech of Nature in Lucretius,' *De Rerum Natura* 3.931–71," *CQ* n.s. 52.1: 291–304.

———. (2005), "The Language of Epicureanism in Cicero: The Case of Atomism," *Proceedings of the British Academy* 129: 151–177.

Reitzenstein, E. (1924), *Theophrast bei Epikur und Lucrez* (Heidelberg).

Richards, I. A. (1936), *The Philosophy of Rhetoric* (Oxford).

Robbins, F. E. (1913), "The Creation Story in Ovid Met. i," *CPh* 8: 401–414.

Roller, D. W. (1988), "The Sources of Lucretius," *LCM* 13: 51–55.

Rösch, H. L. (1911), *Manilius und Lukrez* (Diss., Kiel).

Rose, H. J. (1956), "Lucretius ii.778–83," *CR* n.s. 6: 6–7.

Rosenfeld-Löffler, A. (2006), *La poétique d'Empédocle: Cosmologie et métaphore* (*Echo* 5, Bern and Oxford).

Rosenmeyer, T. G.T (1996), "Sensation and Taste in Lucretius," *Scripta Classica Israelica* 15: 135–151.

Rösler, W. (1973), "Lukrez und die Vorsokratiker: doxographische Probleme im I. Buch von 'De Rerum natura'," *Hermes* 101: 48–64; repr. in Classen (1986), 57–73.

Rossetti, L. (2004), "Empedocle scienziato," in Rossetti and Santaniello (eds.) (2004), 95–198.

Rossetti, L. and Santaniello, C. (2004), *Studi sul Pensiero e sulla Lingua di Empedocle* (*Le Rane* 37; Bari).

Rumpf, L. (2005), "Lukrez und Parmenides," *Philologus* 149: 78–95

Runia, D. T. (1997), "Lucretius and Doxography," in Algra, Koenen, and Schrijvers (eds.) (1997), 93–103.

Rurten J. S. (1982), "Ovid, Empedocles and the Minotaur," *AJPh* 103: 332–333.

Russell, D. C. (2000), "Epicurus and Lucretius on saving agency," *Phoenix* 54: 226–243.

Sallmann, K. G. (1962), *Die Natur bei Lukrez* (ABG 7; Bonn).

Schiesaro, A. (1985), "*Nonne vides* in Lucrezio," *MD* 13: 143–157.

———. (1990), *Simulacrum et Imago* (Pisa).

———. (1990a), "Problemi di formularità lucreziana," *MD* 24: 47–70.

———. (1994), "The Palingenesis of the *De Rerum Natura*," *PCPhS* 40: 81–107.

———. (forthcoming), "Rhetoric, Politics and Didaxis in Lucretius," in S. J. Heyworth (ed.), *Classical Constructions: Papers in Memory of Don Fowler, Classicist and Epicurean* (Oxford)

————, Mitsis, P., and Strauss Clay, J. C. (eds.) (1993), *Mega Nepios: Il destinatario nell' epos didascalico* (*MD* 31; Pisa).

Schindler, C. (2000), *Untersuchungen zu den Gleichnissen im römischen Lehrgedicht: Lucrez, Vergil, Manilius* (*Hypomnemata* 129, Göttingen).

Schmid, W. (1936), *Epikurs Kritik der platonischen Elementenlehre* (*Klassisch-philologische Studien* 9; Leipzig).

Schmidt, E. G. (1975), "Philosophische und Poetische Elemente bei Lukrez," in A. V. Urushadze and R. V. Gordeziani (eds.), *Problems in ancient culture* (Tbilisi), 175–199.

Schmidt, J. (1990), *Lukrez, der Kepos und die Stoiker* (Frankfurt am Main).

Schoenheim, U. (1966), "The place of 'tactus' in Lucretius," *Philologus* 110: 71–87.

Schreckenberg, H. (1964), *Ananke: Untersuchungen zur Geschichte des Wortgebrauchs* (Zetemata 36; München).

Schrijvers, P. H. (1969), "Éléments phychagogiques dans l'oeuvre de Lucrèce" in *Actes du VIIIᵉ Congrès Association Guillaume Budé* (Paris): 370–376; repr. in Classen (1986), 375–381.

————. (1970), *Horror ac Divina voluptas: Études sur la poétique et la poésie de Lucrèce* (Amsterdam).

————. (1974a), "La Pensée de Lucrèce sur l'Origine de la Vie," *Mnemosyne* 27: 245–261; repr. in Schrijvers (1999), 1–15.

————. (1974b): "L'origine du langage" (*DRN* V 1019–1090)" *Mnemosyne* 27: 337–364; repr. in Schrijvers (1999), 55–80.

————. (1978), "Le regard sur l'invisible," in Classen (ed.) (1986), 77–114; repr. in Schrijvers (1999), 183–213.

————. (1983), "Les monstres mythiques (*DRN* v 878–924, ii 700–729) in Συζήτησις: *Studi sull' epicureismo greco e romano Offerti a Marcello Gigante* (Naples), 353–71; repr. in Schrijvers (1999), 24–39.

————. (1996), "Les avortons humains (*DRN* V 837–854)," in G. Giannantoni and M. Gigante (1996), 841–850; repr. in Schrijvers (1999), 16–23.

————. (1999), *Lucrèce et les Sciences de la Vie* (*Mnemosyne* suppl. 186; Leiden).

Sedley, D. (1973), "Epicurus, on Nature Book XXVIII," *Cron. Erc.* 3: 5–83.

————. (1976), "Epicurus and his Professional Rivals," in J. Bollack, and A. Laks (eds.), *Études sur l'Épicurisme Antique* (Cahiers de philologie 1, Lille), 121–159.

————. (1982a), "On Signs," in J. Barnes, J. Brunschwig, M. Burnyeat, and M. Schofield (eds.), *Science and Speculation: Studies in Hellenistic Theory and Practice* (Cambridge), 239–272.

————. (1982b), "Two Conceptions of Vacuum," *Phronesis* 27: 175–193.

————. (1989), "Philosophical Allegiance in the Greco-Roman World," in M. Griffin and J. Barnes (eds.), *Philosophia Togata. Essays on Philosophy and Roman Society* (Oxford), 97–119.

————. (1992), "Empedocles' Theory of Vision in Theophrastus' *De sensibus*," in W. W. Fortenbaugh and D. Gutas (eds.), *Theophrastus: His Psychological,*

Doxographical, and Scientific Writings (Rutgers University Studies in Classical Humanities 5; New Brunswick), 20–31.

———. (1998), *Lucretius and the Transformation of Greek Wisdom* (Cambridge).

———. (2003), "Lucretius and the New Empedocles," *LICS* 2.4: 1–12; also online at www.leeds.ac.uk/classics/lics.

———. (2005), "Empedocles' Life Cycles," in Pierris (ed.) (2005), 331–371.

Seeck, G. A. (1967), "Empedocles B17,9–13 (=26,8–12), B8, B100 bei Aristoteles," *Hermes* 95: 28–53.

Segal, C. P. (1970), "Lucretius, Epilepsy and the Hippocratic on Breaths," *CPh* 65: 180–182.

———. (1990), *Lucretius on Death and Anxiety* (Princeton).

Sharples, R. W. (2002), "Some problems in Lucretius' account of vision," *LICS* 1.2: 1–11, also online at http://www.leeds.ac.uk/classics/lics/volumes.html.

Shea, J. (1977), "Lucretius, Lighting and Lipari," *CPh* 72: 136–138.

Sider, D. (1984), "Empedocles B96 (462 Bollack) and the Poetry of Adhesion," *Mnemosyne* 37: 14–24.

———. (1995), "Epicurean Poetics: Response and Dialogue," in Obbink (ed.) (1995a), 35–41.

———. (1997), *The Epigrams of Philodemus: Introduction, Text, and Commentary* (Oxford).

Silk, M. (1974), *Interaction in Poetic Imagery* (Cambridge).

———. (2003), "Metaphor and Metonymy: Aristotle, Jakobson, Ricoeur and Others," in G. R. Boys-Stones (ed.), *Metaphor, Analogy and the Classical Tradition-Ancient Thought and Modern Revisions* (Oxford). 115–147.

Sinclair, B. W. (1981): "Thucydides, the *Prognostika* and Lucretius: a note on *De Rerum Natura* 6.1195," in G. S. Schrimpton and D. J. McCargar (eds.), *Classical Contributions. Studies in honour of Malcolm Francis McGregor* (Locust Valley NY).

Skutsch, O. (1985), *The Annals of Q. Ennius: edited with introduction and commentary* (New York and Oxford).

Smith, M. F. (1966), "Three Textual Notes on Lucretius (3.961–2, 5.1007–10, 5.1198–1203)," *CR* n. s. 16: 264–266.

———. (1992), *Lucretius: De rerum natura* with an English translation by W. H. D. Rouse; revised with new text, introduction, notes, and index. 2nd. ed., revised reprint. (*The Loeb classical library* 181; London / Cambridge, Mass.).

———. (1993), *Diogenes of Oenoanda, the Epicurean Inscription* (with translation) (Naples).

———. (2003), *Supplement to Diogenes of Oinoanda, The Epicurean Inscription* (Naples).

Snell, B. (1953), *The Discovery of the Mind: the Greek origins of European thought* trans. by T. G. Rosenmeyer. (Cambridge).

Snyder, J. M. (1972), "Lucretius' Empedoclean Sicily," *CW* 65: 217–218.

———. (1980), *Puns and Poetry in Lucretius' De Rerum Natura* (Amsterdam).

————. (1981), "The Web of Song: weaving imagery in Homer and the Lyric Poets," *CJ* 76: 193–196.

————. (1983), "The Warp and the Woof of the Universe in Lucretius' *De Rerum Natura*," *ICS* 8: 37–43.

Solmsen, F. (1950), "Tissues and the Soul," *Philosophical Review* 59: 435–468.

————. (1953), "Epicurus on the Growth and Decline of the Cosmos," *AJPh* 74: 34–51; repr. in Solmsen (1968), 461–483.

————. (1963), "Nature as Craftsman in Greek Thought," *JHI* 24: 473–496; repr. in Solmsen (1968), 332–355.

————. (1968), *Kleine Schriften* vol. I (Hildesheim).

————. (1977), "Epicurus on Void, Matter and Genesis: Some historical observations," *Phronesis* 22: 263–281.

Spoerri, W. (1970), "Zur Kosmogonie in Vergils 6 Ekloge," *MH* 27: 144–163.

————. (1997), "*Crescebant uteri terram radicibus apti* à propos de la zoogonie de Lucrèce (*De Rerum Natura* V 791sqq.), in D. Knoepfler (ed.), *Nomen Latinum: Mélanges de langue, de literature et de civilisation latines offerts au professeur André Schneider à l'occasion de son depart à la retraite* (Genève), 55–82.

Springer, L. A. (1977), "The Role of *Religio, Solvo* and *Ratio* in Lucretius," *CW* 71: 55–61.

Stewart, Z. (1959), "The Song of Silenus," *HSCPh* 64: 179–205.

Striker, G. (1986), "Origins of the concept of natural law," *Proceedings of the Boston Colloquium on Ancient Philosophy* 2: 79–94.

Sudhaus, S. (1892–96), *Philodemus volumina rhetorica* 2 vols. (Leipzig).

Taràn, L. (1999), "Heraclitus: The river fragments and their implications," *Elenchos* 20: 9–52.

Tatum, W. J. (1984), "The Presocratics in Book One of Lucretius' *De Rerum Natura*," *TAPhA* 114: 177–189.

Taylor, C. C. W. (1999), *The atomists, Leucippus and Democritus: fragments: a text and translation with a commentary* (*Phoenix*. suppl.36; Toronto).

Thury, E. M. (1987), "Lucretius' Poem as a *Simulacrum* of the *Rerum Natura*," *AJPh* 108: 270–294.

Tigner, S. S. (1974), "Empedocles' Twirled Ladle and the Vortex-Supported Earth," *Isis* 65: 433–447.

Townend, G. B. (1965), "Imagery in Lucretius," in Dudley (ed.) (1965), 95–114.

————. (1978), "The Fading of Memmius," *CQ* n.s. 28: 267–283.

Traglia, A. (1952), *Studia sulla lingua di Empedocle* (Bari).

————. (1963), "Reminiscenze Empedoclee nei 'Fenomeni' di Arato," in *Miscellanea di Studi Alessandrini in Memoria di A. Rostagni* (Torino), 382–393.

Trépanier, S. (1999), "The Structure of Empedocles' Fragment 17," *Essays in Philosophy* 1.1: 1–21; also online at www.humboldt.edu/~essays/paper1.html.

————. (2003a), "Empedocles on the Ultimate Symmetry of the World," *OSCPh* 24: 1–57.

————. (2003b), "'We' and Empedocles' Cosmic Lottery: P. Strasb. gr. Inv. 1665–1666, ensemble a," *Mnemosyne* 56: 385–419.

————. (2004), *Empedocles: an interpretation* (New York and London).

Turner, M. and Fauconnier, G. (2000), "Metaphor, Metonymy and Binding" in A. Barcelona (ed.), *Metonymy and Metaphor at the Crossroads: a Cognitive Perspective (Topics in English Linguistics)* (Berlin and New York), 133–145; online at http://markturner.org/metmet.html.

Tzifopoulos, I. (1988), "Lucretius on the Seasons: *De Rerum Natura* 5.737–747," Ελληνικά 39: 401–405.

Usener, H. (1887), *Epicurea* (Leipzig).

————. (1977), *Glossarium Epicureum,* ed. M. Gigante et W. Schmid (Rome).

Vander Waerdt, P. A. (1988), "Hermarchus and the Epicurean Genealogy of Morals," *TAPhA* 118: 87–106.

Van Groningen, B. A. (1971), "Empédocle, poète," *Mnemosyne* 24: 169–188.

Vegetti, M. (1983), "Metafora Politica e Immagine del Corpo negli Scritti Ippocratici," in F. Lasserre, and P. Mudry, *Formes de Pensée dans la Collection Hippocratique. Actes du IV Colloque International Hippocratique: Lausanne, 21–26 Septembre 1981* (Genève), 459–469

Vernant, J. P. (1983), *Myth and Thought among the Greeks,* trans. J. Lloyd (London and Boston).

Vlastos (1947), "Equality and Justice in Early Greek Cosmologies," *CPh* 42: 156–178; repr. in D. J. Furley and R. E. Allen (eds.) (1970), *Studies in Presocratic Philosophy I* (London and New York), 56–91.

Volk, K. (2002), *The Poetics of Latin Didactic: Lucretius, Vergil, Ovid, Manilius* (Oxford).

Von Raumer, S. (1893), *Die Metapher bei Lukrez* (diss. Erlangen).

Wacht, M. (1991), *Concordantia in Lucretium* (Hildesheim, New York).

Wallace, R. (1996), "Amaze your Friends! Lucretius on Magnets," *G&R* 43: 178–187.

Wallach, B. P. (1976), *Lucretius and the Diatribe against the Fear of Death. De Rerum Natura III 830–1094* (*Mnemosyne* suppl. 40; Leiden).

Warren, J. (2002), *Epicurus and Democritean Ethics: an Archaeology of Ataraxia.* (Cambridge).

————. (2004), *Facing Death: Epicurus and his Critics* (Oxford).

Wasserstein, A. (1978), "Epicurean Science," *Hermes* 106: 484–494.

Waszink, J. H. (1954), "Lucretius and Poetry," *Mededelingen der Koninklijke Nederlandse Akademie van Wetenschappen, afd. Letterkunde Nieuwe Reeks* 17: 243–257.

————. (1964), "La Création des Animaux dans Lucrèce," *RBPhH* 42: 48–56.

Watson, G. (1971), "The Natural Law and Stoicism," in A. A. Long (ed.), *Problems in Stoicism* (London), 216–238.

Webster, T. B. L. (1954), "Personification as a Mode of Greek Thought," *Journal of the Warburg and Courtauld Institute* 17: 10–21.

West, D. A. (1969), *The Imagery and Poetry of Lucretius* (Edinburgh).

————. (1970), "Virgilian Multiple-correspondence Similes and their Antecedents," *Philologus* 114: 262–275.

————. (1975), "Lucretius' methods of argument (3.417–614)," *CQ* n.s. 25: 94–116.

Westman, R. (1955), *Plutarch gegen Kolotes: Seine Schrift 'adversus Coloten' als philosophiegeschichtliche Quelle* (*Acta Philosophica Fennica* 7; Helsinki).

Wheeler, S. M. (1995), "*Imago Mundi*: Another view of the creation in Ovid's Metamorphoses," *AJPh* 116: 95–121.

————. (1999), *A Discourse of Wonders: audience and performance in Ovid's Metamorphoses* (Philadelphia).

————. (2000), *Narrative Dynamics in Ovid's Metamorphoses* (*Classica Monacensia* 20; Tübingen)

Whitman, J. (1987), *Allegory: the Dynamics of an Ancient and Medieval Technique* (Oxford).

Wiggins, D. (1982), "Heraclitus' conceptions of flux, fire and material persistence," in M. Schofield and M. G. Nussbaum (eds.), *Language and Logos: Studies in ancient Greek Philosophy presented to G. E. L. Owen* (Cambridge), 1–32.

Wigodsky, M. (1995), "The Alleged Impossibility of Philosophical Poetry," in Obbink (ed.) (1995a), 58–68.

Wilford, F. A. (1968), "Embryological Analogies in Empedocles' Cosmogony," *Phronesis* 13: 108–118.

Wilkens, K. (1967), "Wie hat Empedocles die Vorgänge in der Klepsydra erklärt? Bemerkungen zu Fragment B100," *Hermes* 95: 129–140.

Williams, C. J. F. (1982), *Aristotle's 'De Generatione et Corruptione' translated with notes* (Oxford).

Wöhrle, G. (1991), "*Carmina divini pectoris* oder *prodessse* und *delectare* bei Lukrez und Empedocles," *WS* 104: 119–129.

Woltjer, J. (1877), *Lucretii Philosophia cum fontibus comparata* (Gröningen).

Worthen, T. (1970), "Pneumatic Action in the Klepsydra and Empedocles' Account of Breathing," *Isis* 61: 520–530.

Wright, M. R. (1995a), *Empedocles: the Extant Fragments* (London).

————. (1995b), *Cosmology in antiquity* (London and New York).

————. (1998), "Philosopher Poets: Parmenides and Empedocles," in Atherton (ed.) (1998), 1–22.

Index Locorum

A

Achilles
Introduction to Aratus (*Commentariorum in Aratum*, ed. Maass)
  5, p. 34.29–30 (Empedocles DK 31 A 51b): 255
AESCHYLUS
Agamemnon
  1510: 263
AETIUS (*Doxographi Graeci* ed. Diels):
  II 4.10 (Epicurus fr. 305 Us. = *Dox. Graec.* 331,24): 73 (cited)
    6.3 (Empedocles DK 31 A 49b = *Dox. Gr.* 334): 255
    11.2 (Empedocles DK 31 A 51a = *Dox. Gr.* 339): 141–142 (cited)
    13.2 (Empedocles DK 31 A 53 = *Dox. Gr.* 341): 211 (cited)
    13.11 (Empedocles DK 31 A 54 = *Dox. Gr.* 342): 258 (cited), 259
    20.14 (Epicurus fr. 343 Us. = *Dox. Gr.* 350–351): 266 (cited)
  III 3.7 (Empedocles DK 31 A 63b = *Dox. Gr.* 368): 132 (cited)
  IV 9.14 (Empedocles DK 31 A 95a = *Dox. Gr.* 398): 263
  IV 9.15 (Empedocles DK 31 A 95b = *Dox. Gr.* 398): 263 (cited)
  IV 14.1 (Empedocles DK 31 A 88): 264
  V 19.5 (Empedocles DK 31 A 72a = *Dox. Gr.* 430): 15, 35
  V 26.4 (Empedocles DK 31 A 70a = *Dox. Gr.* 438–439): 84 (cited)
  V 28 (Empedocles DK 31 A 95c = *Dox. Gr.* 440): 263
ALEXANDER OF APHRODISIAS (CIAG ed. Bruns)
Quaestiones
  2.23, CIAG Supp. 2.2 72.9–27 (Empedocles DK 31 A 89): 158–159 (cited), 264
ALCMAEON (DK 24)
  A 5: 245, 257
  A 16: 245
  A 17: 245, 266
AMMONIUS (CIAG ed. Busse)
In de interpretatione:
  4.5, 249.1–21: 234
ANAXAGORAS (DK 59)
  A 68: 252
  B 4: 239, 243
  B 9: 239
  B 17: 257
  B 21a: 22
ANAXIMANDER (DK 12)
  B 1: 238
ANAXIMENES (DK 13)
  A 14: 258
  A 17: 266
  B 2: 243
APOLLONIUS RHODIUS
Argonautica
  1.496–498: 258
ARATUS
Phaenomena
  938–939: 253

General Index

A

Aether: in Lucretius: 45, 54, 78, 128, 144, 146–149, 205–206, 218, 237 n. 67; Father-Aether (Air): 81, 86; as exhalation: 146–149; in Ovid: 244 n. 168

air: and bladder in Anaxagoras: 252 n. 86; and soul in Anaximenes: 243 n. 150; bladder as container of: 122–123; in Diogenes of Oinoanda: 226 n. 31; in Empedocles' fragments: 44–45, 73, 101, 111–114, 116, 228 n. 63; in Empedocles' testimonia: 132, 142, 159, 211, 252 n. 79, 255 n. 128; in Epicurus: 52, 123; in Hippocratic *on Breaths:* 117, 251 n. 62; in Ovid: 77, 244 n. 168; in Plato's *Timaeus:* 161; in Pseudo-Plutarch: 217, 255 n. 128, 267 n. 177; in Theophrastus: 119, 123, 135, 227 n. 58

air in Lucretius: 38, 117, 119, 142, 144, 169, 179, 182, 203, 214, 244 n. 168; assimilated with water: 108, 250 n. 46; bladder as container of: 122–123; and creation of the world: 146–149, 217; cloud as container of: 102, 104, 110, 121–123; destructibility of: 208; earth as container of: 126, 134–135, 139–140; as Empedoclean element: 2, 14–15, 47, 67, 72–73, 132, 171, 205–206, 227 n. 58, 228 n. 64; Father- (*see also* aether): 81, 86; and thunderbolt: 119; and transformationist theory: 7; and *Makranthropos* analogy: 77–80; and soul: 134

allegorists: 17

allegory / allegoresis / allegorism / allegorical: 31, 233 n. 6; Epicurus on: 30, 39; in Lucretius: 40–42 (of Venus and Mars), 126 (of furnace and Cyclopes), 193 (of Danaids), 224 n. 8 (of Calliope as harmony); of Magna Mater: 233 n.2; Stoic: 245 n. 180; and Stoics in Philodemus: 233 n. 6, 236 n. 43.

ambiguity / ambiguous style: in Empedocles: 76, 100–101, 149, 238 n. 82, 249 n. 27, 256 n. 11; in Epicurus: 153, 256 n. 5; in Lucretius: 64, 181, 208; in Heraclitus: 200.

Anaxagoras: on ἄδηλα: 22; on language: 257 n. 15; Lucretius on: 3, 50, 54; on mixture: 239 n. 89; Philoponus on: 267 n. 190; on sperms: 243 n. 151; use of bladder as model: 252 n. 86

Anaximander: 238 n. 79

Anaximenes: 243 n. 150, 258 n. 37, 267 n. 185

253 n. 90; furnace as container of:
125–127; as lightning or thun-
derbolt: 118–119, 206, 213–214;
stomach as container of: 253 n.
97; and subterranean water: 215–
217; and sun: 107–108, 142,
147–148, 206–207, 255 n. 136,
261 n. 99; and transformation-
ist theory: 7; as vehicle in simile:
191; and volcanic eruptions: 126,
137–141, 254 n. 122; and wrath:
140–141; *see also* Etna, cloud,
lightning, thunderbolt, volcano
flux (theory of): 195, 198–201, 203, 209,
264 n. 136 n. 140 n. 141; *see
also* flowing water metaphor
foedera naturai: 10, 23, 47, 57–61, 91, 165,
176–178, 187, 202, 239 n. 99,
240 n. 102 n. 106 n. 112, 241
n. 112 n. 124; *fati:* 187, 241
n. 112; in Manilius and Lucan:
106 n. 110; *see also* natural law
formula / formulaic: in Empedocles: 228 n.
60; in Lucretius: 12, 60, 79, 231
n. 98; in Empedocles and Lucre-
tius: 3, 98
furnace: cloud as: 104, 121, 125, 130, 249
n. 36; stomach as: 126–127;
volcano as: 126, 139–140; *see
also* allegory

H

Harmonia (Ἁρμονία): 48, 174, 224 n. 8,
234 n. 24, 237 n. 71, 258 n. 41,
259 n. 68; *see also* Aphrodite,
Love, Venus
harmony: 51, 55, 56, 67, 209, 224 n. 8
Heraclitus: in Lucretius: 3, 7, 50, 54,
200–202, 209, 226 n. 32, 265
n. 149; metaphor of flux in:
199–200, 264 n. 136 n. 137 n.
140; mixing in: 239 n. 89; war
in: 63, 242 n. 130
Hermarchus: 5, 82, 153, 225 n. 28
Hesiod: 48, 237 n. 70, 242 n. 130
Hippocratic, Hippocratic writers, Hip-
pocratics: analogy in: 82, 117,

120, 142, 246 n. 199, 248 n.
6, 251 n. 72, 253 n. 99, 267 n.
179; botanical analogy in: 245
n. 185; Empedocles in: 96; in
Lucretius: 96, 117, 129, 133,
246 n. 190, 248 n. 7; political
imagery in: 238 n. 79;
Homer / Homeric: allegorical reading of: 40;
in Aristotle: 225 n. 23; in Emped-
ocles: 34–35, 44, 48, 56, 97–98,
100–101, 160, 237 n. 71, 248 n.
16, 258 n. 32 n. 41; in Ennius:
26–27; in Lucretius: 28, 66, 68,
98–99, 130–132, 232 n. 123 n.
125, 248 n. 19, 249 n. 22, 251
n. 62; similes in Empedocles and
Lucretius: 95–100, 115, 130–131,
160, 249 n. 24; in Metrodorus:
225 n. 19; in Theophrastus: 131;
in Parmenides: 249 n. 28

I

Iphigenia: 245 n. 186
imagery / images of: erotic: 185–186, 262
n. 107; of mysteries: 23, 231
n. 100; sexual / of friendship:
33–34, 47–50, 94; socio-politi-
cal: 33, 47–48, 50–61, 94, 110,
128, 148, 202, 238 n. 79, 255
n. 138, 257 n. 23, 268 n. 195;
of war: 61–69, 264 n. 142;
legal: 33, 50, 59, 61; oracular: 4;
triumphal: 4; technological (*see
also* technological metaphors):
156, 157, 160, 163, 170, 171,
175, 219; prophetic: 230 n. 91
indivisibility: 6, 53, 162–163, 175, 226 n.
34, 257 n. 22
isonomy (ἰσονομία): 12, 67–68, 115, 146,
239 n. 92

G

God: in Diogenes of Oinoanda: 243 n. 149;
Earth as: 233 n. 2; Empedocles
as: 4, 225 n. 21; in Empedocles:
14, 34–36, 44, 75, 76, 234 n.
20; in Epicurus: 30, 39, 76; in

257 n. 28; Epicurus on Emped-
ocles': 162, 264 n. 134; in Lucre-
tius: 162–163, 212, 230 n. 90;
in Empedocles and Lucretius: 19,
156, 167, 220, 257 n. 19

prolepsis (πρόληψις): 22, 98, 232 n. 110

prophecy: 225 n. 19; prophetic imagery:
230 n. 91, Empedocles as
prophet: 3–4

Pythagoras / Pythagorean(s) / Pythagorean-
ism: 5, 223 n. 6, 224 n. 8, 243
n. 150, 244 n. 169, 260 n. 88

R

Rain: 14, 64, 66, 86, 106, 112, 121–122,
127–129, 132–133, 143, 148,
213, 261 n. 101

reincarnation (*see also* metempsychosis,
transmigration): 94, 245 n. 186

repetition: 3, 12, 224 n. 11, 225 n. 21, 227
n. 42, 247 n. 210, 265 n. 162

roots: in Empedocles: 35, 43–44, 48–49, 51,
55–56, 62, 114, 154, 157, 160,
195–196, 200, 226 n. 33, 234
n. 23, 245 n. 183; in Epicurus
/ Epicureans: 45, 228 n. 61; in
Lucretius: 6–8, 13–15, 32–33,
45–47, 50, 54–55, 60, 64–65,
68, 116, 171, 174, 183, 202,
204–206, 212–213, 226 n. 34,
239 n. 90, 242 n. 142; Lucretian
inferences based on Empedo-
clean: 119–150; Lucretius' vari-
ous containers of: 121–141; in
action in Lucretius: 141–146;
now and then in Lucretius:
146–149; in Ovid: 77; in Theo-
phrastus: 120; in botanical analo-
gies: 80, 91–92, 181, 247 n. 202
n. 203; of wombs: 87–91; *see also*
air, earth, fire, water, wind

S

Sacrifice: 32, 223 n. 6, 245 n. 186

sensory evidence: 6,18, 264 n. 141

similes: extended: 4, 65, 78, 95, 97, 98,
118, 154, 203; Homeric (*see*

also Homer): 95–100, 115,
130–131, 160, 249 n. 24;
multi-dimensional: 100–104,
115, 129, 147; multiple-corre-
spondence: 106–111, 113, 115,
117, 130–131, 143, 155, 232 n.
111, 250 n. 41, 251 n. 70, 252
n. 83, 255 n. 132; of clepsy-
dra in Empedocles: 98, 101,
111–114, 116–118, 132, 149,
247 n. 2, 248 n. 16; of lantern
in Empedocles: 97, 100, 111,
121, 127, 129, 212, 248 n. 16;
of painters in Empedocles:13,
97, 257 n. 23

simulacra: 98, 178, 179, 192, 259 n. 65

soul: in Anaximenes: 243 n. 150; in Dio-
genes of Oinoanda: 180; in
Ennius: 26–27; composition
of soul: 46, 134, 179, 254 n.
112, 265 n. 158; in Lucretius:
82, 181, 184–185, 191–192;
194; connection with body: 80,
179–180, 184; connection with
mind: 181; as vessel: 191; desires
within: 191; in Plato: 191–192,
261 n. 88

sperm (σπέρμα): 71, 198, 243 n. 151

sponge: 121, 125, 127, 155, 210–220, 252
n. 81, 253 n. 90, 255 n. 133,
267 n. 179

spontaneous generation: 83–88

stars: in Diogenes of Apollonia: 267 n. 179; in
Cicero: 76; in Empedocles: 211,
258 n. 42; in Epicurus: 267 n.
177; in Leucippus: 251 n. 66; in
Lucretius: 45, 99, 144, 203, 217,
222; shooting: 214–215

Stoic / Stoics / Stoicism: allegory in Philode-
mus: 233 n. 6, 236 n. 43; ani-
mate universe: 74, 76, 243 n. 152
n. 165; connotations in Lucretius:
79–81, 94, 177, 186–187, 220,
226 n. 32, 241 n. 112, 243 n.
160, 245 n. 180; determinism:
60; and Epicurus: 262 n. 109;
Gods in: 76; image of stomach as